The Rise of Baptist Republicanism

The Rise of Baptist Republicanism

Oran P. Smith

NEW YORK UNIVERSITY PRESS
New York and London

NEW YORK UNIVERSITY PRESS
New York and London

© 1997 by New York University

All rights reserved

Library of Congress Cataloging-in-Publication Data
Smith, Oran P., 1963-
The rise of Baptist republicanism / Oran P. Smith.
p.   cm.
Includes bibliographical references (p.) and index.
ISBN 0-8147-8073-3 (acid-free paper)
1. Southern Baptist Convention—Political activity. 2. Southern
Baptist Convention—History—20th century. 3. Baptists—United
States—Political activity. 4. Republican Party (U.S. : 1854-)
5. Christianity and politics—Baptists—History—20th century.
6. Christianity and politics—United States—History—20th century.
7. Conservatism—Religious aspects—Christianity—History—20th
century. 8. United States—History—1969-   9. United States—Church
history—20th century.   I. Title.
BX6462.3.S65   1997
286´.132—dc21   97-4780
                             CIP

Manufactured in the United States of America

10 9 8 7 6 5 4 3 2 1

To Kristin,
Who Endeavored to Persevere

Contents

LIST OF FIGURES

LIST OF TABLES

LIST OF APPENDICES

Acknowledgments

Though no one besides me is responsible for any factual or epistemological errors that may occur in this book, the better parts of this work would not have been possible without the suggestions and encouragement of a host of political scientists. These include Hal Birch, Earl Black, Robert Botsch, Glen Broach, Lois Duke, Charles Dunn, Betty Glad, Blease Graham, James Guth, Steve Hays, Allan Hertzke, Ted Jelen, Lyman Kellstedt, David Leege, Kevin Lewis, Bill Mishler, Bill Moore, Philip Mundo, Don Songer, Harold Stanley, Robert Steed, Mark Tompkins, Laura Woliver, and David Woodard.

I am grateful also to those outside the political science community who, as participants or observers of fundamentalist politics, provided me with new perspectives: Marion Aldridge, Lee Bandy, David Beasley, Carroll Campbell, James Dunn, Charles Goolsby, Michael Graham, Charles Hamel, Flynn Harrell, Bob Harrison, Gene Hogan, Richard Land, Bob McAllister, Cyndi Mosteller, Richard Quinn, Ralph Reed, Marlea Rhem, Richard Robinson, Mark Ross, Terry Rude, George Shissias, Tom Strode, Chris Sullivan, Byron Verdin, Danny Verdin, Trey Walker, and Trey Ward.

I would also like to express my appreciation to those who helped me obtain data and photographs: Larry Chesser, Jack Harwell, Ron Ingle, Bill Jacoby, Michael Link, Yvette Reyes, John Shelton Reed, Jim Skinner, Joe Smith, Pat Smith, Johnny Stack, Alan Waite, Judy Waite, and Randal Whitten; also to Howard Gallimore and Kelly Bilderbach of the Southern Baptist Convention Historical Commission Library, the staff of the Bob Jones University Library Protestantism File, the staff of the Furman University Baptist History Collection, the Interlibrary Loan and Government Documents staffs of the University of South Carolina Library, the staff of the South Carolina Baptist Convention Reference Room, the staff of the Coastal Carolina University Library, the staff of the North Greenville College Library, the staff of the American Political

Science Association, the staff of the South Carolina Elections Commission, the staff of the South Carolina Republican Party, the Liberty University offices of the president and the chancellor, the Public Relations office of the Christian Broadcasting Network, Unusual Films, and the Bob Jones University office of the president.

Finally, I would like to thank Despina Papazoglou Gimbel, Jennifer Hammer, and Niko Pfund of New York University Press for their guidance and many helpful suggestions during the editing process. Their professionalism proved both challenging and comforting.

The Rise of Baptist Republicanism

1

Introduction

Baptist Republicanism's Cultural Antecedents

The story is told of a little boy selling puppies by the road in the rural South. An elderly gentleman passing by in a wagon, unsure of his failing eyesight, asks the lad what kind of puppies he has. "*Methodist* puppies," the boy quickly replies.

The driver, amused by the boy's apparent religious sensitivity, grins and drives on. A short time later the same commuter again sees the boy with his puppies. Sensing an opportunity to rib the child a bit, the man again asks the boy what kind of puppies he has. But just as quickly as before, the reply comes back this time: "*Baptist* puppies."

"*Baptist* puppies?" the man huffs. "Son, just last week you told me those were Methodist puppies. Why are they now Baptist puppies?"

With a big grin the boy announces, "Well, they's opened their eyes since then, sir."

I first heard the story of the boy with the puppies as a child in South Carolina. The story was recommended to me as a sure-fire way to silence a Methodist friend who thought his parents' denomination was superior. Years went by until I heard the story again, this time from the lips of none other than Strom Thurmond. Taking liberties, like most politicians, Thurmond changed the story a bit. In his version, when the puppies' eyes open, the little canines turn from *Democrat* to *Republican*.

Its tendentiousness aside, the puppy story fits both political and religious contexts. In the last part of the twentieth century, both Baptists and Republicans have used conservative creeds, hardball politics, and powerful personalities to expand membership and win elections in the South. GOP candidates are elected by popular vote at poll sites just like Democrats; Southern Baptist Convention (SBC) leaders are elected by popular vote at huge conventions on a scale larger than any other in Christendom. More moderate rivals—Democrats, Methodists—have witnessed a decline.

The political puppy parable, told by whichever side claims an eye-opening experience, is careful to leave out any hint of the pain that comes with change, however. Real-world change is always much less rosy than what's told in well-intentioned stories. Yes, Southern Baptists and Republicans have exported a Southern brand of gloves-off politics and religion to the rest of the nation, but not without trouble in the ranks. Moderate Southern Baptists, after a decade of serving as the "out" faction, have created a permanent organization with which to co-affiliate, the Cooperative Baptist Fellowship (CBF). Moderate Republicans, whose pro-choice and/or pro-environment views make them unpopular targets at Christian Coalition rallies and business forums, are equally unwilling to go away. The fight over the abortion plank at the 1996 Republican convention is a case in point.

Given these concomitant surges in membership with similar goals and styles (and similar vocal minorities), perhaps it is inevitable that Southern Baptists and Republicans should find each other. The result has been a conservative takeover of the SBC and the GOP. The Republican party and the Southern Baptist Convention (SBC) are not only in firm alliance, they are sometimes indistinguishable from each other (House chiefs Gingrich and DeLay, and Senate chiefs Lott, Thurmond, and Helms are all Southern Baptists). But how coincidental is it that the opposition (President Clinton, Vice-President Gore, House Minority Leader Gephardt) happen to be Southern Baptist as well?

It is a simple statement of fact that, with the exception of Roman Catholic South Dakotan Tom Daschle (the Senate minority leader) and Presbyterian North Dakota native-turned-Texan Richard Armey (the House majority leader), our nation's leaders are entirely Southern Baptist. Most of them are Republican, and the Southern Baptists who are not Republican are friendly to the moderate faction of the Southern Baptists. This is particularly noteworthy considering few Southern Baptists have ever held any of these positions at any other point in our nation's history, much less simultaneously.

My goal in this book is to explore this growth of Republican conservatism in the Southern Baptist Convention and explain the increasing presence of Southern Baptists in positions of power on the national scene. I will also trace the interaction of Convention politics and conservative politics and compare Southern Baptists to other New Christian

Right groups. This is a multidisciplinary study using multiple methodologies to gain an understanding of a captivating political-religious phenomenon.

Religion and Politics?

The very idea of studying a religious denomination in the context of its internal and secular politics is a logical step in terms of modern political science. In recent years, the impact of religious factors on politics[1] has been studied in as many ways as one can study politics: international religious fundamentalism and its impact on global politics,[2] the influence of religious interest groups in American party politics,[3] the influence of religious thought on political philosophy,[4] the effect of religion on the development of the nation's legal and constitutional systems,[5] the importance of political discourse among religious people,[6] and even the impact of religion on political institutions.[7] Each approach, as well as its accompanying methodologies, has been widely used since the 1970s to describe the importance of religion to political science, from the age of John Calvin to the era of Pat Robertson. One of the interesting aspects of the field of religion and politics—its interdisciplinary nature—is often a stumbling block as well. For, in addition to the political science subfields of regional politics, political parties and interest groups, political thought, political theory and voting behavior (each a self-conscious specialty), a study of religion and politics must consider the influences of culture, history, and economics. Religion scholars struggle with the *politics* of religion and politics, while political scientists are called on to show great sensitivity in the often confusing *religious* aspects of the religion-politics amalgamation.

Few categories of political science have received more attention than the study of the politics of religious people. This has been most noticeable in the study of voting behavior, particularly since the advent of the voter survey. These surveys—which ask voters questions related to their religious beliefs, denomination, and church attendance—provide the most intuitive measure of religion's influence on politics. Such research examines religion's *saliency*, the powerful religious factors or variables that explain political phenomena like candidate selection, party identification, and political attitudes. Though some of the early voting-behavior literature ignored religion,[8] or constructed overly simplistic variables to measure the impact of religious belief, scholars have recently been quite successful in making their research applicable to real-world politics.[9]

One of the seminal breakthroughs was the publication in the flagship journal of the American Political Science Association, the *American Political Science Review*, of Kenneth Wald's "Churches as Political Communities" in 1988.[10] The efforts of religion and politics scholars was summarized most recently by the publication of *Rediscovering the Religious Factor in American Politics*, a book whose goal and title are the same.[11] On the popular level, a number of books have appeared as well, including Andrew Greeley's statistical *Religious Change in America*,[12] Garry Wills's dense *Under God: Religion and American Politics*,[13] Harold Bloom's eccentric *The American Religion: The Emergence of a Post-Christian Nation*,[14] and more recently Stephen Carter's blockbuster, *The Culture of Disbelief: How American Law and Politics Trivialize Religious Devotion*, a favorite of President Bill Clinton.[15]

The thesis of each of these works, from the scholarly articles filled with survey data, political philosophy, and theology to the more popular Wills paperback, is much the same—that to understand politics, one must understand religion. In making this point, one author writes that he found "religious styles more predictive of voting patterns in the Populist Era than were the normal data studied (economic, class, regional, etc.)." This finding is corroborated by the nation's best-known pollster, George Gallup, who wrote that "religious affiliation remains one of the most accurate, and least appreciated, political indicators available."[16]

Other sources show that the power of religion as predictor of political behavior is not limited to the usually robust variables, denomination and doctrinal belief. Even regularity of church attendance alone is very potent in explaining voting behavior and ideological predispositions. Regarding the importance of religion in recent presidential elections, Kellstedt et al. argue that "[religious traditions and coalitions] still structure party politics and are quite potent even when economic issues come to the fore. They are likely to be even more important during times of peace and prosperity, perhaps evolving into a more comprehensive religious alignment. For good or ill, observers cannot afford to ignore the role of religion in politics."[17]

Looking at these coalitions from 1960 to 1992, another scholar finds that the more often an American attends church, the more likely he or she is to vote Republican. The most religious (church attending) of Americans also support conservative causes and organizations of all types, while more secular voters support a liberal agenda.[18]

With the rise of the religious right in the late 1970s, the presidential candidacies of the Reverend Jesse Jackson and the former Reverend Marion G. "Pat" Robertson in the 1980s,[19] and the appearance of the Christian Coalition in the 1990s, interest in the political impact of religious belief has stimulated great interest. Religion and politics research has become not only wide but deep in its scope. How else would we have known that supporters of third-party candidacies (of Wallace, Anderson, Perot) are less religious than the average Democrat or Republican,[20] or that there is a difference in political behavior between Pentecostal and Charismatic Christians?[21] This more focused analysis continues to make important new contributions to the field of political science. This research has also stimulated my interest in the religious denomination of my youth, the Southern Baptist Convention, the very symbol of the rising influence of the religious right.

Why Study the Politics of Southern Baptists?

The Southern Baptist Convention presents specific and unique attractions for the political scientist.

There is the issue of size. Though Baptists were tossed out of numerous places in Old England and New England, the sect survived to carve out of an equally hostile South the largest Protestant denomination in the country. Weathering the storm, the SBC soon dominated Southern regional culture and grew to a membership of fifteen million.[22] This fact makes Baptists interesting from a purely demographic point of view, that is, how did a religious denomination start from small numbers in a small state (Rhode Island) and grow to fifteen million? How did a New England sect become the "established church" of white Southern culture?

Size has bearing on politics as well. For example, what was the effect of dramatic growth on the relation of the Convention to civil authorities? How did so large an organization deal with political issues that are of concern to the denomination? What were the cultural effects of growth and/or decline in SBC membership, and how did these affect politics? What ideological shifts accompanied growth, if any? Why has the Convention remained mostly white? What attempts were made to use the Convention for political gain? How did Convention elites or the Convention itself serve as political interpreters or amplifiers for the rank and file? How does the mixture of regional culture and regional religion affect regional politics?

Another attraction, and a much more theoretical one, is the seemingly indelible Baptist connection to what we shall loosely call *democracy*. In a sense this is another form of Baptist republicanism—a republicanism with a lower-case "r." Though there are myriad Baptist sects, most are extremely republican or democratic in church governance, more so than any other organized denomination. Individual Baptist congregations own property, hire ministers, adopt policies, set church budgets, and receive members. Baptists also have the reputation of allowing—even encouraging—the most minor of decisions to be debated by the entire congregation. In one Southern Baptist church, an after-service business meeting was being held to consider a recommendation from the board of deacons that the church purchase a chandelier. As soon as the proposal was announced and opened for discussion, an old farmer from the back of the room stood to his feet and demanded recognition: "I am opposed to the motion, preacher," the elderly gentleman said. "First of all, I can't hardly pronounce it. Second of all, I don't know anyone in our congregation who can play it. And third, what we really need is *lights*!"

In the case of Southern Baptists, this "one man, one vote" church governance is even more pronounced at the national level, where numerous issues are voted upon in convention. (It should be noted that the Southern Baptist Convention is both the name of the denomination and the name of the annual national meeting.) National meetings resemble political conventions, complete with preconvention caucuses, political factions, computerized ballots, slates of officers, campaign speeches, a platform (resolutions), and a keynote address (the Convention Sermon). Given the proper level of controversy, the attendance level rivals that of a major party as well. In 1986, 40,987 delegates (or "messengers" as they are called in the democratic SBC) attended the annual convention.[23] (The highly political nature of the SBC in recent years was taken to its logical conclusion in the amusing but bitterly ironic novel, *The Convention*, by Will Campbell, in which the SBC is renamed the Federal Baptist Church and is by the end of the book indistinguishable from a political party.)[24]

The SBC is worthy of study also because Southern Baptists possess a certain *distinctiveness*. Because of "strong faith" or "wooden-headedness"[25] (depending on whom one consults) the SBC has willfully made itself distinctive, not only from other large nationally based denominations, but from other denominations that operate alongside it in the Convention's native South. An early analyst of the social/political forces in the Convention had this to say:

> The social contributions of Southern Baptists, if considered at all, are usually regarded as insignificant, irrelevant, or hopelessly reactionary. Such easy categorizing, while understandable in part, cannot pass for social history; Southern Baptist life and thought have enough substance to merit careful study. The Southern Baptist Convention, since its founding in 1845, has come to occupy a *distinctive* place in American culture. Southern Methodists, who came from an identical environment, moved up the social scale and eventually reunited with the Northern church. . . . Southern Baptists, however, continued to reach the plain people and refused all overtures of reunion from the North. And unlike Southern Presbyterians, who remained within the former Confederacy, Baptists took their churches to every part of the nation.[26] [Emphasis mine]

In short, the SBC experience was unique. But why did Southern Baptists react differently to a common Southern experience, and why has SBC behavior differed from that of its fellows in the same regional culture?

Part of the reason for the distinction is that, historically, unlike other denominations the SBC has been both *expansionist* and *conservative*, an interesting mix for political analysis. The SBC has always seemed to want to evangelize and grow, but to retain its Southern and low- to middle-class flavor. The SBC has also traditionally tried to be denominational yet evangelical.

Recent history suggests that the SBC is distinctive as the only major American religious denomination to take a giant step to the right. Leaders of the conservative faction agree with leaders of the moderate faction on this point if on nothing else: the snowballing of events that began in 1979 set the SBC at odds with its recent history and with the whole of Protestant Christendom.

Another rationale for a Southern Baptist study is the growing influence of the denomination. The Convention has not always been so influential. There was, in fact, a gap in Southern Baptist representation in high political office. It is not widely known that in the early part of the twentieth century, though the SBC was large and dominated a conservative, homogeneous South, the dominance was primarily among the "plain people." This made being a member of a Baptist church helpful to a politician aspiring to local office. But for the higher offices in the U.S. Congress and Senate, and in governorships, it was better to be a member of a more mainline "upper crust" denomination.[27] The better-educated Methodists and the socially well-connected Episcopalians went to Washington or the governor's mansion more often than the lowly Baptists. Given the SBC's massive size, it was strange that placement of its members in powerful national political office was more difficult for a time than for its smaller counterparts; but the flamboyance of Southern Baptists who *were* elected certainly compensated for their small numbers. Those who went to Washington included Theodore Bilbo, Jimmy Carter, Barbara Jordan, Lester Maddox, Wright Patman, Claude Pepper, Carl Perkins, Gene Talmadge, and Herman Talmadge.[28]

As noted, in recent years there has been a rise in SBC political influence, however. President Bill Clinton (D-AR) and Vice-President Al Gore (D-TN)[29] took office in 1993. When Lieutenant Governor Jim Guy Tucker ascended to the governorship upon Clinton's election to the presidency, the special election to fill his seat was won by a Southern Baptist minister, Mike Huckabee. Huckabee gave up a U.S. Senate bid in 1996 to succeed Tucker, who was indicted on charges related to the Whitewater investigation. Governor Ned McWherter of Tennessee appointed Southern Baptist Harlan Matthews to fill Vice-President Gore's unexpired term in the U.S. Senate from 1993 to 1995. Others include First Baptist Atlanta activist Nancy Shaefer and home-school proponent, lawyer, and minister Mike Farris. Shaefer and Farris were candidates for lieutenant governor in Georgia and Virginia, respectively.

But it was the 1994–96 period that brought Southern Baptists to power in droves. Speaker Newt Gingrich (R-GA), House Minority Leader Dick Gephardt (D-MO), House Majority Whip Thomas DeLay (R-TX), Senate Foreign Relations Committee Chairman Jesse Helms (R-NC), and Senate Armed Services Committee Chairman Strom Thurmond (R-SC), though incumbents, assumed new duties in January 1995. Senate Majority Whip Trent Lott (R-MS) was elected majority whip in 1995 and succeeded Bob Dole as majority leader of the U.S. Senate in 1996. African American Republican J. C. Watts also took his seat in the Oklahoma congressional delegation. Best remembered for his football successes at Oklahoma University by many Oklahomans, Watts is now a Southern Baptist minister. In short, Southern Baptist influence at the national level is no longer weak. With President Clinton, Vice-President Gore, Speaker Pro-tempore Thurmond, and Speaker Gingrich, Southern Baptists are four-deep in constitutional succession.

Defining Our Terms/Crafting Our Concepts

Terms

It seems fitting that before we embark on our journey into the political life of the Southern Baptist Convention, I define certain terms and several concepts. This can be quite tricky. In fact, given the various Convention factions and the SBC's continuing struggle to define itself, defining terms for it may be the most difficult part of this study.

For example, members of the more conservative element which elected its first president in 1979 prefer to be called "conservatives" and consider their opponents "liberals." (The comparison to Republicans is obvious.) Members of the group that lost the power struggle prefer to be

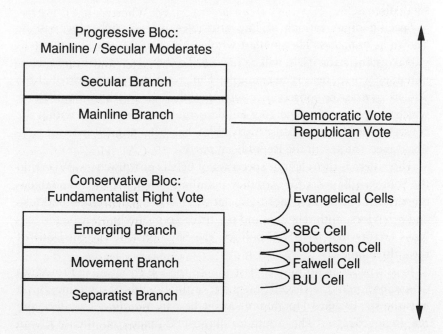

Figure 1.1. Protestant Political Groupings

called "moderate-conservatives" while they label the other group "fundamentalists" or "fundamentalist-conservatives."[30] (Again, note the overtly *political* terminology used.) In this analysis we will please neither side. I will call the rival camps within the Southern Baptist Convention the *conservative faction* and the *moderate faction*.

Also for purposes of this work, the term for political organizations carrying partisan labels will be *parties*, as in Republican party and Democratic party. The term "party" is also used in religious studies to mean "people of like religious-political orientation," for example, the "Souls party," which is evangelical and out to win individual souls, and the "Social Order party," which is egalitarian and seeks to better society as a whole.[31] To avoid confusion, I will in most cases change the religious connotation of "party" to *bloc*, as in the "voting bloc." The two blocs in Protestantism will be known as the *conservative bloc* (roughly following the Souls party parameter) and the *progressive bloc* (the Social Order party). I will avoid the more obtuse "Orthodox Alliance" and "Progressive Public Culture" (proposed by sociologists in an attempt to avoid the loaded term "conservative"). "Conservative" and "progressive" serve nicely for the multiple religious, sociological, and political contexts that I will discuss.[32]

Specific organizations of like attributes within each bloc will be known as *branches*. The smallest whole-unit measurement, for the individual organization itself, will be the *cell*. To show how the proposed terminology works, here is an example. The group that took control of the SBC in 1979 is the conservative *faction* within the Southern Baptist *cell*, which is a part of the Emerging Fundamentalist Right *branch* within the conservative *bloc*. The conservative bloc has been aligned in most elections since 1968 with the Republican *party*.

Then there is the religious spectrum of beliefs and practices. Where do the Southern Baptists fit? Are they mainline, evangelical, or fundamentalist? Each one of these loose associations has certain common outlooks and behaviors, both religious and political. To properly describe the religious factors that feed SBC politics, the SBC must be assigned one of these three labels.

It is a peculiar notion, at first blush, to rule the largest Protestant denomination in the United States out of the bounds of mainline. But it must be so. Richard Hutcheson says it best in *Mainline Churches and the Evangelicals*: "The Southern Baptist Convention, the Lutheran Church, Missouri Synod, and some of the major black Baptist groups, are certainly large denominations with deep roots in American history, but they would be omitted from many 'mainline' lists. Why? Because they are strongly conservative and are not part of the ecumenical movement."[33] Though it is *mainline* in the sense of being long established, the SBC is simply too conservative to be called "mainline" in a religious sense.

Evangelical, a catch-all term for Protestants too moderate to be fundamentalists and too conservative to be mainline, would have fit the SBC during most of the era of moderate faction control. But shortly before its conservative takeover and domination, the SBC was already moving toward the rightward fringe of evangelicalism. Religion scholar Richard Quebedeaux wrote at the time that Southern Baptists were right-of-center evangelicals, near the fundamentalists.[34]

We are then faced with the question: If the SBC is not remotely mainline or truly evangelical, is the current Southern Baptist leadership and its majority conservative faction *fundamentalist*? We face the question with some trepidation because of the political importance of the answer. More than the other two, "fundamentalist" is the most politically loaded of the three categories of American Protestantism. To be a part of religious "fundamentalism" has proven to have numerous political ramifications, making the term problematic for the scholar and the devout alike. The religion faculty of Bob Jones University draws a very small circle for fundamentalism, leaving Jerry Falwell, Pat Robertson, and certainly the SBC on the outside.[35] Southern Baptist conservatives cannot seem to agree among themselves about the label. Some in the conservative faction proudly claim to be fundamentalists because of their *belief* in an inerrant (error free) scripture, while others on the theological right claim that fundamentalism may have been the rage in the North, but there was never a need for a fundamentalist *movement* in the SBC (or the American South).[36] Amid the debate over a fundamentalist movement versus fundamentalist belief, there is one point of agreement, however. Those who embrace the term react negatively to definitions that lump them with the Ayatollah Khomeini and Islamic "fundamentalists."

Bruce Lawrence, in his seminal study of fundamentalism, has done this to some degree. In his research into fundamentalism across religions and cultures (*Defenders of God: The Fundamentalist Revolt against the Modern Age*),[37] Lawrence finds that there are common characteristics of fundamentalism, no matter what the religion. Using Lawrence's framework, we can make several general applications to the SBC, thereby strengthening our case for including the Convention in the fundamentalist circle.

1. *In fundamentalism, there is a reciprocal reinforcement between creedal belief and ritual action.* The chief complaint of the moderate faction is that the SBC under the conservatives has become a "creedal" denomination, turning belief in an inerrant Bible into a litmus test for piety. The moderates argue that the denomination was intended to be based on "soul competency,"[38] the belief that all believing souls are by Christ's death and resurrection made priests and therefore empowered to interpret the scriptures for themselves. Moderates believe that "being Baptist should ensure that no one is ever [to be] excluded who confesses 'Jesus is Lord'" (Philippians 2:11).[39]

This "priesthood of all believers" understanding, which is basic to Baptist theology, is a democratic force. When it works properly, this belief serves as a check against powerful preachers (or politicians) and keeps the denomination in step with the culture. But moderate faction Baptists fear that democracy has been subverted by conservative faction elites who, though democratically elected, once in office have forced allegiance to an unwritten conservative creed. Moderates claim that the conservatives are waving the Bible more but resting on conservative buzz words.

2. *Fundamentalists derive legitimacy by appeal to scriptural authority.* Conservative leaders in the SBC take the Bible literally, including passages from the Apostle Paul which seem to forbid women from assuming church leadership roles. The controlling conservative faction argues that church traditions have no independent authority on faith and practice, and to abandon biblical positions, even those that seem prejudicial, would destroy the legitimacy of scripture.

But to moderates like Marion Aldridge, a Columbia, South Carolina, minister, in interpreting scripture in such a manner, the conservative faction seems to forget that "Jesus' harshest words were against those who claimed 'we are right and all of you are wrong.' Like the Pharisees, fundamentalists in the SBC pray 'Lord I thank you that I am not like those Democrats who abort babies and ordain women.' They think the Moderates are bad people. But how is it *conservative* to say 'God can't speak through a woman?'"[40] Moderates like Aldridge find legitimacy and political advice in places other than scripture, a liberty that is anathema to conservatives.

3. *Fundamentalism encourages Charismatic leadership.* The leaders of the SBC in the post-1979 fundamentalist era (SBC presidents Charles

Stanley, Adrian Rogers, Ed Young, et al.) are to a large degree leaders of "superchurches" (First Baptist Atlanta, Bellevue Baptist Memphis, Second Baptist Houston) that emphasize the need for large membership, huge buildings (with cavernous "worship centers" and mall-like "family life centers") and an extensive schedule of programs and activities, including television broadcasts in which the pastor is the "star." This flurry of activity can be so extensive that many Southern Baptists have little social life apart from the church. The centrality of the church in the life of the believer, compounded with the centrality of the minister in the life of the church, enlarges the role of the pastor in the life of the average Southern Baptist. Preachers are the heads of their little world and in a prime position to provide direction and advice, and give political cues.

The real rub is the matter of the role of the pastor, a role that has changed along with the growing emphasis on "bigness." The old and moderate Baptist understanding of pastor is that he functioned much like a CEO, providing administrative leadership but answering to a policy-making board of directors (deacons). To conservatives, however, the pastor is more the titular head of the church, a prophetlike figure, an administrator and policymaker who turns to the board of deacons for support and prayer but not necessarily guidance. The issue of pastoral leadership and rule through a throwback to a certain Weberian *charismatic authority* has been a side skirmish in the SBC civil war.[41]

4. *Fundamentalism is characterized by a religious ideology that arises out of scripture.* Again, the SBC is scripture oriented, basing an entire belief structure, or *ideology*, around the written word. The SBC logo bears an open Bible. Many SBC churches display an open Bible on the communion table in front of the pulpit. But for Southern Baptists, there is within the pages of scripture the basis for an entire worldview, an ideology. Lawrence claims the fundamentalist ideology is both political and psychological in nature, and that the Bible is so key to this ideology that removing scripture makes fundamentalism "just another social movement."[42]

According to Lawrence, it is a certain separatism mixed with "religious autonomy"[43] (see chapter 4) that produces this "religious ideology." The parameters for this political/ideological portion of fundamentalism are four. Again, we use the template Lawrence provides to assess the SBC on a fundamentalism scale:[44]

1. *Fundamentalists see themselves as advocates of a pure minority viewpoint against a sullied majority or dominant group.* As we shall see

later in this chapter and in the next two, for Southern Baptists the belief that they are somehow lonely "keepers of a flame" began at the time of the American Civil War as the defeated white South in general and Southern Baptists in particular took on a "lost cause" mentality. This regional and denominational self-conception was fueled to scorching heat by the social stresses of Darwinism, the hopelessness of the World War I era, and the scandal of the Scopes trial.[45]

2. *Fundamentalists are oppositional.* The takeover of the SBC was not a pleasant experience for the denomination, and politicized conventions have forced both sides to continue the fight. But there would be no fight without the fundamentalist willingness to continually *confront* their moderate opponents. As such, some fundamentalists gladly call themselves "militant" fundamentalists and continue to keep old wounds open in the name of "fighting the good fight." For the most fundamentalist of Southern Baptists, the repeated calls for peace in the convention and appointment of a Peace Committee were mere calls to compromise, and compromise is a word not in their religious vocabulary.[46]

3. *Fundamentalists are dominated by male elites.* SBC fundamentalists do not allow women to serve as trustees, deacons, or in any role that places a woman in authority over a man—even as Bible teachers to young men. Women are, of course, forbidden from pastoring churches that are a part of the majority conservative faction. The SBC missionary organization, the Foreign Mission Board, has even on occasion withdrawn support from women missionaries who "preach."[47]

4. *Fundamentalists generate their own technical vocabulary.*[48] Southern Baptists have their own language, often referring to their "Baptist life," or "Southern Baptist life." Fundamentalists often refer to each other as "Bible-believing." Moderates have their terms as well, insisting that what fundamentalists might call a doctrinal laxity is a commitment to "move forward."

5. *Fundamentalism has historical antecedents but no ideological precursors.*[49] As we will see, an SBC mentality has been ingrained over 150 years. But SBC fundamentalism is not a true ideology because it is not truly intellectual. In this lexicon, fundamentalism is only a custom developed over time and is hallowed, much like a tale passed down from generation to generation.

For all of these reasons—the perfect match with the Lawrence framework, the takeover by the conservative faction, and the "moderate-conservative" insistence on calling the group that has run the convention for fifteen years "fundamentalist"—we will for the purpose of this book include Southern Baptists in the fundamentalist group and hence in the conservative bloc.[50] In the next few chapters we shall see the political consequences of this ideology.

Concepts

Southernness. The Rise of Baptist Republicanism begins with the concept of Southern Baptist "Southernness," an elusive set of factors that forms the essence of a traditionalistic political culture among white American Southerners. Southernness is a challenge to define. Scholars, novelists, journalists, poets, and even artists and photographers have attempted to grasp what constitutes Southernness. In the study of politics, history, and religion, Southernness must include poverty, defeat, guilt, historical consciousness or "connectedness," white supremacy, passive acceptance, independence, homogeneity, and religiosity. (To this list John Shelton Reed, the foremost sociologist of the American South, would rightly add "vanishing," "rural," and "localistic." Those issues will be considered in chapter 3.)[51]

Right away we observe that the factors that together constitute "Southernness" have a *conservatizing* influence. This is no surprise, given the region's reputation. But "Southern" is not interchangeable with "conservative." A number of the factors enumerated here—particularly poverty, white supremacy, and an individualistic, independent spirit— cut both ways, producing native Southern moderates and a few liberals as well. Home-grown moderates and liberals in the South, however, live a lonely existence or opt for the road, leaving native soil and never looking back.

In summing up the unique white Southern character, some observers look neither left nor right. In a more analytical approach, historian C. Vann Woodward[52] writes in a well-known 1960 essay about a "burden" of Southernness. The "burden," to Woodward, was not only the South's conservatism, but its diversion from and even contradiction of the American Experience. In a land of economic abundance, success, and innocence, the South was dominated by poverty, defeat, and guilt. These burdens over time found their way into the Southern psyche, causing Southerners to suffer the effects of an eclipsed American Experience.

All is not gloomy, however. The irritations and limitations of Southernness have also had positive effects and diminished certain negatives of the American Experience. Though it is the home of the rich and the free, America is a land cursed with abstraction and disconnectedness, a place where few children know the names of their great-grandfathers and old customs die to the *zeitgeist*. Laced with a powerful and unique historical consciousness, Southerners suffer less from this malady than Northerners, who, possessed with a type of spiritual Alzheimer's, envy their Southern neighbors for knowing who they are and from where they have come. The trade-offs are apparent. With the end of war and Reconstruction came defeat, poverty, and racial injustice. But these vices traveled together with a great virtue—the willingness to take a "backward glance." Each facet of Southern life, all connected to the struggle of 1861–65, forms the essence of Southernness over 130 years later.

President Franklin D. Roosevelt said over seventy years after the war that the South was "the nation's economic problem number one,"[53] and the utter hopelessness of the late nineteenth century Southern sharecropper is well documented. Life in the textile mills of the twentieth century provided little escape. In fact, the cotton economy provided the South with the dubious distinction of being the only region of the country to see a net decrease in per capita income from one census to the next. This distinction became doubly painful when it happened *a second time*. Indeed, the South did not begin to truly prosper until the end of World War II and the end of state-sanctioned segregation, almost one hundred years after Appomattox.[54]

Like poverty, a paternalistic white supremacy found its roots in the ante-bellum era as Southern Baptists and other Protestants defended slavery as something biblical. But after the last of the Northern troops left the South and upper-class Southern "redeemers" restored local control, there was peace and some hope for racial healing. This era of good feeling came to an abrupt end, however, as the redeeming Brahmins were forced to give way to a new working-class generation of leaders. With the new governments came a new Jim Crow enslavement, and with it assurances that the biblical "curse of Ham" recorded in Genesis was a God-breathed curse on African Americans. The scripturality of segregation was preached on this passage.[55]

Writing eighty years after the War between the States, political scientist V. O. Key found that old ways still held, that white political behavior was directly related to the presence or absence of the black man. "In its grand outlines, the politics of the South revolves around the position of the Negro," Key wrote.[56] For the South, and particularly for Southern Baptists, slavery, white supremacy, and Jim Crow were classic "slippery slope" issues. Using scripture to justify human bondage in the 1860s placed Holy Scripture in the precarious position of making the institutionalized racial prejudice of the 1960s more acceptable. Unfortunately, the South continued to follow this "scriptural" road, a road traveled by generations of Southerners, some of them quite well-meaning religious people.[57]

Another Southern trait important to our study is conservatism. As alluded to earlier, the Southern brand of conservatism is not purely economic or social (though these concepts spring from it). Much of Southern conservatism is simply a certain passive acceptance of the status quo. Some scholars argue that the South has failed to develop economically and intellectually because the region "lacks well-educated, native critics of the status quo" compared to the rest of the nation. Southerners are conservative and vote conservative in part because they are satisfied with their region. A recent poll reveals this statistically, showing Alabama has a "satisfied" rate of 70 percent versus 29 percent for New York. This carries over to politics: because a loyal opposition to the power barons did not exist, for decades issues were not critically analyzed and reform was not debated, and certainly not passed by any government. Rural-dominated legislatures kept change bottled in committees while reform proposals were greeted with the version of Southern hospitality that met Lincoln's gunboats in Charleston harbor. Lest Southern conservatism appears to be simply ignorance, or the manipulation of the ignorant to preserve the status quo, let us state the matter clearly. Southern conservatism is not artificially contrived, but is real and genuine: a wall of resistance to change and often critique.[58]

Another Southern idiosyncrasy is the incredible homogeneity among white Southerners. Except in Maryland and Louisiana, Baptists and Methodists alone constitute the majority. The diversity of Southern ancestry for several centuries ranged the short distance from English, Scottish, Scotch-Irish, Irish, and Welsh to German, with a smattering of Jews near port cities like Charleston.[59] During a period of open-door immigration in the rest of the country, émigrés from southern Europe, eastern Europe, or Scandinavia were few in the South. (The South was not a part of this growth simply because it was difficult to immigrate there. Not only were there lasting effects of the disruption of railroad transportation due to the Civil War, but the silting of Charleston harbor in the late 1700s also kept out foreign immigrants as well as a not inconsiderable amount of North-to-South economic-development traffic.)[60]

Known as the "backward glance," or the overactive sense of history in the South, in the form of the "Lost Cause" myth Southern historical consciousness is particularly important to our study. The ideas that provided the foundation for the Lost Cause myth were set in motion not in 1865, but in the decade the SBC was born, twenty years before there was a Lost Cause. These ideas, not blue and gray, kept the SBC separate from (and far to the political right of) its Northern Baptist neighbors for decades before Lincoln's presidency.

Because of the extreme spiritual and societal stress brought on by the defense of slavery, coupled with the unique influence of the Bible in the region, the South developed a religious-political national myth as a defense of its way of life—a "Millennial Vision." Based in biblical warnings, this myth had two dramatically different versions, the ante-bellum Millennial Vision and the Lost Cause Millennial Vision.[61]

In the years before the American Civil War, a millennialist myth had already begun to develop, as theologians looked to the scriptures for lessons about the end of the world. With cotton the reigning king, evangelical ministers along with political leaders convinced many Southern elites in an upbeat, positive, "postmillennial" phase that, with its economic and spiritual prosperity, Southern society was so idyllic that this earthly perfection indicated that the thousand-year or "millennial" rein of Christ promised in the scriptures would be ushered in without judgment. Christ would return to earth at the *end* of a millennial reign of peace already begun.

Then came the war. In the postwar phase, as the region lay in ruin, the positive *post*millennialism gave way to dour *pre*millennialism. A devastated South took Confederate defeat as a sign that Christ would soon rapture His church safely out of a world that was getting progressively hostile to His kingdom so that He might judge the sinful world *before* His thousand-year rein. In some sense, the Convention remains in the this latter phase, as deep within Southern Baptist religion and politics lies the notion that the South is separate from the rest of the nation: a little more righteous, a little more virtuous; believers in the absolutes of scripture surrounded by relativists, a Christian nation-state snuffed out by barbarians. (Note the consistency with a portion of Lawrence's definition of fundamentalist political ideology—"advocates of pure minority viewpoint against a sullied majority.") This biblical literalism, born in the searching of the scripture for a defense of slavery and succored on the milk of Confederate defeat and insulation from political change, would take hold and continue to hold sway in the SBC.

Long after the war, the Holy Cause continues to be used to encourage Southerners to keep themselves pure from Northern social and political influence and to resist reunification, liberalization, unionization, and even moderation. The theme found itself from time to time in the well-documented "divide and conquer" strategy of planter and, later, textile elites. An appeal to the old ways was often effective in preventing whites from doing the one thing that would have changed Southern politics forever: joining with blacks in a lower-class workers' alliance.[62]

The myth has its positive uses as well. As Charles Reagan Wilson wrote *in Baptized in Blood: The Religion of the Lost Cause*, the Lost Cause myth was used "to warn Southerners of their decline from past virtue, to promote moral reform, to encourage conversion to Christianity, and to educate the young in Southern traditions."[63]

In either sense, the question arises: Why does the Lost Cause myth remain important? Why is it important for political analysis? Simple. Because the myth lives. According to one cultural critic, "Southern Baptists have been the largest identifiable group of victims of [the Lost Cause] myth." Southern Baptist religion scholar and moderate-faction activist Bill Leonard agrees that the myth is not a dusty fable. He writes that "the way in which Southern Baptist leaders sought to explain the defeat of the South's righteous cause provides insight into their continuing response to divisive theological and cultural issues. The formula seems to be: When in doubt, spiritualize. *That tendency remains a significant element of SBC life*" (emphasis mine).[64]

Closely connected to the Lost Cause myth is a fierce streak of independence in the South. This desire to go its own way has been called a "sense of holy separation," a separation which shielded the denomination from the modernism that found its way into the major denominations of the North.[65] Sociologists have written that a certain individualism and independence have played a role in both the Baptist and Southern heritage.[66] After the war, Southern Baptists were so independent that in spite of the willingness of Northern Baptists to send missionaries into the devastated region to occupy abandoned churches and to rebuild others, Southerners let it be known that they wished to run their churches as best they could without Northern assistance. This independence ran deeper than a poor region's pride. There were intense political ramifications. Helen Turner writes that the conflict was appropriately defined as a clash between two *civil religions*, but significantly that of the North was, despite the postwar efforts of the Yankee churches, less attached to the Protestant institutional structures than in the South. The Confederacy would continue to be a society governed largely by the . . . more established early nineteenth century evangelicals, and neither Yankee victory nor Yankee mission efforts could change that. As the denominations rallied around the myth of the Lost Cause, ante-bellum mazeways seemed to be the only reasonable way of living despite all that had occurred [emphasis mine].[67]

Again, the trait described is magnified with Southern Baptists, for "the very persistence of southern evangelical denominations was for many a sign that the Confederacy had not been completely defeated, and Baptists were particularly noted in this regard because of their numbers. Consequently, of greatest importance in this context is the further development of the SBC's regional identity."[68] Needless to say, proposals for reunification with the North, most notably those of the 1890s, were coldly received in the independent SBC.[69]

"Bapticity." In addition to Southern traits, Southern Baptists have deep in their collective experience certain *Baptist* traits as well. Baptist religion (whether American, Northern, Southern, Northwestern, Southwide, independent, conservative, regular, general, particular, free will, primitive, fundamental, or Bible) has been universally individualistic and independent. These characteristics can be traced from the earliest days as the small sect under Roger Williams suffered religious persecution[70] in a colony that had not yet heard of such enlightened ideas as church-state separation. Conceived as a sect, Baptists have always demonstrated sectlike behavior.[71] However, both *regular* (mainline) Baptists and *separatist* (sectlike) Baptists evolved. Southern Baptists share both traditions. According to Baptist scholar Winthrop Hudson:

> Although there was no uniformity in either section, Baptists in the North tended to be middle class, tended to think in terms of an educated ministry, and expanded westward by the rise of missionaries. Baptists in the South, on the other hand, tended to be of lower social and economic status, exhibited much less interest in an educated ministry, and extended westward by means of farmer preachers. One is tempted to suggest that Baptists in the South had been assimilated to Separatist Baptist emphases, while Baptists in the North adhered to an older Regular Baptist ethos. But this idea would miss the mark.[72]

As for Bapticity, Southern Baptist religion possesses a unique blend of the *sect* and the *established*. This conflict will be a focus of our effort to explain Southern Baptist political behavior.

As already mentioned, Baptists are irrevocably (and as some might say, irretrievably) democratic. Most Baptists, like most Americans, are used to democracy in their institutions and have known little else.[73] It is not simply SBC boosterism or Sunday School Board propaganda to argue that the new nation and the new denomination started from scratch and grew together on the same continent.[74] After all, why shouldn't the most democratic of churches thrive in the most democratic of countries? Winthrop Hudson puts the comparison this way:

> The Baptist emphasis on individual rights, lay control, and local autonomy typified the American spirit. . . . Representation was necessary to accomplish certain ends, but the strength of anti-federalist sentiment made it clear that direct participation in decision making in one's own locality was much to be preferred. This was the popular mood. It was highly individualistic and highly self-assertive. Most [other] denominations scrambled in one way or another to adjust and adapt to the prevailing temper of the people. . . . As the most thoroughly 'American' of all religious groups, it is not surprising that by 1800 Baptists had become the largest religious denomination in America.[75]

The republicanism of Baptists, in the wake of a Declaration of Independence insisting on the *consent* of the governed, made the fledgling democratic denomination the most American church in the new nation. To this day, Baptists dominate no other country to such an extent as in the New World, though the newly democratic Ukraine appears to be fertile territory for Baptists of late.

Southern Bapticity. In some ways, the parts—Southernness and Bapticity—do not sum to the whole, however. There are certain traits common to *Southern Baptists* alone. Southern Baptists are different from other Southern Protestants primarily because of biblical conservatism mixed with revivalism.[76] Aside from the Pentecostals, who are split into many fellowships, of the large denominations in the South—even more so than the very evangelical Methodists—Baptists have been the most fervent "soul-winners." They have expanded their church by converting the "lost," pressing home the claims of Christ one-on-one. Baptists in the North, like other Southerners, are less eager to present the gospel evangelically. For example, as recently as 1993, an SBC study attempted to calculate how many citizens of a certain state would be headed for hell if the Southern Baptist did not bring in the sheaves.[77] The transference of this behavior to politics is not a great leap. As we shall see, converting the lost and converting the liberal seem to be part of the same stroke for many Southern Baptists. David Beasley, governor of South Carolina, is a case in point. A liberal Democrat and Episcopalian, he was converted to the Southern Baptist faith and to conservative Republicanism within a few years of each other. The Republican story in the South, like the Baptist story, has in recent years become a "converts" story of souls won and proselytized.

Summary of Findings

In its simplest form, the thesis of this book, as shown in figure 1.2, is that in the latter half of the twentieth century the SBC has become a barometer of Southern culture and politics by rejecting a reluctant, moderate conservatism, and adopting in its place a militant "go for the jugular" two-party Republican conservatism. Specifically, I will show how the rank and file of the SBC has taken a path from solid Democratic[78] to solid Republican, while SBC elites have moved from political and theological moderation to political and theological conservatism.[79] I will show that this shift contains elements of partisan realignment[80] and the effects of New Christian Right activism,[81] but that a complete picture of this dramatic political shift involves significant conflicts beyond these simple summations, namely: theology and politics (conservative belief vs. moderate polity), denominationalism and politics (sectarian roots vs. churchly values), ideology and politics (Southern mores vs. American ideals), and the politics of social forces (cultural dominance vs. status defense). Figure 1.2 illustrates how these forces combined to effect the unique rightward and Republican shift that is Southern Baptist politics today.

This chapter serves as an introduction, argues the need for a political science of religion (specifically for Southern Baptists), defines terms, and provides a synopsis and plan for the book. The terms and concepts section provides definitions I will use for the terms necessary to avoid confusion in discussing politics in the SBC and outlines certain concepts that play a role in shaping Southern Baptist political identity. The defining of these terms and concepts includes a summary of recent scholarship on

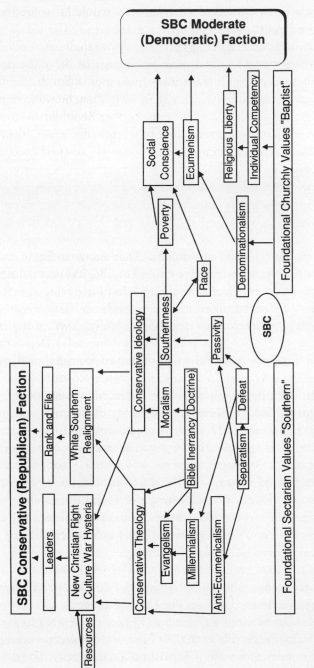

Figure 1.2. Roots of Southern Baptist Political and Religious Factionalism

three key forces at work in the denominational psyche—Southernness, Bapticity, and the baggage the SBC carries into politics independent of the other two forces. The chapter illustrates the cultural and religious factors that must be brought to bear in any discussion of the politics of the SBC. Figure 1.2 diagrams the theoretical model for Southern Baptist political change and charts a strategy for analyzing the SBC in terms of this model.

Chapter 2 traces the political life and events of the SBC during three eras of conservative political agitation—the 1920s, the 1950s, and the 1980s.[82] This analysis identifies eras or "waves" of conservative political activity that come and go and suggests them as signposts for analysis. The chapter shows how a church built to the point of hubris on a blend of conservative theology and moderate polity survived two turbulent political epochs without rancor, only to see these two forces come into conflict at the introduction of secular politics into denominational life in the late 1960s. The series of conservative theological and political reactions in the SBC are compared to the reacting conservatism in Southern and American culture. Conservative and moderate factions are profiled and the critical events that opened the floodgates to politics are explained.

Chapter 3 shows how forces external to the SBC—church-state change, political change, and cultural change—combined with the internal theological struggle to create a structure of political opportunity that propelled conservative elites to convention control and shifted the SBC rank and file to the right politically, abandoning its own Jimmy Carter for Ronald Reagan. The chapter argues that the following led to a "reclaiming movement" in both religion and politics that was dedicated to turning the clock back denominationally and electorally: (1) church-state changes (the First Disestablishment, the Second Disestablishment, the Great Reversal); (2) political changes (the rise of the Republican party in the South and the New Right's "culture war" hysteria); (3) cultural changes (the growth of the middle class), and Convention changes (the loss of SBC cultural dominance, expansion to the non-South). It argues that the South had escaped this fissure twice in times past because the one-party conservative South had no lost conservatism to "reclaim." This chapter includes a large body of original research into U.S. census data and denominational statistics to chart the changing cultural position of the SBC demographically.

While chapter 3 moves from the conservative-moderate struggle in the Convention to the conservative-liberal struggle in the culture, chapters 4 and 5, using a case study of South Carolina, delves more deeply into conservatism itself. It provides a needed contrast between Southern Baptist fundamentalists (classified as part of the *Emerging* Fundamentalist Right) with those in the *Movement* Fundamentalist Right (Robertson and Falwell) and the *Separatist* Fundamentalist Right (Bob Jones). The chapters show theoretically (chapter 4) and practically (chapter 5) that SBC fundamentalists are a hybrid—not truly movement oriented as those in the Movement Right, but not as purely separatist as those in the Separatist Right. The importance of the internal SBC struggle over sectarian versus churchly values in political culture is addressed. Data in this chapter include an analysis of Bob Jones University voting patterns over time and two polls of South Carolina voters, one conducted expressly for this book.

Chapter 6 takes a more quantitative turn, focusing on the changing Southern Baptist rank and file over time (1968–92) through the use of American National Election Study data and Southern Baptist elites over time (1968–96) by analyzing Convention resolutions as political platform planks. The Southern Baptist rank and file are profiled over time beginning with 1968, the year moderate Convention elites unwittingly opened the gate to politics only to be deluged in a tide of militant conservatism. The profile encompasses partisanship, ideology, presidential voting, and political efficacy. Elites are studied based on resolutions passed by twelve state conventions for the year 1993 as well as national resolutions for 1968–96. In this manner, the conflicting elements of conservative and moderate theology and ideology are tracked over time and explained.

Chapter 7 attempts to assess the political impact of recent political and theological alliances in the Convention, showing how a conservative organization adapts to a modern, increasingly secular environment.

Chapter 8 concludes by summarizing the meaning behind the rise of Southerners and Baptists institutionally (particularly in Congress), the connection between Bapticity and Republicanism, and the similar tasks facing the SBC and the GOP in the wake of the end of the moderate Convention and partisan eras and the challenge of recent instability for conservatives in American politics.

In general, the book draws a number of conclusions and makes several contributions to the field of political science.

1. Southern Baptists have deep roots in two distinct religious/political/sociological world views: sectarian and churchly. This cleavage has had and continues to have polarizing political and theological consequences.

2. In the latter half of the twentieth century, SBC conservatism has been dependably *reactive*, just like conservatism in the North in the first half of the century. As conservatism began to lose ground for the first time in the South, Southern Baptists and Southern conservatism became more militant in their respective reactions.

3. Moderate initiatives, the loss of cultural monopoly, and the conservative reaction to that combination opened the door to politics in the SBC. Partisan politics, both secular and theological, produced a two-faction SBC and led to inevitable conservative control of the denomination and its political agenda.

4. Southern-SBC militant conservatism has fed on the Southern-SBC transition from a strictly traditionalistic political culture to a mixed individualistic-traditionalistic political culture.

5. SBC fundamentalism is one cell of the Emerging Fundamentalist Right branch, and differs from the Movement Fundamentalist Right branch (Falwell, Robertson) and the Separatist Fundamentalist Right branch (BJU) politics in agenda, organization, focus, tactics, leadership, and behavior.

6. The three branches of the fundamentalist right often unify behind conservative candidates palatable to all, but the traditional pattern in Republican primaries is a splintering of the three branches among candidates.

7. Religious factors such as fundamentalist unity operate in Republican primaries.

8. In political platforms, Southern Baptist elites have become more moralistic, less socially conscious, and less concerned about separation of church and state as the conservative faction has consolidated control of the political agenda of the convention.

9. The Southern Baptist rank and file was reluctant in its Republicanism until 1988, and reflecting its mixed heritage has proven to be both ideologically conservative and centrist on cultural issues like abortion. Regularly-attending Southern Baptists are more anti-abortion and now lead other Southerners in Republicanism.

10. Southern Baptist political alliances have occurred among theological conservatives, theological alliances have occurred among political conservatives.
11. I draw several conclusions related to Congress. Over the last decade, Southerners, Baptists, Republicans, and African American conservatives have grown in strength in the U.S. Congress. In addition, the new leaders of the SBC face challenges similar to the new leaders of the GOP and the Congress.
12. The theological conservatives who took control of the SBC and the political conservatives who took control of the Southern electorate freely use loaded symbols and shrill rhetoric both because they *could* and because they *had to*.

With the end of segregation in the South and with evangelism secure as the SBC's focus, the conservative, vote-maximizing militant conservatism of insurgent parties is free with its rhetoric, while moderate-conservative, theological-political entities are marginalized. The result has been a one-party organization of the right rather than of the middle, as was previously the case.

Southern Baptist Republicanism is not merely fundamentalist right politics and not only Southern politics. SBC Republicanism is a combination of these forces along with a reactionary politics and theology. This reactionism was produced by unique historical baggage and loss of considerable cultural monopoly, and has been fueled by militant conservative rhetoric. This right-wing rhetorical freedom replaced the hushed moderate political discourse designed to protect segregation in the public square and the centrist ideas that secured a focus on evangelism in the convention.

Like in the South as a whole, two-party Baptist Republican politics has grown from a reluctant Republicanism to a militant one-party GOP conservatism. This conservatism, however, continues to coexist with a moderate minority with equally deep political and theological roots.

Like the fundamentalist right, SBC conservatives are energized to some extent by the politics of the culture war. But they are neither the separatist types who fear political involvement and are culturally small, nor the movement types who see political envelopment as an opportunity to restore a cultural monopoly.

2

Backlash

Baptist Republicanism as Fundamentalist Reaction

The most striking evidence of the strength of the New Religious Right . . . [is] the continuing shift to the right within the Southern Baptist Convention.

> —Jerome Himmelstein, *To the Right: The Transformation of American Conservatism*

About 150 years ago the Mormons began moving West. They traveled by horse and wagon in parties of 30 to 40 families, leaving at intervals of two or three weeks. The first party left in early spring. At the end of every day they stopped to make camp. But before they rested, some of the men unhitched their horses from the wagons, re-hitched them to plows, and began plowing together in the prairie. They did this again the next evening and the next, and the next, until they reached Utah, leaving a chain of little fields across the prairie. Later when the next party passed through, they planted corn in the little fields, carefully covering each seed. Throughout the summer, each subsequent party tended the fields. Even the children would help to pull weeds in the cool of the evening. Sometimes, they erected scarecrows to protect the little fields. All summer they labored faithfully and diligently because they knew the winter was coming.

The winter party left Illinois in October and before long the cold winds blew across the prairie out where there's nothing between you and the North Pole but a barbed wire fence. Snow fell and covered the grass, and the horses began to starve. But the winter party found those little fields, shook the snow from the stalks, and fed the ears of corn to the horses. And they could pull one more day to the next little field, and the next, and the next. The winter party came through because others had taken a turn at the plow.

> —Eldred Prince, Jr., Commencement Address, Coastal Carolina University

As the second decade of the twentieth century drew to a close, in much of the United States religion had been toppled from its lofty pedestal. After being *legally* disestablished in the Establishment Clause of the First Amendment a century and a half before, the church was suffering a second, or *cultural* disestablishment.[1] Whereas the official disestablishment set the church free to compete for parishioners in the marketplace of ideas among free people of free conscience, the second was a negative verdict on the church from popular culture.

Indeed, the church had begun the new century in a weakened condition. America was not as religious as it had been at the end of the American Civil War only thirty-five years earlier. Unlike during the founding era or even during the sectional crisis, Americans were decidedly cool toward religion. A survey conducted of passers-by on a street in any city north of the Mason-Dixon line in the 1910s would have revealed a religious posture dramatically different from that of the last century: a large number of citizens no longer believed that earth and man were created in seven calendar days, and a shrinking ratio revered the Bible as the inspired word of God. Huge waves of immigration from predominantly Roman Catholic countries had begun to undermine the orthodox Protestant consensus as well. Politically, the campaign against rum, romanism, and rebellion had lost its potency. Then came the Great War.

It is at this point we undertake a brief excursion into the political background of the Southern Baptist Convention (SBC), or more properly, we seek to develop a long view of the role of conservative politics in the Southern Established Church. As the opening quotation states, the final shift of the SBC to conservatism was a "striking" event. We start here to understand why.

As shown in the last chapter, for a number of reasons, the South and Southern Baptists in particular have a history of being distinct from the rest of the United States religiously, culturally, and politically. In some cases, as evidenced by immigration patterns, this means that the South simply did not have the same cultural experience as the rest of the nation. This affected politics, with the South supporting the nineteenth-century anti-immigrant American ("Know-Nothing") party[2] and the twentieth-century effort to deny Al Smith of New York, an urban Catholic "wet," the Democratic presidential nomination.[3] In some cases, however, the South experienced the same *inputs*, but Southern society processed them differently, making the *output* at variance with the rest of the country. For example, the twentieth century has seen three waves of fundamentalist uprisings: the 1920s, the 1950s and 1960s, and the 1970s.[4] Each affected religion and politics in both North and South, but not in the same way.

The 1920s: Conservative Rebellion Quelled

In the 1920s, a number of conservative submovements burst onto the American political scene, each having religious overtones.[5] The battle was joined over evolution, the role of political questions in the Convention, and the reliability of scripture, each skirmish having a short- and long-term impact on politics.

One of the most important submovements antecedent to the era, revivalism, is often neglected because of its seeming exclusive impact upon *souls* rather than *society* or politics. But is not society, the electoral polity, made up of individual souls?

In the 1920s, revivalism had been around for at least four decades, with some arguing that it had an even earlier origin, in the army camps of Union and Confederate troops in the Civil War.[6] Most sources, however, trace revivalism, or "soul-winning" crusades, to the Bible/evangelism conference movement that swept the country in the late nineteenth century. These very first crusades were led by Northern fundamentalist evangelists who operated independent of "modernist" denominational structures. The best known among them was the Chicago-based preacher Dwight L. Moody (1837–99). Though indirect in their consequence, the political effects of Moody's preaching and those like him were still potent. One commentator has written that "D. L. Moody, reacting to the reformist message of the social gospel . . . created a conservative cultural crusade designed to defend evangelical values against the forces of liberalism and modernism."[7] Another argues more specifically that the way Moody and those who succeeded him accomplished a political purpose through their preaching was "by presenting morality in terms of individual rather than social reform . . . [which] functioned as a socially conservative force with the practical effect of upholding traditional values and institutions against basic social change."[8] This makes intuitive sense. Religious fervor or personal conversion could have this effect; for example, one who made the religious decision to give up the bottle would make a ready enlistee in a political crusade for temperance, or more broadly, the personal born-again spiritual experience could have the effect of extenuating concern for others as a class or reducing support for programs designed to provide mere temporal benefits. While true for Moody's Midwestern audiences, this mentality took even deeper root in an even more traditionalist Southern culture that had come to expect little from government.

But as explained in chapter 1, the South and the SBC had little need for a "freelance" fundamentalist movement like Moody's. A conservative society and a conservative church left little good soil for planting "reclaiming" crusades of the style and purpose of the great revivalists. Southern Baptists in particular did not have to follow independent evangelists to find conservative religious and social messages. Southern Baptist observer Nancy Ammerman goes so far as to write that a fundamentalist or revivalist movement in the SBC in this era would have been "superfluous" because fundamentalists and revivalists were on every street corner. "There were simply not enough modernists around the Convention to generate a good fight," she writes.[9]

This is not to say that the SBC was not affected by preachers like Moody. The same revivalism that filled auditoriums and brush arbors for independent preachers in Springfield, Massachusetts, and Chicago, Illinois, filled meetings *within* local SBC churches. Because of Civil War camp meetings and meetings called by denominational separatists like Moody, the SBC as a denomination was becoming evangelical and revivalist (or at least more so). Indeed, it is an interesting fact that while to this day there are Evangelical Presbyterian denominations (EPC), an Evangelical Methodist denomination (EMC), and two Evangelical Lutheran denominations (ELCA; EL synod), there is no Evangelical Baptist church. Beginning during this era, Southern Baptists made the term redundant.

It is this revivalism mixed with biblical conservatism that began to distinguish Southern Baptists from other Southern Protestants.[10] This move to revivalism (or the expansion of it) brought a degree of political fallout as well. Southern Baptist moderate faction theologians argue that beginning with the swelling undercurrents formed in this era, Southern Baptists began to "confuse" themselves with fundamentalists. Writing with great angst and disapproval at this departure, Glenn Hinson argues that the onset of an "overt, organized effort of some to spread 'Evangelicalism'" in the convention that was more common to separatist sects led to conservative *revolution* fifty years later.[11] The "great awakening" or "great reawakening" of Southern Baptist revivalism in this era seemed to produce only limited immediate political results, but there is no doubt that the seed was planted in Southern Baptist consciousness for a more aggressive conservative religious-political reaction to a rapidly changing world. Through a sort of religious-political alchemy, the SBC was institutionalizing in Southern culture, through revivalism, the redemption of persons as individuals, not as a society.

The phenomena that shaped Baptist politics in the 1920s, all related to revivalism and conservatism, were the refusal of the SBC to allow politics to distract the convention from its evangelical mission, the identification of the SBC leadership with a national fundamentalist movement in the struggle against modernism, the cultural dilemma over evolution represented by the Scopes trial in Tennessee, and the struggle over the Social Gospel.

The most important consideration about the SBC experience of this era is the lack of a distracting denomination-threatening eruption throughout.[12] While Northern denominations splintered, while the splinters in turn split, and while Southern denominations divided, the SBC survived. This is not to say that the 1920s did not present denominational stress. But given the potential for rupture in the turbulent time immediately after the First World War, Southern religion scholar Samuel Hill explains that it was no small matter that the SBC "could undergo such trauma as sundering forces [did] their punishing worst" and survive intact."[13] (Our calm-during-storm characterization is substantiated to a great degree by the best source for an analysis of the SBC struggles of the period, James J. Thompson's *Tried as by Fire: Southern Baptists and the Religious Controversies of the '20s.*[14] Though Thompson's field is religion, his analysis is very politically sensitive.)

In the fundamentalist-modernist controversy we see the post-World War I appearance of "modernism" (an attempt to merge faith and reason) and "higher criticism" (the belief that the claims of the Bible should be subject to rigorous scientific analysis). Modernism was greeted with little controversy in the SBC. Keeping their eyes on the prize of soul winning, denominational leaders refused to "panic" under pressure of the struggle, "brooking no opposition to their aim of world evangelization," even from self-proclaimed fundamentalists.[15] There were firebrands against modernism and higher criticism in the convention, but hunters were as few as the hunted.[16] This period in the SBC seems similar in spirit with the McCarthy period in the country, when a handful of conservative muckrakers made headlines by planting doubts about a handful of wayward souls (and many innocents) while many equally conservatives leaders stood by the establishment.

The Joe McCarthy of the SBC was the Reverend John Franklyn Norris (1877–1952), who served as pastor of First Baptist Church in Fort Worth, Texas (1909–52), and simultaneously as pastor of Temple Baptist Church in Detroit, Michigan (1935–51).[17] Norris, a well-known convention malcontent, is important politically for several reasons. First, he was a mirror image of the typical Southern Baptist leader. As we have said, to the SBC in the 1920s, *controversy*, and particularly *political controversy*, was to be avoided at all costs. Controversy was a distraction from evangelism. Though a self-proclaimed believer in evangelism, Norris concerned himself less with the future of the denomination and its evangelical reach, and more with what he considered "the fundamentals," premillennialism and dispensationalism.[18] Norris, always called a "fundamentalist," complicates our definitional structure a bit, for in Norris we see a de jure movement fundamentalist who is unhappy in a de facto fundamentalist SBC. The rub here is that the SBC considered itself fundamentalist in theology, but not in need of Norris's Northern-style fundamentalist movement. In this sense, Norris's fundamentalism was more *mentality* than *movement*. His brand of fundamentalism reflected the conservatism of his two pastorates, the individualistic political culture of Texas mingled with the moralistic political culture of the upper Midwest—not the traditionalistic political culture of the South's Convention. Norris is the foreshadowing of a militant, individualistic, Texas brand of fundamentalism that would eventually force itself on the traditionalistic SBC.[19]

Some historians are not as charitable with Norris as we, noting that Norris's "fundamentalism" had much more to do with animus against the emerging Southern Baptist denominational machine in Nashville than with doctrine. But the reaction of SBC leaders to Norris is important as well. Convention conservatives stopped at nothing to prevent his political shenanigans from causing a distracting disturbance. In fact, in a rush of pragmatism, the apolitical SBC "in cleansing themselves of him . . . employed methods more suitable to *politics* than religion (emphasis mine)."[20] Convention leaders resorted to political maneuvering to stop political games. Soon, a fundamentalist became defined in the conservative SBC as "those who turned their discontent inward upon their own denomination."[21] *In a fit of factionalism, conservative SBC leaders reacted to conservative opposition to the peace of the convention by silencing a conservative to defend their conservative purpose—soul winning.*

Norris could claim credit for other events as well. It was in the Norris era that the very independent SBC chose to identify itself with a national defense of fundamentalist theology. Nationally known Southern Baptist theologian and seminary president Edgar Y. Mullins (1860–1928) had already written a chapter in the series of books *The Fundamentals* (published 1910–15),[22] which served as an anthology of conservative theology in reaction to liberalism. But as a result of Norris's activities and others like him, Mullins, acting in his role as Convention president, led the Convention in adopting its first confession of faith in over a century, the "Baptist Faith and Message."[23] The strain produced by modernism[24] caused even the most reclusive among the orthodox (like the SBC) to become "joiners" and coalesce in the fight against theological liberalism. This unification took place within the denomination and across denominations as well.

But there was another controversy in the postwar 1920s. The Darwinian theory of evolution and its implications for theology and public education shook the South and the SBC. Energized by the struggle over human origins, Southern Baptists passed resolutions out of their state conventions and denominational colleges,[25] and many joined the anti-evolution crusade. Because of the active support of Southern Baptists, the anti-evolution movement was successful in banning the teaching of the theory from the classrooms of Oklahoma, Florida, North Carolina, Texas, Tennessee, Mississippi, Louisiana, and Arkansas.[26] Professors in denominational schools were carefully watched as well. The South and the SBC thus mobilized against the threat.

There has always been much debate about the role of the Scopes trial in the context of the evolution battle and its larger impact on American fundamentalism and Southern culture. Some argue that "the Monkey Trial" in Dayton, Tennessee, was a victory for enlightened forces, signaling the end of the fundamentalist movement and the entry of the South and fundamentalists into mainstream national thinking. Others refuse to acknowledge Scopes as even the beginning of the end.

No matter what interpretation one chooses, the showdown was certainly full of symbolism. The fledgling ACLU had been searching the South for years, looking for an opportunity to challenge antievolution laws. When they found John Scopes of Tennessee willing to challenge state statutes, the ACLU put its best attorneys to work and dispatched one of the more famous attorneys of the day, Clarence Darrow. The conservative forces reacted by sending their lawyer, the "Great Commoner" William Jennings Bryan, three-time Democratic presidential nominee, and an aging warrior for both populism and fundamentalism.

In the face of the national media (including noted social critic H. L. Mencken, who informally advised Darrow throughout the trial), Bryan was humiliated. Taking the stand himself, Bryan was cross-examined by Darrow on his fundamentalist beliefs and the Holy Writ from which they sprang. He withstood Darrow's inquisition feebly. He stumbled and dodged. In the form of William Jennings Bryan, in defense of a Southern law, fundamentalism was put on trial and was defeated. The symbolism was irresistible: fundamentalism defeated in the heart of the SBC and the conservative South. It is also symbolic that William Jennings Bryan died within a year of the trial.

The trial and the public discussion of the Darwinian theory of evolution it spotlighted represented a blow to traditional Bible believers. First Copernicus publicly proved that the earth is not the center of the universe, and now Darwin's theory publicly showed humans not to be the center of earthly life.[27]

Some critics argue, however, that Dayton was not the end of the fundamentalist movement, but in many ways the beginning.[28] It is true that fundamentalism was far from dead. Within two years a fundamentalist college, Bob Jones College, would open its doors, and within seven years fundamentalists would effect a Northern Baptist split.

A moderate faction within the SBC was very much alive in the 1920s as well. Often overlooked in the history of the struggle about the theory of evolution are those Southern Baptists who refused to join the crusade against it. Several state conventions, for whatever reasons, refused to pass resolutions condemning the theory.[29] Also, a small group of SBC leaders (primarily editors of state Baptist newspapers)[30] actually accepted a benign "theistic" version of the theory. Theistic evolution argues that God created the basic elements of the heavens and earth in seven days, as recorded in Genesis, but these were not twenty-four-hour days. God allowed heaven and earth to evolve over millions of years, making both the Bible and Charles Darwin accurate. To fundamentalists inside the SBC and out, this pragmatic approach was akin to an "end justifies the means" approach, which was nothing short of heresy.

As with the modernism issue and the Norris controversy, Convention president E. Y. Mullins's concern in the matter of evolution was the opinion voiced by many—a refusal to accept the theory, but an aversion to the political crusading attached to the anti-evolutionary movement. During the height of the controversy, Mullins wrote that "one of the greatest dangers facing us now is that Christian people will be diverted from their task of saving souls into lobbying around legislatures and making out a program for the statute book rather than a program for the salvation of the world." This is a most interesting choice on the part of Mullins. Even faced with the rise of evolutionary theory and the religious questions it raised, Mullins opposed political means to defend religion if those activities shifted the SBC's focus from *souls*.[31]

Things had changed little in the SBC since 1888, when the most temperate denomination in the country ruled a Convention resolution on temperance *out of order* because the issue was too "political"; the purpose of the SBC was soul winning, not politics.[32] No one doubted the Southern Baptist opposition to evolution or support for the temperance movement; but to Mullins and many others, nothing—however good and scriptural in itself—could be allowed to become a distraction. This calculated call for political moderation within a militantly conservative religious-political movement is the key to the rise of Baptist Republicanism and to an understanding of fundamentalist religion and politics.[33]

The social-gospel issue yielded mixed results in the SBC of the 1920s as well. It was during this time that the progenitors of the modern moderate faction took root. But their story in this era is a short one. Seeking to make inroads[34] in the SBC, moderates were defeated by the familiar forces that kept conservative anti-evolution politics from becoming a Convention obsession. The SBC had been inoculated against new leftist or rightist struggles by the threat of controversy[35] and by a myopic emphasis on soul winning.[36]

The Convention was not completely hardened against some of the safer social issues, however. The 1925 Confession contained a "social conscience" clause calling on Baptists to aid the unfortunate among God's children.[37] In numbers, the moderates were not without influence, either, and might have made gains if they had not been so closely watched by Norris and his premillennialists.[38]

The failure of the moderate faction to prevail from the turn of the century until World War II, and the accompanying halt to the influence of the Social Gospel and conscience can be traced to a series of political events within the convention:

1908: Under recommendation of the Committee on Civic Righteousness, a Committee on Temperance is created by the Convention as a standing committee under the conservative leadership of A. J. Barton, a believer in an individualistic outlook on social problems—that social problems can be cured by evangelism.[39]

1913: A Social Service Committee is established under the moderate leadership of W. L. Poteat, a theistic evolutionist and president of Wake Forest College who commits the new committee to a more ambitious social agenda.

1914: Poteat's committee is disbanded, Poteat is relieved, and the committee's duties are merged with Barton's Committee on Temperance. Barton instead of Poteat is chosen to chair the combined agency, a position Barton holds until 1942, forcing the Convention for thirty-four years to deal with social issues as matters of individual social concern.[40]

1920: The name of the Committee on Temperance and Social Service is changed to the Social Service Commission.

1933: W. L. Poteat's nephew Edwin Poteat's proposal for a Social Research Bureau, which would use advanced statistical methods to study society instead of Bartonian pronouncements on the sinfulness of the individual, is defeated. That same year, a resolution condemning "the extraordinary grants of power" extended to President Roosevelt (a part of the Social Service Commission report) is withdrawn when delegates object to dealing with a "political matter."[41]

In short, over a period of twenty-five years the social conscience of the SBC stayed in A. J. Barton's conservative hands,[42] giving moderates little voice. As is often the case in fundamentalism, a single strong-willed leader was key to toeing a conservative line for a whole generation.[43]

But because even a toothless Social Service Commission was able to frighten conservatives and others who feared any diversion from the soul-winning mission, it could survive only by reminding the Convention that the research it provided should not be "used for 'advocation and agitation.'"[44] Defeated moderates, though they occupied positions of strength throughout the Convention, particularly in the denominational press,[45] went underground in 1946 and began to publish a magazine to get their message out.[46]

In the 1920s, even though distinct conservative and moderate theologies and ideologies were already developing, an invisible lid went into place against politics so that no movement from the left or from the right was allowed to undercut "The Message." This lid would not be loosened until the late 1950s.

The 1950s: Conservative Culture Preserved

To understand the SBC of the 1950s, one must understand the 1930s and 1940s, which can be summarized in one word: *growth*. More than any other factor, the phenomenal spread of the Southern Baptist faith in the South in this era, with the accompanying surge of church building, provides the basis for understanding Baptist Republican politics of the 1950s and beyond.[47]

The postwar period was a heady era for the SBC. The Convention saw growth from just over five million members in 1940 to just under ten million in 1960. By comparison, the Northern Baptists (or *American* Baptists after 1950) had stopped growing relative to population growth in the World War I era. The expansion of the SBC, however, at a rate faster than the growth of the Southern population, instilled it with great confidence in its machinery, program, methods, and wealth, as well as in the culture that made it thrive and flourish. The SBC strategy of avoiding creeds and controversies while remaining intrinsically conservative, democratic, decentralized, and evangelical finally seemed to have paid off.

What were the political effects of this Southern Baptist growth? What began simply as natural brand loyalty and confidence evolved into a dangerous hubris, and out of church-building megalomania and a creeping belief that the SBC had a particular "divine mission" came a certain presumption. The SBC had simply became too large and too rich, too fast.[48] With slogans like the Sunday School Board's "a million more by [19]54!" the SBC machinery seemed to encourage this attitude. I recently spoke with a Southern Baptist deacon who told me that this sloganeering continues today.

"Feeling the oats" of a new dominant position in the culture, the SBC externally rejected ecumenism, while internally holding to the belief that the blessing of size indicated a particular divine calling, a manifest destiny to evangelize and proselytize the entire American South. Ecumenism presented few enticing benefits to be sure, and the introverted SBC had already refused to join two mainline organizations, the Federal Council of Churches (now the National Council of Churches) in 1908 and the World Council of Churches in 1948. The SBC rejected unity with fundamentalists and evangelicals as well, opting not to join the American Council of Christian Churches in 1941 or the National Association of Evangelicals in 1942.[49] Refusal to join with other denominations isolated the SBC from other Christians politically, both nationally and regionally. This left the Convention with a political life safe within the bounds of the South, where it faced only success and little challenge to its religious and cultural orthodoxy. The Convention did reluctantly agree to sponsor the founding of the Baptist Joint Committee for Public Affairs (BJCPA) in 1938 as well as the founding of Protestants and Other Americans United for the Separation of Church and State (POAU) in 1947. (The latter organization is now known simply as Americans United.)[50] It is important to note that these were political organizations and not truly ecumenical in nature. The former was strictly Baptist and the latter was only informally supported by the SBC. Both were dedicated not to cooperation among churches for ecumenical religious communion, but to the express purpose of keeping government out of religion.

Such an attitude of isolationism and "chosenness" is fraught with political hazard. Once labeled in a national context as "American exceptionalism,"[51] this mindset is an extreme form of patriotism involving unwavering support for national myths and American ideals and the belief that God has a special place in His heart for the United States. Every war in which the United States has taken part has reinforced these notions.

A similar phenomenon operates in a Southern context. In what I will call "Baptist exceptionalism," when domination of the culture is achieved (whether real or perceived), further Southern Baptist growth is fueled. Eventually the notion of a Christian or even Baptist region becomes a civic religion, a mentality so binding that Southern Baptists begin to think of themselves as the cultural majority with the goal not of rejecting society (as some small, sectlike religious conservatives have done) but of absorbing it.[52] In such a world, Southern Baptist clergy and lay leadership have no interest in taking stands against Southern cultural norms. They are not motivated to oppose the culture or appear unpatriotic about the region, for to a greater and greater extent, they *are* the culture, they *are* the region.

Into this calm utopia came the disruptions of the 1950s—most notably race and the Red scare. This second uprising of political conservatism in America featured the anticommunism of Joe McCarthy and the white Southern reaction to *Brown v. Board of Education.* The key elements of this era, anticommunism and race, had a well-known political impact on the nation and the South. But what of the Convention?

For the blooming 1950s Southern Baptist Convention, even more than for the SBC of the 1920s, the general rule was political inertia, religious focus. There was only one "party" or "faction," so a don't-rock-the-boat policy quietly took effect. Say little about local or convention politics, say a lot about religion. When addressing politics, maintain the civic status quo and do not challenge the culture, but take every opportunity to merge anti-Communism with the gospel. Build the church.

Those who dared to break these various versions of the same fully evolved cardinal rule risked being ostracized. The SBC of the 1950s did have its share of outspoken moderates, but at the end of the decade only those who appealed to evangelism were left standing. The overtly political members frequently lost the internal SBC power struggle. The conservative mentality remained. The only hope of the moderates was in agencies such as the Social Service Commission (now the Christian Life Commission) and the Baptist Joint Committee, where the forces of moderation began to make the first successful attempts at showing to the Convention the world outside of the church walls.

W. A. Criswell: Preacher, Defender of the Old Order

In some sense, W. A. Criswell is still as much the living symbol of the Southern Baptist Convention as he was in the 1950s. Patriotic, confident, a fervent anti-Communist and inerrantist, Wallie Amos Criswell, born in 1909, has never been a force for moderation. The silver-haired orator began his pastorate at the huge First Baptist Church of Dallas in 1944, and at this writing has been a leader in the theological and secular politics of the Southern Baptist Convention for over fifty years.

Criswell has always been a political preacher, and his politics and theology can be found in a well-known sermon he preached in 1950. As was typical of the conservative Southern Baptist stance of the 1950s, Criswell made a plea both for rightist politics and revivalist religion:

> When Judge R. E. B. Baylor, the founder of Baylor University, came to Texas, he held court with both his Bible and his six-shooter on the bench. With the six-gun he kept law and order. With his Bible he preached the gospel. . . . In the way of the ultimate goals of atheistic communism lies

Christian America. As long as there is a strong America, the communists will not triumph. Even the Puritans went to church leading a child by one hand and carrying a musket in the other. But . . . the ultimate answer to the question of whether we live or die as a nation will be found not in the works of Stalin or Mao, but in our willingness to obey God's Holy Word, to repent of our sins, and to follow the way of life everlasting.[53]

Criswell was outspoken on race as well. While traveling on a preaching tour of South Carolina in 1954, Criswell was asked to address a joint session of the South Carolina General Assembly. The segregationist speech was "impromptu," according to Criswell's 1990 autobiography, but became a widely publicized one. In recalling the speech almost four decades after the fact, Criswell was apologetic:

> In my admittedly unwise and untimely address . . . I pled for the continual right to free association in our homes, our schools, but especially in our churches. Reporters rushed to typewriters and telephones. The next thing I knew, banner headlines labeled me as a "hateful segregationist." . . . Making that speech . . . was one of the colossal blunders of my young life. Looking back, I wish with all my heart that I had not spoken on behalf of segregation in any form or in any place.[54]

Criswell's anti-Communist rhetoric and his ready defense of the racial status quo were symbolic of the "one party" SBC conservative politics of the time. The allusions to Judge Baylor indicate that Criswell thought that Baptists were not struggling against the culture, but that Texas Baptists could claim a long history of running the state. The sympathizers with the Communists were the outsiders. The reference to Baylor was an effective bandwagon technique as well. Criswell assumed that the desire to be like the great Southern patriot would be universal among churchgoing Texans. As for his appeal to the South Carolina legislature, a receptive audience, he made a pure defense of the status quo in a Baptist-dominated South. Social justice was as foreign a concept as space travel.

Congressman Brooks Hays

Though it was small in number, and certainly not a challenge to the "one-party" system yet, a moderate opposition to the Criswell group existed in the 1950s and 1960s. These scattered "liberals" ranged from country preachers like Jack Stafford of South Carolina, who naively pursued racial understanding in a small town, to defiant denominational leaders like Brooks Hays of Arkansas, who focused national attention on SBC racial intransigence.

The Brooks Hays case is a most unusual one, if for no other reason than because Hays was simultaneously president of the Southern Baptist Convention and a United States congressman from Arkansas. The moderate Democrat was up for reelection to both posts in 1958–59, and the decision was a split one. While the voters of Arkansas sent the "integrationist" home in the fall of 1958, Southern Baptists reelected him to a second term as Convention president the following year. Arkansas voters simply rejected Hays's support for integration. But Southern Baptists, while concerned about Hays's politics, had to decide which status quo to defend. Though integrationist politics was threatening to the status quo, it was customary to reelect Convention presidents to second terms.[55] As should have been expected, the SBC rejected the idea of pursuing a new policy in regard to its officers, and voted to continue the same leadership.

As to Hays's electoral defeat, the British journal *The Economist* called the outcome "the most lamentable [election] result."[56] In a campaign telling of the politics of the time, Representative Hays was defeated in his Little Rock district by segregationist forces unhappy over his arrangement of a meeting between Arkansas governor Orval Faubus and President Eisenhower to avert a crisis over the integration of Little Rock Central High School.

The Southern Baptist lay leader knew his efforts would be unpopular back home, but thought he had turned back the challenge when he defeated a segregationist in the Democratic primary. But in a surprising break from solid Democratic loyalty, Hays was defeated in the general election by a write-in candidate, Dr. Clyde Alford, a Little Rock school board member who opposed integration. Even the campaigning in Arkansas by the governor of Mississippi, James Plemmon Coleman, was not enough. Coleman visited Hays's district, telling voters in the neighboring state that the "South need[ed] [Hays] in her great struggle."[57] Governor Faubus was reportedly not a bystander, either. He favored the write-in candidate, lending him staff support and allegedly making a number of telephone calls to key supporters. Alford won by 1,200 votes out of 60,000 cast.

Hays knew that his moderate approach was political suicide, but said that he "was so disturbed" that he was "indifferent to [his] political future."[58] For Hays the defeat was *déjà vu*. His father had lost a 1922 bid for the same seat to the candidate who had the endorsement of the Ku Klux Klan.[59]

In his autobiography, *Politics Is My Parish*, Hays reflects on a lifetime as a Southern moderate. Better than anyone else could, Hays paints a picture of the impact of the SBC on late twenties to late fifties Southern politics. It was a period, Hays writes, when "organized religion . . . was too absorbed in unrelated and irrelevant questions to help the distraught lower classes—small farmer and town laborer. The plight of black people did not appear to trouble the white Christian conscience very much."[60] Later in the book, sensing that the reader may not follow this broad characterization, Hays elaborates:

> It may be difficult for those who have not lived in small southern communities to appreciate the extent of the influence of the church on the lives of the people. It is the center of social interests and the stimulus for the cultural life of many people, not limited to religious concerns. The democracy of my church and its gospel of love, anchored to the Bible and Baptist tradition, were the magnets that held me. . . .
>
> [But] the democratic tradition which Baptists appeared to cherish was not a part of congregational procedures. . . . The approaching social crises of the thirties received little attention either in the sermons or in the Baptist literature which plugged for conservative theological views. . . . It was precisely at this point of dealing with social problems that I became somewhat critical of church policy. . . . There was a feeble effort in the period I refer to, even in the Baptist community, but it was a northern influence, chiefly Walter Rauschenbusch's, so it was dismissed as modernistic by many Southern Baptists.[61]

Hays describes a hushed society, a place where the top priority was to preserve the status quo and to keep the church and the community in state of calm.

In later years, Hays would find encouragement in the convention as moderate forces emerged. Writing in 1981, before the effects of the conservative resurgence had become apparent, Hays wrote that "it is heartening to find a new consciousness of these [social] problems in the Baptist community, but the progress must be more rapid if we spare ourselves the tension and suffering that come with the neglect of them."[62] That neglect of social problems produced the factors that led not only to Hays's rejection by the voters, but to the end of a young Southern Baptist minister's career.

The Reverend Jack Stafford

In 1946, G. Jackson Stafford, a World War II marine corps pilot and Bob Jones College graduate, began studies at Southern Baptist Theological Seminary in Louisville, Kentucky. His wife, who was also interested in theology, audited classes at the seminary until she became pregnant with their first child. Stafford graduated from SBTS in 1951 with a Bachelor of Divinity degree. Because he was not particularly good at the networking game that took place among some seminarians, Stafford took longer than usual to land his first pastorate. But after a year he was called to pastor the Batesburg Baptist Church (now the First Baptist Church of Batesburg) in rural Lexington and Saluda Counties, South Carolina, about 30 miles west of the state capital at Columbia.

After the long wait, Stafford was glad to go to Batesburg and was content in his role of country pastor. But the joy of his first pastorate evaporated quickly, as in February 1956 Stafford stood before his small congregation and abruptly resigned, announcing that he had lost the confidence of the deacon board and its chairman, U.S. District Judge George Bell Timmerman, Sr.

Stafford's resignation was not the typical Southern Baptist preacher tail-between-the-legs retreat. Breaking all the "don't rock the boat" rules of Southern Baptist harmony, Stafford not only did not agree to go quietly, but he explained to his flock the issues that forced him out. He even released a statement to the local media, though it was never printed.

The issue was very simple, Stafford said. Like most Southern Baptist ministers, Stafford and his wife, Marguerite, attended the Southern Baptist convention in St. Louis, Missouri, in June 1954. At that convention, numerous votes were taken on resolutions, officers, and reports of SBC boards and commissions. One of the reports considered was that of the Christian Life Commission, the social agency that had, since the end of A. J. Barton's reign in 1942, become the moral and social conscience of the convention.)[63] Inserted into the CLC report at the last hour was a lukewarm commendation of the Supreme Court's few-weeks-old *Brown v. Board of Education* decision. An ancillary paragraph acknowledged "the constitutional guarantee of equal freedom to all citizens . . . with the Christian principles of equal justice and love for all men" and encouraged Christian leaders to "use their leadership in positive thought and planning to the end that this crisis in our national history shall not be made the occasion for new and bitter prejudices, but a movement toward a united nation."[64] Though a spirited debate ensued, Stafford voted with a lopsided majority to accept the report.

But the support for the resolution in the convention hall was not an accurate measure of Southern Baptist opinion on the *Brown* decision, as Stafford found out the hard way. Stafford's wife, Marguerite, recalls:

> We had voted for the resolution to send a letter of commendation to the court. Then we sat down for dinner afterwards with some blacks from Nigeria (which was a big deal then, to sit down and eat with blacks).
>
> When we got back to Batesburg, Jack was confronted [about his vote] by George Bell Timmerman, a federal judge who was Chairman of the Board of Deacons, and the father of [sitting] Governor George Bell Timmerman, Jr. (They lived together in the same house.)
>
> Jack should have dodged maybe, but he defended his position. He then began to cast around for help, but no one would touch him with a ten-foot pole, not even his major professor in seminary.[65]

Though several deacons wanted to support their pastor, Timmerman, a federal judge and father of the governor, was a powerful force in Lexington and Saluda Counties and in the state. The several elected officials who attended the church backed Timmerman as well. When the matter came before the deacons, Timmerman made it clear to the dissenters that the consequences of supporting Stafford would be harmful to them. (Timmerman, Sr., felt directly insulted perhaps because he had ruled in favor of separate but equal in the case *Briggs v. Elliott*, one of the cases that became *Brown v. Board*. Later, it should be noted, the Timmermans became forces for racial healing in the community.)

The Batesburg incident was an interesting one because it was a rare one in the SBC. Though it was rumored that there was another incident, according to Mrs. Stafford there were very few ministers in the Convention who were willing to take any kind of political stand, even among the thousands who voted for the resolution in St. Louis.[66]

After he left full-time ministry in Batesburg, Jack Stafford never served a congregation again. Stafford left to take a job as a chaplain in the U.S. Army. (It was President Truman's desegregation of the armed services that represented the federal government's first efforts at integration.) The Staffords are active Democrats and Southern Baptists, but supporters of the moderate Cooperative Baptist Fellowship (CBF).

Though the Convention vote and Timmerman's reaction to it were racial issues, the incident goes beyond race and provides an illustration for our analysis of partisan politics and political conservatism within the convention. Mrs. Stafford, who seems to be a keen political observer, explains:

> The issue wasn't race, necessarily, but over who would control. The governor wanted to get votes and he got them by being a segregationist. And as he intended, Jack's experience shut the ministers up. Jack never heard from others [with similar experiences]. For when they were confronted [about their 1954 convention vote] [other ministers] had either lied or apologized.
>
> See, Southern Baptists in the 1950s veered away from controversy. Ministers knew what to talk about and what not to talk about in their sermons. There were those who were more liberal and then those who believed "every spoke in Ezekiel's wheel," but there were no burning political issues addressed. Most hid their heads in the sand and spoke the language of the people in the church, even if they didn't believe it.[67]

Judging from the experience of Jack Stafford, politically the SBC survived the 1950s much like it endured the 1920s, by sublimating everything to the work of the church, by a wholesale "veering away," in Mrs. Stafford's words, from both doctrinal and political controversy, except for a Convention-agency policy statement now and then. Moderate Baptist Marion Aldridge, who is almost a generation younger than Stafford, agrees:

> In the 1950s through the 1970s, the SBC reflected the culture. Baptists were "in denial," they wanted *peace* not *admonition*. When faced with ethical issues, like race or women in ministry, the question was always "Will this turn an interested person off?" The attitude was "anything that takes away from building the church is anathema." [It was] evangelism at any cost.
>
> [But] that's not biblical, its schizophrenic. Is there such a thing as a "user-friendly" church? What about a "user-friendly" cross?[68]

Aldridge reflects the frustration of many in the moderate faction as they look back at the lack of dimension to the SBC's gospel at midcentury. The Convention was obsessed with tranquillity, or, in his words, "in denial." But as the 1960s began, the tranquil days were coming quickly to a close.

The 1960s: Conservative Complacency Compromised

After the 1950s, the resistance to change that was characteristic of the Convention and the culture and promoted contentment and stability as seminal goals began to work against Convention conservatives. Without an organized conservative watchdog movement, the SBC began to change a bit with the progressive times, as moderate elements took over the machinery of the Convention. To moderates, it was a "golden age" in which they dominated the convention and progressive political ideas became the agenda of the old Social Service Commission, later called the Christian Life Commission.[69] SBC churches were still conservative, as was the denomination itself (the SBC was one of the most reluctant to condemn the brewing Vietnam War),[70] but moderates very quietly and unobtrusively began to dominate Convention agencies.

The director of the Baptist Joint Committee for Public Affairs[71] (an organization which until recently represented almost all Baptist groups in Washington on religious liberty issues), James Dunn, is himself a moderate faction Southern Baptist. Dunn suggests that the old mentality that smothered controversy in the name of evangelism and church building began to crumble as moderates infiltrated the Convention. The critical year, in his view, was 1968:

> That was a watershed year for Baptists . . . the hired hands, the real spark plugs of the denomination sought in Houston a programmatic commitment to an ecumenical political engagement that was not provincial . . . seeking social justice, a colorblind society, [the development of] an applied Christianity that looked after the poor, and education not indoctrination. [They decided it was] time to join the twentieth century after all . . . to stretch the rubberband as far as it would go.[72]

The seeking of what Dunn calls "a programmatic commitment" was the adoption of *A Statement Concerning the Crisis in Our Nation*, Recommendation #24 from the executive committee of the Convention. The statement was presented as a resolution to the 1968 Southern Baptist Convention[73] at the instigation of Convention agency heads. It had five parts: "We Face a Crisis," We Review Our Efforts," "We Voice Our Confession," "We Declare Our Commitment," and "We Make An Appeal." The document summarized the need for social action in race relations and antipoverty efforts and confessed complicity in the injustice done to blacks. (A motion was made to strike the entire section admitting guilt for racism, "We Voice Our Confession," but it was defeated.) After a healthy debate, the statement passed. The moderates rejoiced, but it proved to be a Pyrrhic victory.

What the presentation of *A Statement* in 1968 represented, in short, was a moderate political awakening. Convention moderates had moved from an irresolute statement in favor of *Brown v. Board of Education* in 1954 to a lengthy, up-front *mea culpa* analysis in 1968 from none other than the executive committee of the Convention. This bold stance represented the first attempt at a political push in the SBC, an aggressive campaign by the middle and left that touched a match to conservative dynamite. Within a few short years, the conservative faction formed and the engine for takeover, the fundamentalist Baptist Faith and Message Fellowship, was being organized.

Until the moderate call to arms at the 1968 convention, conservatives (and everyone else) seemed to be lulled to sleep, content to coexist with a moderate element. This attitude was voiced succinctly by the conservative executive director of the SBC's political Christian Life Commission: "There has been a tremendous shift. When I was growing up in Southern Baptist Churches, one of the most persistent themes was 'Now, we're Southern Baptists. That means we don't get involved in anything controversial. We just preach the gospel.' Well . . . that's an oxymoron!"[74] Southern Baptist resistance to politics became an oxymoron in 1968 when the moderates took their stand and the conservative faction responded. Soon the "one party" SBC would have two militant, ideological factions struggling for control.

The 1980s: Conservative Takeover Completed

In 1979, conservative Southern Baptist layman Charles Goolsby had just come to Washington from his native Texas. Active in the conservative wing of the Democratic party there, numerous internecine struggles had made him a known expert in parliamentary procedure. This reputation followed him to Washington, and shortly before the Southern Baptist Convention in June 1979 Goolsby went to his mailbox to find in it a plane ticket to Houston. Individualistic, movement-oriented Texas conservatism was on the rise again. But unlike the conservatism of J. Frank Norris, this conservative movement was like Goolsby—urban and middle class. The leaders were not country preachers, but Professor Paige Patterson of Dallas and Appeals Court Judge Paul Pressler of Houston. They had made Goolsby's travel arrangements on the recommendation of fellow New Christian Right traveler, U.S. Representative John Conlan, a founder of the Moral Majority. The professor and the judge were making a move on the SBC and needed Goolsby's parliamentary services.

A good soldier, Goolsby willingly made the trip to Houston. His role there was to provide parliamentary advice to Pressler, who stationed himself in a booth above the convention floor.

The first six months had been busy ones for Paul Pressler. In an effort to organize a conservative faction for Houston, the judge often spoke fifty times a week, planning a tight speaking schedule around court dates and taking his legal work on the road and working out of a hotel room. Pressler began his crusade after being invited to talk with a group of Baylor University students about their Old Testament class. According to Pressler, the Baptist-supported university was teaching that the prophesies of the book of Daniel could not be true prophecies, and that the book was a mere human creation. An inerrantist, Pressler was furious. Baylor would have to be changed, and if Baylor needed to return to its fundamentalist roots, so did the Convention.

Pressler's method was not a direct one, but it was quite comprehensive. Along with W. A. Criswell and his protégé Paige Patterson, conservatives would bus in enough delegates or "messengers" to Houston to win the ceremonial Convention presidency. According to SBC rules, the president as figurehead appoints committees that nominate trustees for the numerous Convention boards, such as Baylor University. The boards in turn hire administrators to run Convention agencies, colleges, seminaries, and commissions.

Pressler's plan was to win the presidency for a hand-picked candidate and for the first time to use presidential-appointment power aggressively—to see that conservatives were chosen to sit in every seat on every board in the Convention. Previously appointments had been based on recommendations and consensus as well as the inclinations of the appointer, but no rule forced the president to follow this customary course.

The strategy worked. Adrian Rogers of Memphis was elected, and he appointed the Pressler list to high Convention posts. But the job was far from done. The task had to be repeated. There were so many seats on so many boards, in fact, that the 1979 feat would have to be repeated for ten consecutive years to fully impanel agency boards with totally conservative membership. As of 1996, the Pressler organization has won virtually every recurring presidential election and now controls most every SBC agency.

Charles Goolsby is still a conservative, and still a Southern Baptist. He has since followed Pressler, and become an active member of the Republican party. But looking back over the seventeen years of convention controversy, Goolsby has had second thoughts about his participation in that first "takeover":

> I supported it [the takeover] at the time, but it was a mistake. [The conservatives] had identified the problem—liberalism in the seminaries (and other places)—but their method was wrong. It became too political. When the church becomes political, it is easy to write it off. I agree with [Pat] Robertson and Pressler and others that there is a Christian Counterculture, but there is no such thing as a"Christian polity." The devil is in charge of politics, and we won't beat him there. Politics is a *trap*. The Lord never said, "Let's get control of Rome and pass all these laws." The only way [to change the world] is one soul at a time like Jesus did.[75]

Goolsby's position is not hard to understand, but it is not widespread. He opposed both the stand of the moderate faction in 1968, and he now opposes the 1979 takeover he had assisted for the same reasons: the politicization of the church. Looking back over his Southern Baptist youth in Texas, Goolsby admits that the SBC was involved in supporting Prohibition and blue laws and in opposing gambling, but he defends these as activities that "didn't take over the mission of the church."[76]

Moderate Action, Conservative Reaction

In their analyses of the struggle for Convention supremacy, the moderate James Dunn and the conservative Charles Goolsby agree on at least one very important point: the conservative movement was a *countermovement*. In Goolsby's words: "It was a *response*, just like the Moral Majority was a response to the egregious interference with their freedoms represented by *Roe v. Wade*."[77]

Here's the pattern. The political cauldron churned in the 1920s and the 1950s with "one-party" moderation reigning. But in the 1960s a "militant moderate" political offensive from the convention elite opened the door to politics for the first time and produced a rank and file, equally militant conservative counteroffensive. As with Southern culture, the moderates did enjoy a "Camelot" in the 1960s, but it was a tenuous one. Southern culture, like Southern Baptist culture, naturally tends toward conservatism, and conservative themes resonate with the devoutly conservative. By 1979, the "sweet-spirited and naive,"[78] as one moderate calls them, were swept up in a takeover movement, a political movement developed through the use of "theology by intimidation . . . long and loud [conservative faction] statements on 'let's beat 'em up topics'" that moved the masses to action.[79]

The split became ugly and very public for the first decade. With conservative consolidation, moderates have been driven from positions of leadership within the Convention to find themselves in limbo. They still call themselves Southern Baptists, but pick and choose which programs of the Convention they will support. Furthermore, having given up on regaining control, they have formed a separate moderate organization that includes a seminary, a missions organization, a publishing house, and an annual meeting.[80]

The most intriguing moderate figure in the SBC controversy is Southern Baptist moderate Jimmy Carter. President Carter is a picture of the change twenty years can bring. While Brooks Hays was reelected to the SBC presidency after electoral defeat, Jimmy Carter lost the U.S. presidency and his faction lost control of the convention within eighteen months. Carter's campaign biography, *Why Not the Best?*,[81] was published by the SBC's Broadman Press in 1975, and Carter's "born again" religion and the confessed "lust in his heart" became a major part of his 1976 campaign. But by 1980, opposing abortion but not supporting a ban on the practice[82] was no longer enough for militant conservatives, and Carter was edged out for the middle-right SBC swing vote by Ronald Reagan, dividing Southern Baptists even as they began to awaken politically. Southern Baptists had strong feelings for Carter early on, and he never broke with the Southern Baptist Convention while president. But by 1979, Southern Baptist support for Carter had eroded significantly. The 1980 SBC passed a resolution calling Carter's White House Conference on the Family "a general undermining of the biblical concept of the family."[83]

Theology and Politics

As was illustrated in figure 1.2, Baptist Republicanism contains both a theological element[84] (unbending conservative religious beliefs with numerous historical antecedents) and an ideological element (a mixture of political conservatism[85] and cultural factors). Together they represent a movement to "reclaim" the old ways in the SBC in the face of moderate reforms. Conservative politicians stress the same "reclaiming" themes.

Baptists have truly merged theology and politics. The Cooperative Baptist Fellowship even has a "political officer" and the organ of the moderate faction, *Baptists Today*, has a regular section in its pages entitled "Politics and Corridor Talk."

In merging the theological and the political, Baptist Republicans created a movement of great strength. And, unlike the earlier aborted fundamentalist movements of the 1920s and 1930s, this conservatism was both militant and professional. The leaders of the new SBC conservative faction were rich, powerful, and individualistic, reflective of the Texas political culture from which many of them sprang.[86]

The Theological Takeover of the SBC

The theological submovement of *inerrancy* is the belief in an inerrant, infallible scripture; it holds that the Bible is without error in its original manuscripts. Inerrancy as a movement began in earnest as a reaction to the prevailing moderate establishment of the 1960s SBC. This theological organizing began in the wake of the denominational press's publication of SBC seminary professor Ralph Elliot's *The Message of Genesis* in 1961.[87] In the book, Elliot made use of a wide range of historical and theological analyses to provide a new commentary on the first book of the Bible. The interpretation was not pleasing to conservatives, however, as the seminarian challenged the prevailing orthodoxy on the existence of Adam and Eve and Jonah's survival after being swallowed by a big fish.[88] The Elliot book led to a demand for and adoption of a new "Baptist Faith and Message" (BFM) statement in 1963.[89] This creed, summarizing Baptist doctrine, was adopted to pacify convention conservatives, as it had in 1925.

The BFM of controversy of 1963 was unlike the theological fights of the 1920s, however, in that true calm did not return to the SBC after its adoption. In 1925, the most conservative of the conservatives in the Convention felt secure and returned to their corner. An insecure conservative faction in the 1960s and 1970s, however, was on constant alert.[90] Conservatives perceived moderates as too powerful[91] and refused their offer of a Baptist *pax*. Thus, a theological movement of the discontented was born and the battle was joined at every opportunity.[92]

The theological differences in the two groups cannot be denied. The fundamentalist movement in the 1980s, as in the 1920s, was fueled by a

Bible Conference movement[93] and characterized by strong leadership.[94] In response to a Bible commentary published by the Convention considered liberal by conservatives, the conservative reaction continued with the formation of the Baptist Faith and Message Fellowship, the founding of a newsletter (*Southern Baptist Journal*), and the establishment of a seminary, the Criswell Center. All were used to wage the war for inerrancy in the SBC. There was some social basis for the split, as the more urbanized, educated, and upwardly mobile members tended to support the moderate faction, but the conservative faction had its yuppies as well. Theological distinctions were central to the struggle.[95]

The theology of the moderate faction[96] insists on "discipleship [practical Christian growth] over doctrine"[97] and warns of the entanglement of church and state through the efforts of the fundamentalist right.[98] Moderates stress missionary efforts versus doctrine as a basis for unity.[99] They also revive the doctrine of "soul competency,"[100] which resists the adoption of any type of creed[101] as a move from regular (churchly) Baptist to separatist (sectarian) Baptist traditions (see fig. 1.2).[102] To moderate Baptists, the conservatives are not the true heirs of Roger Williams, who had struggled to found the Baptist denomination, but of his Puritan persecutors. Most moderate faction leaders argue that the move from persecuted New England minority to dominating Southern church has corrupted the theology of Convention conservatives, leading to a weakening of concern for separation of church and state[103] and to too much emphasis on evangelism. One scholar predicts for the SBC a future "immolat[ion] on the pyre of evangelical success."[104]

But the moderates are themselves divided, illustrated best by their reaction to a recent peace statement between seminary presidents and conservative leaders. Some in the moderate faction labeled the statement a sellout, others cheered the newfound peace.[105]

Hinson's swipe at "evangelical success" indicates another difference between the factions in theology. Many supporters of the moderate faction insist that Baptists are not evangelicals.[106] Southern Baptist scholars disagree as to whether the SBC belongs in this camp. Seminary professor Glenn Hinson[107] argues that there is within the SBC not only an *evangelical* strain that produces a commitment to the Great Commission, but a *volunteerist* strain that calls for a commitment to separation of church and state and religious liberty.[108] Being a Baptist, Hinson writes, "refers to that version of Christianity which places the priority of voluntary and uncoerced faith or response to the Word and Act of God over any supposed 'objective' Word and Act of God." It places response over scriptures and creed.[109] Though no conservative, Professor James Leo Garrett disagrees, arguing that Hinson has intellectualized the matter too much. Others disagree, citing the similarity in evangelical and Baptist positions, that is, both are theologically conservative and committed to an active spread of the gospel.[110] (I will continue this discussion in the next chapter as the relationship between the SBC and evangelicalism becomes central to the fundamentalist-moderate struggle in the SBC.)

Convention factionalism entered a second phase in 1990, with a last-straw defeat on the Convention floor and the partial secession of many in the moderate faction to form the Cooperative Baptist Fellowship (CBF). Some joined the more progressive Alliance of Baptists as well.[111] In defeat, moderates have begun to focus what energy they have left on the CBF and the AB. And why not? Indeed, for moderates, the convention is a lonely place. Their demands for more social action, a role for women in church leadership, more ecumenical contact, less conservative politics, more church-state separation, and even a church that behaves like a denomination rather than a sect are unheeded by the dominant conservative faction. As each new president takes office, conservatives continue to dig in at the three major seminaries and Convention boards and commissions. At the seminaries, President Russell Dilday, the last moderate president, was forced out at Southwestern Seminary in Fort Worth in March 1993[112] and replaced by conservative Ken Hemphill in an ugly public dispute complete with student protests. Conservative president Albert Mohler of Southern Baptist Theological Seminary in Louisville[113] has begun to enforce the seminary's 130-year-old doctrinal statement which all professors must sign. Patterson, the theological half of the Pressler-Patterson political-theological takeover movement,[114] was named president of Southeastern Baptist Theological Seminary in Wake Forest, North Carolina, in 1993, completing the takeover of seminary presidencies.

Conservatives have had less success with Baptist colleges and universities, state conventions, and state newspapers. State-level Baptist newspapers, which feature Baptist news from around the state and nation along with a weekly scripture lesson, have huge circulations. Most of these papers are run by state conventions and generally follow state factional trends in editorial content and position.

Institutions of higher education, fearing loss of academic freedom, were the most militantly opposed to takeovers and the focus of recent controversy. Several SBC schools, such as Furman in South Carolina, Baylor in Texas, Wake Forest in North Carolina, and Stetson in Florida, outorganized the conservatives and cut or weakened ties with the Convention, involving Convention floor fights and a lawsuit or two. Others, like Alabama's University of Mobile, cut a deal with the conservatives.[115]

Some states have resisted conservative bids for state convention control for a number of years only to succumb (South Carolina; North Carolina); others have endured years of infighting and bitterness (Texas); still others have remained firmly in the moderate faction (Virginia).[116] Moderates have also been forced out of the Convention's wire service, the Baptist Press (BP), because it is controlled out of Nashville by appointed trustees. Two senior staff members of BP were fired suddenly, causing Southern Baptist Bill Moyers[117] to defend them publicly. This led to the formation of the moderate faction's Associated Baptist Press (ABP).

Since the early 1990s, moderate faction–conservative faction artillery has been all but silenced as the CBF and the SBC have begun to work back to back rather than in each other's faces. Every few months a new issue flares up, such as:

- The failure of moderate forces to see that the fundamentalist Southern Seminary is put on probation by the national seminary accrediting agency;
- The SBC's firing of a missionary couple for supporting speaking in tongues and other Charismatic views;
- Texas fundamentalist faction efforts to set up a rival Baptist Convention in the Lone Star State;
- Americans United for Separation of Church and State's call for a federal investigation of political activities in Second Baptist Church, Lake Jackson, Texas;
- The departure of the theological journal *Review & Expositor* from Southern Seminary and Southern's firing of a popular professor;
- SBC state papers drawing fire for running ads for the CBF;
- The CBF's refusal to take a position on homosexuality;
- Former conservative faction Convention president Charles Stanley's on-again, off-again divorce proceedings;
- Baylor University's lifting of the ban on dancing on campus.

Other than this sniping, the SBC is focusing on implementing a restructuring proposal that will reduce the number of Convention agencies, and the CBF is enjoying its new facilities on the campus of Mercer University and working with the American [formerly Northern] Baptist Churches, USA, on projects of mutual concern.

The Political-Ideological Takeover of the SBC

The takeover of the SBC has a political component as well. The Convention's conservative faction is strongly tied to the Republican party, and the moderate faction is supportive of the Democratic party. The most visible examples of this dual allegiance are the former governor of Arkansas, President Bill Clinton, and the new governor of Arkansas Mike Huckabee.[118] Both are Southern Baptists from Hope, Arkansas. Democrat Clinton has allied himself with the moderate wing, inviting leaders of the Cooperative Baptist Fellowship to the White House for warm fellowship, but suffering through a meeting with SBC leaders that neither side rated productive. Huckabee, a former SBC pastor and a former president of the Arkansas Baptist Convention, is equally attached to the conservative side, appearing at the new conservative-controlled Christian Life Commission's 1994 annual seminar on the same panel with President Reagan's secretary of education, Bill Bennett. Huckabee is best known for igniting a controversy in Arkansas by proclaiming a "Christian Heritage Week" throughout the state. He made the proclamation as acting governor while Jim Guy Tucker was still governor but out of the state.[119]

The Baptist presence on Capitol Hill has faced a similar partisan split in recent years. The Baptist Joint Committee for Public Affairs was until 1992 the political lobby in Washington for all major Baptist denominations, including the Southern Baptist Convention. But citing irreconcilable differences, the SBC sought a divorce from the BJCPA in June 1992.[120] The SBC took with it a majority of the agency's budget and the support of the nation's largest Baptist denomination and set up a lobbying organization of its own on the other side of Capitol Hill. The secession of the SBC from its loyal mouthpiece in Washington, which it had helped found and generously fund, sent an unequivocal message: the bickering in the SBC is no longer a "preacher fight,"[121] and the SBC has changed politically and dramatically.[122]

This shift can be best understood by the politics of the individual players in the conflict. BJCPA director Dunn has long been the progressive reformer, often serving as lightning rod within the SBC for moderates against conservatives. For that reason, Dunn does not grieve a great deal over the departure of his native church from the BJCPA alliance. But because he enjoys the day-to-day give and take of politics more than its financial aspects, he admits that he does not relish "spending more time fundraising"[123] than before. But he is equally earnest about the "freedom" produced by the separation. The bickering over what constituted "the Baptist stand" on public affairs issues is over. Now there are, at least, two "Baptist" stands.[124] Moderate SBC congregations and the CBF still support the BJCPA directly, and the SBC now has a Washington office of its Christian Life Commission (known as the Ethics and Religious Liberty Commission as of June 1997) to make its case.

For Dunn, there is also comfort in the fact that two men he calls "a couple of buddies" came to town in January 1993: the Southern Baptist moderates Bill Clinton of Immanuel Baptist Church in Little Rock, Arkansas, and Al Gore, Jr., of Mount Vernon Baptist Church in Alexandria, Virginia. On the day I visited with Dunn, he told his entire staff that he had arranged for them to go to the White House to attend a welcoming ceremony for the visit of a foreign dignitary. He would need their social security numbers for the Secret Service immediately. This scenario showed that Dunn and the Clinton administration are indeed "buddies." Dunn is often the impresario of numerous functions for religious leaders at the White House, allowing the president to consult regularly with the American clergy.[125] He has also been quite outspoken in his defense of Clinton at the expense of the last two occupants of 1600 Pennsylvania Avenue.[126] In sharp contrast, the SBC leadership and the White House have not been buddy-buddy, with one meeting in the Oval Office among the SBC clergy, Clinton, and Gore ending with little accomplished.[127] Southern Baptists seem much more taken with Speaker Newt Gingrich of New Hope Baptist Church in Fayetteville, Georgia. In short, the political differences among Southern Baptists of late are large.[128]

The estrangement of Baptists like Clinton and Baptists like Gingrich and Huckabee is due to opposite partisan allegiances. In this case, the allegiance is both theological and political, for it is also Bill Clinton's allegiance to the "wrong" theological faction that caused no joy at SBC headquarters in Nashville when he won the election. Like politicians, religious leaders have a stake in election outcomes. The leaders of the ruling conservative faction[129] of the SBC would have preferred anyone else (even Episcopalian George Bush) besides a member of the moderate faction of the SBC to be president of the United States.

Because we have had only three Southern Baptist presidents—Harry S. Truman of Missouri,[130] Jimmy Carter of Georgia, and Bill Clinton of Arkansas—it is difficult to measure the relative warmth of relations between the denomination and each president. However, it is hard to imagine cooler relations than those existing between Clinton-Gore and the SBC.[131] *Insight*,[132] the newsletter of the National Association of Evangelicals (NAE), told the NAE membership in the first year of the Clinton presidency that since his election to the White House, President Clinton has snubbed the entire evangelical community. The newsletter's list of complaints included the claim that during the president-elect's transition in Arkansas, no meetings were held with Little Rock clergy, that the Cabinet and White House staff do not contain any self-professed evangelicals, and that an invitation to speak at the March 1993 meeting of the five-million-member NAE went unacknowledged. Southern Baptists in particular are sore that they have not been invited to National Prayer Breakfasts, to meetings with national church leaders, or to interfaith breakfasts.[133] One of the members of the Clinton transition team, former vice-president of the National Council of Churches and former executive director of the NAACP, Benjamin Chavis, told the *Washington Monthly* that the reason for the refusal to acknowledge the NAE's invitation was the organization's "irrelevancy." "It's not because anyone is shutting the door in their face, but because their ideology increasingly does not apply to the American condition."[134]

Evangelicals in general and Southern Baptists in particular are not without their shots at the administration. At a recent Southern Baptist Convention, forty resolutions were presented to the resolutions committee, eighteen of which were attacks on Clinton and Gore. The committee combined the separate entreaties into one resolution blasting Clinton. It passed overwhelmingly, along with resolutions opposing homosexuality, abortion, and the appointment of an ambassador to the Vatican. These actions would have been enough to make the point to the White House that the SBC sought repentance. But when each "messenger," or delegate, from Clinton's home church was required to go before the Credentials Committee and swear his or her opposition to homosexuality before being seated, the call for repentance began to resemble an inquisition. One conservative faction messenger, demanding more drastic action, called for the Immanuel Baptist Church of Little Rock to be disfellowshiped, that is, tossed out of the SBC. Clinton's church has been picketed, and Convention programs have been developed to ask Southern Baptists to pray specifically for the president for ninety-day periods.[135]

It is interesting to consider now how much stronger were the actions of the 1992 and 1993 Conventions opposing the 1992 Democratic nominees than the 1988 Convention was to the 1988 nominees. Michael Dukakis, who has been called "the first truly secular candidate we ever had for the presidency," once told friends that he never thought of death or the afterlife.[136] Dukakis was treated with kid gloves compared to the reception given the candidate who sang in the choir in his home church and whose campaign and 1995 State of the Union theme was "The New Covenant." (Before his crucifixion, Jesus held a Last Supper of bread and wine with his disciples in which he called the wine "the new covenant in my blood.") One of his 1996 campaign themes, best articulated at the Chicago Democratic convention, was the restoration of "American faith." President Clinton also preached "faith" and "values" to the Progressive National (African American) Baptist Convention, confessed to the sins of anger and gluttony, and argued that he searched scripture and could find no scripture proscribing abortion. A search of the archives of the Clinton presidency at the website of Texas A & M Univeristy shows that Clinton used the word "faith" in 256 speeches, from his inauguration through December 1995. He used "covenant" seventy times in three years. Clinton quoted scripture[137] so much during his two presidential campaigns that he was said "to know the language of Zion."[138]

This meant nothing to the Southern Baptist leadership or to the convention that condemned him. Perhaps they thought his religious training made him more accountable for his theological and political mistakes, that "to whom much is given, much is required."

Moderate Faction Politics

Moderates and Conservatives have shared in creating an extremely political Southern Baptist Convention. Much of this obsession has its roots in the early years of the schism. In this polarization, the antics of the Republican-aligned conservative faction have been well reported—from SBC president Bailey Smith's "God does not hear the prayer of the Jew" spoken at a 1984 Texas Republican *political* rally, to the picketing of churches.

The equally passionate political motivations of the convention moderates have been given less attention. Perhaps this is because they have been the losers in the recent struggle. In search of outspoken moderation we again turn to James Dunn, head of the safe haven for moderates, the Baptist Joint Committee on Public Affairs.

Because the BJCPA lobbies Congress on a variety of political and ethical issues on behalf of ten Baptist denominations, moderates find the cooperation and partnership that exists among the Baptist groups through the BJCPA extremely important. Particularly helpful is the opportunity for fellowship with the black National Baptist Convention and the "Northern" Baptists, the American Baptist Churches (ABC). The BJCPA is (was) a symbol for moderates of the commitment of the SBC to break out of its evangelical subculture[139] and to interact with more mainline Baptists, a position moderate faction Baptists have been urging since the turn of the century.[140] Demonstrating this mindset, the moderate faction's Southern Baptist Alliance became the Alliance of Baptists, and the official moderate organ, *SBC Today* magazine, became the more ecumenical-sounding *Baptists Today*. Also, a number of moderate churches, including the First Baptist Church of Washington, D.C., hold joint SBC/ABC affiliation.

As already noted, much of the SBC conservative faction's distaste for the BJCPA has been generated by its executive director, who is as much a source of hope to progressives as a thorn to conservatives. James Dunn was for a time a member of the board of directors of Norman Lear's Moral Majority alternative, People for the American Way,[141] and has from time to time set the Joint Committee on the opposite side of the religious right's Capitol Hill agenda, particularly on the issues of school prayer, the "Grove City" Civil Rights Bill, abortion, and various nominations to the Supreme Court.[142] (In recent years, Dunn has also angered conservatives by including representatives of the Cooperative Baptist Fellowship, but not the Southern Baptist Convention, at White House prayer breakfasts.)[143]

Dunn, as a central figure in the moderate faction, recently summarized his political and religious positions in a review of the book *The Baptist Identity, Four Fragile Freedoms* by Walter Shurden. His words are worth quoting here:

> President Bill Clinton, Al Gore, Bill Moyers, Marian Wright Edelman, Martin Luther King, Jr., and Marian Anderson. . . . I contend that the six persons above are among the *real* Baptists in contrast to the many *faux*

Baptists that regularly muddy the media. . . . Dr. Shurden has hit the heart of what makes a Baptist a Baptist. He has touched the spiritual and theological marks, the distinctives, the convictions, the ideals. These are beliefs shared by President Clinton and countless citizens who resonate to the rhetoric born of his faith.[144]

Dunn and the BJCPA have not been alone in their more Democratic sympathies. The newspapers of certain state Baptist conventions[145] are holdouts for the moderate position. Reporting on the impact of the 1992 election for the *Baptists Today*, Marse Grant, the editor emeritus of *Biblical Recorder*, the newspaper of the North Carolina Baptist Convention, wrote:

> These two fine Baptist laymen achieved their victories with absolutely no help from the SBC inner circle which featured Republican speakers on convention programs for the past decade. . . . Where will the Clinton-Gore administration turn to when church-state issues arise? It won't be the Washington political office of opportunistic SBC Christian Life Commission executive director Richard Land. It will be the Baptist Joint Committee and its veteran executive director James Dunn. His considerable influence is enhanced by the election of Bill Clinton. Land's underlings can't carry Dunn's briefcase when it comes to influence on Capitol Hill. . . . What impact will the election have on the SBC? Very little. The fundamentalists [conservative faction] are too deeply entrenched for any significant change in this century. . . . The [moderate faction's] Cooperative Baptist Fellowship is young and growing. Many of its strongest supporters are in the same age group that put Bill Clinton in the White House. It is the wave of the future in Baptist life.[146]

Other prominent Southern Baptist moderates include Jimmy Allen, a former Convention president and close friend of former President Carter;[147] Vice-President Al Gore;[148] former ten-term Alabama congressman and People for the American Way director James Buchanan; former Dunn BJCPA assistant and Alliance of Baptists director Stan Hastey; former Cooperative Baptist Fellowship director Cecil Sherman; and Will Campbell, civil rights activist and author of *Brother to a Dragon Fly, Stem of Jesse,* and *The Convention,*[149] a novel about the conservative SBC resurgence. Most wrote columns celebrating the end of the Reagan-Bush era, celebrating the presidency of Bill Clinton, and bragging that the president is not only a Southern Baptist, but their brand of Southern Baptist.

Bill Clinton has seen his presidency lead to a shoring up of moderate Baptist Democratic support as well. One Southern Baptist pastor decided to seek a slot as delegate to the Democratic National Convention after receiving a notice in the mail entitled "Why You Cannot Be a Christian and Be a Democrat."

Conservative Faction Partisan Politics

The conservative faction is tied to the Republican party probably more than the moderates are tied to the Democrats. At the time of the 1979 conservative faction takeover of the SBC led by Pressler of Houston and by Patterson, both men were working with other New Right preachers and for other Republican causes as well. There were National Affairs Briefings in 1980 led by Tennessee Baptist layman Ed McAteer's Religious Roundtable and a rally at W. A. Criswell's First Baptist Church in Dallas, where candidate Ronald Reagan told the "bipartisan" meeting, "You can't endorse me, but I endorse you." It was Pressler who joined with preachers like Tim LaHaye, laymen like Ed McAteer,[150] and conservatives like Joseph Coors to found the organization that became the Council for National Policy in 1981. The purpose of the organization is not well known. When Pressler was asked about the Council by Bill Moyers in a documentary in late 1987 and early 1988, Pressler ended the interview abruptly, telling Moyers that he had agreed to be interviewed about the Southern Baptist Convention and its politics, not about secular politics. Along with Coors, Pressler and Patterson have also helped to raise funds for Howard Phillips's Conservative Caucus[151] in Texas. In addition, Patterson's wife has served on the national advisory board of the New Right group called Concerned Women for America along with the wives of conservative faction Convention presidents Adrian Rogers and Charles Stanley.[152] Judge Pressler was about to be nominated by President Bush to head the office of Government Ethics in 1989 when the nomination was withdrawn.

Convention presidents have had a hand in endorsing U.S. presidential candidates. Jimmy Draper, president of the SBC from 1982 to 1984, mailed an endorsement for Pat Robertson for president to 125,000 Southern Baptists before the Super Tuesday primaries in March 1988.[153] Pressler, LaHaye, and former or future SBC presidents Jerry Vines, Adrian Rogers, Ed Young, and Morris Chapman also attended a meeting with George Bush during the 1988 campaign, along with Jerry Falwell and other New Christian Right leaders.[154] Since that time, the GOP-SBC connection has been more open; Presidents Reagan and Bush addressed national conventions regularly.

With victory in eighteen straight convention presidential elections, the conservative faction has shifted its political focus from the convention presidency to the activities of two other organizations that have supported conservative faction activism. The Public Affairs Committee of the SBC[155] (which represented the SBC on the BJCPA but has long been dominated by conservative Republicans) is now free to pursue its own agenda apart from the Joint Committee. Past PAC members have included Samuel T. Currin, a former aide to Senator Jesse Helms; former Alabama Republican congressman Albert Lee Smith; and Les Csorba, Judge Pressler's son-in-law and head of the movement's conservative group, Accuracy in Academia. All were appointed by the committee on nominations, which is appointed by the SBC president.[156] The Public Affairs Committee awarded Senator Jesse Helms the Religious Liberty Award in 1990.[157]

The Christian Life Commission (the Ethics and Religious Liberty Commission as of June 1997), is headed by Richard Land, a Pressler ally and former aide to Texas Republican Governor Bill Clements. Land moved from membership on the PAC to head day-to-day operations at the CLC both in Nashville and Washington in the post-BJCPA era. (This was a promotion, for the Christian Life Commission is composed of trustees elected by the SBC and has power to perform certain tasks on its own. The Public Affairs Committee, before merger with the CLC, was an SBC committee of members who had no decision-making powers outside the convention meeting.)[158] Land's position is almost as conservative as Dunn's is progressive. He commented shortly after the 1992 election that "a significant number of unborn babies [will] die unless God changes Bill Clinton's mind and heart."[159]

In addition to these agencies and individuals, paid political consulting has been part of the SBC fight as well. We have already documented the flying in of a parliamentarian for the 1979 SBC, and the conservative faction has, since it beat the moderates to the punch in organization right from the start, taken on a few hired guns. Conservatives in Texas hired Jesse Helms's protégé, Barry McCarty, in November 1991 to provide parliamentary advice in their showdown with Baylor University.[160] The moderates are not to be left out on this score. North Carolina moderates retained Randolph Cloud, former director of development for the North Carolina Democratic party, to help organize moderate delegates in the Tarheel state in 1985.[161] This is a most telling phenomenon in the age of the political consultant—that a religious denomination would be so divided by factionalism that it would turn to paid partisan strategists. Charles Goolsby told me that moderate outgoing Convention president Jimmy Allen screamed at one point during the takeover in 1979 that Judge Pressler was "trying to run [the SBC] like a national political convention."[162]

Conclusion

Looking back on her experience at Batesburg Baptist Church in 1956, and her subsequent intense involvement in secular, Convention, and local church politics, Marguerite Stafford sees a pattern:

> In our local church, it's like it used to be in the Convention. We're divided, but we get along because our pastor has decided not to make it an issue. Our [suburban south Georgia] church is growing. It has lots of fundamentalists in it, but we're as diverse as we can be. Fundamentalists in the church haven't tried to take over. Again, we're just "going along."[163]

Mrs. Stafford thinks it is tragic that the Convention has been politicized and is divided into warring factions. Most Southern Baptists would no doubt agree with her, save those moderates[164] who are proud of the strength of the companion moderate organizations,[165] and conservatives who feel the purge is God's will.

But as figure 1.2 in chapter 1 showed, the split was inevitable. There was and is within the SBC a distinct moderate and conservative theology and a distinct moderate and conservative political ideology, each with their own antecedents, one more Baptist, one more Southern; one more libertarian, one more traditionalistic; one more "churchly," one more "sectarian"; one more Democratic, one more Republican. Without engagement in secular politics and secular-type political organizations and strategies, or as Mrs. Stafford puts it, by just "going along" and "not making [politics] an issue," there might be harmony and unity in the largest religious denomination in America, and factions would not have formed.

One thing is certain. The halcyon days of the 1920s, when there was one-party (faction) rule and the fiercest controversies were subsumed in the name of soul winning, are over. The succeeding 1950s SBC that turned a deaf ear to social concern and fostered a benign politics in the name of church building is gone as well. Just as in the founding of America, with political parties came polarization, forcing every citizen (or parishioner) to choose a side. As the anecdote at the beginning of this chapter indicates, it was because conservative and moderate factions have each taken their turn at the plow through successive political seasons (the 1920s, the 1950s) that the struggle was given sustenance for the winter phase of the 1980s. In that phase, Southern Baptists were forced by militant "parties" to confront their own political history or remain painfully astride a widening chasm.

As figure 2.1 illustrates, at the turn of the century the goal of Southern Baptist politics was not engagement with the issues in the culture, but a focus on its evangelical mission. The spigot of secular politics and political issues was kept tightly closed for decades, even in the face of intense pressure. When needed, statements were passed to assuage the concerns of the most conservative, concerns usually about issues outside the Convention, such as evolution or modernism. The goal was to preserve unity and the cultural and Convention status quo.

As the world changed, however, moderate forces in the SBC attempted to change the organization, and conservatives began to react to internal concerns. Moderate Social Commission proposals were defeated or co-opted by conservatives. Calls for social concern were converted into another kindling of evangelical fervor. As figure 2.1 also shows, each moderate initiative was stymied by a conservative reaction that led to adoption of an equally conservative treatise or action immediately afterward. Every moderate initiative in the top half of the figure was followed by a conservative reaction below and slightly to the right on the time line. This is true of the nation as well. But it was the opening of the *political* door in 1954 and 1968 and the demand that the SBC address the issues of social justice that destroyed the moderate equilibrium and produced the permanent right-wing backlash of the present era. After 1968, conservatives would no longer be persuaded by arguments that moderate initiatives should be tolerated to prevent *distraction* from evangelism, and a conservative faction organized itself and took over. As a result, the Convention is playing to only half of its political heritage (see fig. 1.2).

In short, whether in American culture, Southern culture, or in the SBC, each moderate action has had an equal and opposite conservative reaction—each with greater force as "liberals" exerted influence from

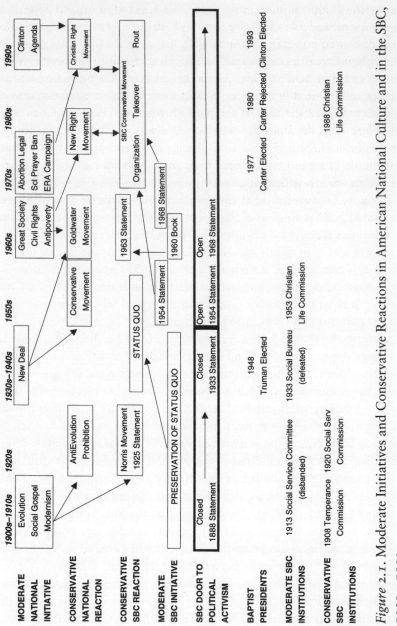

Figure 2.1. Moderate Initiatives and Conservative Reactions in American National Culture and in the SBC, 1900–1992

outside the Convention, then inside, then advanced to official positions. The latter proved too much for the conservative faction, and the explosion of 1979 occurred in Houston.

But Baptist politics does not operate in a vacuum. In the next chapter we will examine how religious, political, and social change across state and denominational boundaries, mixed with a changing relationship of the SBC to the culture, fueled Baptist Republicanism. We have seen that, unlike previous movements, the 1979 uprising was (1) a "reclaiming" movement, not a pure defense of the status quo, (2) a middle-class movement, and (3) an individualistic movement as well as a traditionalistic one. With the "restructuring" of American religion, this is a familiar description. One no longer checks one's politics at the door of the worship house, and politics and religion have become perpetually fused in the nation as well.

3

Culture War

Baptist Republicanism as Cultural Defense

As shown in the last chapter, both theological and political aspects contribute to Southern Baptist political change. These changes have come to the denomination through internal political struggles between organized factions of the middle and the right. But internal squabbling aside, what about factors external to the Convention? Is the rise of Baptist Republicanism not also due to external pressures as well? Do these pressures not spring from a changing religious and political culture?

This chapter will, using social movement theory, explore the changing politics of the Southern Baptist Convention as brought on by the changing relation of the SBC to its external environment. Because of the size of the Convention, social movement theory (which is often reserved for small sects or minorities) may seem inadequate at first blush. But the women's movement and Christians, both of which constitute a majority of Americans, have been the subjects of enlightening social movement–style analyses in recent years. Though I am not a sociologist, I have consulted the literature of these movements to arrive at the following conclusions. I have also conducted classic social movement research on political minorities.

Cultural Defense and Political Opportunity

Social Movement Political Models

Alienation. Most classical models of social movements rely on a causal process beginning with social strain, then discontent, followed by protest. One such model, "alienation," a type of classical model, is based on the earliest of political and social theories.[1] These theories hypothesize that industrial societies, urbanized and dominated by large impersonal organizations, do not provide the personal emotional security enjoyed in traditional agrarian society. This disconnectedness, a phenomenon that grew with the nineteenth-century industrial revolution, produces in the individual a sense of alienation, isolation, and anxiety. In the political realm, this means that as societies become industrialized, people begin to feel distant from their government: they begin to feel that political institutions are run by unsympathetic elites and that their vote can do little to dislodge them. One theorist went so far as to suggest that the ultimate outcome of this sense of alienation will always be irrational behavior, or "extreme behavior [in order] to escape," along with an outright distrust of governmental institutions.[2]

Theorists suggest that it was mercantilism and industrialization that introduced alienation to America. This is from where the *agrarian myth* springs. According to this notion, since the early days of the republic, there was in the average rural American a strong attachment to an unwritten belief that agrarianism was the normative state—the natural order of things—and this attitude bled into beliefs about government. As one author put it, "Any government was a failure that did not foster the interests of the agricultural class." As the story goes, when the government in Washington proved "discouragingly indifferent to their demands," agrarians lost faith in the national government. A detachment from their constituted government led to the rise of Jacksonianism in the 1830s, and reappeared in the late 1890s as populism. The Jacksonians and the populists were alike in that they considered the industrialization of America "an alarming tendenc[y]" and "looked backward with longing to the lost agrarian Eden" *and its government*.[3]

The alienation experienced by the Jacksonians and the populists appeared once more, late in the nineteenth century, as progressivism. Progressives, according to the historian Richard Hofstadter, "suffered from the events of their time not through a shrinkage in their means but through the changed pattern in the distribution of deference and power." "The whole cast of American thinking in this period," he continues, "was deeply affected by the experience of the rural mind confronted with the phenomena of urban life, its crowding, poverty, crime, corruption, impersonality, and ethnic chaos. To the rural migrant, raised in the respectable quietude and the high-toned moral imperatives of evangelical Protestantism, the city seemed not merely a new social form or way of life but a strange threat to civilization itself."[4] These farmers, with the

mindset of the last century, newly arrived in the city, longed for a civilization that for them was no more. In terms of the South, social theorist
Richard Weaver has written that atomization and alienation have been
long-standing characteristics of the fundamentalist South in particular.[5]
In the nation as a whole, the supporters of Senator Joe McCarthy shared
a similar, if less agrarian, disillusionment.

The tie to fundamentalist Christianity is all but intuitive. Alienation has
its effects on the spiritual as well. Research testing the concept of alienation as an explanation for fundamentalist involvement[6] finds that conservative Christians feel a certain resentment toward, and feel left out of,
the larger culture, even despised. The theory of political alienation
hypothesizes that fundamentalist right politics is another example of
alienation "boiling over." Fundamentalists become politically active
because they are unhappy with their government and have for too long
felt powerless to change it. This view of very conservative Christians as on
the fringe of American culture (and by their choice not totally socialized)
is consistent with religious history.[7] Fundamentalist doctrine teaches the
biblical precepts of "come out from among them and be ye separate," and
"love not the world neither the things that are in the world."[8] The rise of
a post-Civil War secularism in America, seen most notably in Tennessee's
Scopes trial, where the fundamentalists' beliefs about the origin of
humankind and their champion, William Jennings Bryan, were ridiculed,
drove "Bible believers" farther underground. This is the traditional image
of fundamentalist Christians—not the rabble-rousing pulpiteers of the
1980s and 1990s broadcast by satellite, but Amish-like believers who fear
becoming too closely tied with materialistic things.

As we saw in chapters 1 and 2, even though this alienation might
apply to the more separatist conservative branches of the conservative
bloc, or to Northern fundamentalists who divided denominations over
doctrine, it does not seem to be the historic experience of Southern Baptists. The SBC has been known as a dominating presence in the region,
and conservatives have always been strong in the organization. So, does
alienation theory shed light on the SBC? At first glance, both the cultural
domination and conservatism of the SBC in a conservative region seem
to conflict with the tenets of alienation theory: that conservative Christians are politically anxious or feel despised by the culture.[9]

Status Politics. A second classical theory is very similar but focuses on
pure discontent rather than alienation. The "status politics" (or "status

defense") model is developed from the concept of status in the writings of Max Weber.[10] Weber wrote that there are status hierarchies in society, with each social group occupying a position on a status scale and possessing the degree of political power that is in accordance with that position.[11] Weber and later Seymour Martin Lipset stress the separation of social movements into groups with materialistic versus nonmaterialistic social goals.[12] Those with nonmaterialistic goals are defined as "status groups." That is, they are defined in terms of their way of life, not their role in the economy.

Conservative Christians in this revised model are a "status group," not because of their economic status, but because of their distinct lifestyle. These ideas are employed by Joseph Gusfield in his research into the temperance movement.[13] Gusfield suggests that the temperance crusade began when native white evangelical Protestants felt they were losing their *status*, their prestige (their *cultural monopoly*, in Weber's terms), to recent immigrants. So they sought to ensconce a part of their political culture legislatively, to enact a law that would draw a line between them and hard-drinking new Americans. Gusfield stopped short of attaching any permanent significance to the temperance movement, however, calling the crusade a "symbolic effort." Others, interpreting Gusfield, wrote that temperance crusaders were seeking "control of the means of symbolic production."[14]

But there are a number of problems with Gusfield and with the "status politics" model. Some critics have difficulty with the fact that according to Gusfield the *consequences* of the temperance movement can be used as an explanation of the *motives* of the crusaders, though he gives no empirical evidence (nor has any been found since) that the temperance movement wanted to improve their status.[15] Steve Bruce presents a second objection, noting that there is no evidence that the crusaders shared a common social status.[16] This does not seem to be a valid criticism, however, because, as noted, the issue in this revised theory of status politics is nonmaterialist in nature.[17] But, as stated earlier, social status was Weber's primary concern in the original theory.

Politics of Lifestyle Concern. A modification (and an improvement, some would argue) of the status politics/discontent model has produced the "politics of lifestyle concern (PLC) model." According to these theorists, Weber means that conservative Christians will involve themselves in politics not because of status concern necessarily, but to defend their view of national culture against a perceived threat. The PLC model, which is also called the "collective behavior model," reflects a reaction not because of alienation or status, but because of the strain brought on by social change making lifestyle concern instead of status the motivating factor.[18] "To focus on status is theoretically to put the cart before the horse," one scholar writes.[19] Another author further presses home the claims of the PLC model: "A style of life can be maintained or propagated only to the extent that its adherents exercise some control over the means of socialization and social intercourse. Life style concern is most clearly evident when fading majorities come to recognize the eclipse of their way of life through loss of such control."[20] This interpretation and this theory are well developed in the Ann Page and Donald Clelland study of fundamentalist organization in a school textbook controversy in West Virginia[21] and in Louise Lorentzen's work on a fundamentalist's bid for political office in Virginia.[22] Page and Clelland find little status concern among those fighting the allegedly bad textbooks, but a great deal of concern among conservative Christians about their ability to continue to instill their "cultural fundamentalism" into their children and through the public schools, and continuing to realize their hope of "socializi[ng] youth to their own construction of social reality." According to Page and Clelland, instead of abandoning the public schools, parents fought the educational system, the mass media, and even liberal churches to maintain their ability to control what "constitutes meaning" for their children by attempts to "build and sustain moral orders which provide basic meaning for human lives."[23]

The "politics of lifestyle concern" differs from the old "status politics" model in that PLC theorists do not see fundamentalist political activism as directed to merely symbolic goals. As one author suggests, why should conservative Christians in their pursuit of nonmaterialist goals be satisfied with only symbolic victories if those with materialist goals are not?[24] Lorentzen agrees, stressing the *issue-orientedness* of PLC: "An issue relatively narrow in scope may stand for and serve to reinforce a way of life—a system of belief."[25]

How do these classical theories—alienation, status politics, the politics of lifestyle concern—square with Southern Baptist history and behavior? SBC scholar and sociologist Nancy Ammerman, in her *Baptist Battles*, writes: "A fundamentalist *movement*, I would argue, does not arise out of theology alone. Only when conservative beliefs lost their cultural dominance was it necessary for people to organize and identify themselves specifically as holders of those beliefs" (emphasis hers).[26] Page and Clelland argue that PLC is triggered when "fading majorities recognize the eclipse of their way of life."[27] These theoretical concepts seem to call Baptists in the changing South by name. Baptists once dominated the culture, but now they run into opposition when they attempt to conduct personal evangelistic work. Southern Baptists look with horror on cases like the public-school mother in Ecru, Mississippi, who fought the school board in an attempt to prevent her Lutheran son from being subjected to "Southern Baptist prayers."

Resource Mobilization. A less psychological and more political approach to the study of social movements is represented by the resource mobilization model. This model focuses not on the discontent and irrationality of action by the rank and file, but on organization—specifically upon leaders and their ability to build organizations around rational preexisting concerns. According to this elite model, resources in the form of volunteers, allies, and money are drawn to a successful movement until the level of resources reaches that needed to produce change. Movements decline when resources and allies dry up.[28]

Resource mobilization theory is a challenging alternative to the "status politics" and PLC models, pointing out that the grievances cited as causes in classical theories are constant[29] and are necessary but not sufficient for explaining rank-and-file involvement. Jerome Himmelstein has used the resource mobilization approach to explain the transformation of conservatism in general and the New Christian Right in particular. He writes that "the rise of the New Religious Right . . . fed on several of the conditions that theories of social movements generally emphasize—heightened discontent, a growing capacity for collective action, and the *intensified efforts of social-movement professionals*"(my emphasis).[30]

These "social movement professionals" are those who serve as the *mobilizers*, whether by television broadcast (as Falwell did), through political field work in the churches (as the Bob Jones fundamentalists have done), or by direct mail (as the Christian Coalition often does). The role of the mobilizer is key to resource mobilization theory. For unlike previously discussed models, resource mobilization argues that social movements do not spontaneously combust, but need a little kindling.

Danger lurks in making extreme interpretations, however. Some resource mobilization theorists, who focus on mobilization of resources (of funds and people), have ignored psychological motives altogether. The best approaches do not assign a priori roles to either motives or resources, but emphasize the working of *grievances* and *mobilization* in tandem.[31]

Critics have questioned the elitism of resource mobilization theory on a number of counts, including its suggestion that outside elites provide resources to movements only in order to co-opt them, its belief that the rank-and-file members of a movement are impotent and would do nothing without this infusion of outside support, and its view that indigenous resources are not worthy of consideration.[32] But the resource mobilization model seems applicable in the short run to the SBC. As noted in the last chapter, a well-organized machine under the political tutelage of Judge Paul Pressler and the theological coaching of Paige Patterson stirred the conservative embers of the heartland of the Convention and in 1979 moved to take over a sleeping organization by electing a charismatic leader.

But in the long run, after effecting sixteen consecutive presidential-election wins, how does resource mobilization fare? Has the SBC been co-opted as resource mobilization theories predict? One might say no, for though the New Christian Right was supportive of the conservative surge in the SBC and Pressler and Patterson were Reagan organizers, there was some question about who was using whom in this arrangement. Southern Baptists close to the Republican White House were made uncomfortable when leaders of the SBC in May 1988 considered withdrawing an invitation to President Reagan to address the Convention after reports that he and his wife, Nancy, followed astrology.[33] Similarly, in June 1991, delegates to the Convention publicly rebuked President Bush for supporting the National Endowment for the Arts the day before he was to address the Convention.[34]

The power of the conservative faction's rank-and-file and their indigenous resources should also not be overlooked, as resource mobilization theorists tend to do. Though the pump was primed by a militant leadership that declared itself ready to "go for the jugular,"[35] the conservative side has found many enthusiastic enlistees as state conventions and denominational agencies have been flooded by the new conservative faction.[36]

Political Process. In recent years, the "political process" model has arisen to challenge "resource mobilization" theory in an attempt to address some of the criticisms leveled against it. Though it has made no attempt to analyze the New Christian Right in terms of political process theory per se, the theory has proven useful in explicating other political movements, most notably the civil rights movement[37] and the women's movement.[38]

The political process model, like the resource mobilization model, accepts an elitist theory of political power. Such a framework accepts (though not necessarily celebrates, as some have claimed) that social and political change ultimately take place because of the interaction of elites. The spontaneous whim of self-mobilizing masses alone simply cannot bring reform. Therefore to some degree, both resource mobilization and political process theories accept that factors both external and internal to the interest group must interact to produce social movements.

Political process theorists argue that after holding grievances over a long time, the aggrieved population develops an organizational "readiness" and a feeling of efficacy and confidence called "cognitive liberation." The cognitively liberated understand that their problems have political antecedents. When this consciousness meets certain conditions or a requisite "structure of political opportunities," an organization is achieved and movement activism begins.[39] The theory stresses infrastructure in the form of associational networks to promote mobilization, interpersonal rewards derived from membership in association, effective communication networks, and strong leadership. But perhaps the most intriguing point in the political process model is the notion that, given the right political *circumstances*, certain interest groups in the population can take on a new "consciousness" (mentality) in which "the system" (the way things are) loses its legitimacy for them. (Rush Limbaugh tapped into this post-1992 anti-Washington, anti-Clinton mentality in his book, *The Way Things Ought to Be*.) Soon these disaffected people are rejecting fatalism, asserting their rights and opinions, gaining a sense of power and efficacy, and winning political battles—and the snowball begins to roll. Then the cycle of power-membership-resource expansion begins.[40]

Like the preceding models, this one is a simplification of a complex theory. But the fit with the fundamentalist right in general and the SBC in particular is strong and demands an analysis of the "structure of political opportunities" in the SBC.

Theologically and politically, the paradox in the SBC is that the first rumblings of organized-movement, "two-party" (two-faction) conservatism in the SBC coincided with the development of two parties in

Southern politics,[41] and that the ultimate victory of the conservative faction preceded the fall of moderate Southern Baptist Jimmy Carter from the presidency by eighteen months. As noted briefly in the last chapter, fundamentalist faction influence in the Convention has been directly related to political events. In this case the events operated in the country as a whole but were most pronounced in the South.

Social movement theories are most helpful to us when the interaction of events is uniquely fitted to the political process model of social movements and their mobilization.[42] Though the theories of political participation as social movements are as complicated as the disparate groups in them, the claims of all movement models can be summarized into several basic points. Namely, (1) a political awakening often finds its roots in strain or discontentment; (2) discontent can be heightened by a concern about the status or lifestyle of the group; and (3) the political climate of the times can produce a structure of opportunity that offers rank-and-file members of the group an opportunity and a motivation to become involved in politics, which (4) often plays into the hands of semiprofessional organizers who call on them to rise and defend something unique to them, their culture, their way of life, their status, and their community.

The remaining sections of this chapter will test the assumptions gleaned from the various theories by examining SBC change in relation to Southern and American culture, and by dissecting the political opportunity structure presented to the SBC at the time of these cultural changes.

Baptist Politics and Cultural Defense

Decline and Cultural Defense

Many of the notions of social movement theory can be used as a framework for understanding the sea change in Southern Baptist political thought. These models confront us with alienation, perceived threats, cultural defense, and mobilization—all suggestive of minority status. But what is the position of the Southern Baptist Convention in its home, the South? Does the SBC constitute a majority of white Southerners? A large percentage? How does the SBC rank from one Southern state to another? How have these relationships changed over time? Using data collected by the Census Bureau[43] and obtained from the Southern Baptist Convention

Historical Commission itself,[44] we arrive at some useful statistics that reflect the status of Baptists.

Because SBC Historical Commission statistics report only church *membership* (usually adults and older children, since Southern Baptists are not confirmed), and because Southern Baptists are overwhelmingly white, we must adjust U.S. Census figures to permit comparison. We first remove from the total population the total number of black Southerners.[45] We must then remove those not of church-joining age. Unless they have professed their faith publicly and joined the church, children are not counted. We will estimate then that the average age required for church membership in the SBC is ten years old. Using census counts, we subtract all children aged birth to nine years old. We can then compare accurately over time the percentage of Southerners calling themselves Southern Baptists.

When we examine the claims of movement theories in light of table 3.1 and figure 3.1, we see that there might be some credibility to the claim that Southern Baptists behave as they do because they have lost ground culturally. The theories of status defense and the politics of lifestyle concern suggest that the steady climb in Southern Baptist membership from 1930 to 1960, followed by a decline through the 1990s, leaves members concerned about preserving a "way of life" or, in Weber's terms, a "cultural monopoly." Facing what Page and Clelland term a "fading majority," it is likely that a movement might form to defend the traditional view of the national or denominational culture.[46]

Mobilization comes into play here as well. After seminary student Paige Patterson and Texas appeals court judge Paul Pressler met in the late

TABLE 3.1.
Southern Baptists as Percentage of Southern Population, 1930–1990

	1930	1940	1950	1960	1970	1980	1990
Deep South	25%	27%	32%	36%	35%	32%	31%
Peripheral South	15%	16%	21%	23%	22%	19%	17%
South	19%	20%	25%	27%	26%	23%	21%
Border	11%	13%	18%	21%	22%	22%	23%
Greater South	17%	19%	24%	27%	26%	23%	22%

Note: White adults only.
Sources: U.S. Census and SBC Historical Commission.

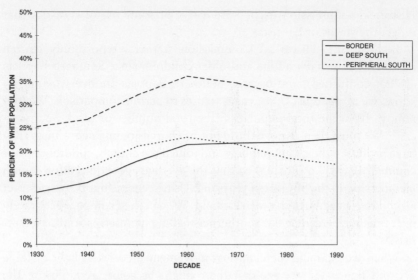

Source: U.S. Census and SBC Historical Commission.

Figure 3.1. SBC% of Population, 1930–1990

1960s at the Café du Monde in New Orleans to discuss their mutual con-cern about a rising tide of liberalism in the SBC, the organization of cadres to take over the Convention began.[47] Their meeting—and their traveling show which soon followed—coincided with the decline of the Conven-tion's strength. In an era of stagnancy, Patterson and Pressler began to organize people and collect funds to effect the eventual takeover in 1979.

But as the political process theory argues, *timing* is important as well. Potential recruits to the Patterson-Pressler movement had to be ready to make changes in the Convention. To their minds, the time for talking had to pass, the Convention power structure as it was had to lose its legiti-macy, and they had to assert their rights as members.[48]

The state-to-state dynamic is important to notice. Most of the oldest state conventions in the Deep South and the Peripheral South (Alabama, Georgia, North Carolina, South Carolina, Tennessee, Texas, and Vir-ginia) reported steady increases from the 1930s through the post-World War II era, with membership reaching a peak by 1960. Every decade since then, SBC membership has been on the decline on the eastern seaboard. Only Florida reached a peak much earlier (and therefore declined more quickly), in 1950, and the westernmost states of Arkansas, Mississippi, and Louisiana were still growing. (The tremendous popula-

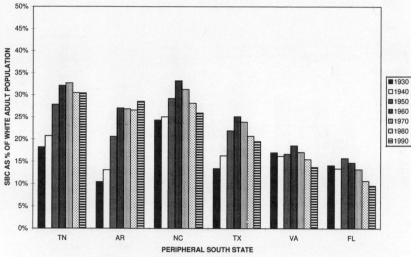

Source: U.S. Census and SBC Historical Commission.

Figure 3.2. SBC Membership in Peripheral South States, 1930–1990

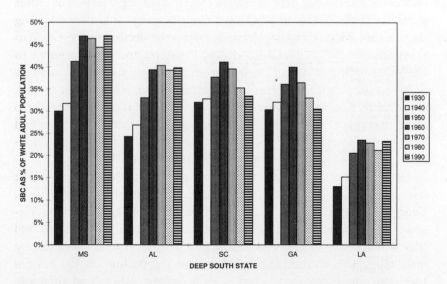

Source: U.S. Census and SBC Historical Commission.

Figure 3.3. SBC Membership in Deep South States, 1930–1990

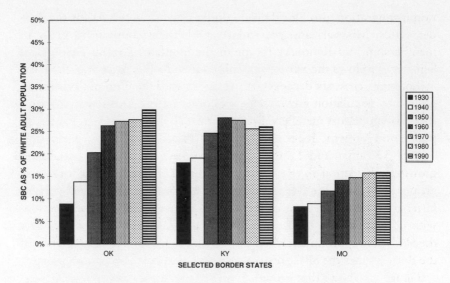

Source: U.S. Census and SBC Historical Commission.

Figure 3.4. SBC Membership in Border States, 1930–1990

TABLE 3.2

SBC Growth and Population Growth in the South, 1930–1990

State	Population Growth	SBC Growth	SBC > POP
Deep South			
Alabama	51%	70%	19%
Georgia	65%	66%	0%
Louisiana	59%	77%	18%
Mississippi	47%	66%	19%
S. Carolina	67%	68%	1%
Peripheral South			
Arkansas	39%	78%	39%
Florida	92%	88%	-4%
N. Carolina	63%	65%	2%
Tennessee	54%	72%	18%
Texas	70%	79%	9%
Virginia	69%	61%	-7%
Border South			
Kentucky	38%	58%	19%
Missouri	29%	63%	34%
Oklahoma	32%	80%	48%

Note: White adults only.
Source: U.S. Census and SBC Historical Commission.

tion in-migration into Florida is no doubt at work here.) As for the Border states, Missouri and particularly Oklahoma continue to grow in membership, but Kentucky (home of the Southern Baptist Theological Seminary) follows the 1960-peak-subsequent-decline pattern of the East.

Looking across six decades with an eye toward the ratio of Convention growth to population growth, one sees other trends. Our research shows that though Baptist membership in most states has merely kept pace with population growth, membership in Arkansas, Mississippi, Tennessee, Texas, Alabama, and Louisiana has grown in relation to population growth in the period 1930 to 1990. The Border South states show an even greater spurt, with the Oklahoma Baptist Convention growing 48 percent faster than the population of the state.[49] Missouri and Kentucky follow with 34 percent and 19 percent, respectively. Taken as a whole, in the South the SBC grew approximately 4 percent faster than the population, while in the Border states the SBC grew 45 percent faster than population growth.

Figure 3.5 shows that growth from 1930 to 1990 was at best uneven. Georgia's Baptist population is holding at 30 percent of its total population. Membership in Florida and Virginia is declining, and the rest of the

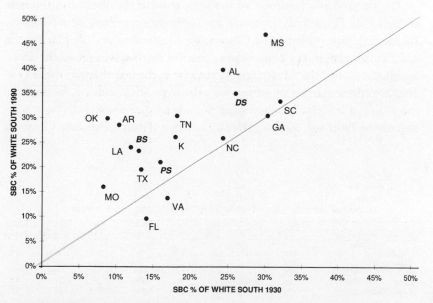

Source: US Census SBC Historical Commission.

Figure 3.5. SBC % of South 1930 vs SBC % of South, 1990. by State

South is still growing. Showing the most dramatic growth are Oklahoma, Arkansas, Mississippi, and Alabama. Of the three regions, the Peripheral South is weakest in growth; its older cousin in SBC longevity (the Deep South) and its younger sibling (the Border South) each outpaces it.

Table 3.3 shows that although the Border states were growing, the percentage of Baptists residing there fell by approximately 4 percent over the period 1930 to 1990. This drop, coupled with a 5 percent decline in the South (a 9 percent drop in the Deep South and a 4 percent rise in the Peripheral South), yields a 9 percent increase in SBC membership ratio from the North, Midwest, and West. As of 1990, over 25 percent of the SBC membership is in states other than the Deep South and the Peripheral South.

The trends we find here thus reveal that the Southern Baptist Convention is still making progress in increasing its membership compared to sixty years ago, but it has stagnated during the last decade. It is not hard to see how this slowdown, together with memories of a growth spurt and an ever so subtle shift of the Convention away from its Deep South roots, might produce a "cultural defense" reaction from the fundamentalist right.

The cultural phenomenon of the shift toward the West and the new influence of Texas and Tennessee by 1968 are something of a paradox. By moving into positions of Convention leadership and displacing the old Eastern group, the conservative faction further weakened the Deep South and gained the advantage. As we saw in the last chapter, these Texans, as representatives of an individualistic political culture, brought to the national leadership a new energy and, among conservatives, a willingness to fight for control. By 1979, when Texans Pressler, Criswell,

TABLE 3.3
Southern Baptist Membership by Region, 1930–1990

Year	1930	1940	1950	1960	1970	1980	1990	Net
Convention Membership	3,850	4,949	7,080	9,732	11,630	13,607	15,044	Change
Deep South	45%	44%	42%	40%	39%	37%	36%	-9%
Peripheral South	33%	35%	37%	37%	37%	37%	38%	4%
South	76%	76%	76%	74%	73%	71%	71%	-5%
Border	19%	18%	17%	16%	15%	15%	14%	-4%
Greater South	97%	97%	96%	93%	91%	89%	88%	-9%
Rest of U.S.	3%	3%	4%	7%	9%	11%	12%	9%

Note: White adults only, in thousands.
Source: U.S. Census and SBC Historical Commission.

and Patterson made a run on the Convention, new, non-Deep South leadership had already been developing. As table 3.4 shows, with the exception of Atlanta's Charles Stanley, the Deep South hasn't had a convention president since 1974.

Marginalization and Cultural Defense

Other factors contribute to a Southern Baptist sense of discontent, loss
of status, and cultural defense as well. These go beyond the ratio of
Southern Baptists to Southerners and are related to the position of organized religion (particularly conservative bloc evangelical Protestantism)
in American culture, and the SBC's reaction to it.

As argued in the last chapter, a nationwide sea change took place in
the United States in terms of religion during the 1940s through 1970s.
SBC fundamentalists may have missed the turn-of-the-century denominational splits and fundamentalist-style movements to reclaim a lost
orthodoxy in the North (1900–1930),[50] but by the end of World War II,

TABLE 3.4

Home States of SBC Presidents, 1968–1997

Year	President	State
1968	H. Franklin Paschall	Tennessee
1969	W.A. Criswell	Texas
1970	W.A. Criswell	Texas
1971	Carl E. Bates	North Carolina
1972	Carl E. Bates	North Carolina
1973	Owen Cooper	Mississippi
1974	Owen Cooper	Mississippi
1975	Jaroy Weber	Texas
1976	Jaroy Weber	Texas
1977	James L. Sullivan	Tennessee
1978	Jimmy R. Allen	Texas
1979	Jimmy R. Allen	Texas
1980	Adrian P. Rogers	Tennessee
1981	Bailey E. Smith	Oklahoma
1982	Bailey E. Smith	Oklahoma
1983	James T. Draper	Texas
1984	James T. Draper	Texas
1985	Charles F. Stanley	Georgia
1986	Charles F. Stanley	Georgia
1987	Adrian P. Rogers	Tennessee
1988	Adrian P. Rogers	Tennessee
1989	Jerry Vines	Florida
1990	Jerry Vines	Florida
1991	Morris H. Chapman	Texas
1992	Morris H. Chapman	Texas
1993	H. Edwin Young	Texas
1994	H. Edwin Young	Texas
1995	James Henry	Florida
1996	James Henry	Florida
1997	Tom Eliff	Oklahoma

Source: SBC Convention Annuals, 1968–1996.

the steadfastly orthodox South would no longer be immune to the religious changes taking place in the rest of the nation. Interstate highways, jet airplanes, business conglomerates, economic expansion, television, radio, the wide distribution of blockbuster motion pictures, and national magazines would carry the national culture into the South. Suddenly the SBC longed for the good ol' days and found itself in the midst of a "reclaiming" movement of its own, similar to that of Northern fundamentalists of a generation or more earlier.

Restructuring

According to the two-party theory[51] (or, translated into the terms we adopted in chapter 1, the two-*bloc* theory), American Protestants can be classified into two blocs: those who have traditionally been concerned with saving individual souls, and those who direct their activities toward improving the collective social order. This division developed very early in U.S. history as Protestants became divided into those concerned with social justice and national mores versus those who separated themselves from the world and sought to convert *individuals* rather than improve society at large. Noted religion scholar Martin Marty uses this conceptualization in a number of his works, but puts it best in an introduction to Jean Schmidt's *Souls or the Social Order*:

> [One] party thought that one met society's ills and problems by transforming individuals and calling them to serve. The [other] party, the social Christians or the Social Gospelers, did not disdain the role of the individual. But they believed that the structures of society themselves were in need of redemption and that people who professed and worked for the coming Kingdom of God could make the difference.[52]

The Marty theory was an accurate portrayal, particularly for Southern religion. W. A. Criswell put it bluntly to a reporter in his first news conference upon being elected SBC president in 1968, an exchange Criswell records in his memoirs:

> "What's your goal for the nation's largest denomination?" a newsman asked.
> "I would like to lead our convention into a great evangelistic and missionary effort," I replied. "I want to get lost people to God."

"But what about social action?" the same man shouted, implying that I had no social concern. "What about the poor, the homeless, the hungry?"

"You cannot divorce faith and works," I shot back at him. "You cannot divorce morality and ethics from evangelism and missions. You can't put a man's head over here and his heart over there."[53]

Criswell, in refusing to "divorce" the two, serves as an apt illustration of the old theoretical notions about souls versus social concern. In 1968 Criswell saw two choices beckoning for his allegiance: either the Social Action party (bloc) that the reporter seemed to demand he join, or a Soul-winning party (bloc). Criswell chose the latter. (See figure 1.1.)

But much has changed since 1968. With the rise of the New Christian Right, a number of variations on these theoretical arguments have developed, including notions of a "restructuring" of religion in America.[54] According to this characterization, parties (blocs) are composed not of separatist fundamentalist soul winners versus activist feeders of the poor, but *liberals* and *conservatives*. Robert Wuthnow argues that in this "restructuring," both fundamentalists and social Christians are now active in the political arena, but are greatly polarized in ideology and type of activism. This pervasive political activity has produced declining "brand loyalty"[55] to denominations and a plethora of "para-church organizations," umbrella organizations not aligned by denomination but by right- or left-wing religious clusters of political activity. Sociologist James Davison Hunter agrees with the Wuthnow characterization, writing that old divisions have been replaced with an "orthodox" versus "progressive" culture war[56] with groups of Baptists (and Methodists, and Presbyterians) on *each* side of the divide, not on *either* side.

Political science confirms these religious-sociological perspectives. The simplistic Protestant-Catholic-Jew[57] formulation perished long ago, and political scientists have since used better-defined denominational and doctrinal groupings.[58] But as some have noted, there is an ever-widening gap in Protestantism between what are loosely called "evangelicals" and "seculars." The result is a political struggle in American religion between two alliances, the fundamentalist-evangelical and the mainline-secularist.[59] Some observers have gone so far as to argue that this is true for the entire American experience, with several well-defined "theological tension eras and American political epochs." According to this analysis, the labels have changed over time but the struggle has been much the same.[60]

The appearance in recent years of a number of books directed at a lay audience signals the heightened interest in religious ideological polarization among the general public. These works include Os Guinness's *The American Hour*[61] and Yale Law School professor Stephen L. Carter's *The Culture of Disbelief.*[62] Guinness and Carter, conservative and liberal respectively, agree with the revised two-bloc characterization. Guinness, a Briton, goes so far as to describe the struggle in the same terms as the American Civil War—that of a traditionalistic, legalist, strict constructionism against a progressive egalitarianism with notions of a "higher law."

In addition to these works are those that focus on only one of the ideologies—fundamentalist-evangelical politics. Political scientist Michael Lienesch, in researching *Redeeming America*, found that over the last decade and a half the subject of the New Christian Right has been approached as "cultural, historical, organizational, political, psychological, sociological, and theological" using theories of "collective behavior, resource mobilization, status politics, organizational transformation and pluralist coalition-building."[63] But for all this research, Lienesch laments, the missing element is a meshing of religious, sociological, and political observations and theories. Religion and sociology scholars have seemed unable to make this synthesis, writing with little understanding of politics or using sound arguments that are valid but have been seen in political science journals for decades.

Paradoxically, political scientists have seemed unwilling to bridge the gap, perhaps fearing accusations of "soft" research. In this sense, *Redeeming America* attempts to combine elements of all of the above theories and approaches. In doing so, Lienesch concludes in this study of New Christian Right beliefs and values that the conservative Christian political movement has been mistakenly assigned a high and a low point, much like a meteor (which burns brightly and then falls helplessly to the earth) when it should be seen as cyclical, much like a comet (which appears boldly, then fades, only to return equally as bright).[64]

Reversal, Disestablishment, and Culture War

Indeed, there are cycles of a cometlike New Christian Right over time. One scholar describes it as "accommodation, activism, and alienation." It was first set in motion with a national cultural phenomenon known as

the "Great Reversal," the period from 1900 to 1930 when formerly passive conservatives became activists, first in the religious sphere under
revivalist preaching, and then politically in response to crusaders like
William Jennings Bryan. At the same time, longtime activist progressive
bloc Christians seemed to cool in their desire for social change.[65] This
reversal has filtered to the South since 1930 as more of a "Great
Arousal," because there were few moderate elements in the South with
whom conservatives could trade places.

There is also a matter I touched on briefly earlier: the overall decline
of religion nationally, the "disestablishment" of the church. One theorist
wrote that the "disestablishment" is "a qualitative change in the relationship between church and culture." True, involvement in church has
increased proportionately since the nation's founding, but in the 1960s
the trend began to reverse and, like the SBC, the church nationally
became "disestablished" in the national culture much as it had been in
law since 1833.[66]

Given this "post-Christian" reality, the pendulum continues to swing.
At some time, conservative Christians will produce a movement with
social, moral, and intellectual components.[67] As noted in the previous
chapter, there have already been three waves of conservative activism—
the 1920s, the 1950s, and the 1980s. With each new cycle, the movement
has reappeared more mature, more politicized, more coherent, and more
sophisticated.[68]

In fairness to the older "two-party" theory, we must concede that two
such parties may have existed and may still exist in an intellectual sense.
Benson and Williams, in *Religion on Capitol Hill*,[69] found certain distinctions in the thought processes of conservative religious members of
congress and the liberal ones. Religious conservatives were much more
individualistic in their religion and in their politics, while those who were
members of liberal denominations were much more likely to be community oriented.[70] As we saw in chapter 2, it was certainly true of the SBC
until politics turned the denominational head. The old SBC of the first
thirty years of the twentieth century was personified by A. J. Barton, who
used the Temperance Commission to call for a greater effort in saving
souls, not the social order.[71]

In the Restructuring, the Great Reversal, the Second Disestablishment,
and the three orbits of the Christian right it is evident that the SBC is
divided, like American religion as a whole. Following the Second Disestablishment and a role reversal, polarization set in. The conservative bloc

and the progressive bloc are each composed of activist and pietistic members who effect movements having cyclical, cometlike behavior, depending on which faction has the upper hand. Each cycle includes roughly decade-long eras of activism and confrontation followed by approximately twenty-year eras of a more personal, pietistic focus.[72] Both religious ideologies contain those who pray and those who organize, and the restructuring of religion in the United States has caused denominational lines to follow ideological lines.

In terms of social and cultural change, the SBC has seen a decline in its strength in the regional culture and the injection of a national secular culture that features the disestablishment and polarization of religion. These factors, operating as pincers, would be enough, it seems, to produce alienation and discontent, and in many ways they were responsible for the rise of the conservative faction within the Convention. But to translate these notions into explanations for conservative politics, the proper structure of political opportunity is needed—the development of the proper political climate for militancy, a series of events to serve as a "lever," or an organizational push led by professionals. All of these presented themselves in the 1980s.

Baptist Politics and Political Opportunity

The restructuring of American religion and its Second Disestablishment, along with the specific decline in Southern Baptist strength in the culture and the rise of a conservative theological/political faction in the SBC, created, according to the political process model, quite a "political opportunity structure" for conservatives. To borrow a phrase from another context, the SBC was "ripe for realignment."[73] For by 1970, it was surrounded by the conservative trends and "liberal" bogeymen of the New Southern politics, including the full implementation of the Voting Rights Act, the development of a suburban Southern middle class, and the rise of the Republican party.

In the 1940s and 1950s, V. O. Key was already writing that Southern politics would change dramatically, and soon. Key was predicting that the "Democratic solidarity of the South . . . could not survive another New Deal," that because of outside influences, the Republican party would grow in the South, that modernization (urbanization and industrialization) would bring political change, and that race (which had dominated Southern politics since the first black slaves arrived in the New World in chains) would not be a dominant issue after the 1948 Thurmond Dixiecrat campaign.[74]

In their examination and extension of the points raised by Key, Earl Black and Merle Black in *Politics and Society in the South* find that Key was correct on most points. The second New Deal (the Great Society programs of Lyndon Johnson) changed Southern politics forever, according to Black and Black:

> Lyndon Johnson's administration (1963–1969) combined racial,economic, and cultural liberalism in domestic affairs with ineffective intervention in foreign policy. These unpopular policies divided the southern Democratic party into antagonistic and sometimes irreconcilable factions. . . . Republican presidential candidates had many salient issues that could be used to fashion southern victories.[75]

White Southerners were driven away from the Democratic party, Republicans attracted them on several tracks, or "streams," as James Sundquist calls them.[76] A growing middle class or "leadership class" of white Southerners (particularly in the Peripheral South states of Florida, Tennessee, Texas, and Virginia, and in some Deep South cities) were attracted to Eisenhower, Nixon, and to some extent Goldwater (1952–64). In Donald Strong's words, these Southerners were "acting like Yankees," that is, they were voting their pocketbooks. In the wake of the New Deal, the Fair Deal, the New Frontier, and the Great Society, many Southern whites turned to a more conservative Republican party, which by this time had begun to oppose redistribution of wealth and federal social programs.[77] Working-class whites (particularly in the Deep South states of Alabama, Georgia, Mississippi, Louisiana, North Carolina, and South Carolina, and in some rural areas of the Peripheral South) were more attracted to the effort of non-Democrats Barry Goldwater and George Wallace (1964–68).

As early as 1963, this combination caused observers to see the coming of a Southern political earthquake. The Democratic "Solid South" would not survive the one-two punch of civil rights activism and increased social-spending programs.[78] By the 1970 gubernatorial elections (the first year of sizable black participation in Deep South Democratic politics, according to Sundquist), a majority of both working, or middle-class white Southerners in both the Deep and Peripheral South, had shifted in party identification to the Republican side or, in more cases, to independency. Two years later, Nixon swept the region and carried forty-nine states, and the South led in the nation's realignment. The Republicans have lost few presidential elections since. Relieved of the pressure of gaining supermajorities in the North (the GOP strategy since the time of Lincoln) to offset the Solid South, the Republicans turned to the South as a *base*, forcing the Democrats to turn to the North for success.[79]

Economically and culturally, with the end of segregation and Jim Crow, the South became the "Sun Belt"—the non-union, low-tax, low-wage haven for American (and foreign) businesses. The average native Southerner became more middle class and more urban, and non-native Southerners began to move in, bringing their Republican allegiances with them. By 1980, the South was the largest electoral region; it was in full realignment, and with Super Tuesday it became the new linchpin to winning the White House.[80] But as the Republican plurality grew in the South, the party siphoned off conservative Democrats. This made the Democratic party more liberal, which produced the Reagan landslides of 1980 and 1984, a trickle-down, local-level Republicanism in the 1980s and 1990s, and the congressional Republican revolution of 1994.

It was in this 1960s–70s era that a conservative (New Right) movement within the Republican party, led by the Goldwaters, Reagans, and Buckleys, for the first time merged economic conservatism at home with the rolling back of communism abroad (as compared to the isolationism of the old GOP). This proved to be an attractive position for many pro-military (pro-violence?) Southerners and provided another ideological magnet for the GOP in the South. The Republican coalition in the South was no longer composed of only the rich plus the very rich (a loser), but of hawks and the anti-Communists as well (a winner). Then came the fundamentalist right. The appeal of the GOP in the 1980s and 1990s, as in the 1960s and 1970s, traveled on two tracks. But the one-two punch was no longer economics and race, but economics and *morality*. The success of the New Right replaced overt racial appeals with moralistic social issues that energized conservative voters for the GOP, and also energized fundamentalist Baptists (Jerry Falwell and Bob Jones), then Pentecostal Baptists (Pat Robertson), and finally Southern Baptists.[81]

But the end of Jim Crow and the rise of the fundamentalist right did not mean the end of racial politics, and it is on this point, according to Black and Black, that Key made a rare inaccurate prediction. To win the White House or any election, parties must attract "ticket-splitters."[82] Neither party has enough straight ticket voters to win every election. In recent years, the Republicans have won the swing white (moderate independent and conservative Democratic) voter by loaded symbols and conservative ideology: the "L" word, fear of big government, strong national defense, gun-control hysteria, communist expansionism, welfare freeloading rhetoric, and even the pledge of allegiance.[83] (Perhaps they had no choice but to resort to such tactics: as late as 1968, only 30 percent of self-identified Southern conservatives called themselves Republicans.)[84] Republicans found their winning strategy by focusing not on race or economics, but on ideology and ideological symbols. On this basis, Southerners switched to the GOP, leaving the less-ideological voters to the Democrats.[85]

Unfortunately, ideological politics again makes Southern politics *racial* politics, in that there is a deep ideological split on race, particularly on the role of government in dealing with it. Whites *of all classes* are less interested than blacks in a role for government in fighting poverty and serving as a catalyst for economic opportunity.[86] The split along ideological lines and the need to win the Swing White vote led to the constant pounding that Carter, Mondale, Dukakis, and Clinton received on "meaty" conservative issues, many of which were more *symbolic* of ideology than true ideology. The strategy worked virtually every time in the South, particularly in the Deep South, even in 1992. Though defeated nationally, in Mississippi George Bush won a true majority of votes against two opponents, even with the largest black voting population of any state firmly behind the Democratic nominee.

There is a strong parallel in the SBC for using ideology and ideological symbols to win elections. With a set of symbolic issues of their own, the conservative faction won control of the "sweet spirited and naive" majority in the Southern Baptist Convention. These symbolic issues included religious issues such as liberalism in the seminaries and liberalism in Convention agencies, and political issues such as *Roe v. Wade*, school prayer, the ERA, and even the spread of atheistic communism. These "beat 'em up" issues (as moderate faction preacher Marion Aldridge calls them)[87] were used in the SBC much like the race issue had been used in V. O. Key's South to manipulate the simple for political gain. "[H]uman beings are symbolic creatures," one sociologist wrote, and this *symbolism* is part and parcel of the conservative backlash.

This is certainly true of the takeover of the SBC where "liberal" and "conservative" found new meaning. Symbolic politics favors Republicans (and in the SBC context, conservatives) and has been key to the realignment of the South. Republicans are free to speak openly of their conservatism, particularly on issues such as law and order, while Democrats must walk a tightrope because of their biracial (bi-ideological) coalition. In politics as in theology, liberals speak in hushed tones south of the Mason-Dixon line. But ideology cuts both ways. With Democrats quietly securing 90 percent of the black vote no matter what Republicans may do, the GOP must raise the symbolic/ideological banner in every redneck bar and country club, fighting to get the astounding 65 percent of the white vote to win.[88]

The best work on symbolic politics in recent years is that of Murray Edelman. Edelman defines symbols as "that facet of experiencing the material world that gives it a specific meaning."[89] Armed with symbols and the meaning they construct for people, political power can be achieved through "manipulating people by manipulation of the symbols that engage them."[90] This is possible because symbols can be important when they stand for larger issues. If used effectively, the symbol "makes their polity meaningful and it gives them status." And of status, Edelman claims, "these are values for which men fight hard." Symbols can be useful in commanding political troops as well, for "it is the conventional responses to such words as 'liberal,' 'conservative,' 'regulation,' and 'law,' that constitute the prevailing political sign structure, providing an order that permits groups to act, to anticipate the responses of others, and to acquire status."[91]

With this basic structure, Edelman centers his constructions on a number of factors useful to our analysis, the most significant being the role of *issues, leaders, adversaries* or enemies, and *organizations. Emotional appeals* are best used when concealed "under the guise of defining issues."[92] *Leadership* can be effective when "[m]en's anxious search for direction in a world many of them find alien encourage them to accept . . . gestures of leadership as valid and effective."[93] And finally, *constructing adversaries* is important, because "[t]he evocation of a threatening enemy may win political support for . . . prospective targets [and] people construct enemies who renew their own commitment and mobilize allies."[94] *Organizations* are important because "their creation is also a guarantee that the threats will continue to be taken as real."[95]

There is much here to explain the rise of the conservative faction within the SBC. As early as the late 1960s, conservatives began to rally a searching SBC membership to their *leadership* and to build an *organization* by keying in on emotion-concealed *issues* that presented their *adversaries* as apostates to truth. *The Baptist Faith and Message* statement was adopted, the Baptist Faith and Message Fellowship was formed, "inerrancy" and "conservatism" became the rallying cries, and campaigns against those in charge in Nashville began at the grassroots. Armed with the symbolic/ideological issues of inerrancy of the Bible and political conservatism, all other questions became moot, and the revolution had begun.

Not surprisingly, the general style and progression of Southern politics is also reminiscent of Convention politics. Southern politics in the 1940s and 1950s consisted of decades of "extension" of the New Deal one-party system, while the 1960s and 1970s were an era of "rending" it.[96] As we also saw in chapter 2, and as suggested in figure 3.1, the 1940s and 1950s were a growth era for the SBC and a "one-party" nonpolitical era in the Convention. When left-right "bipartisan" politics first appeared in 1954, the Convention was in its last growth decade. In 1968, the rending began in earnest as the moderate faction exerted its influence and provoked a conservative backlash. It was also in 1968 that, for the first time, the percentage of self-identified Democrats among Southern whites dipped below 50 percent. By 1979–1980, conservative politics was in full swing in the Convention and in the South. With the introduction of "two-party" politics, polarization began as the conservatives took over the SBC by beating up the moderates on symbolic secular and religious politics, and the conservative Reagan defeated the moderate Baptist Carter in the same manner. Just as the conservative Baptist faction came to the Convention in Houston in 1979 calling for a return to the old ways to reclaim the SBC, Ronald Reagan came to his convention in Detroit in 1980 saying he would "make America great again," and return the country to the values of his youth. The appeals of the Convention right and the Republican right were, as Southern Baptists often say, "off the same page in the hymnbook." By 1984 both the Washington Republican establishment and the Nashville SBC structure were "programmatically" conservative. Moderates began to be purged, and the word "compromise" dropped out of the respective party and convention lexicons.[97]

Rise of the Conservatives

The change in the ruling faction in the Southern Baptist Convention appears to be a logical step when one looks at the changing politics of the South. In the post-Great Society era, white Southerners, both middle and working class, switched their party allegiance from Democratic to Independent to Republican. More specifically, white Southerners, conservative by a ratio of 3:1 and happy in their religious and culturally homogeneous region, left what has been called the "core white Democrat" constituency for "core white Republican" and "swing white."[98] This fulfilled V. O. Key's prediction that the one-party Democratic South would not survive another New Deal.[99] The "one-party" SBC did not survive the decade, either. Recent politics and historic Southern culture each played a role in these shifts.[100]

The 1970s–1980s Shift

Southern Voters.
CONSERVATIVE SOUTHERN VOTERS, PREVENTED FROM FORCING
MODERATES TO LEAVE THE DEMOCRATIC PARTY (THE ONLY PARTY)
AND BECAUSE OF THE NEW PRESENCE OF BLACKS REACT
   LEAVE THE DEMOCRATIC PARTY TO BECOME INDEPENDENTS
      OR REPUBLICANS
   (PAST FORGOTTEN, DEMOCRATS FORCED OUT OF OFFICE)

Southern Baptists.
CONSERVATIVE SOUTHERN BAPTISTS REACT
   FORM A CONSERVATIVE RELIGIOUS / POLITICAL MOVEMENT
   FORCE MODERATES TO LEAVE THE CONVENTION
   (PAST FORGOTTEN, MODERATES FORCED TO SURRENDER
     CONVENTION INFLUENCE)

As sketched in the above headlines, the two shifts are not so different. White Southerners, faced with a new electorate after 1970 or so, are unable to outnumber or expel "liberals" from the Democratic party and turn their backs on their historical party to become Republicans. Though some elements were attracted by Strom Thurmond and the Dixiecrats in 1948 and George Wallace in 1968, or Eisenhower-Nixon in 1952 and Barry Goldwater in 1964, by 1980 the South was a Republican prize, helping oust Jimmy Carter from the White House and establishing a twelve-year Republican reign. Similarly, in the late 1970s, the SBC's conservative faction, turning its back on an old alliance, was able to outnumber and/or expel the moderate faction from true Convention power and establish a conservative dynasty.

Conclusion

In terms of the sociological theories we have presented, Southern Baptists were the perfect mark for the fundamentalist right and the new conservative Republican party. While feeling the strain of a loosening grip on the culture of its native region, SBC conservatives began to be alienated from the *national* culture with the Second Disestablishment of religion in the 1960s. SBC conservatives were then faced with the polarization brought on by an external culture war and an internal war provoked by a newly emboldened moderate faction.

Then came the political threat. From 1960 to 1980, more black than white voters joined the electorate, and the Democratic party began to play to these potential new voters.[101] Southern conservatives felt betrayed as LBJ turned "traitor"[102] to the South on race, and Jimmy Carter proved weak on conservatism, challenging the new social and economic status of the white Southerner. The final straw in the religious-cultural-political-ideological-racial turmoil for Southern Baptists, illustrated in figure 3.6, came with this "betrayal" by Jimmy Carter. Though LBJ was a Southerner, it was in Southern *Baptist* Jimmy Carter that Southern Baptists felt most disappointed. As Carter moved slightly to the left to keep primary opposition at bay, Southern Baptists chose to become born-again as Republicans, jettisoning the Georgian to join the

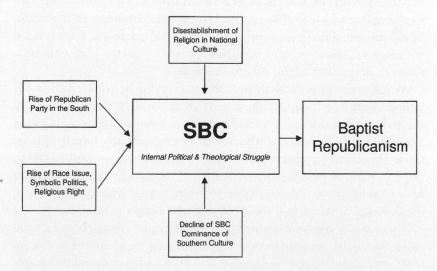

Figure 3.6. Elements of Southern Baptist Political Shift, 1968–1996

Reagan "reclaiming" movement of 1980. SBC conservative elites in turn became a part of the fundamentalist right establishment (see chapter 4).

An interesting question here is how Carter could sink so far with Southerners in only four years. According to James Sundquist, part of the answer lies in the great weakness masked in Carter's 1976 Southern sweep. Though in the final count they supported Carter over Gerald Ford, white Southerners split along class lines. Upper-class Southerners voted overwhelmingly for Ford, and middle-class voters leaned Republican as well. Only lower-class whites supported Carter, at a rate of nearly 60 percent. Carter's weakness is also manifest, Sundquist argues, in that "the percentage of vote won by Carter was almost exactly the same in the South as in the rest of the country."[103] This should not have been the case for the Southern Baptist candidate. By 1980, Ronald Reagan was finally "unraveling . . . the political class coalition that Franklin Roosevelt has put together" as these lower-class voters, "swayed by [symbolic] issues that had nothing, or very little to do with class," voted Republican.[104]

It is highly likely that many of these lower-class swing voters were Southern Baptists. According *Religion at the Polls*, in 1975, the year before Carter was elected, only 22 percent of Southern Baptists earned over $15,000 per year. This was the lowest percentage of all Protestants. Forty percent of Episcopalians exceeded that level of income, 43 percent of Presbyterians, and 38 percent of Methodists. Furthermore, broken down regionally, 58 percent of all Baptists lived in the South (compared to 28 percent of Methodists, 25 percent of Presbyterians, 22 percent of Episcopalians, and 10 percent of Lutherans.)[105] Here we are provided with factors contributing to the defeat of Jimmy Carter, and with more evidence of the shift of the SBC to the right.

As for political process theory, there seems to be some truth in the notion of unstable political alignments contributing to social change. In the wake of the instability of being a white Southern Democrat in the 1960s through 1980s and the rejection of Southern Baptist Jimmy Carter, Southern Baptists became Republican, one change feeding on the other in a transferred legitimacy of sorts.[106] For the Southern Baptist, it became simultaneously acceptable to be frustrated with Jimmy Carter, the Democratic party, and the moderate leadership of the SBC.

The issues of discontent/alienation remain valid as well. Not a sociologist, Sundquist nevertheless cites two "streams" of "Southern discontent," and argues that a "discontent and alienated" white South became Independent in the 1960–1980 era and Republican thereafter. Southern

Baptists were in realignment on a number of fronts, motivated by their discontent over recent cultural, religious, economic, and political change.[107]

It is not a great stretch from this point to also argue the most fundamental assumption of political process theory, the notion of "political opportunity." At the end of the decade in which the SBC had experienced its first no-growth decade, moderate Southern Baptist Jimmy Carter sat in the White House, and moderate Southern Baptists ran the entire Convention structure. But political events and political-type campaigns within the SBC such as school prayer and the Equal Rights Amendment (ERA)[108] played to the fundamentalist movement's advantage. The house cleaning of seminaries and colleges soon followed during the later Reagan years. Indeed, often the religious and the political seemed to blur, and SBC president Bailey Smith stood at a Republican rally to say: "God Almighty does not hear the prayer of the Jew."

4

Fundamental Differences
Baptist Republicanism's Political Partners

The building blocks of any party system are issues and structures, or more formally, the platform of the political party and the people who organize around it under the party label. In some European countries, the meaning of *party*, as defined by the core agenda and voter groups associated with it, has changed little in the space of one hundred years.

In Great Britain, laborers are Labour, and conservatives are Conservative, as it has always been. When I quizzed a mechanic from Warwickshire about his affiliation, he said, "I'm a working man, so I must be for Labour, you see." Almost three out of four Britons strongly identify with a political party, compared to only one out of three Americans.

In the United States, parties regularly shift back and forth across the ideological spectrum, and groups of voters change party affiliation at will. Blacks leave the party of Lincoln in droves and Teamsters become Reagan Democrats.

At least a couple of factors are at work here. First, there is the concept of party realignment, also called "shift in party balance," or a "redefinition of the basis of party cleavage." The definition of realignment, depending on the approach, involves changing party composition as well as changing party strengths.[1] Scholars point to numerous examples of realignments, each not a single election, but a series of partisan contests in which a watershed shift takes place. The disappearance of the Whigs, the rise of the Republicans, and the Depression–New Deal eras are good examples.

A second concept is that of party porousness. Unlike British parties, for example, American parties are able to take in new groups of voters with their own unique agendas on a regular basis. Some would see this as a weakness. But others believe that by this porousness American parties have turned their openness into strength. Leon Epstein writes:

Party membership is loosely defined, often by state law that allows access without dues or organizational commitments. Parties so constructed are less meaningful than parties elsewhere . . . [but] . . . they provide labels that candidates seek and that officeholders use for certain collaborative purposes. . . . Such absorption, after all, is a kind of effectiveness.[2]

Though it is curious to the European advocates of strong, rigid parties, the weak party model of American politics has within it a curious strength based on its fluidity.

There is no better illustration of realignment and the great porousness of American political parties than the rise of the fundamentalist right. Once afraid of partisan politics, self-identified born-again evangelicals now make up almost half of the Republican primary vote, and a quarter of those are members of the Christian Coalition.

But the realignment of Christians to the Republican party is often oversimplified, and the degree of porousness needed has thereby been underestimated. The spectrum is narrow in a sense. The road from the SBC to Bob Jones to Pat Robertson to Jerry Falwell may be quite short in the grand scheme. But the value of this type of study is the discovery of nuances that define these important groups and their contrasting behaviors in Southern and American politics. Each comes to politics with unique motivations, each has a religious and political history of its own, and each fundamentalist group responds to different political stimuli.

Diversity of the Conservative Bloc

The very title of one of the early studies of voting behavior, *Protestant, Catholic, Jew*,[3] is a powerful summary of the typical partitioning of the electorate by religion that is found in the classic works on voting behavior[4] and in more recent works that follow in the classic tradition.[5] The title shows how far we have come. Early works study religion and its impact on political behavior by including in their models tests designed to discover if identification as a Protestant, Catholic, or Jew has an impact on a voter's decision. Divided into Protestant/Catholic/Jew, political and religious group identification and group cohesiveness are tested[6] in this literature, as is religion and its relationship to the presidential vote.[7] Other early studies examine religious and political opinions and their impact on issues,[8] and even political differences within each of the three religious groups based on ethnicity (e.g., Polish Catholics versus Irish Catholics).[9]

But the simple Protestant/Catholic/Jew division proved much too broad. The term "Protestant," for example, assumes a unified Protestant vote: Episcopalians and snake handlers, Anglo-Catholics and Amish in a single political monolith. The toppling of this assumption was the first breakthrough, as two distinct methods emerged to subdivide the Protestant vote. Some looked for distinctions among Protestant *denominations*.[10] Others chose to use *doctrinal* positions in finding explanations. The latter approach has surpassed the former in recent years, and the literature seems to validate the superiority of the doctrinal approach.[11] This approach has allowed us to find that doctrinal camps within modern American Protestantism transcend denomination, and we gain a richer understanding when proceeding on this theoretical basis.

One of these doctrinal groups, the evangelicals, defined by their conservative doctrine and high level of cultural engagement, has been growing at a faster rate than other Protestant groups since 1980. This is important politically because evangelicals have shaken off their aversion to political action.[12] Increased political involvement has led to a renewed interest in evangelicalism and its politics as distinct from mainline denominations (those who are Protestants but not harder-line evangelicalists or fundamentalists.) Voting patterns have been analyzed in depth,[13] and a sorting out of the differences between Evangelicals and "mainliners" has taken place.[14]

The "conservatives within the conservatives," or fundamentalists, have an even more deep-seated distaste for politics. For that reason and because of their formerly small numbers, fundamentalists were for decades overlooked in research on political involvement among religious groups. But work on fundamentalists finds, among other things, a distinctiveness in ideology,[15] in level of partisan political involvement,[16] and in attitudes toward "out groups."[17] Though very similar to evangelicals, fundamentalists are religiously distinct, and conservative Christians are careful to call themselves either one or the other.[18] (Fundamentalism is considered an extreme form of evangelicalism; fundamentalists are evangelicals, but evangelicals are not fundamentalists.)[19] Samuel S. Hill, a Southern religious scholar, constructs the best distinction: fundamentalists are "truth-oriented" while evangelicals are "conversion-oriented," and "for Fundamentalists religion is something you *believe*, while for the Evangelical religion is something you *get*."[20]

There *is* a difference and a distinction. Followers of fundamentalist Jerry Falwell are much more conservative and much more politically

active than the followers of evangelical Billy Graham.[21] Fundamentalists
are also stronger in their party identification and more conservative in
ideology and on selected issues.[22] Fundamentalists are also much more
Baptist-dominated, much more participatory, and more likely to translate their religious conservatism into political conservatism than are
evangelicals.[23] Fundamentalists and evangelicals even behave differently
as campaign contributors.[24] There are differences between the two in theology, age of the members, ideology, and in opinions about religious
leaders and the Moral Majority. Their positions on certain foreign policy and social issues differ, as does the importance of religious convictions in their voting decisions.[25] Several outstanding case studies of fundamentalism show the world of Protestant fundamentalists, revealing the
importance of politics to these most conservative of believers.[26]

The analysis represented in this chapter will attempt to take this progression in the literature one step further, but with a slightly different
categorical strategy. Instead of dividing Protestantism into parts and
analyzing the distinctions, or comparing the fundamentalist to the evangelical within the conservative bloc, I will attempt to blend what we
have learned from the voting-behavior literature[27] with interest group
and social movement theory to analyze politically active conservative
bloc Christians in a more political fashion—by the differing complexion
of the political behavior of groups *within* the fundamentalist bloc. (See
fig. 1.1.)

Jerry Falwell, Bob Jones, Pat Robertson, and the leadership of the
Southern Baptist Convention do not seem to us so different religiously
and politically. All call themselves fundamentalists.[28] All have Baptist
ties. Each has a rigid Bible-based view of the world that drives his political attitude. Each believes that a proper interpretation of the scriptures
meshes best with a right-of-center political philosophy.[29] All are conservative Republicans. To varying degrees, each holds a Manichean
view of the world in which there are blacks and whites but few grays.
There is little doubt also that all are *political* creatures. Falwell,
Robertson, the Joneses, and conservative Southern Baptist preachers
pepper their sermons with political references and current events, particularly in relation to the end of the world. Each reveals a keen interest, if not obsession, with politics. But surprisingly, all fundamentalist
Protestant conservative Republicans are not created equal in style or
substance—a key element to understanding the politics of Southern
Baptists.

The Separatist Fundamentalist Right

Members of the Separatist Fundamentalist Right (SFR) are conservative in voting behavior and are active Republicans, but are simply too committed to a *religious* movement to join a *political* movement. In the SFR, militant fundamentalism is historically the only movement. In South Carolina, the Bob Jones cell (the University, Sr., Jr., and III) is perhaps the best example of this position. Bob Jones College was founded in 1927 by evangelist Bob Jones in Florida, and then was moved to Cleveland, Tennessee, before settling as Bob Jones University (BJU) in Greenville, South Carolina, in 1947. Jones, Sr., one of the foremost evangelists of his day at the time he founded BJC, died in 1968. His son, Bob Jones, succeeded his father as president and is now chancellor. Bob Jones, III, grandson of the founder, is now president of the independent Christian university. (Bob Jones, IV, is a graduate student at the University of Notre Dame, an affiliation that caused quite a stir.) With just short of four thousand students (85 percent of whom are from out of state), BJU is South Carolina's largest private school. The university, through the strong signals it sends to its worldwide corps of graduates and its near total domination of local elective and party politics, makes BJU a "pacesetter" for fundamentalist politics. BJU has its loyal as well as not so loyal critics. Others in the fundamentalist right often accuse BJU of being "hyperseparationist" and more likely to work with nonbelievers than other Christians in politics, whom they consider "beneath" them. Though its founder was Methodist, BJU functions as a denomination (in terms of publishing, missions board, etc.) for a network of independent Baptist churches. It was Bob Jones who virtually founded the Christian school movement; it is a leader in home school publishing and in Christian satellite teaching technology as well.

The SFR branch has been described sociologically, but is seldom placed into the larger picture politically.[30] Southern Baptist scholar Nancy Tatom Ammerman discusses Separatist Fundamentalists in terms of "churchly" and "sectarian" religious distinctions developed in the late 1920s, arguing that "churchly" Christians are "more accommodated to the culture, in tune with the surroundings," while the sectarians are "'in tension' with the larger culture, adopting practices and safeguards that set them apart from the dominant tradition."[31]

This is the distinction at work here. The Bob Jones cell is much more separatist than the others, voting Republican beginning with Goldwater in 1964, but never attracted to movement conservatism because of its religious particularity.[32] To the Bob Jones Republican of the Separatist Fundamentalist Right, there is no political "movement" and no movement mentality except for the religious movement (fundamentalism) that launched Bob Jones University two years after the Scopes trial. One BJU ministerial graduate unintentionally explained the SFR position in an Independence Day sermon. "Making more Christians by the spread of the gospel is America's only hope," the young preacher said. "We don't need to return to 'the good old days of traditional American values,' we need to return to Jesus Christ. Our duty is to glorify God and to advance the kingdom of God."[33]

Bob Jones, III, and Bob Jones agree with their graduate. Movement Christian politics is not their way. During the halcyon days of the Moral Majority, Jones III put it very directly to the *Arizona Republic*:

> Ecumenism serves the Antichrist. It came along with Billy Graham who accommodated everything to soul-winning. The charismatic movement accommodated everything to the spirit of love, and now they [Falwell's Moral Majority] are accommodating everything to morality. . . . I can unite only with those with whom I agree. Christians should work within the framework of their own beliefs toward social goals, without any ecumenism. I could appear with someone like Jerry Falwell in a purely political context, without any religious dimension at all. But realistically, how can someone like myself or Falwell do that? We cannot separate ourselves from our identity as preachers.[34]

But Jones does not advocate cave dwelling. He strongly supports direct political involvement by fundamentalists and even evangelicals, as long as no religious borders are crossed. He is in fact concerned about the lack of impact the church seems to be having on politics, telling *The Evening Press* in Binghamton, New York, that "the so-called 'wall of separation' between church and state is a liberal fabrication to try to put churches out of a place of influence in political life."[35]

The Jones position seems confusing at first: on the one hand he favors separate fundamentalist and nonfundamentalist involvement, but on the other he does not want to organize or unify the two for secular purposes. His is the separatist political understanding taken to its logical conclusion. Our intricate analysis of evangelicals and fundamentalists and other groups within conservative Protestantism would be a waste of time to Jones, for in his view (1) there are fundamentalist Christians and non-fundamentalist Christians, (2) the fundamentalist circle does not include Falwell, and (3) political associations among Christians, just like religious ones, should be doctrinally pure.[36] The oft-cited scripture is Amos 3:3: "Can two walk together except they be agreed?" In the opinion of Bob Jones, III, fundamentalists join only with fundamentalists *religiously* (hence the referenced split with Billy Graham, who will join with any religious leader as long as *he* gets to preach), therefore they may only join movements with other fundamentalists *politically*.

The Movement Fundamentalist Right

The Movement Fundamentalist Right is the most vocal of the New Christian Right and has been given the most attention in the last decade in the secular press. Most of this attention is due to the dramatic shaking-off of the theological and cultural impediments to political organization, still at work in the Jones separatism.[37] After decades of unwillingness to organize, various demographic and social changes (see chapters 1 and 2) turned these previously passive Christians into a potent political force for the Republican party. The Pat Robertson and Jerry Falwell cells are the most influential examples.

In their zealotry, their agenda, and their resistance to the establishment GOP, the Falwell and Robertson battalions are reminiscent of the post-Eisenhower "New Southern Republicans," the "programmatic conservatives" who rallied behind Goldwater and formed the modern Republican party. Political-parties scholar James Sundquist describes them this way:

> They were determined to have done with defeatist minority politics and to build an effective political instrument for conservative ideas. . . . they were young, energetic, concerned with program rather than patronage, disinclined to compromise on party principle. Just as the programmatic northern liberals were more liberal than the Democratic party as a whole, so the programmatic southern Republicans stood to the right of the center of their national party—many of them near the extreme right of the whole liberal-conservative spectrum. . . . Out of the Goldwater crusade in both sections of the South . . . came a legacy of revived Republican organization.[38]

The Sundquist characterization of the 1960s Movement Right is strikingly similar to the 1970s and 1980s Movement Fundamentalist Right. By changing only a few words and by substituting "Christian" for "conservative" and "fundamentalist" for "Republican" and "party," we have an apt description of the Movement Fundamentalist Right. As we shall see, the style of these aggressive but green political operatives was similar to Goldwater's supporters. The reaction of regular Republicans to these new political players in the 1980s and 1990s was similar to the chilly reception the Goldwater supporters received in the 1960s from the Eisenhower-Nixon-Rockefeller crowd as well.

Independent Baptist Jerry Falwell of Lynchburg, Virginia, struggled with political activism. Because of the separatist mentality he inherited, he resisted political involvement for twenty years. But when many Catholic clerics and only a few conservative Protestant pastors led the fight against abortion in the immediate wake of *Roe v. Wade*, Falwell began to wrestle with the part of his separatist theology that kept preachers out of secular politics. In his autobiography, Falwell wrote a firsthand account of his struggle:

> I began to preach regularly against abortion. . . . However, it soon became apparent that this time preaching would not be enough. To stop the legalizing of death by abortion, opponents of *Roe v. Wade* were protesting in the streets. For the first time in my life I felt God leading me to join them. But such a step was entirely against my nature. So I began to reread the Biblical passages that might inform me. . . . And I tried to stay open to the truth even when it seemed to threaten my convictions.
>
> . . . It wouldn't be easy for this Baptist preacher to become politically active. I had always tried to be a responsible citizen in the privacy of the voting booth. But my teachers had taught me the concept of separation of church and state. Somehow I thought the separation doctrine existed to keep the church out of politics.
>
> . . . [W]hen my son Jerry Jr. decided to study law, my daughter had to convince her Grandpa Pate that one could be a lawyer and a Christian at the same time.
>
> "But your mom and dad spent their wholes lives teaching you children to tell the truth," Grandpa protested, "and now Jerry Jr. is going off to law school, where they teach you how to lie."
>
> . . . Grandpa Pate represented generations of fundamentalist Christians for whom getting involved in law and government was out of the question. I had inherited those generations of tradition.[39]

Falwell's decision to break with the past and take to the streets began a six-year crusade for morality led by a multidenominational Moral Majority. By the time Falwell came along, the Goldwater group, the

Buckleys, and the *National Review* subscribers formed the *Old Right*. Falwell represented the religious arm of the *New Right*, an interlocking group of organizations that were the Conservative Movement.

As his name became a household word, Falwell began to be criticized by fundamentalists as well as those associating themselves with the group "People for the American Way." He was welcomed at the Reagan White House, however, and was asked to pray at the Republican National Convention in Dallas in 1984. But the Moral Majority was not to last. By October 1986 the organization began to fade as Falwell changed its name to the Liberty Federation, turned the organization over to one of his associates, and returned to preaching at Thomas Road Baptist Church and running Liberty University.

Even as Jerry Falwell's Moral Majority was founded during the Republican shuffle to succeed Jimmy Carter, Pat Robertson founded his organization as Republicans scrambled for a successor to Ronald Reagan. Both Christian movements were born in a leadership vacuum and thrived on it for a time; Falwell walked into a true Christian political vacuum, and Robertson stepped into the vacuum left by Falwell. Robertson took up where Falwell left off, starting an organization of his own that coincided closely with the demise of the Moral Majority.

But the Robertson organization extended the Moral Majority, focusing on attracting not the merely *morally conservative* American but the *Christian* American. The early literature featured a trampled Christian flag with the message, "Are You Fed Up?" Robertson's Freedom Council was closed in 1986 to make way for Americans for Robertson; some of the Freedom Council staff were hired at AFR, but a number were laid off. The Christian Coalition formed in February 1990. The Coalition has been more grass-roots oriented, not being content with grandstanding and direct mailings like the Moral Majority had been, but seeking to build an organization in every state and county in the country. This mobilization, which began as early as 1985, came with the help of not only preachers but professional political consultants and staffers who were veterans in the political arena. These included Marc Nuttle, the campaign director; Mary Ellen Miller, the national field director; and Marlene Elwell, one of the best grass-roots organizers in the pro-life movement.

Though Robertson's message had always been thoroughly political since the founding of the Christian Broadcasting Network (CBN) in the 1970s, this son of a Virginia senator began sounding the alarm for Christian political involvement most pointedly in his 1986 book, *America's Dates with Destiny*. Selecting twenty-three dates in American history that he considered vitally important to the national civic religion, Robertson wrote a chapter on each, culminating in a final chapter dedicated to "Election Day 1988." Robertson encouraged Christians to be ready for that day by registering new voters, studying and discussing political issues, joining together with other concerned Christians and with other churches, and getting involved at the precinct and primary level in a political party: "imagine what could happen in America's 175,000 precincts if just ten evangelical Christian volunteers could be mobilized to assist in each one! The American political process would be revolutionized, and the future of the nation would be changed forever." He went on:

> The nation stands at another crossroads. During the twentieth century, America wandered off the course established by her forefathers. In this past decade we have been finding our way again. But we must not relax our vigil. It was not enough that 500 thousand Americans prayed for the nation's renewal on the Capitol Mall in Washington, D.C. We must continue to pray for the nation in small groups and in huge rallies all across America. It is not enough that Ronald Reagan has begun the journey back toward our spiritual and conservative roots. We must continue and advance the work he has begun.[40]

The Falwell and Robertson cells within the movement branch are obviously similar, but there are subtle differences in focus and strategy. For example, when beginning their crusades, both men wrote books outlining their plan of action. But in contrast to the Southern Baptist-turned-Charismatic Robertson's *America's Dates*, which is mostly political, the Independent Baptist Falwell's *Listen America!*[41] was a 50-50 mix of politics and preaching, with its closing chapter calling for prayer, national repentance, a facing of national sins, and "moral involvement." The moral involvement factor included becoming registered to vote, becoming informed (by joining the Moral Majority), and becoming mobilized. But in contrast to Robertson's emphasis, by *mobilization* Falwell emphasized mostly active participation in the party of one's choice. Robertson seemed to call for a "meeting before the meeting" type of strategy, a banding together for maximizing political muscle within the political party, that is, the formation of a *movement*.[42] Christian Coalition executive director Ralph Reed quite frequently speaks of "the movement" and "joining our movement" in his speeches.[43]

Though it is parenthetical to our study, it is important to note the contrast. It is also important to recognize submovements within the Falwell and Robertson camps. Falwell's Moral Majority was so intertwined with the New Right, a competing *political submovement* of sorts, that it is often difficult to distinguish the two. Like Richard Viguerie, the National Conservative Political Action Committee (NCPAC), Phyllis Schlafly, Howard Phillips, and Paul Weyrich, Falwell's group was just another political action committee that sent out mail in bundles from a Washington address, asking all those supporting his agenda to send in a check.[44] Falwell simply provided the moral element to the movement and gave emphasis to the most moral of the social-issues agenda. Robertson's first foray into political organizing seemed to be linked to his bid for president, a *personal submovement* driven by his own personality. (After all, he was the son of a United States senator and a descendant of several presidents.) Americans for Robertson and the Freedom Council were much the same from the beginning. As it was difficult to separate the Moral Majority from the New Right, Robertson's movement was inextricably linked to Robertson himself.

Like every political movement, the Movement Fundamentalist Right has gone through changes over fifteen years, and has attracted critics. But according to evangelical political observer Os Guinness, all has not been productive. Guinness is a disciple of the late Francis Schaeffer, the Christian philosopher who in his 1970s books, *The Great Evangelical Disaster* and *The Christian Manifesto*, gave Christians permission to be politically active. Like his mentor, Guinness does not mince words, lamenting that from the 1980s to the 1990s the fundamentalist right changed from "the sleeping giant of American public life to the poor little whipping boy at the mercy of liberal forces." Conservative Christians are complainers now, he writes, whining about "their decreasing status, the increasing bigotry against them, and the hardening closure of the political process to their influence."[45]

Guinness sees what I see—a shift from the Falwell activist tradition to the Robertson version. Though neither was particularly winsome, the Falwell style was pompous, militant, and polyester, while Robertson is the pleading martyr in the thousand-dollar suit. One reason for the contrast could be that, as already noted, Falwell in the early days seemed always to act as an adjunct to the New Right, while Robertson has been more the Lone Ranger. With complaints ranging from a decrease in Christians' status to bigotry against them, and a diminishing of their influence, Guinness is concerned that conservative Christians are beginning to travel the path long abandoned by the civil rights movement—concentrating on victimhood and corraling resentment to achieve special privileges.[46] Though there is no space here, it could be argued that the independent Baptist-Pentecostal contrast is at work here politically. Robertson's bedrock followers are Pentecostal and charismatic and lean to the evangelical-accommodationist side of the fundamentalist right. Falwell is supported by a more militant independent Baptist base. Contrasting theological worlds are manifesting themselves in varying political styles and attitudes among the Movement Fundamentalist Right, with Robertson and Falwell as good and bad cops respectively.[47] Falwell was always the more militant in tone, winning a lawsuit against the NCAA so that his Liberty University football players could continue to pray in the end zone after a touchdown. Indeed, after all that Robertson and Reed have done, it was *Falwell* whom President Clinton singled out by name as an enemy in a call to a talk show on KMOX in St. Louis. Calling from Air Force One, the president spoke for twenty-three minutes, assailing Falwell and Rush Limbaugh for their personal attacks on him.

Since Christians have been involved in politics, from the earliest days to Falwell to Robertson's Christian Coalition, opposition to their organization and their agenda has mounted in the larger culture. As described in Stephen Carter's *Culture of Disbelief*,[48] this has contributed to a "reframing" of issues in the public mind causing the fundamentalist right to lose ground among the more moderate members of the conservative bloc. This has left some Americans with the notion that fundamentalist right activism is nothing short of the politicization of the church. Others applaud the entrance of a new group of conservative voters to the electorate. These secular debates, too, have had an impact on the delayed involvement of the culturally dominant Southern Baptists, the Emerging Right.

The Emerging Fundamentalist Right

The Emerging Fundamentalist Right, a group that includes the Southern Baptist cell, are those conservatives who, as we saw in chapters 1 and 2, are not *secular*, in that they are Christian and conservative, but remain too *dominant in the culture* to join a political movement.

Politically and theologically, these "churchly" Christians, as Niebuhr would call them (in contrast to the "sectarian" separatists), are much the same as other conservatives, but they are less prone to be movement join-ers because of their stronger position in the culture.[49] Unlike students at BJU, for example, members of the Emerging Fundamentalist Right have had little exposure to a Northern-style separatist fundamentalist move-ment subculture.[50] The Emerging Fundamentalist Right is the mirror image of the Separatist Fundamentalist Right. Emerging Fundamentalists refuse to be attracted to political movements because of their large num-bers; likewise, Separatist Fundamentalists prefer a virtuous smallness and isolation. (See fig. 1.1.)

This three-branch concept is illustrated graphically in figure 1.1. There is the progressive bloc vs. the conservative bloc, each with its own particular branches, the several cells within each branch, and the divid-ing line of partisanship. Then there is the interplay of other movements such as the old BJU-type fundamentalist separatist *religious* movement that left little room for movement politics; the *political* movement led by Jerry Falwell, which was more New Right than Christian Right;[51] the *personal* movement of Pat Robertson, which culminated in his run for president; and the *cultural* movement, which led to the takeover of the Southern Baptist Convention.[52] The Southern Baptists are shown as a part of the conservative bloc but not entirely captive of the Christian right. The Southern Baptist moderate faction (listed for reference pur-poses here) is both a faction within the Convention and a cell within Protestantism. SBC moderates are in the progressive bloc, which wants no part of traditionalistic fundamentalism.[53]

Interaction: The Fundamentalist Right and the SBC

The attitudes of other fundamentalists toward Southern Baptists are a consideration when placing Southern Baptists within the conservative bloc. Jerry Falwell bends over backward to attract Southern Baptists,[54] writing in his history of fundamentalism that "[o]ne cannot describe the Fundamentalist Movement without studying . . . the Southern Baptist Convention."[55] Falwell has also featured former SBC president Bailey Smith's son, a ministerial student at Liberty University, in full-page ads for the school in SBC publications, while dedicating an issue of his now defunct *Fundamentalist Journal* to SBC president Jerry Vines and the "conservative surge" in the SBC.[56] Then again, half of Liberty's board of trustees is Southern Baptist.[57]

Bob Jones fundamentalists, on the other hand, argue that Southern Baptists are not fundamentalists by their own definition because of the doctrine of separation.[58] Separation requires that fundamentalists refuse to form leagues (religious or otherwise) with nonfundamentalists, or even to associate with those who keep company with nonfundamentalists. The SBC conservative faction may be admirable in many respects, but it is yoked in the Convention to the moderate faction. The BJU leadership also thinks that conservative Southern Baptist leader Judge Paul Pressler (who is remembered for announcing that he would "go for the jugular" to take over the SBC)[59] moved too slow in his purge. In *SBC: House on the Sand?*, BJU professor David O. Beale makes his case for SBC softness by quoting the less than fundamentalist view of moderate-faction SBC agency heads, most of whom have since been purged by the conservatives.[60] The BJU books and tracts on the SBC seem incomplete, or at least dated. For every moderate SBC pronouncement in the Beale book, there is a hard-right inflammatory quotation from a Southern Baptist like Bailey Smith, who has cheered the throngs at Falwell's Liberty University. It is not difficult to see the political effect of this attitude. The Separatist Fundamentalist mentality sees the circle around the flame of truth as small and getting smaller, whereas the Movement Fundamentalist mentality trumpets the growth of fundamentalism.[61] However, it must be noted that some of Jerry Falwell's best friends in the Baptist Bible Fellowship (BBF) have been at least as hard on the SBC as the BJU press. The most strident in the campaign to expose liberalism in the SBC are book peddlers R. L. Hymers and John R. Rice. The dust jacket of the Hymers book on the SBC screams, "You Will Be Shocked and Jolted on Virtually Every Page!" The late John R. Rice's book bears the admonition, "Southern Baptists Wake Up!"[62] Both of these tract masters are in the Baptist Bible Fellowship, another cell of the Separatist Fundamentalist Right. The BBF follows in the footsteps of a preacher mentioned earlier in this work, Southern Baptist secessionist J. Frank Norris.[63]

To emphasize again a point made in chapter 1, the contrast in Northern and Southern fundamentalism is worth noting in the BJU-Falwell-Robertson-SBC distinction. I would argue along with Yance that "although Southern Baptists have other qualities, their most evident feature is Southernness. Consequently, they have a central role in the South's folk religion."[64] It was this southernness,[65] mixed with an almost inseparable individualism,[66] that formed a bulwark against progressive tendencies, factors not found in all Protestant denominations. This is a key to understanding how and why conservatives stayed within the Convention when other denominations, primarily Northern ones, were splintering. It is worthy of note also that in the 1970s–1990s schism, progressives were Baptists first and Southern second, while conservatives were Southern first and Baptists second. The Northern-Southern distinction is not lost among the SBC leadership, either, as during the first advent of the New Christian Right former Christian Life Commission director Foy Valentine begged the media in 1976 not to lump him and his denomination in with "Yankee fundamentalists."[67]

5

Bible Belt

Baptist Republicanism in the
Palmetto State

"Tip" O'Neill once explained that "all politics is local." He was right. But had the Speaker been a member of the fundamentalist right (quite a stretch), he might have further explained that "all religious politics is local too, but not monolithic." At least that is what South Carolina governor Carroll Campbell told me.

In the three branches of the fundamentalist right we gain a unique understanding of politics and its varying tactics. No grasp of Baptist Republicanism can be achieved without understanding these simple distinctions. Our "local" setting is South Carolina. Our conclusion is that Southern Baptists are neither Bob Jones fish nor Robertson fowl.

The Separatist Fundamentalist Right Branch

Bob Jones University Conservatives I: 1976

In the state of South Carolina, as in the nation at large, the politics of the fundamentalist right is often linked to takeover attempts and party "raiding."[1] A group associated with largely independent Baptist Bob Jones University became active in South Carolina politics with much controversy in 1976. Though numerous BJU faculty and staff had long been active as individuals in the Greenville County Republican party (since the 1964 Goldwater campaign, according to Governor Carroll Campbell), in "the year of the evangelical," 1976, a faction of younger, more militant BJU politicos made an attempt at outright control of the local party. Their exact goals were unclear, but many were energized by a pro-Ronald Reagan campaign film shown in several churches friendly to BJU. Some wanted to help the conservative Reagan take the Republican nomination from moderate President Ford. Some had gone to Moral Majority–type meetings and had adopted Falwell's political manuals as their own. Others were concerned about protecting their church-affiliated parochial schools from government interference. (BJU itself and local church schools in Ohio and Texas had been singled out for attention by the IRS and state agencies beginning in the early 1970s.)[2]

The takeover plan was to take the county organization precinct by precinct. Fundamentalist conservatives would seize precincts, and precincts would elect fundamentalist convention delegates. Fundamentalists would then, holding a numerical majority among delegates, control the proceedings of the county convention in Greenville's Textile Hall. The next step would be to send conservative/fundamentalist delegates to the state convention in Columbia to pass a pro-Reagan, pro-conservative party platform.

Executing their plan, the organization took the sleepy Greenville County GOP by storm in the hundred or so precinct meetings in the county, ousting veteran pro-Ford moderate leaders in some precincts and organizing precincts not heard from in decades in other parts of the county. At the county convention, county Republican chairman Mike Spivey was defeated for reelection by BJU conservatives and their non-fundamentalist Reagan allies, some of whom carried walkie-talkies for coordinating floor strategy. Ironically, Spivey would switch sides in less than a decade and become a county Robertson organizer in league with his former foes. As in the Spivey case, wounds would heal by the mid-eighties. But the 1976 scene was not a pleasant one for the Greenville County Republican party. Former South Carolina governor (then a candidate for the South Carolina Senate) Carroll Campbell remembers the events well.

> The county convention threw out the officers! In Greenville in 1976, there were precinct meetings where they would talk theology for three or four hours. There were good [BJU] people like [staff member] Gilbert Stenholm, but there were others who liked to fight more—they treated the platform like the constitution!
>
> One of the problems [with the latter group] was that their people skills were not great. One lady screamed at me while I was on stage: "When were you born again?" But she was the exception.[3]

Many Bob Jones graduates and supporters in other parts of the state who were active in the Republican party followed much the same strategy.

But Greenville, the home county of BJU, was the hotbed of controversy. Carroll Campbell continued to find himself in the middle of the struggle, and in many ways his political life and that of the Separatist Fundamentalist Right would thereafter be intertwined.

But as Campbell said, things began to change. After their defeat at the hands of the BJU group in 1976, a small group of old-guard Greenville County Republicans (mostly supporters of President Ford) seceded from the county party to form the Piedmont Republican Club. The BJU group also became aggressive, running candidates for state and county office. All of them lost. In time, cooler heads among the BJU crowd emerged, and a group of conservative pro-Reagan "regulars" joined with them to elect a county party chairman in 1978, the same year Carroll Campbell went to Congress.[4]

The Campbell-fundamentalist interplay was a factor in state politics again in 1980. That year, Congressman Carroll Campbell was seeking to consolidate power statewide in preparation for future political ambitions. Campbell's plan was to see that his candidate won the state party chairmanship and would then install his protégé, Warren Tompkins, as executive director of the state organization. With the help of fundamentalist conservatives statewide, Campbell and his team saw to the defeat of incumbent state chairman Dan Ross and, as planned, new chairman George Graham hired Tompkins. (Ironically, Ross later became a leader in the Christian Coalition.) Campbell repaid his Separatist Fundamentalist Right allies with a negotiated share of delegate slots at the Republican National Convention and a relatively free reign in drafting the state party platform.[5]

Bob Jones University Conservatives II: 1980–1996

With the county and state parties mending, 1980 presented an important opportunity for the Bob Jones University conservatives: a second phase. With their newly discovered political efficacy, the BJU vote in Greenville County and the BJU fundamentalist vote statewide became a Republican plum. The party was at peace, but many local Republicans wondered how these new Republicans would behave as *voters*. Would they support the candidates of the moderate Republican establishment (who usually had a better chance of winning), or would they again attempt to run for office themselves and support candidates regardless of the candidate's chances? More bluntly, would the fundamentalists stand alone against the rest of the county and state party, or would they cooperate?

An analysis of the BJU vote answers these questions. Residents of the Bob Jones University campus (which includes the homes and apartments for many of the faculty and staff)[6] vote in the Greenville 27th and 28th precincts (before a 1984 reapportionment, these boxes were known as Greenville 1 and Greenville 2, and I have compensated for this). An analysis of the election returns from these two boxes in comparison to the county and state Republican primary vote reveals a distinct voting history, which I will call *the BJU vote*. The period I have chosen, 1980–96, is the era in which the BJU vote came of age and the choices for South Carolina Republicans expanded dramatically. The choices were few in 1980. But in 1994–96, the GOP primary season pitted very different types of Republicans against one another, presented a number of options for the BJU vote, and provided a test of the behavior of the Separatist Fundamentalist Right.

In 1980, as in 1976, Ronald Reagan was the hero of the Bob Jones vote, winning 72 percent to John Connally's 17 percent, with only 11 percent for George Bush in that year's presidential preference primary. The county gave Reagan only 60 percent because Connally and Bush fared a bit better countywide than in Greenville 1 and 2. Statewide, Bush was significantly stronger at 30 percent, which held Reagan to 55 percent. True to the Falwell-Jones split, Christian conservative and Falwell protégé Charlie Rhodes won 35 percent of the BJU vote, about what he got statewide, but well-funded regular Republican Marshall Mays picked up 60 percent of the campus ballots.

With Ronald Reagan in the White House, Strom Thurmond in the U.S. Senate, Richard Riley, a popular Democrat, as governor (and later secretary of education in the Clinton Administration), and Carroll Campbell in Congress, the next major test of the BJU vote would not come until 1986. Carroll Campbell had decided to run for governor that year and was popular with most elements of the party. But it had been the boyhood dream of another South Carolina congressman, Tommy Hartnett of the Lowcountry, to be governor. Hartnett announced that he, too, would be interested in a gubernatorial campaign. But after months of stand-off, even after receiving a supply of "Hartnett for Governor" bumper stickers, the Charlestonian succumbed. Campbell's political network in Republican circles in Washington, his organization in the state, his history as a tireless fundraiser, and Lee Atwater's commitment

TABLE 5.1

Bob Jones University Precincts Republican Primary Voting, 1980–1996

Campaign 1 1980 US President				Campaign 4-B 1986 US Congress Runoff		
	BJU	County	State		BJU	County	District

	BJU	County	State
Bush	11%	17%	15%
Connally	17%	22%	30%
Dole	0%	0%	0%
Reagan	72%	60%	55%
Stassen	0%	0%	0%
Baker	0%	1%	1%
Fernand	0%	0%	0%
Belluso	0%	0%	0%
Total	100%	100%	100%
	1,637	19,741	145,501

Campaign 1 — 1980 US President

	BJU	County	State
Bush	11%	17%	15%
Connally	17%	22%	30%
Dole	0%	0%	0%
Reagan	72%	60%	55%
Stassen	0%	0%	0%
Baker	0%	1%	1%
Fernand	0%	0%	0%
Belluso	0%	0%	0%
Total	100%	100%	100%
	1,637	19,741	145,501

Campaign 2 — 1980 US Senate

	BJU	County	State
Carley	6%	14%	23%
Mays	60%	56%	43%
Rhodes	35%	30%	34%
Total	100%	100%	100%
	446	2,733	33,045

Campaign 3 — 1986 US Senate

	BJU	County	State
Jordan	63%	49%	47%
McMaster	37%	51%	53%
Total	100%	100%	100%
	754	12,959	51,859

Campaign 4-A — 1986 US Congress

	BJU	County	District
Adams	43%	23%	20%
Marchant	28%	23%	23%
Rigdon	7%	8%	8%
Workman	23%	46%	49%
Total	100%	100%	100%
	763	13,427	17,267

Campaign 4-B — 1986 US Congress Runoff

	BJU	County	District
Adams	60%	46%	45%
Workman	40%	54%	55%
Total	100%	100%	100%
	718	12,303	15,184

Campaign 5 — 1988 US President

	BJU	County	State
Bush	25%	45%	49%
Dole	13%	19%	21%
Kemp	49%	16%	11%
Roberts	13%	20%	19%
Dupont	0%	0%	0%
Haig	0%	0%	0%
Stassen	0%	0%	0%
Total	100%	100%	100%
	946	26,803	195,292

Campaign 6 — 1988 US Congress

	BJU	County	District
Adams	43%	43%	43%
White	57%	57%	57%
Total	100%	100%	100%
	860	18,373	26,520

TABLE 5.1
(continued)

Campaign 7
1990 SC Lt. Governor

	BJU	County	State
Martchink	11%	30%	49%
McMaster	89%	70%	51%
Total	100%	100%	100%
	660	10,493	95,994

Campaign 8
1992 US President

	BJU	County	State
Buchanan	48%	31%	26%
Bush	50%	64%	67%
Duke	2%	5%	7%
Total	100%	100%	100%
	708	18,345	148,358

Campaign 9-A
1994 SC Governor

	BJU	County	State
Beasley	82%	62%	47%
Hartnett	13%	23%	21%
Ravenel	6%	16%	32%
Total	0%	100%	100%
	995	27,831	253,719

Campaign 9-B
1994 SC Governor Runoff

	BJU	County	State
Beasley	92%	79%	58%
Ravenel	8%	21%	42%
Total	100%	100%	100%
	965	24,145	232,076

Campaign 10-A
1994 SC Lt. Governor

	BJU	County	State
Clyborne	37%	28%	23%
Jordan	31%	19%	27%
Peeler	32%	54%	49%
Total	100%	100%	100%
	969	27,568	240,350

Campaign 10-B
1994 SC Lt. Governor Runoff

	BJU	County	State
Jordan	63%	38%	41%
Peeler	37%	62%	59%
Total	100%	100%	100%
	946	23,905	219,689

Campaign 11-A
1994 SC Attorney General

	BJU	County	State
Condon	33%	37%	43%
Eckstrom	46%	36%	29%
Hamm	21%	27%	28%
Total	100%	100%	100%
	926	26,406	238,872

Campaign 11-B
1994 SC Attorney General Runoff

	BJU	County	State
Condon	31%	45%	58%
Eckstrom	69%	55%	42%
Total	100%	100%	100%
	929	23,342	221,014

Campaign 12
1994 SC Supt. of Education

	BJU	County	State
Nielsen	36%	43%	51%
Rawl	8%	11%	19%
Stiles	56%	46%	30%
Total	100%	100%	100%
	937	26,647	171,851

Campaign 13
1996 US President

	BJU	County	State
Alexander	4%	9%	10%
Buchanan	44%	34%	29%
Dole	34%	42%	45%
Forbes	4%	12%	13%
Keyes	13%	3%	2%
Lugar	0%	0%	0%
Total	100%	100%	100%
	1,122	37,463	276,741

Source: South Carolina Republican Party, Greenville County, Greenville [S.C.] News.

to "consult" the campaign persuaded Hartnett that he could not win a statewide primary. Hartnett agreed to seek the lieutenant governor slot instead.

BJU-affiliated conservatives were united behind Campbell's gubernatorial bid, but not in the race for his successor in Congress. Dividing the fundamentalist camp for the first time were two state representatives friendly to the Joneses who represented state house districts near BJU in the general assembly (Representatives Rick Rigdon and Tom Marchant), the popular mayor of Greenville (Bill Workman), and a political newcomer (airline pilot Ted Adams). Marchant seemed to have the official Jones family endorsement, Adams was most popular among BJU students (who provided manpower), Workman had the support of many of the veteran BJU Republicans, and Rigdon had the rest. Rigdon, the least active of the candidates (and the lone BJU graduate) was least popular with fellow alumni, in large part because of his newly found charismatic faith: speaking in tongues is anathema to BJU conservatives, so they gave Rigdon only 7 percent.[7] Former John Birch Society member Adams, however, received almost a majority of the campus vote (43 percent), leaving the mayor with 23 percent. Countywide and districtwide the reverse was the case, as Workman came within an eyelash of winning the nomination outright with 49 percent and Adams finishing last among the active candidates with 20 percent. In the runoff, Marchant stepped aside to allow Adams to face Workman. Workman was outdistanced by Adams 60 to 40 percent at BJU, but he won the nomination easily with 55 percent. The divisions from the primary never healed, however, allowing the Fourth District seat in Congress to turn Democratic in 1986.

The Republicans had another primary in 1986, an election to find a candidate to face veteran senator Ernest Hollings. BJU voted even more like movement conservatives in this contest, giving the surgeon, Vietnam War pilot, and political newcomer Henry Jordan 63 percent of its votes against the former United States attorney Henry McMaster. McMaster won the nomination with just over half of the county and statewide vote. The race for Congress in 1986, in which the BJU vote was divided, in some ways signaled a return to the more individualistic politics of earlier years to a Separatist Fundamentalist Right organization, but the story of the U.S. Senate primary contradicted that trend—it was all movement conservatism.[8] The BJU vote seemed to be up for grabs, but was likely to land in the pocket of whoever was the most conservative Republican running.

BJU Republicans divided again in the 1988 Republican presidential primary and in the campaign for Congress. BJU gave strong support to Jack Kemp (49 percent) and grudging support to George Bush (25 percent) while soundly resisting the claims of Pat Robertson. The rejection of Robertson was so complete in the campus vote that the charismatic televangelist received a lower percentage of the vote in the two BJU boxes than he got state or countywide.

In the race for Congress, the campus also leaned toward a more "regular" candidate, turning back movement conservative Ted Adams in his second campaign for Congress and supporting city councilman and former Campbell staffer Knox White at the same ratio as the rest of the county and congressional district. During the campaign, questions had been raised in the fundamentalist community about Adams's church affiliation and the strength of his fundamentalist commitment. This hurt him in the BJU boxes, and White received the nomination. After the campaign, Adams left the Republican party in frustration with BJU and other conservatives, joining the U.S. Taxpayer's party. In the wake of Adams's defeat, his supporters and other non-BJU religious conservatives openly complained of the rumors spread about Adams's faith and about the BJU vote's increased willingness to accommodate the Campbell-establishment wing of the Republican party.

The BJU vote has always frustrated Movement Fundamentalist Right organizers by settling for "making a contribution" but not (after 1976) dominating or truly *changing* local and state politics. To use the analogy Earl Black has used to illustrate party factions, the BJU group just wants to make sure they are on the bus, they don't care if they don't happen to be driving it. One fundamentalist leader told me that BJU had a "plantation mentality," a willingness to help the regulars in return for free reign on the platform and for state convention delegate slots. The same leader-observer admits, however, that by refusing to focus on takeovers, BJU is out of danger of having "utopian notions of bringing in the kingdom of God by voting," which many in the Movement Right have fallen prey to.

In 1980 and 1986, BJU fundamentalists seemed willing to support "movement conservative" candidates, provided the candidate gave them no *religious grounds* on which to object to his candidacy. Robertson and Adams fell into the latter category.

This pattern held in 1990 when Henry McMaster fared better with the BJU vote when he ran for lieutenant governor. Unlike in his 1986 U.S. Senate campaign, he was the most conservative candidate. Against moderate (pro-choice) Charleston state senator Sherry Martschink, McMaster won 89 percent of the campus vote and 70 percent countywide to defeat the Low Country legislator and win the nomination with 51 percent of the vote statewide. Likewise, in 1992 Protestant incumbent president George Bush edged out Roman Catholic columnist Pat Buchanan by 2 percent to win the BJU boxes. Bush beat Buchanan much more soundly statewide (67 percent to 26 percent). Buchanan had spoken to the student body, as had Vice-President Dan Quayle. Both were warmly received. Conservatism has its limits, however, and former Ku Klux Klan grand wizard David Duke received less support in the Bob Jones community than countywide or statewide, as campus boxes gave David Duke only 2 percent, much lower than the county (5 percent) and the state (7 percent) percentage. The rejection of Duke is particularly telling given that BJU did not admit its first unmarried black students until 1971, and the school retains a strict policy of no interracial dating or marriage, although its tax exempt status has been pulled by the IRS because of it.[9] BJU says that biblical commands are behind its dating policy and no racial prejudice is involved. In any case, David Duke's poor showing with BJU should lay to rest arguments for a connection between BJU fundamentalist politics and David Duke–style racial campaigns.

Carroll Campbell was not a bystander in 1990, 1993, 1994, or (as we shall see) 1996. His organization was known to favor Senator Martschink, and though McMaster was the lieutenant governor nominee, the Campbell-McMaster ticket never materialized. For the Bush campaign, Campbell was Southern regional chairman, and he spent a number of days as surrogate speaker both in the region and in the state, rallying support for the beleaguered president. As for 1994, by process of elimination it is simple to determine the Campbell candidate. Two of the three Republican candidates, Hartnett and Ravenel, were old Campbell rivals. The third, Beasley, hired Campbell's former chief of staff, Warren Tompkins, to run his campaign.

The 1994 picture nevertheless was a complicated one for Bob Jones voters, and also the most complicated in the history of South Carolina's fundamentalist right politics. Much of the complexity came out of the growth of South Carolina Republicanism. Fourteen years earlier, Separatist Fundamentalist Right voters had few choices. With a selection of several good candidates, the August 9, 1994, primary would test their loyalties all around. In the race for governor, the Christian Coalition backed David Beasley, a Southern Baptist lay preacher who was both a born-again Christian and a born-again Republican. Beasley had changed lifestyles and parties in the four years leading up to the primary, having served as majority (Democratic) leader of the South Carolina House and having never been elected as a Republican. Beasley professed a born-again experience based on listening to the Bible on cassette tapes distributed by the South Carolina Association of Christian Schools and Hampton Park (Independent) Baptist Church at a legislative breakfast. Beasley was invited to speak both at the Greenville church and at BJU chapel services. Unafraid to inject religion into the campaign, his performances quickly endeared him to the Bob Jones vote. Beasley's appearance at BJU was a significant shift away from an earlier policy that allowed politicians to address the assembled students and faculty about their campaigns but held a stricter standard for *preachers*. Ronald Reagan, John Connally, Dan Quayle, and others had *spoken*. But *preaching* was for independent, Separatist Fundamentalists only. The school's president, Bob Jones, III, seemed to underscore the significance as he told the students that Beasley wasn't there to make a political speech, but to give his Christian testimony. He may have been the first Southern Baptist to "preach" at BJU for decades.[10]

Beasley's opponents were Charleston congressman Arthur Ravenel, one of the founders of the South Carolina Republican party who was pro-choice on abortion and openly hostile to the Christian Coalition, and former congressman Tommy Hartnett, who had been defeated narrowly two years before by Ernest Hollings for the U.S. Senate and had been the losing half of the 1986 "dream team" ticket of Campbell-Hartnett. (The winning half, eight-year incumbent governor Campbell, was barred by law from seeking a third term.) Both Ravenel and Hartnett would make religion an issue against the Coalition-backed Beasley. In the heat of the campaign, Hartnett, a Roman Catholic, complained to his diocese's newspaper that he had met with Bob Jones leaders who told him that they would support Beasley because he had been "born again."[11] Ravenel would base his two-week runoff campaign against Beasley largely on his Coalition connection.

But BJU gave Beasley strong support: 82 percent in the primary and an incredible 92 percent in the runoff, the latter outpacing the level of support for Ronald Reagan. Though not by an eight to one and nine to one margin, Beasley also performed well countywide in the primary and the runoff (62 percent and 79 percent, respectively) and the state (47 percent and 58 percent). (Greenville County, the county with the highest concentration of Separatist Fundamentalists and various Movement Fundamentalists was the pivotal county in the general election as well, where

Beasley, the former coastal legislator, beat Democrat Nick Theodore in Theodore's home county by 8,000 votes—49,000 to 41,000.)

The contest for lieutenant governor in 1994 presented a tougher choice. Howell Clyborne, a member of the South Carolina House from Greenville County, who represented much of the BJU community in the state legislature, faced the owner of a household-name upstate dairy business, Bob Peeler. The movement conservative Christian Coalition backed surgeon Henry Jordan. The entrance of Jordan temporarily complicated the fundamentalist political situation when it appeared that Beasley and Jordan had secretly agreed to run as a team for governor and lieutenant governor. But the Campbell organization informed Beasley that the lieutenant governor candidate of choice was Representative Clyborne. Jordan's telephone calls to Beasley began to go unanswered as Beasley seemed to agree with his handlers among the Campbell alumni that a fundamentalist "Christian Coalition" GOP ticket would have little success.[12] But Jordan and the other Christian right candidates, David Eckstrom (attorney general) and Gerald Stiles (superintendent of education), would not be moved and stayed in their respective races.

The BJU community seemed comfortable with the realigned "ticket," though many smarted from Clyborne's unseating of their graduate, Representative Terry Haskins, for minority leader of the South Carolina House. Clyborne blunted much of this opposition by appearing to be only a water carrier for speaker pro-tempore Representative David Wilkins, who enlisted him to run against Haskins to reduce partisan tensions and thereby help the cause of Wilkins for speaker of the South Carolina House. And after all, Clyborne was the state representative for much of the campus. But BJU conservatives had been friendly to Henry Jordan (an Evangelical Presbyterian–turned–Southern Baptist), and a BJU graduate served as press secretary in his campaign for Congress in 1988. In the first race, BJU voters cast the most votes for the local representative, with the movement conservative finishing last and the dairyman in between. Dairyman Peeler won the county and the state. In the second race, with Clyborne eliminated, the campus vote switched to the conservative, giving Jordan almost two-thirds of the vote. Countywide and statewide, dairyman Peeler won by close to the same ratio.

In the attorney general's race, the contest was similar to the lieutenant governor's race in that a perceived Christian Coalition candidate won enough votes to advance to the runoff, only to be soundly defeated there. Lexington County (Midlands) School Board member David Eckstrom, the endorsed candidate, vied with former Charleston solicitor (prosecutor) Charles Condon and the state-appointed Consumer Affairs advocate, Steve Hamm of Columbia. Though no liberal, Hamm was perceived to be the least conservative of the three. The Roman Catholic Condon won the state and county with percentages near 40 percent but finished second to evangelical Eckstrom among Bob Jones voters, 46 percent to 33 percent. In the runoff, BJU gave Eckstrom more votes (69 percent), but Condon won the state at 58 percent.

The Republican primary for superintendent of education was the only one that featured an incumbent. Barbara Nielsen, the first Republican superintendent since Reconstruction, faced a challenge from the right by Columbia International University (formerly Columbia Bible College) education professor Gerald Stiles. Stiles accused Nielsen of being too liberal for the Republican nomination—supporting Outcome-Based Education and Goals 2000–type programs. Stiles was tapping into a widespread concern among the fundamentalist right about education issues (second only to abortion to most in the Christian right). Stiles won the BJU boxes with 56 percent of the vote, but he and a third candidate came a percentage point short of denying the incumbent the nomination outright, so no runoff was necessary.

1994 was significant in that for the first time BJU gave a candidate running a movement-backed campaign (David Beasley) its overwhelming support. But the campaign presented a contrast in that local ties seemed to come into play for the first time as well in the case of the race for lieutenant governor. The attorney general's race seemed to indicate that Roman Catholicism might still be a disadvantage in courting the BJU vote, but Pat Buchanan erased this assumption. As in 1992, Buchanan finished strong in the BJU boxes—and won them this time. The Buchanan plurality in the BJU boxes was almost as thorough a drubbing of Dole as the Dole margin of victory over Buchanan statewide (44 percent Buchanan, 34 percent Dole at BJU, 45 percent Dole, 29 percent Buchanan in South Carolina).

The Movement Fundamentalist Right Branch

Pat Robertson Conservatives I: 1987–1988

In order to see that Vice-President George Bush had the utmost advantage in the 1988 presidential campaign, South Carolinian and Bush campaign manager Lee Atwater conceived a plan agreed to by Governor Campbell and dutifully executed by his minions in the South Carolina GOP. According to the Atwater scheme, the South Carolina Republican party would begin to reorganize itself not in even-numbered years, when governors and presidents are nominated, but in odd-numbered years, when there is no other political activity. George Bush's campaign manager sold the idea as an opportunity to build the party when there was less distraction from campaigns and as a method for getting a one-year headstart on the Democrats in organization.[13] Atwater also proposed that the date of the South Carolina Republican presidential preference primary be advanced closer to those in New Hampshire and Iowa to provide better exposure and greater importance to the Palmetto State. Both proposals passed with little opposition. Bush was set to take advantage of a huge lead and a supportive organization in a crucial primary state. But the Atwater plan was not to be executed without complications.

Taking a chapter from the Bob Jones 1976 playbook and discerning Bush's intentions for South Carolina, the Pat Robertson organization sprang into covert action. Led by political organizer–preacher Ray Moore, Jr., Robertson secretly developed a South Carolina structure for months. (A similar organization was pieced together in Georgia.) Hundreds of fundamentalist Christians, primarily members of charismatic or Pentecostal churches, quietly organized, then dominated the 1987 state party reorganization, taking control of numerous precinct, several county, and at least one congressional district organization.[14] The Robertson precampaign organization was a strong one. Robertson hired Ronald Reagan's 1980 primary media consultant for South Carolina, Richard Quinn, to handle organization. Though not a part of the original plan, Charismatic Christians even elected two of their own to the statehouse: Carole Wells of Spartanburg (1986) and Alva Humphries of Richland (1987). But the play for control of the state organization was turned back on a number of fronts. A lawsuit against the Richland County Republican party protesting refusal to seat Robertson delegates was withdrawn when the Robertson forces determined the litigation was harming Robertson's prospects for a good primary showing. Regular Republican Tommy Hartnett was elected chairman of the state convention in 1987, blocking a floor fight, and the Robertson choice for state party chairman, Van Hipp of Spartanburg (later of Charleston), was elected but refused to endorse Robertson. Then came the final blow, the devastating 1988 South Carolina Republican primary defeat—19 percent for Robertson to 48 percent for Bush. Robertson had hovered at between 25 percent and 30 percent in most campaign polls, but experienced a drop in the final two weeks. Campaign aides suggested to me that this was the falling away of BJU Separatist Fundamentalists and other conservative bloc Christians, which helped Kemp.

The appeal to a broader conservative bloc by the Robertson campaign proved unsuccessful, with many Southern Baptists voting for Bush and most Separatist Fundamentalists supporting Kemp. Bush won the South Carolina primary, the turning point in the 1988 campaign, because he was able to capture the establishment GOP vote and a large number of Southern Baptists, whereas Robertson and Kemp split the non-Southern Baptist fundamentalist right vote.

Pat Robertson Conservatives II: 1988–1996

Though the Robertson forces would make another attempt at prominence in the South Carolina GOP with the nomination and slim defeat of Robertson's state coordinator Roberta Combs of Berkeley County for Republican national committeewoman in 1988 (as a consolation, the Robertson-dominated executive committee named her treasurer in 1989), following Robertson's defeat in the presidential primary the Robertson organization became dormant for almost three years. Incumbent Representative Alva Humphries was defeated in the Republican nomination for his House seat during this slump, oddly enough by the son of the political consultant who handled Robertson's South Carolina campaign.

There was a strong suspicion by many party regulars that the Robertson phenomenon would fade away and that most supporters would not maintain active participation in the Republican party. But the fervent hopes of the moderate Republicans were dashed. As with the Separatist Fundamentalist Right BJU Republicans in 1976, Movement Fundamentalist Right Robertson Republicans were there to stay. Enter the Christian Coalition. It was in 1992, through the national leadership of the newly formed Christian Coalition (directed by Republican operative Ralph Reed),[15] that the South Carolina Robertson effort became the South Carolina chapter of the Christian Coalition, still in the hands of Roberta Combs. One of the first projects of this chapter was the distribution of 200,000 copies of the now infamous *Christian Coalition Voter Guide '92* in the Fourth Congressional District. These flyers featured a national issues survey comparing Bush, Clinton, and Perot on one side and South Carolina U.S. Senate and congressional district candidates on the other. When candidates refused to respond, "positions of candidates were verified or determined using voting records and/or public statements."[16] The campaign was most damaging to Fourth Congressional District incumbent Democratic congressman Liz Patterson of Spartanburg, who was defeated by Christian Coalition–backed Bob Inglis 50.4 percent to 47.4 percent. (Inglis was a virtually unknown Greenville attorney.) Patterson summed up the entire campaign and the participation of the Christian Coalition when she told the *Washington Post,* "I can't believe they would question my life, my God, my religion."[17] To former Representative Patterson, the *Voter Guide* was the culprit, though many close to her acknowledge that she simply took the Republican candidate lightly. In late 1996, the Federal Election Commission filed suit against the Christian Coalition for the *Voter Guide,* specifically citing South Carolina's flyers as an example of improper activities under the Coalition's nonprofit, nonpartisan tax status.

1993 was another active year for Combs and the Coalition as they endorsed conservative former U.S. attorney Henry McMaster of Columbia for state party chairman over moderate-conservative Greenville County chairman Knox White. The McMaster-White campaign divided the fundamentalist right in a "friends and neighbors" way, as White enjoyed significant support in the BJU community, goodwill held over from his 1988 campaign for Congress.[18] A late entry was moderate former state representative Joyce Hearn of Columbia. McMaster won in a close election, but the day of the convention he faced a secessionist movement of great proportions led by his predecessor, Barry Wynn of Spartanburg (a Knox White supporter) and party stalwart George Shissias of Columbia (a Hearn supporter). Unhappy with the outcome of the election and the influence of the Coalition, Wynn, Shissias, and a number of state legislators (including Representative June Shissias, wife of George) formed the Republican Leadership Council and asked regular Republicans to withhold contributions to the McMaster-led state GOP and to send the money to them instead.[19]

Following close on the heels of the secessionist movement in 1993, as "The Coalition" became a state bugaboo, a controversy arose involving *purported* Coalition influence. McMaster found himself under serious pressure when, only weeks after his election as state chairman, he sought support for a one-item legislative agenda. Learning that the state had recently granted autonomy to Coastal Carolina University (formerly a branch campus of the University of South Carolina) and that a board of trustees would be elected to govern the new school, McMaster asked House Speaker Pro-tempore David Wilkins of Greenville (a moderate Republican) for his assistance in helping to elect a slate of *conservative* candidates. McMaster provided the slate on a typed index card. As did other alert political observers, the new Republican chairman saw the creation of a new board as an opportunity to place a state agency in conservative hands. Wilkins, however, proved to be a poor choice to captain the McMaster effort, allowing the typed listing of the slate, labeled in McMaster's hand "Conservative Coalition Candidates," to fall into the hands of the Democratic party floor leader in the House and *The [Columbia] State* newspaper, both of which had been conducting watchdog efforts in regard to "Coalition" activities.[20]

In the days before the trustee election, conservative Democratic support for McMaster's conservative slate evaporated as rumors of a "Christian Coalition list" were rampant on the House floor. The McMaster effort ended in a greater drubbing than anticipated when on the day of the election *The State* published the list. All but one of the candidates were defeated—a defeat administered by the mere specter of "The Coalition."[21]

McMaster's woes continued with the actual Coalition. Attempting to include representatives of all factions on his new staff, McMaster had appointed a Combs confidant to his staff in the state headquarters. The relationship was short lived, however, for when the Coalition representative began faxing confidential party documents to the Coalition office in the dead of night, McMaster had no choice but to terminate the employee. The incident very quickly found its way into the newspapers.

Smarting from the secessionist effort, the trustee election, and the disloyal pol, McMaster sought to distance himself from the Coalition by showing a firmer hand to the Coalition-controlled state executive committee. This move drew the immediate fire of the Coalition when its leadership made a surprise play in the committee for control of the day-to-day operations of the party. McMaster lost the surprise vote, seeing his staff in effect replaced by committees set up by the Coalition. McMaster ultimately won the war, however, by refusing to recognize the rival structure and forcing the Coalition to heel.[22]

Then came election year 1994. The Coalition was geared up. It had a statewide organization, a fresh face, and a simple agenda: elect David

Beasley governor. At the state Republican convention over a year before the 1994 election, generic Republicans put the former state representative in a three-way tie for second place behind "undecided," at 17 percent.[23] Those identifying with the Christian Coalition, however, already supported him at a rate of 62 percent.

The Coalition leadership's enthusiasm for Beasley seemed to come from several motivations, including the fact that $20,000 in consulting fees were paid by the Beasley campaign to MBI Special Events, a company owned by Michele Combs, daughter of state Coalition director Roberta Combs. Beasley for Governor also paid a firm named MPR $8,350 for consulting. MPR shared a post office box address with Coalition officer Drew McKissick.[24]

In the fall of 1994, David Beasley was elected governor of South Carolina by a slim margin. The new governor moved quickly, sprinkling his administration with appointees who were outspoken Christians, but none of whom was a puppet of the Christian Coalition leadership. This strategy proved to be enough to make the Republican establishment nervous, but not enough to satisfy the Coalition. Cyndi Mosteller of Charleston, an activist in the Charleston area pro-life movement, was appointed to the board of the Department of Health and Environmental Control, prompting a showdown in the state senate over her confirmation. A BJU graduate and organizer for the upstate campaign was hired in the scheduling office, and a deacon in one of the largest conservative faction Southern Baptist churches in the state was named legal counsel. But the idea of appointing Gerald Stiles, the former candidate for superintendent of education and a Columbia Bible College professor, to the post of gubernatorial adviser on education matters was squashed. The Coalition spent little time lobbying for appointments, however, settling for input to Beasley through informal channels. After all, there were other battles to fight.

With only faint outlines of the 1996 presidential campaign discernible, Roberta Combs began to plan. First, she continued to wage a cold war with party chairman McMaster, and worked behind the scenes with the new governor and the former governor (Campbell) to find a replacement for the independent-minded chairman when his current term ended in May 1996. Combs relented only when no candidate emerged and when McMaster received the endorsement of every county party chairman and nearly every Republican elected official. By November of 1995, Campbell and Beasley had added their names to the list and Combs was forced to surrender.

The next step was to attempt to position the Coalition simultaneously in the camps of presidential candidates Buchanan, Dole, and Gramm. Combs spent most of her time with Dole, the candidate whom Pat Robertson declared "conservative," and whom Ralph Reed seemed to favor. Beasley endorsed the Kansas senator along with former governor Campbell. (The Beasley endorsement is interesting in that his debt to Campbell, a potential Dole running mate, left him little choice. On the same trip that Beasley met with Dole in Washington about coming aboard, he stopped off in Virginia Beach to appear on Pat Robertson's *700 Club* program. In a matter of hours, the South Carolina governor faced the national symbols of the two not-always-harmonious factions that came together to elect him governor months earlier.)

As the Dole effort went forward, Combs's lieutenants joined the Buchanan and Gramm efforts to hedge bets. Combs offered advice to all comers, agreeing to provide key contacts and pointers on how to win Coalition support. It was Bob Dole, however, who enjoyed the advantage of free access to Coalition lists. One South Carolina Republican who joined the Coalition by dialing the national coalition office received a great deal of mail from both the national and state offices, but only one official Coalition telephone call: an invitation to join Bob Dole for a rally on his behalf put on by the Coalition for the South Carolina primary.

By stopping conservative Christians from voting *en bloc* for any candidate (Buchanan), and by picking off much of the Christian bloc vote for Dole, the Coalition was successful in South Carolina. With Dole's Gramm/Buchanan-ending triumph, Roberta Combs, David Beasley, and Carroll Campbell were well positioned. All that was left to decide was the pro forma: who would go to San Diego to vote South Carolina's thirty-eight votes in the coronation? All was unity and camaraderie, then Combs struck again.

Here is what happened. Before the Republican state convention in May 1996, Beasley, his aides, and Combs met several times and spoke by conference call. During their deliberations, they were able to hash out a list of delegates and alternates who would be designated the gubernatorial/Coalition slate. The slate represented a cross section of the party, mostly Christian conservatives, but with a number of elected officials as well. (In a sense this was a favor to the governor, for based on the results of the previous year's statewide precinct organization, Combs had the votes to select whomever she wanted.) When convention day arrived,

Outspoken Baptists

Figure 1. W. A. Criswell, First Baptist Church, Dallas, and SBC president, 1969–1970. Pioneer conservative. (Photo by Greg Stephens. Reprinted by kind permission of *Baptists Today.*)

Figure 2 (LEFT). Brooks Hays, Arkansas congressman and SBC president, 1958–1959. Pioneer moderate. (Reprinted by kind permission of the Baptist Historical Collection, Furman University.)

Figure 3 (RIGHT). Paul Pressler, Texas judge and conservative-take- over mastermind. (Reprinted by kind permission of *Baptists Today*.)

Figure 4. Paige Patterson, Texas theologian and conservative-take- over mastermind. (Reprinted by kind permission of *Baptists Today*.)

Figure 5. James Dunn, director, Baptist Joint Committee. Moderate leader.
(Reprinted by kind permission of James Dunn.)

Figure 6. Richard Land, executive
director, SBC Christian Life Commission. Conservative leader.
(Reprinted by kind permission of
Baptists Today.)

Our Baptist Government

Figure 7. Bill Clinton, president of the United States, attends Immanuel Baptist Church, Little Rock, Arkansas, with his wife, Hillary. (Photo by Greg Gibson. Reprinted by kind permission of AP/Wide World Photos.)

Figure 8. Al Gore, vice-president of the United States, attends Mt. Vernon Baptist Church, Mt. Vernon, Virginia.

Figure 9. Newt Gingrich, speaker of the House of Representatives, attends New Hope Baptist Church, Fayetteville, Georgia..

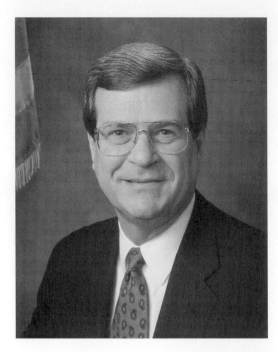

Figure 10. Trent Lott, majority leader, U.S. Senate. (Reprinted by kind permission of Trent Lott.)

Figure 11. Tom DeLay, minority whip, U.S. House of Representatives.

Figure 12. Strom Thurmond, president pro-tempore, U.S. Senate.

Figure 13. Richard Gephardt,
minority leader, U.S. Congress.

Figure 14. J. C. Watts, U. S. Congress. (Reprinted by kind permission of J. C. Watts.)

Moderate Baptists and Democratic Politics

Figure 15. Former President Jimmy Carter declares his support for the Cooperative Baptist Fellowship (CBF) and endorses their revolt against the SBC, 1993. (Photo by Fred Prowser. Reprinted by kind permission of *Baptists Today*.)

Figure 16. Baptist Joint Committee director James Dunn (*center*) joins President Clinton for the signing of the Religious Freedom Restoration Act. (Reprinted by kind permission of James M. Dunn, Baptist Joint Committee.)

Figure 17. Vice-President Al Gore (*left*) and Baptist Joint Committee director James Dunn plot legislature strategy. Reprinted by kind permission of *Baptists Today*.

Fundamentalist Baptists and Republican Politics

Figure 18 (top). Then-President George Bush addresses the Southern Baptist Convention in Atlanta in 1991. (Reprinted by kind permission of *Baptists Today.*)

Figure 19 (bottom). David Beasley, governor of South Carolina, addressing S.C. Baptist Convention. Convention president Steve Hogg is on the right. (Reprinted by kind permission of the Baptist Historical Collection, Furman University.)

Figure 20. Mike Huckabee, governor of Arkansas, succeeded Jim Guy Tucker, who succeeded Bill Clinton. He is a former Southern Baptist pastor.

Figure 21. Christian Coalition leaders Ralph Reed (*left*) and Pat Robertson (*right*) wait their turn at a coalition rally with South Carolina Governor David Beasley (*center*). (Photograph by Pam Royal. Reprinted by kind permission of the Columbia, S.C., *State* newspaper.)

Fundamental Differences in the Fundamentalist Right

Figure 22. Bob Jones III, president of BJU (*far left*), with Ronald Reagan in 1980. (Reprinted by kind permission of Unusual Films, Bob Jones University.)

Figure 23. Pat Buchanan speaking to the student body at BJU. (Reprinted by kind permission of Unusual Films, Bob Jones University.)

Figure 24. Newt Gingrich (*right*), with Jerry Falwell, speaking at Liberty University. (Reprinted by kind permission of Liberty University.)

Figure 25. Clarence Thomas (*second from right*), with Jerry Falwell (*far left*), at Liberty University. (Reprinted by kind permission of Liberty University.)

Fundamentalist Right
Political Literature

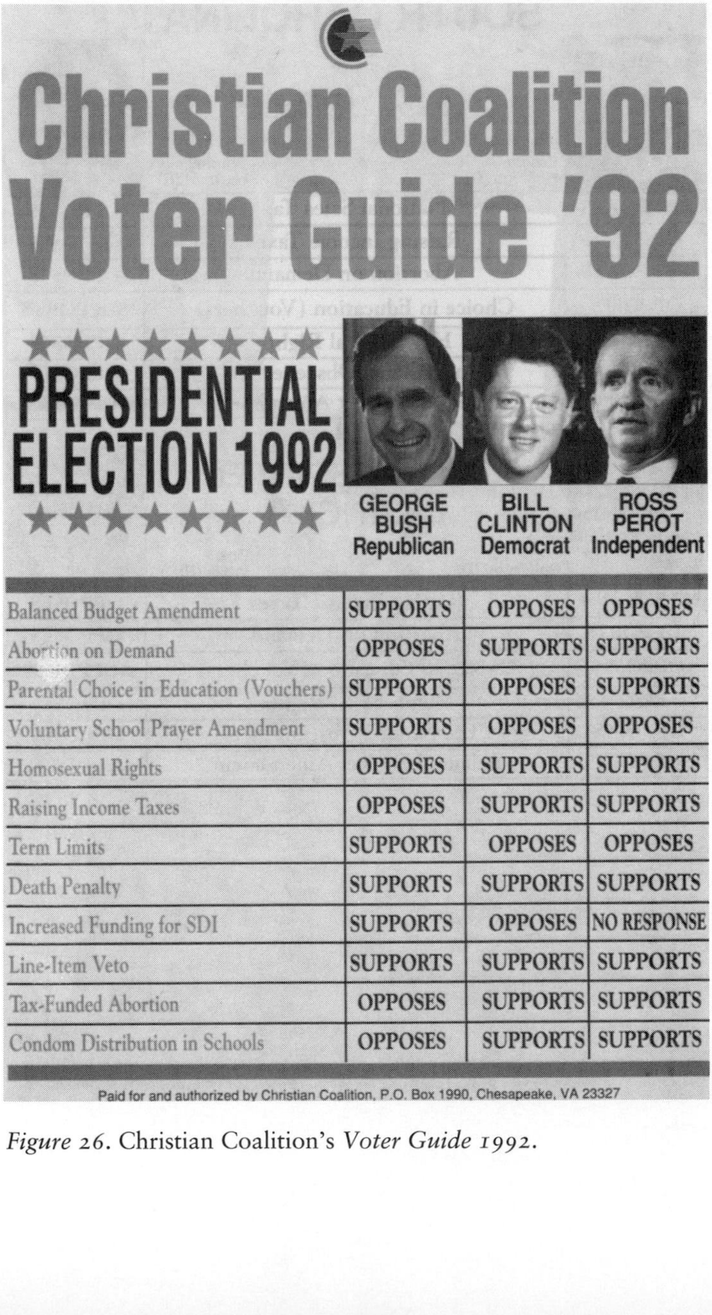

Christian Coalition Voter Guide '92

★★★★★★★★★★
**PRESIDENTIAL
ELECTION 1992**
★★★★★★★★★★

	GEORGE BUSH Republican	BILL CLINTON Democrat	ROSS PEROT Independent
Balanced Budget Amendment	SUPPORTS	OPPOSES	OPPOSES
Abortion on Demand	OPPOSES	SUPPORTS	SUPPORTS
Parental Choice in Education (Vouchers)	SUPPORTS	OPPOSES	SUPPORTS
Voluntary School Prayer Amendment	SUPPORTS	OPPOSES	OPPOSES
Homosexual Rights	OPPOSES	SUPPORTS	SUPPORTS
Raising Income Taxes	OPPOSES	SUPPORTS	SUPPORTS
Term Limits	SUPPORTS	OPPOSES	OPPOSES
Death Penalty	SUPPORTS	SUPPORTS	SUPPORTS
Increased Funding for SDI	SUPPORTS	OPPOSES	NO RESPONSE
Line-Item Veto	SUPPORTS	SUPPORTS	SUPPORTS
Tax-Funded Abortion	OPPOSES	SUPPORTS	SUPPORTS
Condom Distribution in Schools	OPPOSES	SUPPORTS	SUPPORTS

Paid for and authorized by Christian Coalition, P.O. Box 1990, Chesapeake, VA 23327

Figure 26. Christian Coalition's *Voter Guide 1992.*

Baptist Political Humor

Figure 27. The moderate faction has often used humor to help them deal with the takeover of the denomination. (Reprinted by kind permission of *Baptists Today.*)

Figures 28 and 29. You say you want a resolution? Resolutions passed by Southern Baptist Conventions, the denomination's de facto platform, have attracted much attention, particularly those on homosexuality, women, race, and Walt Disney. (*Left:* ©1995 Joel Pett/The Lexington Herald-Leader Co. *Right:* Cartoon by Mike Peters. © Tribune Media Services, Inc. Reprinted with permission.)

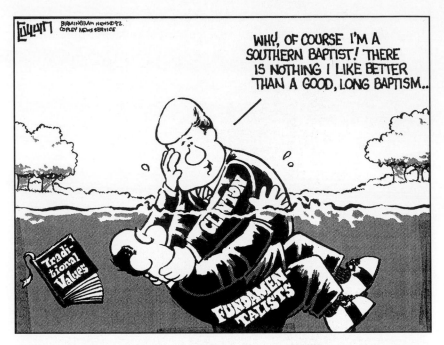

Figure 30. Bill Clinton's politics and his denominational affiliation have come into conflict of late, a situation not ignored by cartoonists. (Cartoon by Mike Cullum. Reprinted by kind permission of Mark Cullum and Copley News Service.)

May 4, 1996, Combs gubernatorial staffers and others handed out the official slate. Printed on 8-1/2 by 11-inch paper, it was unmistakable and flagrantly distributed with the title "Recommended Slate of Merit Candidates for At-Large Delegates to the National Convention." But to the governor's surprise, a second list was being distributed by Coalition county chairmen. This was a far different list, printed on a card easily slipped into the palm and containing the names of Christian Coalition members and friends only—except for the governor and Senator Strom Thurmond. Cyndi Mosteller, the Beasley Health Board appointee and chair of the 1996 platform committee is an unusual case. An anti-abortion activist and member of the state SBC Christian Life Commission, she became alienated from Combs because of her willingness to work with non-Christian Coalition conservatives. Mosteller had the distinction of being an official Coalition-endorsed candidate *on her home county's slip (the one she would have access to)*, but not on those distributed in the other forty-five county delegations.

Important to our study is that by making the slate in Charleston, Mosteller gave Southern Baptists representation on a Coalition slate that was almost completely dominated by the Charismatic portion of the Movement Fundamentalist Right and a few members of the Separatist Fundamentalist Right from Greenville. The Coalition is still alienated from members of the Emerging Fundamentalist Right SBC, even those who fight abortion in their spare time.

As for the delegate selection, when the ballots were counted, several unknowns finished with more votes than former governor Campbell and Congressman Floyd Spence (neither of whom had made the Coalition list). Another of the state's four Republican congressmen had to settle for alternate, as did the Republican National Committeeman for South Carolina. The other South Carolina RNC member, the Republican National Committeewoman, failed to make alternate and would not go as a delegate to a convention she helped plan. As for Combs, there seems to be some difference of opinion as to whether she finally agreed to the "unity slate," but not among members of the governor's staff.

In late 1996, the Coalition's hold over the party began to slip even more as even a Coalition majority was not enough to unseat the party treasurer and secretary and elect Coalition members. Members of the executive committee allied with the Coalition, faced with divided loyalties, chose the incumbent officers over the challengers from their own ranks. Now that they were veteran members of the body, and satisfied with McMaster's leadership, even Coalition members found themselves "regularized." Their leader had no such compunction.

Jerry Falwell Conservatives

The Moral Majority burst on the scene nationally with great exposure in 1979, and recent years have seen sales of anti-Bill Clinton videos peddled with great success nationally on "The Old Time Gospel Hour."[25] But very little has been heard from Jerry Falwell in South Carolina, especially since the disbanding of the Moral Majority. Although a number of South Carolina churches are tied to Falwell and help supply Liberty University with students, independent Baptist Falwell is in some ways crowded out in the state by Bob Jones on the right and by conservative Southern Baptists slightly to Falwell's left. Politically, this has translated into few appearances except perhaps in Charlestonian Charlie Rhodes's U.S. Senate primary campaign in 1980 (the heyday of the Moral Majority). In that year, Rhodes printed in his campaign brochure language that resembles Falwell's:

> In 1892, the Supreme Court ruled that America was a Christian nation. Yet, today, they have banned prayer from the classrooms of our schools. America has been great because she had been good and Charlie Rhodes believes that we, as a people, must return to that greatness or we shall perish as a nation.[26]

Rhodes was defeated that year by regular Republican Marshall Mays in the Republican primary. Mays was then trounced by the incumbent senator, Ernest "Fritz" Hollings. Another Falwell-motivated candidate, Charlestonian Tom Moore, was defeated by Tommy Hartnett for the Republican nomination in the First Congressional District. Hartnett won two-thirds of the vote against Moore, went on to defeat Charles "Pug" Ravenel, and served three terms in Congress.

More recent efforts of Falwell supporters have not been as overt, as they are conducted by candidates who do not emphasize their Falwell connection, nor do they use Christian themes. An example is the perennial candidate in S.C. House District 79, Michael Letts. Letts, a Liberty University graduate and friend of Falwell, has on two occasions run in a Republican primary against moderate to conservative Representative (now Judge) Roland Corning of Richland County. Corning's district comprised the affluent Spring Valley neighborhoods north of Columbia.

Letts has fared poorly against Corning, and found less room to Corning's right after Corning's much publicized anti-abortion legislation and his infamous question to fellow Representative June Shissias during House debate on the matter: "Have you ever had an abortion?"[27] According to a Corning campaign manager who has also served as a county chairman in the upstate of South Carolina:

Letts kept running against Roland [Corning] saying in direct mail that Roland "wasn't the pro-life candidate," so Roland introduced all that pro-life legislation. Other than that, Letts' campaigns against Roland were pretty standard, not Christian Coalition style. His consultant was Rod Shealy, who can hardly be identified with the Coalition. Letts had Christian volunteers, though. I sent one of our guys into the Letts headquarters to "volunteer," just to find out![28]

Letts, associated with Falwell, was a hybrid, more in character with a typical South Carolina conservative campaign with a few Christian Coalition–style campaign themes included, but not like the Coalition, Bob Jones, or Southern Baptist fundamentalist–style.

The Emerging Fundamentalist Right Branch

Southern Baptist Conservatives

Because of their dominating numbers, the story of Southern Baptists in South Carolina is little different from the story of white Southerners in general—a wholesale shift from solid Democratic to solid Republican. But until a short time ago, progressive, Democratic-leaning Baptists and independents in South Carolina were in firm control of the state organization. That is no longer true. One of the supporters of the progressive countermovement to the conservative resurgence is former South Carolina Baptist Convention president Flynn Harrell. Harrell was for a number of years on the staff of the South Carolina Baptist Convention as well, and is one of the most "theologically aware" Southern Baptist laymen in South Carolina. He had this to say about the new state leadership of the SBC:

The fundamentalists have won several elections in a row in South Carolina. That makes me a bit uncomfortable, but not because of secular politics or personalities. The new leaders are my friends. The difficulties I have with them are primarily theological.

The church-state separation issue is where we moderate-conservatives [moderate faction] differ most with the fundamentalist-conservatives [conservative faction]. Then there are the important issues of soul competency and the priesthood of the believer and the Baptist belief that everyone should be able to read and interpret the scriptures for himself or herself under the leadership of the Holy Spirit. That is the real divide as I have experienced it.[29]

Harrell's concerns about the future of the South Carolina Baptist Convention are similar to those expressed by a number of moderate faction Baptists. But much like the conservatives, no matter how hard each side seems to try to discount it, the divisions in the state convention generally touch secular politics in some way. One moderate Baptist leader told the author in the middle of a theological discussion that he couldn't understand how a Christian could be a Republican "if they read either U.S. history or the 25th chapter of Matthew."[30]

Because of the size of the Convention, both elites and the rank and file are worth analyzing. Southern Baptist scholar James Guth and others have shed great light on the growing strength of the Republican party and the fundamentalist right among Southern Baptist ministers in the nation as a whole.[31] This is true in South Carolina as well. But except for ministers, Southern Baptists among active fundamentalist right political elites in South Carolina have been few until recently. State senators Mike Fair and David Thomas, both of Greenville, have Southern Baptist backgrounds, with Thomas holding a Southwestern Seminary degree. But both have moved toward the Bob Jones fundamentalist camp in recent years.[32] Former Representative Dell Baker, a close friend of Thomas and now a powerful lobbyist, has done much the opposite, switching from a BJU-friendly independent Baptist church to a Southern Baptist congregation. This indicates how conservative Southern Baptists have become, in that even image-conscious political leaders can shift easily from Southern (Emerging Fundamentalist) Baptist to independent (Separatist Fundamentalist) Baptist with little concern. This fluidity is representative of the closeness and easy transition now possible between a more conservative convention and an ever more "regularizing" BJU fundamentalist community.

As for a barometer of the more rank-and-file Southern Baptist in our case-study state, a poll of South Carolina citizens conducted in 1990 by the Institute of Public Affairs at the University of South Carolina[33] offers us insightful results. The attraction of the USC research

TABLE 5.2

Religious Denomination and Party Affiliation, South Carolina, 1990

	SBC	Baptist	Protestant	Catholic	Other
Strong Democrat	8%	14%	5%	12%	6%
Weak Democrat	8%	14%	11%	8%	9%
Ind-leaning Democrat	8%	7%	8%	8%	13%
Independent	0%	10%	14%	12%	6%
Ind-leaning Republican	13%	14%	15%	8%	6%
Weak Republican	29%	21%	26%	28%	44%
Strong Republican	33%	20%	21%	24%	6%
n =	24	163	178	25	16

Note: Whites only.
Source: 1989 Policy Survey, Institute of Public Affairs, University of South Carolina.

TABLE 5.3

Religious Denomination and Opinion of Abortion, South Carolina, 1990

	SBC	Baptist	Protestant	Catholic	Other
Legal any circum	12%	17%	26%	24%	31%
Legal only certain	71%	66%	63%	60%	31%
Illegal in all occur	17%	17%	11%	16%	38%
n =	24	165	181	26	16
	SBC	Baptist	Protestant	Catholic	Other
Accept for birth defects	58%	69%	72%	77%	56%
Not accept for birth defects	42%	27%	24%	19%	44%
Don't know	0%	4%	4%	4%	0%
n =	24	165	181	26	16

Note: Whites only.
Source: 1989 Policy Survey, Institute of Public Affairs, University of South Carolina.

for our purpose is the open-ended question for religious affiliation (see Appendix A). Typical of a very Protestant Southern state, the religious-affiliation question generated numerous responses, ranging in specificity from answers such as "Protestant" to "Baptist" to "Southern Baptist." The latter group seems most interesting. The results from the questions on partisanship and abortion show that just short of 75 percent of these self-conscious "*Southern* Baptists" identified themselves as Republicans, indicating a very present conservative element within the SBC in South Carolina. This subgroup also strongly opposes abortion.

A second poll, conducted for me by First Impressions, Inc.,[34] reveals another dimension of the Southern Baptist vote. Table 5.4 shows that in spite of the fact that David Beasley was the Christian Coalition candidate and that it was widely reported that he had paid the Coalition leadership for "consulting," Southern Baptists interviewed chose him over *two* Republican challengers at a rate of 66 percent. Table 5.5 indicates a bedrock SBC base for Beasley, who received half of his support from fellow Southern Baptists. When I asked Beasley shortly after the primary whether his identification as a Southern Baptist helped his campaign, he thought my question odd at first, but upon reflection answered:

> I think in the same way that being a good doctor or a good lawyer helps you [among doctors and lawyers]. Southern Baptists knew me from before the campaign from being a lay preacher and the parliamentarian [of the state Baptist convention].
>
> When [Democrats joked that I would get the "snake handler" vote] then it came out that I was a Southern Baptist, so everyone knew. That helped I guess. There are almost a million Southern Baptists in South Carolina.[35]

Beasley ran his campaign to attract Christians, not necessarily Baptists, though in South Carolina there was little difference between the two.

TABLE 5.4
South Carolina Republican Primary, 1994, Support for Gubernatorial Candidates by Denomination

	Beasley	Hartnett	Ravenel	Total
Baptist	66%	3%	31%	100%
Methodist	55%	8%	37%	100%
Presbyterian	49%	20%	31%	100%
Episcopalian	7%	20%	73%	100%
Lutheran	23%	8%	69%	100%
Catholic	22%	39%	39%	100%
Statewide	51%	11%	38%	100%
n =	118	27	88	233

Note: Whites only.
Source: First Impressions.

The Real Fundamentalist Coalition

Returning to our interview with Carroll Campbell, who in addition to being governor for eight years was a participant-observer during the rise of the fundamentalists in Palmetto State politics, we are reminded of the diversity of fundamentalist political behavior:

> In 1993, many of those BJ[U] folks [who threw out the "regulars" in 1976] were thrown out by the Christian Coalition. The differences weren't religious. Its just they weren't their crowd. The CC was working for a takeover, which is very different than working for long term governance. Also, the term "Christian" used in "Christian Coalition" has been appropriated and this creates resentment. But *"Christians in politics" is not monolithic.* [Emphasis mine][36]

In the previous chapter, I summarized what many others have said—that the two-party, activist-liberal, separatist-conservative thesis no longer fits the realities of American politics. I also suggested in that analysis that the various theories of a "culture war" seem accurate but are lacking in that they do not seek to uncover the subtle differences within the traditionalist camp. Therefore, we have seen a brief history of the Separatist Fundamentalist Right, the Movement Fundamentalist Right, and the Emerging Fundamentalist Right in contemporary South Carolina politics. As Carroll Campbell told me: "'Christians in politics' [and in con-

TABLE 5.5

South Carolina Republican Primary, 1994, Denominational Composition of Candidate Support

	Beasley	Hartnett	Ravenel	Statewide*
Baptist	49%	9%	33%	40%
Methodist	15%	9%	14%	16%
Presbyterian	14%	25%	12%	13%
Episcopalian	1%	9%	11%	4%
Lutheran	2%	3%	9%	5%
Catholic	3%	28%	9%	7%
Other	16%	16%	13%	15%
	100%	100%	100%	100%
n =	140	32	101	493

Note: Whites only.
* Includes those undecided.
Source: First Impressions.

text he seems to mean conservative *Republican* Christians in particular] is not monolithic." [37] There is some diversity among fundamentalists.

Figure 1.1 in chapter 1 presented a framework for how differences have been manifested. Bob Jones University fundamentalist Christians, the most religiously separatist in the spectrum, became allied with "Regular Republicans" only two years after their storming of Greenville's Textile hall with walkie-talkies. Though they are kingmakers in a party chairmanship fight, they made few demands. Their new strategy, which unfolded in the eighties with the rise of new leaders, returned to the notions of individualistic politics. BJU graduates, like political pioneer Representative Terry Haskins, ran for office as individuals and were elected during this period. Other BJU graduates, former students, or members of BJU-friendly churches who have been elected since this change in policy include Senator Mike Fair, Senator David Thomas, Representative Rick Rigdon, Representative Dan Tripp, Representative Mike Easterday, the late Representative Dick Herdklotz, Representative Glenn Hamilton, County Councilman Scott Case, County Councilman Paul Wickensimer, City Councilman Dayton Walker, and U.S. Senator Tim Hutchinson of Mississippi.

All these men were elected in an era of widespread and high-percentage participation by fundamentalists in the local party, but with little extra-party fundamentalist political organizing and no takeover attempts. The visibility of BJU graduates, faculty, staff, and students was as great as in 1976, perhaps greater, but the tone was much milder and cooperative. There has been little controversy since, and candidates for chairman who have been given the nod by all factions have run unopposed in party elections for a over a decade.

Perhaps the BJU group has been "regularized" to some extent. It has certainly been taken under wing of the governor of the state, the mayor of the city, and the chairmen of county and state Republican organizations from time to time. As we have seen, BJU voters cast their lot with local state Representative Howell Clyborne for lieutenant governor in 1994, a "regular." This left movement conservative Jordan the last of three. The coziness of this newfound regularization seems to work against a Robertsonesque *Movement* Christian Right mentality from the opposite direction, from the old separatist influences that still keep BJU from cooperating with ecumenical conservative political movements.[38] Now a part of the power structure, BJU Republicans have a *political* reason to oppose the Christian Coalition as well as a doctrinal one.

By contrast, over six years after their first foray into South Carolina

Republican politics, Pat Robertson's Movement Christian Right remain outsiders, not regarded by regulars as "real" Republicans who are committed to the GOP for the long term, but as zealots sworn to enact a short-term Pat Robertson–Ralph Reed agenda. As ugly as the 1987 run on the state GOP was, it did not prevent a second takeover move in 1993. Perhaps Governor Campbell put it best when he said that the distinctiveness of the Coalition (compared to BJU, the SBC, and Falwell) is that their goal is "takeover . . . not long-term governance."[39] The problem of failure to "mainstream" is a concern for the Christian Coalition's Ralph Reed, who has of late called for a broadening of the agenda[40] to include economic as well as moral issues. But Robertson forces are still very closely tied to the personal agenda of Robertson, which functions as a personal submovement of this most movement-oriented group of conservatives.

Ralph Reed is growing in influence, however, and is pleased to have built an organization that is grass-roots oriented, avoiding the problems that plagued the Moral Majority. Falwell's organization was nothing more than a direct-mail and soapbox operation. Reed has built on his early direct-mail appeals by naming directors in each state who are charged with creating the county-by-county, community-by-community, church-by-church structure. But for all of this planning, the Coalition has yet to join the mainstream in South Carolina. It is quite a paradox that the much more religiously separatist Bob Jones group has been much better at blending than Robertson's forces, even given the headstart enjoyed by the BJU group.

Jerry Falwell has disappeared politically in South Carolina, his political fortunes ending with the top-down-oriented Moral Majority campaign which was in reality a mere adjunct to the New Right campaign of the late 1970s–early 1980s. A confession in his autobiography that he was reluctant to become involved with the Moral Majority's political agenda and happy to return to Thomas Road Baptist Church and Liberty University reflects the tug of his independent Baptist separatist roots.[41] However, the administration of Bill Clinton has worked as a tonic for Falwell like the administration of Jimmy Carter had a decade and a half earlier. Returning to limited political involvement by attacking the gay lobby and President Clinton's role in the Whitewater affair has proven to be a money-maker in direct mail.[42] But this straddling leaves Falwell half in and half out of the Movement Fundamentalist Right and less a factor in Christian fundamentalist politics.

Southern Baptists in some ways seem to manifest characteristics that are a mirror image of the BJU group, not too separatist to join a Christian political movement, but too contented and dominant in the culture to "stoop" to support such activities. After all, what would the ladies at the garden club or the men at the Rotary think if Joe Southern Baptist were to become a "true believer" and join a *movement* of any type?

This is changing, however. Fundamentalist Southern Baptists in South Carolina have been distracted a bit from organized politics by an internal religious-cultural movement of their own.[43] But this introversion is wearing away as victorious conservatives consolidate control. According to one observer, Southern Baptists in South Carolina were showing a new face in 1994:

> Southern Baptists were real active here in Bob Cantrell's campaign [a conservative candidate for Congress who lost the Republican primary in 1994] and David Beasley's campaign for governor, so much so that the county party chair said she was "surprised" or "amazed." But she's in with the Christian Right herself, and she doesn't say that one of the organizers for [Henry] Jordan [1994 Lt. Governor candidate of the movement] was working for Cantrell.
>
> Southern Baptists are getting politically active not in an organized movement, but on their own. Before the active Christians were almost exclusively the independents, the fringe, and the non-denominational fundamentalists that were politically active. I wonder if there will be a turf war soon?[44]

Again, Southern Baptists seem ready for politics, but not for membership in the Movement Fundamentalist Right.

David Beasley and the Fundamentalist Right

Even given the diversity and the very different history of these four groups, there was no disagreement on a candidate for governor. Why? First, David Beasley was the perfect candidate for the BJU vote. He was a Christian, a Protestant, and not a charismatic. He was openly endorsed by the "regulars" (including the Campbell organization) but not at first by the regulars that BJU didn't trust. He won almost nine out of ten BJU votes. The Robertson organization liked him, too. His style appealed to them, as did his willingness to dole out consultant contracts. Active in Southern Baptist denominational affairs and lay preaching in Southern Baptist churches, the emergent conservatives in the SBC saw him as one of them as well. Even the Falwell confidante, Michael Letts, in yet another run for state house District 79, won the first round primary with support coming from the same precincts that voted heavily for Beasley.

The story of 1994 is that for the first time since the three branches of the fundamentalist right became politically aware (since the rise of Falwell and Robertson, the post-1976 maturing of the BJU vote, and the SBC conservative takeover in South Carolina) Fundamentalist conservatives from Separatist Fundamentalist Right to Emerging Fundamentalist Right were on the same team—a fundamentalist coalition. This was an odd coalition, however. A silent one. No one controlled it; the partners barely knew each other. And in the case of some, its seemed best that they didn't.

As a footnote to the 1994 primary, it should be clarified that this seminal unity allowed Mr. Beasley a great deal of latitude in dealing with criticism. Beasley risked the endorsement and active support of the Christian Coalition, never making excuses for their work on his behalf. He took this risk because he knew that whether they were members of the Christian Coalition or agreed totally with its goals, the fact that for the first time there was so much unity among conservative Christians in South Carolina (BJU, Falwell, SBC as well as CC) would help blunt the attacks of his opponents and help him win. But in the final analysis, he would win not necessarily because of the support of the Christian Coalition, but because of the reaction of conservative Christians (perhaps many of whom were teetering Southern Baptists) to the attack on the Coalition by the other side. The Beasley strategy worked.

Perhaps Beasley's campaign knew (returning to our South Carolina poll) that even though 40 percent of likely primary voters were mainline, 60 percent went to church every week and 40 percent were Baptist. Using the Coalition as a straw man for "Christian" and turning the opponents' attacks into a Holy War would drive church-going people away from Hartnett and Ravenel and to Beasley by default. Beasley explained it this way:

> When we were criticized for the Christian Coalition, we didn't defend the Coalition but asked "why they were attacking *Christians*" . . . that they were Christian-bashing. They attacked George Allen in Virginia [for Coalition support as well]. Virginia has only about half as many Southern Baptists as South Carolina. We won't bring it up against [the Demo-

cratic nominee] Theodore, but will use it as a defense if attacked [in the general election].[45]

In short, David Beasley coasted to an easy victory in the South Carolina Republican primary by taking advantage of recent, subtle changes in the Christian vote—from the SBC's new warmth for conservative Republican politics to BJU's "regularized" new tolerance of Southern Baptists. His was the first campaign to take advantage of a genuine, however invisible, fundamentalist coalition—Separatist, Movement, and Emerging Right.

TABLE 5.6

South Carolina Republican Primary, 1994, Support for Gubernatorial Candidates by Regularity of Church Attendance

	Beasley	Hartnett	Ravenel	Total
Every week	61%	8%	31%	100%
Almost every week	43%	20%	37%	100%
Few times year	28%	12%	60%	100%
Seldom	24%	18%	59%	100%
Never	38%	13%	50%	100%
Statewide	51%	11%	38%	100%
n =	137	30	99	266

Note: Whites only.
Source: First Impressions.

TABLE 5.7

South Carolina Republican Primary, 1994, Regularity of Attendance and Composition of Gubernatorial Candidate Support

	Beasley	Hartnett	Ravenel	Statewide
Every week	75%	44%	53%	60%
Almost every week	15%	33%	18%	19%
Few times year	5%	10%	15%	11%
Seldom	3%	10%	10%	8%
Never	2%	3%	4%	2%
	100%	100%	100%	100%
n =	137	30	99	475

Note: Whites only.
Source: First Impressions.

TABLE 5.8

South Carolina Republican Primary, 1994, Support for
Gubernatorial Candidates by Religious Self-Identification

	Beasley	Hartnett	Ravenel	Total
Fundamentalist	66%	6%	28%	100%
Evangelical	67%	3%	30%	100%
Charismatic	75%	0%	25%	100%
Main Line	41%	17%	42%	100%
Statewide	47%	14%	40%	100%
SC	51%	11%	38%	100%
n =	132	30	94	256

Note: Whites only.
Source: First Impressions.

TABLE 5.9

South Carolina Republican Primary, 1994, Religious
Self-Identification and Composition of Gubernatorial
Candidate Support

	Beasley	Hartnett	Ravenel	Statewide*
Fundamentalist	23%	10%	14%	15%
Evangelical	17%	3%	11%	11%
Charismatic	7%	0%	3%	4%
Mainline	33%	60%	48%	40%
Something else	20%	27%	24%	30%
	100%	100%	100%	100%
n =	132	30	94	460

Note: Whites only.
* Includes those undecided.
Source: First Impressions.

Fundamentalist Politics: Nationalizing the South Carolina Study

South Carolina is only one case, a representative sample for studying the impact of fundamentalist political activity and the contrasting behavior of the several "cells" of fundamentalism in one state. But our brief survey into the Christian right in the Palmetto State can lead to the development of broad, national concepts.

Level of Activism

We have seen that although at the polls they may agree more than disagree of late, over time the following of Jones or Falwell or Robertson or Southern Baptists contrast in their eagerness for movement-style activism. As figure 5.1 shows, while BJU has remained Separatist for seven decades, Falwell and Robertson have moved into the Movement Fundamentalist Right branch. More recently, the SBC has begun to straddle the Movement-Emerging line. BJU had a brief foray into activism, as illustrated, but has since returned to much less militant involvement. Falwell and Robertson appear and reappear over time but are regularly *activist*. The new SBC elites have taken their rank and file on a march toward greater involvement, edging toward activism since taking over the Convention in 1979.[46] There remains some division of focus for SBC politicos, partly due to continuing state-level denominational brush fires. But a number of Southern Baptists have taken their places as chairs of platform committees and in other ideological posts. Some are the newest foot soldiers in the GOP. Some have actually joined the Christian Coalition. Wherever they are, Southern Baptists are more important to the Republican party than ever.

The role of "balance of power" is important to consider in this change. Southern Baptists in South Carolina so dominate the cultural landscape that there is little to stimulate them to organize to oppose a

| | Branch of Fundamentalist Politics | | |
	Separatist	*Movement*	*Emerging*
1969–1979		BJU	SBC
	Falwell		
	Robertson		
1979–1989	BJU	Falwell	SBC
		Robertson	
1990–	BJU	Falwell	
		Robertson	
			SBC

►◄

TENDENCY

Weak   Strong

Figure 5.1. Level of Political Activism by Cell

culture they greatly influence.[47] The lowering of tensions in county and state Republican politics is a numbers game as well. After being viewed as an interloper by dominant moderate Republicans for years, BJU has seen the party move its direction since the end of the Ford-Rockefeller era and since the trickling down of Reaganism to the local party level in the 1980s and 1990s.

This has not assisted in the regularization of the Christian Coalition, which remains militant, choosing, for instance, to resist the leadership of Henry McMaster, Jack Kemp's 1988 state chairman and one of the most conservative statewide candidates in state history.[48] But unlike BJU or the SBC, due to the nature of the organization, the end of *confrontation* might be the end of the Christian Coalition. This is the nature of the organization. The SBC and BJU, on the other hand, have no political organizational budgets to meet and can afford accommodation. The Coalition, with a huge overhead, must keep the troops and contributors at fever pitch to keep funds coming in.

As for Southern Baptists, a move toward a genuine organization and the Movement Fundamentalist Right by the leadership (perhaps in a looming state lottery fight) could possibly change the political complexion of the state, energizing a large group of conservatives. But such an effort would be a tightrope walk in a state Baptist convention still populated by a number of Democrats and more regular Republicans.

The principle for the national level here, as shown in figure 5.1, is the effect of time. Depending on religious characteristics, cultural characteristics, leadership, and the nature of the organization, some fundamentalist political groups become activist, while some resist activism. Groups may even resist activism for opposite reasons.

Local and National Organizations

In comparing fundamentalist political groups, it is important to consider the effects of national versus local organization. BJU has never organized its graduate network into a *national* political organization but has had some level of local organization since 1976. Falwell had a national soapbox with little grass-roots organization from 1979 to 1986. Pat Robertson has been organized on the national and grass-roots levels since the preparations for his bid for elective office in 1987. Robertson's success on the local level has been mixed. One of his worst defeats occurred in his own hometown of Virginia Beach,

	LOCAL / STATE POLITICAL ORGANIZATION?		
NATIONAL POLITICAL ORGANIZATION?	**YES**	YES	NO
		ROBERTSON RECENT SBC	FALWELL
	NO	BJU	HISTORIC SBC

Figure 5.2. National vs. Local Political Organization

where in 1994 all five of the candidates he backed for the school board lost.

The SBC began to use its Christian Life Commission as a political functionary in 1990,[49] and it began a drive to start similar state-level commissions in 1992. But then again, it would not be so strange to hear a Baptist say, "I'm not a member of any organized church, I'm a Baptist." And so, much of the political organizing among Baptists has an ad hoc nature to it. These risings include the Henry County, Georgia, Baptist fight against a beer license for a convenience store close to a church; the Mississippi Baptists organizing against casino gambling on the Mississippi and along the Gulf Coast; the Richton, Mississippi, fight against a women's retreat center run by a lesbian couple from Ovett; and the numerous political blazes in Cobb County, Georgia (including the resolution that drove the Olympics out).

As for the future, Falwell and BJU could at any time attempt to build a genuine national grass-roots organization with local chapters. They have graduates in every state as well as sophisticated media resources. But neither has chosen to do so. BJU does distribute a flyer with political news entitled *What in the World!* to churches for use as bulletin inserts or handouts, but the newsletter is just that: news. Subheadings include "Government," "Religion," and "Society." There is no attempt to organize voters or to score candidates. The disclaimer describes its purpose: "Published by Bob Jones University, Greenville, South Carolina 29614, to help believers know what the devil is up to." As for the Southern Baptists, they seem poised for such a move, but are in an informational stage for now, keeping members informed about pressing political issues through conventions, seminars, and publications, and assisting local risings when needed.

In considering local and national organization, the role of leadership is crucial. Leadership is predominant in the on-again, off-again Falwell interest in politics, and the shift of the SBC to the right both nationally and in South Carolina. To many, leadership is the main reason that the Christian Coalition has been well organized nationally under Ralph Reed, but overly personalized nationally by Robertson and marginalized in South Carolina by Roberta Combs. As for BJU, it could easily be surmised that after the 1976 takeover fiasco, the BJU administration sent out informal word that the university and its mission were being hurt by these political activities and that they should cease if they are so divisive. Indeed, according to one supporter of Ted Adams's campaign for Congress in 1986, after the 1976 debacle there were attempts to impose order by "operatives" in the BJU administration. These efforts were derailed by the Adams-Workman-Marchant split that year, but took root by the next election cycle. "[1986] was the first fragmentation [of the BJU vote]. University leaders were for three men. The opposition to Workman caught Republican leaders in the University by surprise. By the second Adams campaign [1988] there was more order by the operatives, and many asked Ted [Adams] not to go [through with the second campaign]."[50] To extrapolate this nationally, strong leadership can often have as much effect as religious and sociological factors in determining whether a certain fundamentalist group will have a national organization, a local grass-roots organization, both, or neither—and whether that organization will be cooperative or obstructionist.[51] The BJU group, led by prominent faculty members and administrators, have used their leadership skills to accommodate state and county Republican leaders and to assuage their fears about fundamentalism. Roberta Combs of the South Carolina Christian Coalition wants very much to be regarded as a power in South Carolina Republican politics. Though her tactics have mellowed a bit, her usual strategy has been a battering-ram approach, both in her quest for party office and in her behind-the-scenes work.

Evangelical versus Conservative Movements

In our South Carolina analysis we also uncovered the phenomenon of competition from another movement. In the case of BJU (figure 5.3), fun-

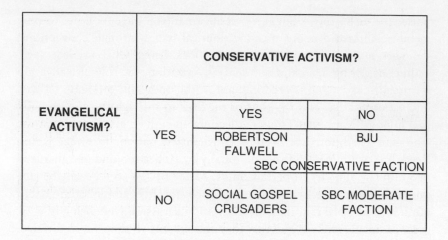

Figure 5.3. Evangelical vs. Conservative Movement Activism

damentalism is the competitor. And because the fundamentalist movement is *the* movement, political movements present no siren song. To
BJU, political participation, even the seeking of elective office, is the duty
of the Christian. But in the end, evangelism overshadows politics.

There are examples in American history of the similar competitions
that ended differently. Nineteenth-century proponents of the Social
Gospel favored a social approach to Christian witness, choosing the politics of reform to improve the lives of the needy, handicapped, and
enslaved, but not "soul winning." The movement for them became an
amalgamated political-religious one focused on society at large.

By contrast, Pat Robertson and Jerry Falwell find themselves equally
active in both movements: conservative politics and evangelism. Southern
Baptist moderates and the mainline, more supportive of teaching than of
evangelism,[52] are active to a lesser degree in each. Southern Baptist conservatives have traditionally been a part of the evangelical, "soul-winning"
movement, but of late vary from congregation to congregation and from
state to state, and they straddle the line of low and high political activism.

Given this scenario, those seeking to form a national conservative Christian movement composed of dues-paying members would be wise to work
with Robertson first, Falwell second, Southern Baptists third, and BJU last.
BJU's energies will not be rechanneled, Falwell and Robertson want to
have it both ways, and the SBC is at a crossroads in its political life.

RELIGIOUS SEPARATION	SOCIOLOGICAL SEPARATION		
	HIGH	MODERATE	LOW
HIGH	BJU		SBC CONSERVATIVE FACTION
MODERATE		FALWELL	
LOW		ROBERTSON	SBC MODERATE FACTION

Figure 5.4. Sociological and Religious Separation by Cell

Theological versus Sociological Separation

Important politically, too, are two kinds of separation: theological and social. BJU scores high in both categories, the mainline and SBC moderates low. Dedicated to the public school system and public colleges but reluctant to join in ecumenical dialogue, SBC conservatives are religiously separated but sociologically interactive. Sociologically, Robertson and Falwell are neither as socially integrated as the SBC or as distant from mainstream culture as BJU (though that call is difficult). Religiously, Falwell's Moral Majority seemed to reach out more to Roman Catholics in its brief existence than Robertson's Christian Coalition did at its inception. But Robertson has shown less sectarianism in his programming at the Christian Broadcasting Network (CBN) and the focus at the Christian Coalition has broadened of late, even to the point of openly courting Catholics. Robertson is also moving out of his religious Pentecostal circle.

Nationally, the groups at the extremes of the diagram attract our attention—the Southern Baptists and BJU. We see the seeds here both for Southern Baptists as the Emerging Fundamentalist Right[53] and BJU as the Separatist Fundamentalist Right to reject membership in the Movement Fundamentalist Right. Neither has anything to protest. One remains influential in political life, the other prefers to concern itself with the next world.

Agenda Size and Specificity

Because, as Governor Campbell has said, the BJU campus has had some regular political activity since 1964, the age of the BJU political agenda is as old as the conservative movement that merged anti-Communism abroad with conservative social policies at home.[54] In comparison to the rest, the Old Right leaders of BJU are more likely to continue to rail against trilateralism and in favor of a general overarching cultural conservatism than to speak out against more trendy neo-conservative targets like Outcome Based Education (OBE).

The other three conservative cells are new in comparison. Falwell and Robertson, the *programmatic* conservatives, arrived in the eighties with an agenda of specific issues. Falwell touted school prayer, Robertson stressed a list of social issues. The Southern Baptists are often just as specific of late, of course, but as figure 5.6 shows, the SBC has a broader social concern by tradition. This is not to say that Robertson and Falwell have not been socially conscious. Robertson's Operation Blessing, a campaign to feed the hungry, and Falwell's alliance with the African-American Revelation Corporation of America indicate each is serious about helping the poor through private sources. But the SBC, unlike BJU, Falwell, and Robertson, has since the founding of its Christian Life Commission almost thirty years ago focused on progressive issues like hunger, social justice, and race. The conservative agenda (including pro-life and other socially conservative themes) has been grafted in with the coming of the conservative era. Falwell, Robertson, and Jones have been slow to

		AGENDA ISSUE SPECIFICITY	
	SPECIFIC	MODERATE	GENERAL
AGENDA AGE OLD			BJU
MIDDLE AGED		SBC MODERATE FACTION	
RECENT	FALWELL ROBERTSON	SBC CONSERVATIVE FACTION	

Figure 5.5. Agenda Size and Specificity by Cell

AGENDA CONTENT		
CONSERVATIVE	MIXTURE	PROGRESSIVE
BJU FALWELL → ROBERTSON	SBC CONSERVATIVE FACTION	SBC MODERATE FACTION

Figure 5.6. Agenda Content by Cell

let *any* progressive themes crowd their agenda, though Falwell and Robertson are adding economic conservatism to social conservatism for variety. Perhaps, however, a special designation should be added to BJU, which far outpaces the other two in shunning progressivism.

Conclusions

As Figure 5.7 summarizes, there are four political fundamentalist groups in America, each bringing a particular religious and sociological heritage to politics. With the stamina of the Southern Baptists, the aggressiveness of Falwell, the ambition of Robertson, and the consistency of BJU, each has its own approach. Each can easily be placed in the appropriate category: Separatist Fundamentalist Right, Movement Fundamentalist Right, or Emerging Fundamentalist Right.

In the 1920s H. L. Mencken wrote about the Scopes trial that if one were to toss an egg out of a Pullman window almost anywhere in America, it would hit a fundamentalist. This is not as true today, but as religion scholar Randall Balmer has observed: "Pullman cars are obsolete in America today. Fundamentalists are still around."[55]

In fact, fundamentalists have awakened. In the turbulent decade of the 1960s, Jerry Falwell was concentrating on "saturation evangelism" and building his Thomas Road Baptist Church, which had recently been established in the old Donald Duck orange juice bottling plant. Bob Jones was burying its founder, undertaking an expansion of its campus, and arm wrestling the New Evangelicalism of Billy Graham. Pat Robert-

	BJU	FALWELL	ROBERTSON	SBC CONSERVATIVES
FUND RIGHT BRANCH	SEPARATIST	MOVEMENT	MOVEMENT	EMERGING
POLITICAL ORGANIZATION	SOME LOCAL	NATIONAL	NATIONAL LOCAL	NATIONAL SOME LOCAL
LEADERSHIP	COOPERATIONIST	MILITANT	MILITANT	COOPERATIONIST
MOVEMENT MEMBERSHIP	RELIGIOUS	RELIGIOUS POLITICAL	RELIGIOUS POLITICAL	RELIGIOUS SOME POLITICAL
OTHER MOVEMENTS	FUNDAMENTALISM	PERSONAL	PERSONAL	SOCIAL / CULTURAL
TYPES OF SEPARATISM	SOCIAL RELIGIOUS	MOD SOCIAL MOD RELIGIOUS	MOD SOCIAL MOD RELIGIOUS	MOD RELIGIOUS
AGENDA AGE	OLD	NEW	NEW	NEW
AGENDA SPECIFICITY	GENERAL	SPECIFIC	SPECIFIC	SPECIFIC
AGENDA CONTENT	CONSERVATIVE	CONSERVATIVE	CONSERVATIVE	CONSERVATIVE MODERATE

Figure 5.7. Summary of Fundamentalist Group Political Characteristics

son was being ordained a Baptist minister and signing on with a one-camera Christian television station called WYAH, named after "Yahweh," the Hebrew name for Jehovah. The Southern Baptist Convention was in the middle of a growth spurt, focusing on evangelism and church building. But as the sixties came to a close, fundamentalists found themselves in a very different world from the pristine past. By the mid-1970s, discontent with the changing culture led to varying degrees of political involvement, which has been magnified in the 1980s and 1990s. Falwell, Robertson, Jones, and the SBC have little empires now, influencing large groups of followers, most of whom are now registered to vote—and doing so.

6

The Pew and the Pulpit
Baptist Republican Mass and Elite Politics

The SBC schism, though possessing its own unique characteristics, is a part of a general split within American Christendom. Reacting to changes in the culture, the Convention and the country, a conservative faction has arisen within the SBC bent on controlling the affairs of
the fifteen-million-member organization, aligning its elites informally
with the fundamentalist right political agenda and working Christian
conservative politics down to the rank and file. Moreover, in terms of its
preacher elite, the SBC is the embodiment of one side of what one Southern Baptist scholar has called a "'two-party' mobilization in American
Protestantism between 'modernist this-worldly clergy' and their 'traditional other-worldly colleagues.'"[1] The SBC is part of one bloc of a dual
mobilization that comes from politics and theology.[2]

If the SBC fissure is more than theological (i.e., social, cultural and
political), logically, then, this split should play out not only in the open
political arena (where Bill Clinton and Al Gore, who are Convention
moderates and political Democrats, clash with the leadership of the
Southern Baptist Convention) but in the private political attitudes of
Southern Baptists in the pew and pulpit.

Research has already shown that Southern Baptist elites (pastors),
though not all are enlisted in the army of the Emerging Fundamentalist
Right, have been influenced by fundamentalist right trends, becoming
more activist, conservative and supportive of the two Bush-Quayle tickets. Baptists also have a history of allowing their pastors to take an active
part in politics.[3] Southern Baptist lay persons and pastors agree with the
statement "it is good that groups like the Moral Majority are taking a
stand for Christian principles" at a rate of 60 percent.[4]

Given this scenario and based on this research, three questions present themselves. First, beyond "playing an active role" and "taking a stand for Christian principles," what is the political platform of Southern Baptist elites, and how has this agenda changed over time? Second, where should we place the average woman or man in the SBC pew politically? Which party attracts his or her allegiance? What trends appear in SBC partisanship and ideology over time? Are Southern Baptists more politically conservative than other Americans? Are they more conservative than other Southerners? Third, how do Southern Baptist elites compare politically with the Convention rank and file? Is the parishioner more conservative than the average preacher, or vice versa? What does this comparison tell us about the future of Baptist politics and the interaction/connection between the politics of preacher and parishioner?[5]

The Changing Politics of the Southern Baptist Rank and File

We take the second question first, the politics of the SBC *rank and file*. To answer this question, we have selected data from the American National Election Study (ANES). The ANES, conducted by the University of Michigan's Center for Political Studies, provides a body of data that is very useful for this type of research.[6] Because of the comprehensive nature of the research, a significant number of Southern Baptists are included in the study.[7] In addition, as a part of the biennial survey, randomly selected individuals are asked a number of standard questions, which remain the same over the twenty-four years in question.[8] This consistency adds to the integrity of our analysis and will help us to determine which political pole most closely suits Southern Baptists, and how this relationship might have changed over time.[9]

Using data from this survey, we will seek to plot Southern Baptist political opinion along several dimensions: partisanship, ideology, national voting patterns, abortion issues, interest in campaigns/politics, and religious self-identification. Southern Baptists will be compared with a random sample of white Americans, a random sample of white Southerners, white Southerners who regularly attend church, and Southern Baptists who regularly attend.[10]

Partisanship

Not surprisingly, in the national sample we find Southern Baptists becoming more and more Republican from 1968 to 1992. Until 1988, the

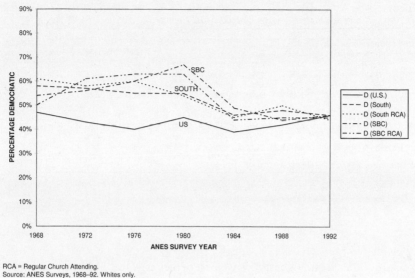

RCA = Regular Church Attending.
Source: ANES Surveys, 1968–92. Whites only.

Figure 6.1. Democratic Party Identification in United States / South / SBC

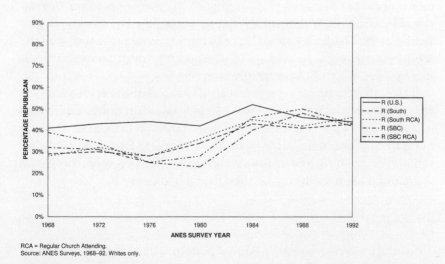

RCA = Regular Church Attending.
Source: ANES Surveys, 1968–92. Whites only.

Figure 6.2. Republican Party Identification in United States / South / SBC

TABLE 6.1
Party Identification in United States / South / SBC, 1968–1992

	1968	1972	1976	1980	1984	1988	1992
Democratic							
United States	47%	43%	40%	45%	39%	42%	46%
South	58%	57%	55%	55%	46%	48%	46%
South (RCA)	61%	58%	60%	54%	45%	50%	44%
SBC	54%	56%	60%	67%	49%	44%	46%
SBC (RCA)	50%	61%	63%	63%	44%	45%	45%
Republican							
United States	41%	43%	44%	42%	52%	46%	44%
South	29%	30%	28%	34%	43%	41%	43%
South (RCA)	28%	32%	28%	36%	45%	42%	46%
SBC	32%	31%	25%	23%	40%	48%	42%
SBC (RCA)	39%	34%	25%	28%	46%	50%	43%

Note: Whites only. RCA = Regular Church Attending.
Source: ANES Surveys, 1968–92.

pecking order from highest to lowest in percentage Republican was Americans / Southerners / Southern Baptists. Southern Baptists were reluctant Republicans, particularly in the Jimmy Carter era. In the late 1980s, though, Southern Baptists caught up with the region and the nation in Republican identification, leaving all five groups clustered around 45 percent by 1992. The story is, of course, much the mirror image for Democratic identification, with Southern Baptists being the last "yellow dogs." But by 1988, Southern Baptists were becoming as disenchanted with the Democratic party as the average Southerner. All categories of voters settled by 1992 at 45 to 50 percent Democratic.

This shifting partisan loyalty leaves SBC voters at the end of a rollercoaster ride in which they were more Republican than other Southerners in 1968, less Republican than other Southerners in the Carter era, and more Republican again in the late 1980s. Southern Baptist Republicanism dipped again slightly in 1992 to bring the SBC to a conformity with the nation not seen since 1968, though at a higher level.

Ideology

Ideologically, the Southern Baptist pattern is similar to that of partisanship with but one exception. Even while voting for Jimmy Carter, Southerners and Southern Baptists were leading the nation in conservatism. However, it appears that although both groups hovered at an all-time high conservative percentage of 70 percent in 1984, Southern and

TABLE 6.2

Ideology in United States / South / SBC, 1972–1992

	1972	1976	1980	1984	1988	1992
Liberal						
United States	20%	11%	18%	28%	22%	24%
South	15%	13%	16%	29%	18%	19%
South (RCA)	11%	9%	9%	25%	13%	15%
SBC	14%	10%	18%	29%	16%	20%
SBC (RCA)	12%	6%	17%	26%	13%	14%
Conservative						
United States	42%	47%	71%	69%	47%	45%
South	50%	53%	52%	65%	50%	50%
South (RCA)	58%	61%	64%	71%	56%	56%
SBC	43%	62%	47%	67%	53%	51%
SBC (RCA)	52%	74%	65%	67%	56%	61%

Note: Whites only. RCA = Regular Church Attending.
Source: ANES Surveys, 1972–92.

Southern Baptist conservatism fell in 1988 along with that of the rest of the nation. In the era 1972–92, Southern Baptists leapfrogged Southerners, and Southern Baptist regular church attenders surpassed Southern regular church attenders in conservatism, indicating a convention moving at a brisker pace than the region to the starboard side. In short, Southern Baptists were erratic in embracing "conservative" as a label, but as convention and secular politics pressed the issue of ideology, they grew more comfortable with the term.

Before leaving ideology, we should note that 1976 was a true liberal nadir. With conservative Ford vs. progressive-conservative Carter, liberalism was truly out of vogue, particularly in the Convention. Among SBC regular attenders, a grand total of 6 percent of respondents called themselves slightly liberal, liberal, or extremely liberal.

National Vote

Figure 6.3 presents another era of Southern Baptist contradiction, the presidential election. From 1968 to 1972, Southern Baptists became much more Republican, but not at the phenomenal rate of the rest of the South. Both Southerners and Southern Baptists were the least Republican in 1976. But in the 1980s, an interesting split opened along attendance lines, with regularly attending Southerners and regularly attending Southern Baptists (the more "active" Christians) being more Republican than other Americans, while average Southerners and Southern

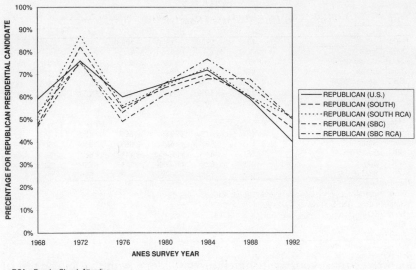

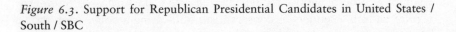

RCA = Regular Church Attending.
Source: ANES Surveys, 1968–92. Whites only.

Figure 6.3. Support for Republican Presidential Candidates in United States / South / SBC

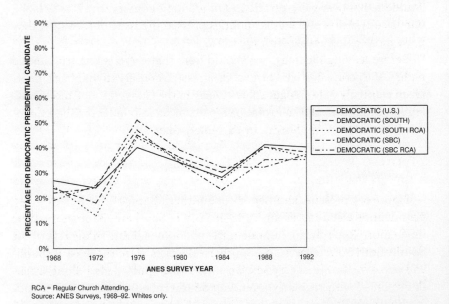

RCA = Regular Church Attending.
Source: ANES Surveys, 1968–92. Whites only.

Figure 6.4. Support for Democratic Presidential Candidates in United States / South / SBC

TABLE 6.3
Support for Presidential Candidates in United States /South / SBC, 1968–1992

	1968	1972	1976	1980	1984	1988	1992
Republican							
United States	59%	76%	60%	66%	72%	59%	40%
South	48%	82%	55%	64%	70%	60%	46%
South (RCA)	51%	87%	56%	65%	73%	60%	51%
SBC	47%	76%	49%	61%	68%	68%	50%
SBC (RCA)	53%	75%	53%	66%	77%	65%	50%
Democratic							
United States	27%	24%	40%	34%	28%	41%	40%
South	24%	18%	45%	36%	30%	40%	38%
South (RCA)	25%	13%	44%	35%	27%	40%	36%
SBC	22%	24%	51%	39%	32%	32%	37%
SBC (RCA)	19%	25%	47%	34%	23%	35%	35%
Non-Democratic							
United States	73%	76%	60%	66%	72%	59%	60%
South	76%	82%	55%	64%	70%	60%	61%
South (RCA)	75%	87%	56%	65%	73%	60%	63%
SBC	78%	76%	49%	61%	68%	68%	64%
SBC (RCA)	80%	75%	53%	66%	77%	65%	65%

Note: Whites only. RCA = Regular Church Attending.
Source: ANES Surveys, 1968–92.

Baptists were less Republican. By 1988, Southern Baptists were as Republican as SBC regular attenders. In 1992, Southern Baptists, SBC regular attenders, and Southern regular attenders gave Bush a majority, while Southerners and Americans gave Bush less than a plurality of their votes.

The category "national vote" shows the most interesting trend of the twenty-four-year period, a phenomenon related to the two Southern Baptist presidential candidates. From the ANES pre-election interview to the post-election interview, there was a twenty-point dip in Jimmy Carter's support among Southern Baptists in 1980 (from 59 percent to 39 percent). If we can assume that the respondents were being forthright, it appears that although Southern Baptists supported Carter early in the campaign, something snapped later, causing them to turn on the Georgian and his party, never to turn back. Perhaps Southern Baptists liked the Carter style but not the Carter performance. Or perhaps 1976 was a sign, as Southern Baptist regular attenders were already giving the edge to Ford. As for Bill Clinton, it appears that with the SBC, his Southern Baptist membership was worth an increase of only 5 percent among Southern Baptists over Dukakis's showing four years earlier. Support for Clinton dropped about 6 percent from the pre- to the postelection interview among Southern Baptists—a slight margin—but second only to Carter's 1980 decrease in this 1968–92 window.

Abortion

The Southern Baptist position on abortion is a difficult one to define based on our data, but some patterns do emerge that illustrate the division within the SBC. In general, moderation seems to be the rule, with approximately 10 percent favoring a ban on abortion across all categories from 1972 to 1992. From 1980 to 1988, however, as the issue heated up, a cleavage began to develop following a logical order: SBC regular attenders were most in favor of a ban, followed by Southern regular attenders, Southerners, Southern Baptists, and Americans. This gap closed as support for the anti-abortion position fell across the board, but regularly attending Southerners are about as likely to favor a ban as regularly attending Southern Baptists.

Not surprisingly, the compromise abortion positions (acceptable for rape, incest, or to save the life of the mother) taken together consistently dominate other categories over time, with degree of support following the reasonable order from warmest (Southern Baptist regular attenders)

TABLE 6.4
Position on Abortion in United States / South / SBC. 1972–1992

	1972	1976	1980	1984	1988	1992
Ban						
United States	8%	7%	10%	13%	12%	10%
South	7%	7%	11%	18%	14%	11%
South (RCA)	5%	7%	14%	21%	18%	14%
SBC	7%	8%	11%	16%	12%	8%
SBC (RCA)	9%	6%	15%	22%	14%	10%
Choice						
United States	23%	26%	36%	31%	36%	43%
South	15%	20%	32%	24%	31%	37%
South (RCA)	10%	17%	26%	14%	22%	25%
SBC	14%	18%	27%	19%	26%	31%
SBC (RCA)	8%	11%	21%	8%	21%	20%
Restrictions						
United States	69%	67%	54%	56%	53%	47%
South	78%	73%	58%	58%	56%	52%
South (RCA)	85%	76%	59%	65%	60%	61%
SBC	79%	74%	63%	65%	62%	60%
SBC (RCA)	84%	83%	63%	69%	65%	70%

Note: Whites only. RCA = Regular Church Attending.
Source: ANES Surveys, 1972–92.

to coolest (Americans). The same order is followed in reverse for choice. Southern Baptists remain least likely to support the pro-choice position, but after hovering around 20 to 25 percent for a decade, the pro-choice figure broke 30 percent in 1992 among Southern Baptists. Regularly attending Southern Baptists, at 20 percent, remain distant: 11 percent behind the SBC and 23 percent behind the nation, but significantly above their 1972 level of 8 percent.

Interest in Politics

One of the supposed effects of the rise of the fundamentalist right was an increased interest in politics by conservative Christians. According to this notion, the fundamentalist right energized previously nonparticipating voters, particularly in the years of its greatest influence, 1980 and 1984.

In the national picture, several trends seems to emerge. First, both categories of regular attenders are across time more interested in politics than the other three groupings. (This is consistent with what the classic book, *The American Voter*,[11] says about the effect on political awareness and

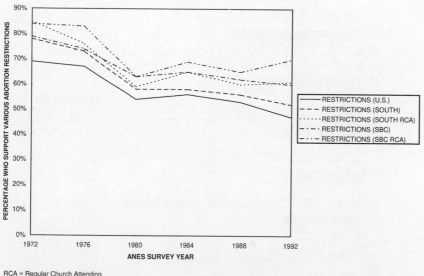

RCA = Regular Church Attending.
Source: ANES Surveys, 1972–92. Whites only.

Figure 6.5. Support for Restrictions on Abortion in United States / South / SBC

interest of civic involvement of any type, including church.) Southern interest grew along with others in 1976, and Southern Baptist interest grew more than others in 1984. But the most dramatic figure is the increase in Southern Baptist interest in 1992. At 17 percent, it is the second highest rate of growth in interest of any group in our twenty-four-year survey.

Evangelical versus Fundamentalist Identity

Besides the better denominational battery, the greatest innovation in the 1992 survey for those studying religion is the new question using "words that best describe" one's religion. These include fundamentalist, evangelical, mainline or liberal, and spirit-filled. In the predictable order, respondents range from the Southern Baptist regular attender category (which contains the most fundamentalists and the fewest moderates) to the general United States category (which has the most moderates and the fewest fundamentalists). Southern Baptists have a greater liking for "evangelical" and "fundamentalist," the two most conservative terms, than any other group—more evidence of a shift to the right in the SBC, though a reluctant minority is still present.

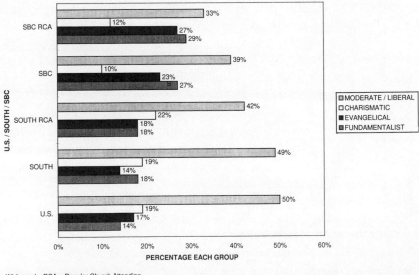

Whites only. RCA = Regular Church Attending.
Source: ANES Survey, 1992.

Figure 6.6. Religious Group Identification in United States / South / SBC

The Southern Baptist Mass Perspective

Since the bottom fell dramatically out from under Jimmy Carter in the fall of 1980 among his SBC brethren, those who identify with the SBC have maintained their affinity for GOP candidates, even with the two Southern Baptists heading the 1992 and 1996 tickets. Though 1992 tempted them much more than 1988, Southern Baptists, like other white Southerners, are still preponderantly Republican as presidential voters and somewhat more Republican in party identification. But the Democratic party is not dead. "Conservatism" in this sense is two-edged. There is a still significant Democratic allegiance present in the South, making Southern Baptists reluctant to let go their traditional Democratic identification even while voting overwhelmingly Republican for president. Generational difference is sure to play a role in this anomaly.

There is a strong but hard-to-define moderate element still present in the SBC as well. We see this in the difference between the "Southern Baptist" and the "Baptist" responses in the earlier South Carolina survey and between the regularly attending Southern Baptists and Southern Baptists in the ANES poll. The abortion question provides more evidence: our research shows that there is a moderate element that opposes a ban (or choice) but favors restrictions. Religious self-identification is middle-of-the-road in the Southern established church as well, with parishioners not totally identifying with the term "fundamentalist," embracing "evangelical" with near equal enthusiasm. Those in the SBC who prefer the moderate/liberal label are certainly more moderate than liberal. It is unfortunate that moderate and liberal were not separate categories.

There is a conservative element in the SBC also. These *Southern* Baptists, who would probably agree with SBC leader Richard Land that "Lyndon Johnson was the first president elected after the Civil War who didn't have an accent,"[12] are very self-consciously Southern and quick to link Southern and conservative.[13] The *Southern* Baptists and regular attenders are more conservative in every respect and much more Republican. Our national survey reveals a recent element of activism present in the SBC as well, with Southern Baptists suddenly outpacing others in interest in politics and campaigns. The origin of this phenomenon is in doubt, but is assumed to be in the conservative direction as the SBC voted 49 percent to 37 percent for Bush over Clinton in a nation that voted 43 percent to 38 percent for Clinton and Gore.

As to the debate between those who hope to make the SBC look representative of America and those who would like to open a new SBC branch of the fundamentalist right: both are likely to remain frustrated. We must remember that Southern Baptists led the fight both for separation of church and state and for temperance. Though neither belief may still endure, in the Southern Baptist Convention of the late 1990s the Baptist spirit of moderation that forced the separation of church and state in the seventeenth century seems to coexist with the nineteenth-century Baptist conservatism that crusaded for temperance.[14] It is this straddling that produced the moderation that caused the conservative faction to take over a decade to force the moderate faction out of the Convention that has seldom, in thirty years, strayed from the belief that the Bible has "truth without any mixture of error for its matter."[15] Perhaps the tension between Convention leaders and followers is a factor here. In any event, rock-ribbed conservatism is now in the driver's seat of a denomination that just a decade and a half ago was presenting denominational service awards not to Jesse Helms but to Jimmy Carter.

The Changing Politics of Southern Baptist Elites

Now we turn to the Southern Baptist elites, the preachers and denominational bureaucrats who attend the functions and run the organizational machinery. Because of its history, the SBC is a *Convention* and not a *Church*—a matter not of mere semantics, but explanatory of the original ad hoc structure of the organization. In the SBC, the convention (annual meeting) runs the Convention (permanent structure). Indeed, we find in the proceedings of the convention itself not only the elements that led to the political changes in the SBC, but the best source for political analysis: the resolutions passed by the delegates or "messengers" to the annual convocation. (Messengers are elected from individual churches as delegates to the national meeting. In most cases, there are enough slots available for any church members who are willing to attend and can afford the trip.)

Analyzing resolutions and official statements from religious denominations is not a new research design, but there is less precedent for an in-depth analysis. The few existing works study political statements across churches. We will delve deeper, examining the resolutions passed by one denomination over time. In doing so, we will be able to track how the agenda of SBC elites has changed over the last thirty years.

Tracking Change I: SBC Convention Resolutions by Content

In searching for the political opinions of the elite who control the Southern Baptist Convention at any particular time, the best source has become the body of annual resolutions.[16] Though it was not their original intention, these statements in recent years have become the de facto political *platform* of the organization.

We begin our analysis with the 1968 convention. After conversations with leaders of the SBC, it was determined that 1968 represented in many ways the "coming out" of the SBC politically. It was in that year, as described in chapter 2, that the moderate faction began aggressively to push a social agenda for the SBC. By beginning with 1968 we get over a decade of resolutions before the "takeover" to show the progression of political "platform" changes.[17]

For added precision, resolutions passed by the convention since 1968 have been coded as "internal" or "external" in scope. *Internal resolutions* relate to matters within the Convention. *External resolutions* are concerned with society at large. Internal resolutions are coded as fitting into one, two, or three church-oriented categories: formalistic, doctrinal, and evangelical. *Formalistic* resolutions are those expressing sentiments without politically or religiously loaded content of any kind. *Doctrinal* resolutions make statements about theology. *Evangelical* resolutions urge gospel or "soul-winning" appeals.

External resolutions are coded with categories from a list that includes moralistic, religious liberty, and socially conscious contents. *Moralistic* content is indicated by a call for higher moral standards in the nation without any reference to spiritual antecedents for that moralism (for such a resolution would be Internal in nature and coded Doctrinal). *Religious liberty* content is indicated by an appeal to the historic Baptist ideal of strict separation of church and state. *Socially conscious* content is determined by social gospel–type calls for helping the physical and emotional needs of the poor without calls to meet spiritual needs.

Resolutions that are primarily *formalistic* include those that range from appreciation to convention officials, appreciation to host cities, appreciation to the news media, salutes to certain types of ministers, and support for convention agency themes. Resolutions that lament the rise in cost of second-class mail and recognize a thousand years of Christianity in Russia fit in the "formal" category as well. All relate to the machinery or structure of the denomination or the church and are noncontroversial.

Resolutions that are primarily *doctrinal* include seminary doctrinal issues, local church autonomy, priesthood of the believer doctrine, doctrinal integrity, the New Age movement, ministerial integrity, the biblical role of women (when not connected to political issues regarding women), or the observance of the Lord's Day.

Resolutions that are primarily *evangelical* may cover prayer for spiritual awakening, evangelism at Olympic games, evangelism at Southern Baptist Convention meetings, personal sharing of the gospel, opportunities for new mission work, support for individual missionaries, and support for the Cooperative Program (the Southern Baptist fund for financing mission projects).

Moralistic resolutions include abortion, gambling, homosexuality, media sex and violence, pornography, public school morality, and substance abuse.

Religious liberty resolutions may include opposition to the appointment of an ambassador to the Holy See, equal-access legislation, First Amendment pleas, reaction to IRS rulings, religious liberty and employment issues, school prayer, tuition tax credits, and constitutional issues.

Socially conscious resolutions include those concerning criminal justice system reform, the environment, family farming, hunger, help for the mentally handicapped, peace, refugees, racism, and welfare.

Results

The results of this analysis find that, judging from the political and religious issues it chooses to address and the official opinions stated, the Convention has changed to a marked degree in twenty-five years. As we see in table 6.5 and in figures 6.7 and 6.8, in the moderate era—from 1968 to the takeover in 1979—most of the content of internally focused resolutions was of a formal, even pro forma type. Leaders were applauded, and institutions and agencies were recognized in 38 percent of statements. Doctrinal issues finished last of the three categories, with 23 percent, and evangelical issues were in between, at 25 percent. By the transition era—from 1980 to 1989, when conservatives solidified control—formalistic resolutions had, compared to the rest, fallen. But doctrinal and evangelical resolutions were virtually unchanged. In the conservative era, the impact of conservative control is becoming evident as theological purists and newcomers to convention politics press for more statements, including doctrinal and evangelical language, and fewer formal, institutional credos.

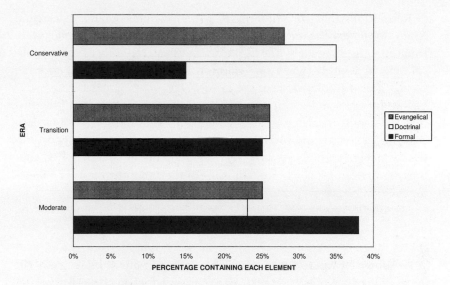

Source: SBC Annuals, 1968–93. Data compiled by author.

Figure 6.7. Content of Resolutions Passed by SBC (Internal Matters), 1968–1993

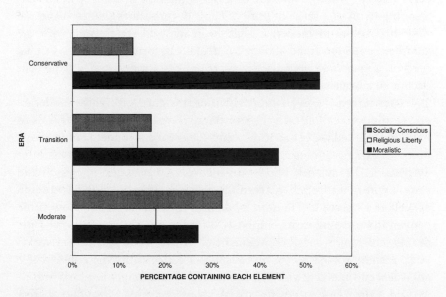

Source: SBC Annuals, 1968–93. Data compiled by author.

Figure 6.8. Content of Resolutions Passed by SBC (External Matters), 1968–1993

TABLE 6.5

Resolutions Passed by SBC Annual Conventions, by Content and by Era, 1968–1996

	Moderate 1968–1979	Transition 1980–1989	Conservative 1990–1996	Trend Mod - Cons
Internal				
Formal	38%	25%	24%	-14%
Doctrinal	23%	26%	26%	3%
Evangelical	25%	26%	22%	-3%
External				
Moralistic	27%	44%	50%	23%
Religious Liberty	18%	14%	15%	-3%
Socially Conscious	32%	17%	18%	-14%
Totals by era	174	162	74	410

Note: Resolutions contain multiple elements. Percentages do not add up to 100%.
Source: Resolutions from SBC Annuals, 1968–96. Data compiled by author.

As shown by figure 6.7, from the beginning of our study in 1968 (in the middle of a moderate era) to 1993, a period when conservative-faction control was at its height, formal resolutions fell 23 percent, doctrinal resolutions rose 12 percent, and evangelical resolutions rose 3 percent. This is a strong indicator of a denomination in flux, of a convention in pursuit of a sense of purity. Table 6.5 indicates that by 1996 the ratio had begun to moderate slightly in internal statements, with the complete 1968–96 trend showing a decline in formal resolutions of 14 percent, a 3-percent increase in doctrinal resolutions and a 3-percent decline in evangelical resolutions.

External resolutions are more significant (figure 6.8). In the moderate era, resolutions calling on Southern Baptists and government officials to help the poor led the list at 32 percent. Pleas for a stronger stand against immoral practices (mostly alcoholism) in the public culture came in at 27 percent. The historic Baptist distinction of separation of church and state, expressed through concern for religious liberty, showed strength as well at 18 percent. The shift evident in the transition era showed the convention slipping in its emphasis on religious liberty, and dropping dramatically in its social consciousness. (Most of the loss was made up in an equally robust rise in moralistic resolutions.) By the conservative era, the trend was set, with continuing calls for stronger national morality and a drop in concern for social issues and First Amendment freedoms.

From 1968 to 1993, moralistic resolutions rose 26 percent while social-conscious resolutions fell 19 percent. Religious liberty statements dropped 8 percent. For 1968–96 (table 6.5) moralistic resolutions increased 23 percent, social-conscious resolutions fell 14 percent, and religious liberty resolutions fell 3 percent. The new leaders of the SBC represented a new faction, but not in the old sense. In the old Southern politics, a faction represented personalities or even geography, but never carefully reasoned positions on meaty issues. The SBC factions were much more clearly separated. A glimpse into the resolutions passed in the era controlled by each faction tells the story. Moderates stressed formalism, liberty, and social concern, giving new voice to historic platitudes. The conservatives are concerned with the politics of moralism, taking into the public square its resolve against sin and its consequences. The religious divide is implicitly partisan, the moderate agenda being a variation on a theme by President Lyndon Johnson, the conservative a page from the Reagan scrapbook.

Tracking Change II: SBC Selected Resolutions by Type

Though the body of resolutions is quite revealing, it is important to track individual issues and their impact as well. We have already seen from this analysis and that of others[18] that in the late 1970s Southern Baptists were moderate on social issues. What issues make up the moderate and conservative platforms now? How has the SBC position changed with each changing faction? On selected issues that received marked attention in the period from 1968 to 1993, the following resolutions evolved:

ABORTION

(Resolutions were passed in 1971, 1974, 1976–80, 1982, 1984, 1987, 1989, 1993–96.)[19] In the numerous resolutions passed on the abortion issue, the position had changed incrementally over the twenty-five-year period. The 1971 resolution, using some pro-life language but alluding to the need for choice, took a middle-ground position. The 1974 resolution reaffirmed the 1971 resolution by name and called for prayer for guidance. By 1976, abortion was "terminat[ing] the life of an innocent human being,"[20] but the political content of the resolution was identical. The 1978 and 1979 statements merely affirmed the 1976 position.

There is a shift in opinion on abortion in the transition era of the 1980s. Resolutions included clauses opposing abortion except to save the life of the mother, arguing that life begins at conception, and calling abortion a "national sin" that leads to child abuse and euthanasia (1984:8).[21] Elements of other abortion resolutions supported legislation to protect pro-life hospitals, take the Supreme Court to task for *Roe*, ask all Southern Baptists to observe an annual "Sanctity of Human Life Sunday," and call on SBC agencies to expand care for unwed mothers and to appoint coordinators for pro-life political activities.

In the conservative era the litmus test for abortion's appropriateness has become the much more stringent *"imminent* death of the mother" (emphasis mine; 1989:3).[22] The SBC has also gone on record supporting pro-life legislation and amendments, opposing "morning after" pills and experimentation with fetal tissue and patenting of genes, opposing legislation aimed at abortion clinic protesters, opposing surgeon general nominee Henry Foster, calling on both parties to adopt pro-life platform planks, and chiding President Clinton for vetoing the partial birth abortion ban in a letter sent to the White House calling on the president to "repent" of his veto. The SBC also demanded on two occasions (1993:4; 1994)[23] that abortion not be covered in any health care bill passed by the Congress, and a recent resolution (1993:4) alludes to a "Biblical prohibition against abortion."[24]

CHURCH AND STATE

(Resolutions with church and state content were passed every year in the moderate era except in 1973, but not in the transition and conservative eras in 1984 and 1987–90.)[25] In the moderate era, resolutions had supported the Supreme Court school prayer ban (1969:11),[26] fought against public aid for all-white church schools (1970:6),[27] opposed appointment of an ambassador to the Vatican, and resisted a perceived "elite" in the nation that opposes church-state separation. This era also saw statements opposing EEOC and IRS regulations thought to threaten church-state separation.

The transition era continued much of the sentiments of the previous era opposing IRS regulation, ambassadors to the Vatican, and aid to parochial schools. Church and state issues were much fewer in the conservative era, and the SBC did proactively stray from its separationist path, calling on the courts to expand "equal access" legislation for schools and to avoid too strict an interpretation of the Establishment Clause in regard to public schools. In the late 1980s, a school prayer resolution, taking the opposite stand from the 1969 Convention support of the Supreme Court ban, was said to have been written by the religious liaison of the Reagan White House and shipped to the convention site for consideration. A resolution at least as strong was passed in the 1996 convention as the issue resurfaced in the form of the Armey Amendment (authored by House Majority Leader Richard Armey, R-TX, which prohibits federal and state governments from denying anyone "equal access to a benefit, or otherwise discriminating against any person on account of religious belief, expression, or exercise." The stance of the resolution and support of the Armey Amendment is a far cry from the late 1960s worries about separation. The Convention also went on record in this era against new EEOC guidelines on religious harassment in the workplace as being dangerous to religious liberty, and it supported resolutions demanding protection for Americans sharing the gospel abroad.

HOMOSEXUALITY

(Resolutions were passed in 1976–78, 1980, 1985, 1988, 1993, and 1996.)[28] This issue is given attention here, not for the number of resolutions but for the noticeable shift in language from the moderate to conservative regime. The earliest resolutions treaded lightly, preferring that churches not ordain homosexuals, but fearing to step on local autonomy and quickly getting to the point: that homosexuals can be "saved from the penalty and power of sin through Jesus Christ" (1976:5).[29] Beginning in 1977, the resolutions became progressively more negative, however, moving from a description of the life-style as simply "sin" to "an abomination." All but one of the seven resolutions offered hope similar to the 1976 statement, stressing the need for forgiveness. But the late-transition-era 1985 resolution was all stick and no carrot, forgetting to offer a way out through Christ, stressing only the sin and opposing "special rights" for homosexuals (1985:11).[30] The infamous resolution on the Disney Company and the accompanying resolution on homosexual marriage contained the strongest wording yet. The homosexual marriage statement, at nearly 1,400 words, is one of the longest passed by the Convention. The Disney resolution, an indictment against Disney on numerous charges of anti-Christian bias, is reproduced in the Appendix.

RACE

(Resolutions were passed in 1969–74, 1978, 1981–84, 1986, 1988, 1989, 1993, 1995, and 1996.)[31] Though it was a bit of a surprise in the South, racial resolutions have presented a less substantive contrast across eras than other matters, with Southern Baptists always going on record against racism directed at both blacks and Jews during these years. Resolutions also regularly called on SBC officials to seek out qualified minorities for service in Convention affairs, and they stressed that there is "no racial distinction to God" (1982:24).[32] The difference between eras on the issue of race is more one of attitude, but it is still significant. In a couple of resolutions in the moderate era, Southern Baptists admitted that the "[SBC] has failed to take a stand against anti-Semitism" (1972:5)[33] and that there was a need to "purge [our]selves of racism" (1978:11).[34] Until 1995, transition era and conservative era resolutions stopped short of admitting such guilt, concentrating on seeking out qualified blacks for Convention leadership, sharing the gospel with African Americans, seeking to "establish friendships" with those of other races, and encouraging blacks to attend SBC seminaries. But race became the central topic of the 1995 Convention meeting, culminating in a resolution of apology and an interesting, evolving conservative biracial alliance. The ramifications of this alliance are discussed in the next chapter, and the complete text of this resolution can be found in the appendix. Consistent with 1995, the Convention passed a strongly worded resolution in 1996 on arson of African American churches.

SUBSTANCE ABUSE

In the twenty-three substance-abuse resolutions analyzed in this research, the Southern Baptist Convention position is consistently hardline and (unlike with school prayer and other church-state issues) much more open to government involvement. From calls for warning labels on alcohol to bans on "happy hours," the SBC's historic moralistic militancy, dating from the temperance movement, is seamless.

MILITARY/PEACE

Military and peace issues present another ideological contrast. Moderate era resolutions spoke in terms of "the universal dream of peace for mankind" (1968:10)[35] and the need to spend less on war and more on social needs in the federal budget (1972:8)[36] or, more eloquently, to "shift funds for armaments to human needs" (1978:5).[37] The transition era spoke of the tension between peace and deterrence (1980:22),[38] support for arms control, and the new national-defense emphasis (1981:14),[39] and supported an arms control agreement with the USSR if "mutually verifiable" (1983:4).[40] (The quoted words were added in a conservative amendment from the floor.) In the conservative era, the SBC, in a strongly evangelical statement, commended the president and honored the dead of Desert Storm but mentioned *peace* much less than in the former eras (1991:9).[41]

To these categories, we should add *ecumenism*, though Baptists would do so reluctantly. Ecumenical resolutions called for closer involvement with other Christian groups or cooperation with other agencies (whether Christian or secular) that shared the goal of a particular resolution. Not surprisingly, little ecumenism was expressed in the SBC, though in the moderate era one resolution expressed that the "image of God was in every man" (1971:10).[42] Conservative era "ecumenical" resolutions, by contrast, are primarily concerned with cooperation *among fundamentalists* in preaching the gospel and encouraging Bible reading. The Convention turned the corner in 1996, choosing no longer to ignore but to oppose the ecumenical movement as usually understood by moderates and progressives, and calling on Southern Baptists to support the work of their local church and of the Convention, striving for "*biblical* unity." A 1994 resolution cautioned Southern Baptists against alliances with Roman Catholics. (For a complete discussion of SBC–Roman Catholic dialogue, see chapter 7.)

Another couple of trends seem worth noting as well. In the moderate era, resolutions were always passed in numerical order, often with debate. In the transition era, as conservatives and moderates struggled, resolutions were often tabled or amended, with controversial resolutions often passing immediately before adjournment no matter what number they bore. In the conservative era, fewer amendments and less debate have restored passage of resolutions to numerical order. A *pax moderatum* followed by strife, followed in turn *by pax conservatatum*. Conservative era resolutions in the late 1990s have taken on a broader range of topics as well, specifically on education—supporting "parental choice in education" and opposing outcome-based education.

Tracking Change III: State Convention Resolutions

Individual Southern Baptist state conventions pass resolutions as well, following the national pattern. But because these state conventions are held in each state and travel costs are much lower than travel to a national event (though, like the national convention, it is dominated by preachers), we presume a much more democratic participation. With these official statements, we can know if a pattern is present, and if states have also entered a conservative era. As the SBC resolutions give us a moving picture, these resolutions give us a snapshot.

The sample we have selected consists of the total number of resolutions passed by ten Southern states in 1992. (In addition to these ten states, which constitute a majority of Convention membership, there are thirty other state conventions. The remaining thirty are much smaller and include northern states as well as combined states such as Kansas-Nebraska, Maryland-Delaware, New England, Pennsylvania–South Jersey, and Utah-Idaho.)

We chose 1992 because of the year's *political* significance. Most of the state Baptist conventions were held in November 1992, days after the victory of the double SBC Clinton-Gore ticket. The sixty-five resolutions are classified in a similar manner as that used for the SBC, except, because of their simpler content, state convention resolutions were assigned only one category of the six. Therefore, the percentages when totaled equal 100 percent.

What we find in this analysis is strength for moralistic and formalistic agenda items, with the former holding the preponderance of resolutions at almost 54 percent of the total. But when the very *pro forma* formalistic agenda items are removed, the moralistic agenda percentage rises to 76 percent. These moral statements include not only the regular Baptist concerns of abortion, alcohol, and gambling, but also euthanasia, television and movies, and sexual issues (including homosexuality). President Clinton is mentioned in eleven resolutions, with every state convention but Texas passing at least one resolution on the president-elect.

Because of the number of Clinton resolutions, these were in turn placed in two classes. Those simply calling on Baptists to pray for the president were coded "formal." Mississippi, North Carolina, and Virginia passed such motions.[43] The resolutions passed by Alabama, Arkansas, Florida, Georgia, Louisiana, and South Carolina were quite different, ranging from "that President Clinton be encouraged, in all deliberations and in all decisions, to be guided by prayer and by Biblical principles" (South Carolina)[44] to a "call upon fellow Southern Baptist Bill Clinton to renounce his stated intentions to promote abortion on demand and minority status for homosexuals" (Florida).[45]

The agenda of the state conventions, even more than that of the national SBC, reveals a strong bent in favor of external affairs (83 percent of the resolutions when formalistic resolutions are removed), a waning interest in religious liberty and social consciousness, and a surprising unwillingness to use resolutions for doctrinal and evangelistic statements as the national organization does.

Tracking Change IV: CLC Seminar Agenda

But we go deeper into the SBC political elite. If the SBC has an official apparatus for the systematic application of Christian principles to politics, it is the Christian Life Commission (known as the Ethics and Religious Liberty Commission as of June 1997). Founded in 1954 with what was thought to be mostly a change in name from the old Social Service Commission, the revamped agency, like its predecessor, was charged with being the *ethical* arm of the Convention.[46] From its revamped beginning, the CLC took an aggressive approach, asking tough questions and probing controversial issues. The CLC became a true commission in the late 1960s, reflecting its full-time duties and leaving behind the old ad hoc committee mentality of the past. (The name had been changed from Social Service *Committee* to Social Service *Commission* in 1947).

Charged with promoting social ethics and a concern for the moral and social climate of the nation,[47] the leadership of the CLC grew restless merely with cheerleading, producing reports, and making recommendations to the Convention annual meeting. So it began an annual seminar. Though not the focus of the CLC's work, the seminar has in many ways became the CLC's most important political project, and its most controversial. The annual seminar has become an opportunity to bring together thoughtful individuals from various backgrounds to discuss burning political issues of interest to Christians. The seminar provoked a fire storm almost immediately with its regular presentation of both sides. For example, the editor of *Playboy* magazine appeared at its third seminar (on morality).[48]

The CLC has always had a progressive tilt, only recently becoming strongly conservative under the leadership of Richard Land, former aide to Texas Republican governor William Clements.[49] Land was chosen when Larry Baker,[50] director since 1987, resigned in opposition to a plan to merge the CLC with the Public Affairs Committee, a standing committee of the Convention created in 1987 by conservatives dissatisfied with the moderate-faction-dominated Baptist Joint Committee on Public Affairs.[51] Land has wasted no time in changing the tenor of the conference, held annually since 1968.

One of the most popular topics for the annual CLC is Christian citizenship. This topic is selected roughly every four years, and the seminar is usually held in Washington, D.C. Because of their proximity to the Capitol, these conferences always feature a number of political figures, though not politicians exclusively. A quick overview of the citizenship conferences will show the change that has taken place at the CLC in twenty years.

The first conference, in 1968, drew President Lyndon Johnson, Representative Jim Wright (D-TX), and Senator John Sherman Cooper (R-KY). By 1976, the conference had a more extensive agenda, and featured Senator Hubert Humphrey (D-MN), Senator Edward Kennedy (D-MA), Senator George McGovern (D-SD), Representative Barbara Jordan (D-TX), Representative Les Aspin (D-WI), Representative Andrew Young (D-GA), and Representative John Anderson (R-IL). Also participating were Senator Howard Baker (R-TN), Senator John Tower (R-TX), and Senator Mark Hatfield (R-OR). The 1980, 1984, and 1988 conferences on citizenship were much the same in partisan balance, including Representative Newt Gingrich (R-GA), Representative Walter Fauntroy (D-DC), Senator Robert Dole (R-KS), Representative Claude Pepper (D-FL), as well as return appearances by Senator Hatfield and Representative Wright.

By 1992, the citizenship conference, and the CLC annual seminars in general, began to take on a different cast. Most of the politicians were gone, and in their places were William J. Bennett, Cal Thomas, Beverly LaHaye, and a Republican anti-obscenity lawyer, along with the president of the SBC and the president of the executive committee of the SBC.[52] The pre-1996 citizenship seminar featured O. S. Hawkins of Dallas, who applied Jeremiah 7:9 to President Clinton: "Will you steal, murder, commit adultery, swear falsely, burn incense to Baal and walk after other gods whom you do not know and then come and stand before Me in the house that is called by My name?" A far cry from the seminar that welcomed Lyndon Johnson, McGovern, Kennedy, and Pepper. The new regime had taken hold with a vengeance of the political agency in the conservative era. Gone were the elected officials, replaced by the leaders, scholars, and politicos of the fundamentalist right.

Conclusions

The history of the Southern Baptist Convention from 1968 to 1993, viewed from the ideological position of its rank and file and through the official statements of its elites, reveals a once apolitical denomination becoming politically aware—in some cases militantly so. Its leaders at the state and national levels stand energized for movement conservatism, and followers in the pews are only a step behind.[53]

The leadership of the conservative faction seems important here. As with any movement, the leaders or "professionals" can provide the necessary organizational force for keeping the struggle alive, or they can torpedo success. As has been documented, a leadership that is willing to be "co-opted" will siphon off strength. But militant leaders, by representing the rank and file, by refusal to be "bought," or a combination of the two, can achieve political power for their organization. The result can be a rallying of grass-roots support to the new leadership, or simply silence from the opposition within the organization and those unwilling to take a position. In either case, an unbending leadership can provide the needed edge to a struggling movement. This leadership cadre is essential to understanding the Southern Baptist Convention's changing theology and politics.

In light of the demographic data and political history presented earlier, it is important to note that the SBC began to move away from its religious liberty and socially conscious heritage and toward a more solely moralistic bent at exactly the time it became both "bipartisan" internally (moderate and conservative factions developed) and less cultural significant. As the Convention entered its first no-growth, "two-party" decade, a healthy skepticism of church-state cooperation as well as a heart for meeting temporal human needs no longer diluted the regular listing of national sins common to official statements. Internally, doctrine and evangelicalism began to dominate the institutional focus that built one of the largest, most cohesive denominational bureaucracies in the nation. Our state-convention-by-convention analysis of a year in the conservative era reveals that, unlike the transition era, the conservative era is not only wide but deep, with even the historically moderate North Carolina and Virginia conventions passing thinly veiled "pray for the president" resolutions. As represented by the quadrennial citizenship seminars of the Christian Life Commission, conservative polemics has begun to supplant the *search* for political truth that characterized the left of center annual meetings of the political agency. No longer do delegates hear prominent liberal and conservative politicians debate policy from an institutional perspective. A new crowd now gathers to hear the fundamentalist right agenda, presented by policy activists associated with the Republican party. (But taking hold only in the early nineties, the change at the CLC, unlike that reflected in Convention resolutions or at the ballot box, has been the latest in coming but the most militant.)

The double-quick march to the right among the rank and file began in earnest at about the time of the decline of the SBC in the culture and the rise of two "parties" in the Convention as well. Though we are hampered by a decennial census and a quadrennial ANES survey, we say with some confidence that the 1968–72 era was an important one. As the church declined and elites began to shift hard right, so also did the mass of the SBC become more conservative, more Republican, and more likely to vote for Republican presidential candidates.

As for the future of Baptist Republicanism, the strain of an organization shifting from moderate to conservative brings to mind the social critique of James Davison Hunter. According to Hunter, "the Orthodox Alliance" of which the SBC is a part is at a distinct disadvantage in growth potential vs. "the Progressive Public Culture"[54] in interpreting the past and setting the agenda for the future[55] because the former are surrounded by a hostile culture and are, therefore, forced constantly to adjust their faith.[56] In short, in Hunter's "culture war," progressive culture will in the end bring down orthodox communities.[57] This is the struggle with which the SBC will have to wrestle. In a milieu in which the church has for thirty years become progressively less dominant and at the same time more conservative both at the elite and mass level, can the denomination do what it must to survive? Can it simultaneously change, grow, and remain orthodox?

Or will the SBC prove Hunter wrong, using its size and energy to do religiously what the Republicans have done politically, *proselytize* disaffected conservatives from the competition as the competition moves left? The SBC, by moving right, as the last chapter suggests, is in a position to tap groups slightly to its right as well, such as the "yuppie" portion of Falwell-type fundamentalists who might see the SBC as a way to return to mainstream Southern culture without sacrificing ideological and doctrinal purity.

7

United We Survive
Baptist Republican Alliances

In the last six chapters, we have traced the unique formation of an attraction between Southern Baptists and the Republican party through that attraction's many antecedents. Along the way, we have found that Southern Baptists embody American Religion. It is in the United States that Baptists have grown so phenomenally. Their church government is historically so democratic that they have earned the label "hyper-Americans."[1] If Southern Baptists are hyper-American, then, to coin another term, they must be "hyper-Southerners" as well.

- In their rigidness and conservatism, Southern Baptists have taken a path opposite to that of their northern brethren, preaching to their Southern Zion a narrow theological message with immense social and political implications.
- We have noted also that, like the Southerners they are, Southern Baptists are large in number but provincial in their consciousness.
- Southern Baptists are *fundamentalists*, but because of their size not truly *separatists*.
- Southern Baptists are Southern, but they are growing fastest outside the old Confederacy.
- Southern Baptists are culturally strong but socially defensive. There is a "churchlike" and a "sectlike" quality to the SBC as it relates to politics.[2] The convention sees itself as large and community-spirited, almost Rotarian-like, while simultaneously bearing on its shoulders a small chip of fundamentalist sectarianism. This causes both separatist and worldly strains to coexist in the SBC.
- Southern Baptists are a paradox politically, filling the ranks of the fundamentalist right but without a desire to lead it.
- Southern Baptists are politically conservative, but have both ultra-conservative and moderate strains.

- Because the social upheavals of the North arrived in the isolated South one generation later, Southern Baptist reaction to social and political changes has taken place mostly in the last twenty-five years.
- Southern Baptist elites and the rank and file have awakened from their sleep as Emerging Fundamentalist Right Republicans with the development of a two-party (faction) convention and a two-party South.

This disparate picture of Baptist Republicanism has been laced with a number of overarching themes that seem appropriate to summarize and expand here. In summarizing the past and seeking to predict the future of the SBC, we arrive at two important questions: (1) Is it true that, as sociologists have predicted, groups like the SBC will struggle *internally* to grow and maintain a conservative political impact?[3] and (2) As political scientists have already noted, is the SBC indeed finding that many of the strategies that led it from its "one-party" moderate "don't rock the boat" moorings to militant movement Republicanism are at work in the national electorate as well?[4] The first factor concerns the elites who lead the SBC, the second relates to the rank and file parishioner/voter.

To Survive and Stay Right: The Strain of New SBC Alliances

Sociologists think that fundamentalist religious groups like the SBC may be headed for extinction in the long run. According to James Davison Hunter, as the culture becomes more progressive, "orthodox" groups like the SBC will be hard pressed to find new members and keep old ones. Modern Americans and new generations will be turned off by the anachronistic biblicism of fundamentalists and their poorly crafted attempts to come to terms with an increasingly irreligious America.[5] Taking his thinking a step further, we may also assume that in our electronic, scientific age, in which the earth revolves around the sun, humankind is descended from lower forms of life, and separation of church and state (including in public schools) is the law of the land, American culture will turn increasingly secular.

This scenario seems most alarming for Southern Baptists. At fifteen million adherents, they push the envelope for growth. An added concern is the challenge of being in a rapidly growing and changing region. The

statistics can be confusing here, but as we have seen, the SBC is still growing, but at a slower rate than before, and at a much slower rate than population growth. In financial terms, there is both good news and bad
news. The SBC Convention *Annual* shows that monetary giving is down,
but a recent Congregational Giving Survey funded by the Lilly Endowment shows Southern Baptists to be among the most generous givers.[6]

The changing South, of which the SBC is a part, presents two internal
challenges for the Convention. It must defend its post-1979 conservative
worldview against an ever-encroaching secular culture, and it must grow
or be consumed by that culture. The Southern Baptist reaction to these
two challenges seems worth noting here. First, the SBC conservative faction leadership, as Michael D'Antonio has written, is "obsessed" with
"*certainty* and *success*." Their orthodoxy gives them assurance that right
is right and wrong is wrong, and that their brand of militant conservative religion can succeed. Second, it is the firm belief of the SBC leadership that forsaking their conservative theology for something more palatable would endanger the health of the denomination, a position directly
opposite to that of secular sociologists.[7]

Political Alliance: Conservative Baptists and Catholics

In May 1994, a group of conservative Protestant and Catholic leaders
released "Evangelicals and Catholics Together: The Christian Mission
in the Third Millennium"[8] (hereafter known as *Together*). An ecumenical document, *Together* was drafted chiefly by evangelical Charles Colson (a Watergate conspirator and later founder of a Christian prison
ministry) and neo-conservative author Richard John Neuhaus, a
Lutheran pastor turned Roman Catholic priest. Participating in the two-
year drafting of the statement were fifteen leading lights of Christian
political conservatism, both Catholic and Protestant, including the
chancellor of the Archdiocese of Boston and officials with the National
Association of Evangelicals. An additional list of twenty-five
"endorsers" included First Amendment lawyer William Bentley Ball
(who handled the BJU defense against the IRS), Christian Broadcasting
Network and Christian Coalition founder Pat Robertson, John Cardinal O'Connor, and Presbyterian theologian J. I. Packer. Others, including Ralph Reed of the Christian Coalition, signed shortly after release
of the accord.

No Protestant group was more well represented in the signers of *Together* than Southern Baptists. In addition to the chief Protestant organizer, Charles Colson (who attends a suburban Washington, D.C., Southern Baptist Church), Richard Land of the Christian Life Commission and Larry Lewis of the Home Mission Board were among the council of fifteen who not only endorsed the document, but assisted in the actual drafting of it.

The SBC participation was historic. The Convention had taken part in some ecumenical dialogue in its history (particularly through the Christian Life Commission), but never any of this magnitude, and certainly not since the conservative faction took over. Ecumenical resolutions seldom made it to the floor of the Convention meeting and the issue of CLC ecumenism under the old regime had been used by the organizers of the conservative faction to promote its takeover effort, a tactic that played well to a long-standing Baptist resistance to cooperation with non-Baptists of any stripe. Rumors of alliances with non-*Protestants* bordered on heresy and helped propel the new management into power in 1979.

So why did conservative faction CLC leaders feel safe to sit down with Roman Catholics? The participation of so many other groups provided cover, or a bandwagon effect, but this is only part of the explanation. The difference between the ecumenical dialogue undertaken by the moderate faction in its halcyon days and that of the Richard Land–conservative faction variety is simple. The former was of a religious nature, the latter was purely political.

As figure 7.1 shows, the purpose for *Together* was simply this: to put in writing an alliance of politically conservative Catholics and politically conservative evangelicals, to seal a commitment to lay aside religious differences to more effectively fight the devil, for sure, but mostly to fight the left wing. With *Together*, the conservative political elites of the Convention were drawn to the conservative political elites of the Roman Catholic community.

The document is certainly neo-conservative, but it is a bit paleo-conservative as well,[9] proclaiming that Christians should "resist the utopian conceit that it is within our power to build the Kingdom of God on earth" and stating the goal of "contend[ing] for the truth that politics, law and culture must be secured by moral truth." The accord attacks "relativism," "nihilism," abortion, pornography, "the deviant," multiculturalism, the entertainment industry, and "anti-intellectualism." By signing, each commits to support choice in education, "a renewed appre-

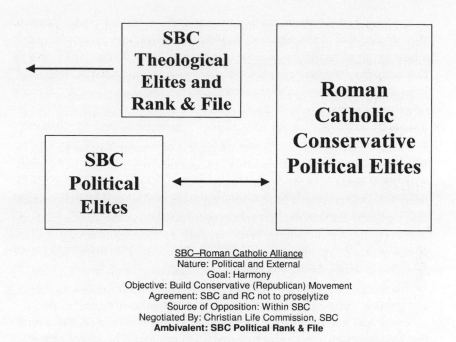

Figure 7.1. Southern Baptist and Roman Catholic Political Cooperation

ciation of Western culture," a market economy, freedom of religion, and "mediating structures in society" such as the family and the church. The document is eclectic; a mixture of the rhetoric of the Republican National Committee, the Heritage Foundation, and the old Christian Anti-Communism Crusade.

Given this broad agenda, two caveats are in order, one naturally following the other. First, the document is not without religious content. It laments "the scandal of conflict between Christians [which] obscures the scandal of the cross, thus crippling the one mission of the one Christ," asserts the "infallible Word of God," affirms that "Evangelicals and Catholics are brothers and sisters in Christ," and acknowledges that "unity and love among Christians is an integral part of our missionary witness to the Lord whom we serve."[10] It also calls proselytizing (Protestants seeking to convert Catholics and vice versa) "neither theologically legitimate nor a prudent use of resources." But this is not the central thrust of *Together*. The religious content of the document comes at the beginning and the end, sandwiching the centrality of the political focus.

Second, because there is religious content in the document (content that argues that Catholics and Baptists are both part of one invisible Church) the participation of Southern Baptist leaders Land and Lewis in this political document touched off a firestorm of criticism among theological conservatives both elite and rank and file (again, see fig. 7.1). A Southern Baptist medical doctor placed on the Internet a critique of *Together*, arguing that the accord was "ambiguous and overly ambitious." Though sharing the conservative political views of the signers, this Southern Baptist layman thinks the article is nevertheless politically and theologically weak. If it had been a political document only, he argues, it would have been acceptable had it gone a step further. "[T]he most obvious absence is the homosexual agenda . . . one trusts this is an oversight and not a subtle acquiescence to a vocal and aggressive pressure group," he writes.[11] As for the political sections, the conservative faction apologist is not impressed:

> The document pretends to have found common ground between Roman Catholics and Evangelicals when in actuality it appears that all that has been found is that both oppose abortion and pornography. . . . For Roman Catholics and Southern Baptists to march in pro-life rallies and to protest abortion together does not require that either change or compromise doctrine or theology. . . . The most powerful alliance for influencing of the general society with the message of Christ is not a *political* alliance, it is the alliance of the message of the Gospel ministered through a changed life. [Emphasis mine][12]

In a paper released soon after the storm of criticism hit, CLC director Land again argued that readers should focus on the political nature of the document:

> [W]hile listing agreement on social issues such as being for religious liberty, the sanctity of human life, the reaffirmation of family and church in society, and being against abortion, euthanasia, pornography and racism, the document lists serious *theological* disagreements. [Emphasis mine][13]

Presbyterian J. I. Packer, one of the harshest critics of Roman Catholic theology and the most prolific living writer on Protestant Reformation theology, in "Why I Signed It," turns to political arguments. Packer writes that he liked the treatise because it "declares war on anti-Christian statism and specifies social values that must be fought for . . . grassroots 'co-belligerence' is its theme. . . . It identifies common enemies and pleads that the counterattack be cooperative."[14]

By early 1994, less than one year after the release of *Together*, Land and Lewis were back peddling, signing a statement of clarification in January authored by half a dozen Protestants and assuring fellow Southern Baptists once again, in March 1994, that "[it] was not and is not primarily a theological document, it is an attempt to consolidate the influence of Catholics and evangelicals on the most serious moral and social concerns of our day."[15]

The straw that broke the back of *Together* for the SBC was the decision of ninety-five Hispanic Baptist leaders in Texas (who are the focus of SBC mission work among Roman Catholics) to oppose the document, calling it "theologically flawed." In attempting to convert Catholics, the Baptist pastors were having the accord's proselytizing clause quoted to them by prospective converts.[16] In mid-1995, Land and Lewis removed their names from *Together*. Colson thanked them nevertheless for "seeking unity in the church . . . and defending the truth in today's relativistic culture."[17]

The rise and fall of Baptist participation in *Together* is illustrative of current political views in the convention. Most would agree with the Internet physician that Baptist political alliances are acceptable, but not if they sacrifice theology. Land believes that his codenominationalists have missed the forest for the trees, however, in refusing to cement an impressive political alliance of religious conservatives through which to fight the common liberal enemy in the culture war.

Religious Alliance: Conservative Baptists, Black and White

If the short-lived alliance of the Southern Baptists with the Roman Catholics was a *political* alliance with a strong *religious* element, the rapport of 1995 with African American Baptists is a *religious* alliance with a strong *political* element (see fig. 7.2). As with the Roman Catholics (whom Baptists have considered an enemy for three hundred years) Southern Baptists led by Land's CLC are seeking to patch things with black Baptists, a group alienated for almost as long with Southern Baptists.

Immediately after the 1994 Southern Baptist Convention in Orlando, Florida, leaders of African American Southern Baptists and the Christian Life Commission began to discuss the need for dealing with the race issue in the upcoming sesquicentennial convention. This led to a May 22,

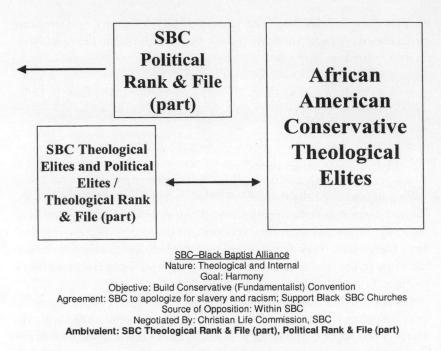

SBC
Political
Rank & File
(part)

SBC Theological
Elites and Political
Elites /
Theological Rank
& File (part)

African
American
Conservative
Theological
Elites

SBC–Black Baptist Alliance
Nature: Theological and Internal
Goal: Harmony
Objective: Build Conservative (Fundamentalist) Convention
Agreement: SBC to apologize for slavery and racism; Support Black SBC Churches
Source of Opposition: Within SBC
Negotiated By: Christian Life Commission, SBC
Ambivalent: SBC Theological Rank & File (part), Political Rank & File (part)

Figure 7.2. Southern Baptist and African American Religious Cooperation

1995, meeting at Christian Life Commission headquarters in Nashville, Tennessee.[18] Cohosted by Land and black Southern Baptist Convention vice-president Gary Frost (pastor of the Rising Star Baptist Church in Youngstown, Ohio), the meeting of fourteen black and white Southern Baptists produced a resolution that was presented to the 1995 convention. Though it received some opposition, the resolution was adopted overwhelmingly on June 19, 1995, in Atlanta.[19]

As in the Catholic pact, the opposition that the statement generated was not with "out" groups, but within the ranks of the SBC. In this case, with the reversal of elements (see fig. 7.2), the conservative theological elements supported the Southern Baptist–black Baptist alliance while conservative political elements opposed it. But similar to the Catholic pact and unlike previous ecumenical and interracial pow-wows of the moderate faction, the common ground was *conservatism*, in this case theological conservatism.

Perhaps the most controversial element of the resolution on race was the linking of modern racism with chattel slavery. According to the Baptist Press, one African American participant in the meeting was particularly pleased with this "new thing" that connected the two. The clause in the resolution read in part:

> [W]e lament and repudiate historical acts of evil such as slavery from which we continue to reap a bitter harvest, and we recognize that the racism which yet plagues our culture today is inextricably tied to the past; and . . . we apologize to all African Americans for condoning and/or perpetuating individual and systemic racism in our lifetime; and we genuinely repent of racism of which we have been guilty, whether consciously (Psalm 19:13) or unconsciously (Leviticus 4:7). [20]

These references aroused Southern Baptist political conservatives. Wes Pruden, an Arkansas native, a self-proclaimed Southern Baptist, and editor of the conservative *Washington Times* newspaper, poked fun at his fellow Baptists in a column entitled "When the Baptists Freed Their Slaves." Echoing the concern of many liberals, Pruden argued that "preachers easily make fools of themselves when they venture into politics." Sounding like a separatist, Pruden wrote that "if a man is authentically called to the noblest task of all, to preach the Gospel of Jesus Christ, he's poaching on God's time if he descends into the political arena." To Pruden this issue was clear. The resolution "condescends to blacks and panders to neurotics and history illiterates."

The reason for the strategy in Pruden's mind is because Southern Baptist growth "has subsided in recent years and there is a concern about how to retrieve the momentum." Seeming to point directly at Land, Pruden wrote: "Bureaucrats everywhere, in government or out, are always on the scout for more turf. The euphemism for this is 'opening the door wider to evangelizing among blacks and other ethnic groups.'"[21] (To be fair, the SBC has gained so much African American Baptist turf already that the Convention recently surpassed the black Progressive National Baptist Convention in number of African American majority churches.)[22]

Except for accusing the Southern Baptists of "political correctness," the conservative *Washington Times* editor echoes the cynical concerns printed in the editorial pages of many moderate newspapers and commentators, that Southern Baptist leaders will say anything to lure members.[23] African American columnist Carl Rowan misunderstands as well, thinking Southern Baptist support for affirmative action and race-based scholarships are in the offing.[24] Both miss the point.

This resolution, like the Catholic pact sponsored by the new conservative leadership, actually goes farther than earlier efforts (in this case the racial resolution of 1968) that provided ammunition for the conservative takeover (see chapter 2). This did not escape one conservative member of the committee that drafted the resolution, who acknowledged the danger on the floor but told the Baptist Press: "This is not the same convention we were in 1968." Another commission member said the difference between the 1968 and 1995 racial resolutions is that the rank and file "trust" the Christian Life Commission now.[25]

What we have then, is a classic case of "only Nixon could go to China" syndrome or "only Reagan could go to Moscow" principle. The Southern Baptist Convention pastors and delegates (the theological conservatives) and some political conservatives (see fig. 7.2) *trust* the Christian Life Commission to deal with racial problems properly. This trust is built on the militant stands the CLC takes on other issues and the hard right political agenda it has begun to push—an agenda which dwarfs ad hoc pacts with blacks and Catholics (see chapter 6).

In 1964, recalls a moderate faction CLC executive director, President Johnson called a CLC group together in the White House Rose Garden to tell them that "no group of Christians has a greater responsibility in civil rights than Southern Baptists. Your people are part of the power structure in many communities. Their attitudes are confirmed or changed by the sermons you preach and by the lessons you write and by the examples you set."[26] By 1968, the Johnson program was in place, but the advice of the father of the Great Society had gone unheeded by most Southern Baptists. In 1995, a much stronger resolution passed much more easily. Part of the reason was due to changing times. But the smooth passage is also due to the belief of rank and file Southern Baptists that the call for racial apology was coming from fellow political conservatives. The situation is reminiscent of the story told about the follower of the man we will call Evangelist Jones. A church member approached a follower of Jones and the following conversation took place.

> "I hear they are going to move Stone Mountain."
> "That's ridiculous. Stone Mountain can't be moved!" was the indignant retort.
> "*Evangelist Jones* says they're going to move it," the first parishioner responded.
> Without batting an eye the follower then replied, "Wonder where they're gonna put it."

Often the receptiveness to the message depends on the messenger. Moreover, we should not overlook the following:

1. The resolution also contained elements reflecting the very conservative political and religious common ground black and white Southern Baptists shared, for example: "We affirm the Bible's teaching that every human life is sacred," and "proclaiming that the Gospel of our Lord Jesus Christ is the only sufficient ground upon which redeemed persons will stand together in restored family union as joint-heirs with Christ."[27] African American historian John Hope Franklin told *Time* magazine shortly after announcement of the pact that it seemed natural to him that Southern Baptists and blacks "share . . . a very strong belief in fundamentalism."[28]

2. The day following the adoption of the apology, a resolution was adopted opposing the nomination of Dr. Henry Foster, an African American, as surgeon general, an act not without certain racial overtones. But several black Southern Baptists, including Rickey Armstrong, pastor of Central Baptist Church in Syracuse, New York, were among the harshest critics of the Clinton administration for the nomination. Armstrong opposed Foster even though both are black:

> Are black Christians so intense in their efforts to refute racism that they overlook obvious violations of sound biblical teachings? . . . Is the practice of abortion, even if it is performed under the conditions of Dr. Foster's rhetoric (safe, legal, rare), morally right?[29]

This statement, and the Christian Life Commission's dissemination of it certainly, seems consistent with efforts to build on the theological alliance with a black-white Southern Baptist conservative *political* alliance. It also seems to indicate that the racial "deal" enacted in the SBC seems a bit different than the attempts at racial unity of other denominations.

The SBC maintains separate black and white churches for the most part, particularly in the South. Also, the black SBC pastors are more conservative. Some mainline churches have attempted strategies similar to that of interracial Oakhurst Presbyterian Church in Decatur, Georgia, where the white minister wears an African sash with his traditional robe, the music is mostly black gospel, and the sanctuary's stained glass windows include both a black and a white Jesus.[30] Such has not been the case in the SBC, as the Convention has targeted more traditional, conservative African Americans.

3. Newly elected Oklahoma congressman J. C. Watts, one of two African American Republican Congressmen, who represents a district that is 84 percent white, is a Southern Baptist minister. Watts said in the CLC newsletter, *Light:* "I don't want to be a black leader. . . . I want to be a leader, period."[31] Watts has proven to be a conservative leader already, voting for virtually every item in the Contract with America, including a vote for an amendment that would have made deeper cuts in funding for the National Endowment for the Arts (the amendment failed as Republicans divided 152–75).

Conclusion

Recent Southern Baptist pacts with blacks and Catholics have been designed to keep conservatives together, to allow them to huddle and fight with unity as "co-belligerents" in the culture war on the side of the conservative bloc. The strategy is a wise one but will face internal challenges. Only time will tell if the new conservative faction can do what the moderate faction could not do on its watch: move the SBC out of its shell and to alliances with strangers who share similar goals. If this is accomplished by a conservative regime, another paradox will appear: a conservative crusade for ecumenism.

8

Conclusion
Baptist Republicanism, Southern Conservatism, and American Politics

As the Baptist South Goes . . .

Is there a link between Bapticity and Republicanism in *American* politics? That is not a simple question to answer, but there are a number of religious forces at work in *Southern* politics that have national ramifications, and Southern religion is inevitably Baptist influenced.

As table 8.1 shows, the first Clinton-Gore ticket was unpopular among white Southerners in general. Given the percentage the Democratic candidates received in each Southern state and voter registration statistics by race, white support can be calculated by state. This is determined by multiplying *composition* by *cohesion*. If percentage of those voting who are black is multiplied by their cohesion (assumed at 90 percent), and if this figure is subtracted from the total, we have the white portion of the Clinton-Gore vote. When this figure is then divided by the percentage of those voting who are white, we have the portion of the white population supporting the Democratic ticket. Our results show that by state, between 53 percent and 79 percent of Southern whites voted *against* Bill Clinton and Albert Gore in 1992. In 1996, the range was 50 percent to 76 percent. Clinton-Gore received 40 percent of the white vote in Gore's home state of Tennessee in 1992 (42 percent in 1996) and 47 percent in Clinton's home state of Arkansas (50 percent in 1996). Only with the strong support of the black community was the Clinton-Gore ticket able to win the electoral votes of Arkansas, Louisiana, Georgia (1992), Tennessee, Missouri, Kentucky, and Florida (1996).

This anti-Clinton statistic, the *not*-Clinton vote, which was the sum of Republican and Perot support, showed white Southerners to be strongly opposed to the agenda of white Southern Baptist Bill Clinton.

TABLE 8.1
The SBC and the GOP, 1980–1994

Southern State	Black Reg %	Black Dem't Cohesion (estimated)	Black Contrib to Clinton (calculated)	White Reg %	White Dem't Cohesion	White Contrib to Clinton	Total Clinton %	1992 White Vote Anti-Clinton	1996 White Vote Anti-Clinton	%SBC in State	% SBC Growth 1980–1990	% GOP Congress 1996	% GOP Congress 1980	1980–1996 Change
SC	28%	90%	25%	72%	21%	15%	40%	79%	72%	33%	8%	63%	63%	0%
MS	26%	90%	23%	74%	24%	18%	41%	76%	76%	47%	9%	71%	43%	28%
LA	25%	90%	23%	75%	31%	24%	46%	69%	66%	23%	9%	56%	20%	36%
AL	22%	90%	20%	78%	27%	21%	41%	73%	70%	40%	7%	56%	44%	12%
GA	22%	90%	20%	78%	31%	24%	44%	69%	69%	30%	10%	69%	17%	52%
NC	19%	90%	17%	81%	32%	26%	43%	68%	66%	26%	5%	57%	46%	11%
VA	17%	90%	15%	83%	31%	26%	41%	69%	61%	14%	3%	46%	91%	-45%
TN	14%	90%	13%	86%	40%	34%	47%	60%	58%	30%	7%	64%	40%	24%
AR	14%	90%	13%	86%	47%	40%	53%	53%	50%	29%	12%	50%	33%	17%
FL	11%	90%	10%	89%	33%	29%	39%	67%	56%	10%	19%	64%	29%	35%
TX	11%	90%	10%	89%	30%	27%	37%	70%	69%	20%	14%	50%	23%	27%
MO	9%	90%	8%	91%	39%	36%	44%	61%	53%	16%	5%	55%	42%	13%
KY	6%	90%	5%	94%	42%	40%	45%	58%	55%	26%	5%	75%	33%	42%
OK	6%	90%	5%	94%	30%	29%	34%	70%	62%	30%	13%	100%	25%	75%

Source: *Statistical Abstract of the U.S.*, 1981–82, table 799, p. 488, table 791, p. 484; *Statistical Abstract of the U.S.*, 1993, table 457, p. 285;
CQ Weekly Report, 12 November 1994, 3301; SBC Historical Commission; America Votes; AllPolitics-CNN-Time Exit Polls.

In 1992, South Carolina led the Deep South in anti-Clinton vote, with Mississippi close behind. The two states traded places in 1996. In the Peripheral South, Texas led, followed closely by Virginia and North Carolina. In the Border region (for our purposes, Missouri, Kentucky, and Oklahoma), Oklahoma diverged from the other two, giving a higher level of opposition to the Democratic ticket. Table 8.1 also shows the growth of the Southern Baptist Convention, by state, from 1980 to 1990 and the growth in Republican members of Congress by state from 1980 to 1996.

As table 8.2 indicates, there is some degree of concomitant change in these statistics. The states that are among the strongest in the anti-Clinton vote—Mississippi, South Carolina, Alabama, and Georgia—are the most Southern Baptist. Of the five fastest *growing* Southern Baptist states—Florida, Texas, Oklahoma, Arkansas, and Georgia—three (Oklahoma, Florida, and Georgia) have the most Republican Southern congressional delegations in 1997. The same three have the fastest-growing Southern Republican delegations.

Southern Surge in Republican Congresses

On the elite level, Southern, Republican, and Southern Baptist influence have grown hand in hand as well. One method for assessing Baptist Republican strength among Southerners is to analyze whom they send to Congress. An interesting comparison in that regard are the 1997–98 Congress and the last Congress controlled by the Republicans, the 83rd

TABLE 8.2

The SBC and the GOP, 1980–1996 (Rank Order)

1996 % Anti-Clinton			1990 % SBC			1980–1990 % SBC Growth			1996 % GOP in Congress			1980–1996 % GOP Growth		
RANK	STATE	%	RANK	STATE	%	RANK	STATE	%	RANK	STATE	%	RANK	STATE	%
1	MS	76%	1	MS	47%	1	FL	19%	1	OK	100%	1	OK	75%
2	SC	72%	2	AL	40%	2	TX	14%	2	KY	75%	2	GA	52%
3	AL	70%	3	SC	33%	3	OK	13%	3	MS	71%	3	KY	42%
4	TX	69%	4	GA	30%	4	AR	12%	4	GA	69%	4	LA	38%
4	GA	69%	5	OK	30%	5	GA	10%	5	TN	64%	5	FL	35%
5	LA	66%	5	TN	30%				5	FL	64%			

Note: Boxes indicate SBC-GOP commonalities.
Source: Data compiled by the author from sources listed in table 8.1.

(1953–54). With demographic and political changes, the Congresses are dramatically different in geopartisan composition. As figure 8.1 shows, Republicans have since 1953–54 moved from holding nine Southern seats in the entire Congress to holding a majority. But as table 8.3 shows, in the intervening years demographics have helped the South as well. In the forty-four years since Republicans last ran Capitol Hill, the South has gained seventeen seats due to reapportionment, making it the largest single regional block, a position long enjoyed by the Midwest. The Northeast, conversely, has lost twenty-seven seats, losing 10 percent of its number in Congress.

In terms of caucus, the 1953–54 Democratic caucus was dominated by the South, with 52 percent of all Democratic seats. The Midwest control over the Republican party was almost as complete, with 43 percent. In the 1997–98 Congress, the South provides the largest bloc in the GOP but has lost half of its strength in the Democratic caucus. The Midwest is now second to the South for Republicans. The effect of the 1996 elections was dramatic. The Northeast, though small, in 1997 replaced the South as the largest regional bloc among Democrats. The South replaced the West in 1997 as the region with the greatest Republican majority. In the 1953–54 Republican Congress, every region was Republican except the South. In 1997–98, the South leads in congressional Republicanism.

Baptist Surge in Congress

Though Southern Baptists got a late start in partisan politics,[1] the denomination has become much more likely to see its members go to

TABLE 8.3
Republican Congresses by Region

1997–1998 CONGRESS (105th)						
Region	Democrats	Republicans	Congress	Democrats	Republicans	Congress
Northeast	59%	41%	96	28%	17%	22%
Midwest	49%	51%	108	26%	24%	25%
South	39%	61%	137	**26%**	**37%**	**32%**
West	46%	54%	93	21%	22%	21%
			434	203	231	434

1953–1954 Congress (83rd)						
Region	Democrats	Republicans	Congress	Democrats	Republicans	Congress
Northeast	36%	64%	123	21%	36%	28%
Midwest	29%	71%	133	18%	**43%**	**31%**
South	92%	8%	120	**52%**	5%	28%
West	33%	67%	57	9%	17%	13%
			433	211	222	433

Source: *Congressional Quarterly Weekly Reports; AllPolitics.*

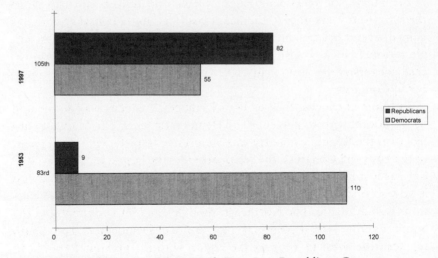

Figure 8.1. Republican Growth in South Since Last Republican Congress

Congress. Our research shows most Protestant denominations, whether in terms of the South or the nation as a whole, have seen the percentage of members decrease over the last thirty years. Much of this is due to the growth of Roman Catholic, Jewish, and to some degree Mormon membership.

Across the South, we see a slight increase in Lutheran and Presbyterian influence, with the Church of Christ and Baptists off slightly and

TABLE 8.4
Denominational Rankings in Congress

	South		United States	
	1963	1995	1963	1995
1	Methodist	Baptist	Methodist	Baptist
2	Baptist	Presbyterian	Presbyterian	Methodist
3	Presbyterian	Methodist	Baptist	Presbyterian

Source: *Congressional Quarterly Weekly Report,* 4 January 1963, 18 January 1975, 5 January 1985; *Almanac of World Politics,* 1996–97.

Methodists down by 12 percent. Nationwide, the trend is similar, but here Baptists show the only Protestant increase while Methodists, Presbyterians, Episcopalians, and the Church of Christ have lost ground.

In terms of change in ranking among Protestants, Methodists dominated the South and the nation in the 1960s Congresses. Baptists have now taken over the top slot regionally and nationally. In the South, Presbyterians have moved to the second slot, leaving Methodists at the bottom. In the nation as a whole, Methodists have slipped as well, but only to second place. Perhaps it is no coincidence that moderate Methodists dominated the moderate Congresses of the 1960s, and that in the conservative 1980s and 1990s conservative Baptists have taken over.

Consistent with the other trends we have tracked, we find that Baptists in Southern congressional delegations and in the Congress as a whole have become much more Republican. As shown in table 8.5, Baptist senators and representatives in the South are now 59 percent Republican, up from 3 percent in 1963. In the decade of the 1990s, for the first time a larger percentage of Southern Baptist members of Congress are Republican than Baptist non-Southerners. Perhaps this is because a larger portion of Baptists come from the less Republican North than before. The percentage of congressional Southern Baptists has dropped from 75 percent of Southerners to only 61 percent in thirty years.

In terms of race, while the several black Baptist denominations are quite strong in the South, most African American members of Congress from the South are *not* Baptist but members of the African Methodist Episcopal (AME) Church. Congressional Baptists are numerous in the Northern delegations, however, where Baptists now make up a majority of Northern black members of Congress.

Another revealing analysis goes one step further, tracking Southern Baptist congressional representation *by state*. As table 8.6 shows, some states have consistently sent Baptists to Congress, particularly Ken-

TABLE 8.5

Southern Baptists in Congress by Party and Region

	South		United States				
	D	R	D	R	S	NS	n
1963	97%	3%	80%	20%	75%	25%	60
1975	78%	22%	73%	27%	73%	27%	56
1985	66%	34%	65%	35%	59%	41%	49
1995	41%	59%	49%	51%	61%	39%	67

Note: D = Democrat; R = Republican; S = SC, MS, LA, AL, GA, NC, VA, TN, AR, FL, TX, MO, KY, OK; NS = all other states; n = number.
Source: Congressional Quarterly Weekly Reports, 4 January 1963, 18 January 1975, 5 January 1985; Almanac of World Politics, 1996–97.

TABLE 8.6

States with Most Southern Baptists in Congress

	1963	1975	1985	1995
1	SC	KY	KY	KY
2	AR	NC	NC	OK
3	KY	MS	MS	AL
4	GA	GA	GA	MS

Source: *Congressional Quarterly Weekly Reports,*
4 January 1963, 18 January 1975; Almanac of World
Politics, 1996–97.

tucky, Georgia, Mississippi, and, to some extent, North Carolina. In the 1995–96 Congress, Southern Baptist and Republican Mississippi, and somewhat Southern Baptist and Republican Kentucky led in Baptist presence. The very Southern Baptist and Republican Alabama, and the growing Southern Baptist and Republican Oklahoma, make first appearances.

The South has voted more Republican in presidential and congressional politics in the strong or growing Southern Baptist areas. As Southern influence in Congress has grown, Republican and Baptist strength has grown accordingly. As stated in chapter 1, the SBC is certainly well represented in the new Republican leadership; Gingrich, DeLay, Lott, Thurmond, and Helms are all Southern Baptists. When one includes President Clinton, Vice-President Gore, Minority Leader Gephardt, and Minority Whip Wendell Ford are added, few elected executive or congressional leaders are left who are not SBC. But Baptist and Southern influence is not always only an institutional matter. A more ephemeral Southern Bapticity, and what it contributes to American politics, is important as well.

Lost Moderation: The SBC and the USA

In the face of the dramatic changes in the Southern Baptist Convention in the last twenty-five years, the moderate faction, though out of power, has not been without a voice. As we saw in chapter 3, these loyal SBC critics have created a presence, producing a newspaper, staffing a seminary, holding an annual meeting, and operating a publishing house.[2]

One moderate faction critic argues that recent changes in SBC life stem from a broad, universal withdrawal from *moderation*, both *theological* and *political*. This notion is consistent with our findings. Former SBC official Grady Cothen writes that from 1890 to 1965 (or as we argue in chapter 2, from 1968), "the moderate leaders showed the ability to divert the energies of the denomination from the growing problems to evangelism and missions. The rise of astute fundamentalist leaders . . . created increasing problems. These people were unwilling to settle for the centrist theology that had dominated the convention from the beginning."[3]

The rub is this: after decades of moderate (and conservative) refusal to upset the SBC apple cart for the sake of preserving the ultimate goal of evangelism, an immoderate attitude began to develop, and a militant conservative faction started to mobilize. This conservative mobilization, as explained elsewhere in this book, was in effect the creation of a second party (faction). But the creation of an alternative faction involved the generation of heated controversy. "Peace," or a lowering of shrill voices, encouraged a continuation of "one-party" moderate faction policies and control, which, in Cothen's opinion, kept the Convention focusing on the ultimate goal of evangelism. For Cothen, the conservative disruption was personally upsetting. The centrism he promulgated was a Convention-saving goal, not a milquetoast strategy for bureaucratic survival. The Convention was evangelistic and growing, with few theological liberals calling the SBC home in 1979. Moderate apologists are both very careful to tie their theology and politics to that of *Baptists* in a general sense (not always to *Southern Baptists*). They argue that from the very beginning, the Baptist idea was to band together for one purpose: to support missions. The theology or politics of each member of that cooperative was never to be an issue. Personal theology was to be left to the individual's conscience. Politics was not a matter for the church to address.

All this began to change in the late 1960s, coming to a head in 1979 with the conservative takeover. But the conservative faction (party) platform was not all *theology*. The battleground was clearly religion *and* politics. The theological issue was the inerrancy of scripture, while the original political issues were women's rights, abortion, and prayer in the public schools. To conservative faction leader Paige Patterson, the specific issues, and whether they were political or theological, made little difference. He was in effect forming a party and developing a strategy, an attitude that would win the battle for the hearts and minds of those in the pew. Patterson, always brazen about his goals and methods, told the *[Oklahoma] Baptist Messenger* early in the controversy that "the Convention's actual posture is far more conservative than most of its leadership on social and moral issues. . . . I think [abortion will] go over nearly as well as the Inerrancy thing."[4]

As with inerrancy, Patterson found in abortion a hot-button issue. To this would soon be added many more pressure points, including homosexuality and even national defense. As table 8.7 indicates, if Patterson's goal was to reach the grass roots and energize conservatives there, he chose an effective strategy. Members of the Southern Baptist rank and file, even in the moderate faction stronghold of North Carolina (whose responses to such issues appear in table 8.7), were much more conservative than other Protestants on a smorgasbord of theological and political issues from which Patterson could choose. One observer even argued that political issues were *more* important in the takeover, writing that "the tragedy of the Southern Baptist Convention is the result of a purely political and social conspiracy that still masquerades as a religious movement."[5] Using issues such as these, the conservative faction was able to alarm the masses, seize the convention presidency, and run the agencies of the denomination through its boards.

The Patterson strategy—to draw sharp lines of demarcation, to present ideas in stark liberal-conservative terms, to mix religion and politics, and to use loaded symbolic issues—reflects the Southern (and perhaps even Southern Baptist) contribution to American politics. In some sense, however, it is difficult to separate the chicken from the egg. According to one authority, the "spirit of politics [was] infused into every corner of American life" in this era, and the rise of what we call a "two-party" South/Convention made opposing "the system" legitimate. The "system" could take the form of the one-party moderate faction Southern

TABLE 8.7
Southern Baptists and Social Issues

Question	All Respondents	Southern Protestants	Southern Baptists
Believe more should be spent on welfare	24%	26%	15%
Believe more should be spent on defense	29%	31%	38%
Believe premarital sex is always wrong	45%	43%	63%
Believe homosexuality is always wrong	74%	76%	90%
Believe abortion is always wrong	31%	23%	33%
Believe that they have been born again	57%	56%	87%
Believe that the Bible is the literal word of God	55%	52%	65%
Believe they share same relig faith as community	53%	61%	64%

Source: Compiled by author from 1988 Values & Beliefs Study, UNC-Chapel Hill.

Baptist Convention system, or the one-party Southern courthouse Democrat system. SBC analyst Arthur Farnsley argues that there was a "parallel between southern populism, southern democracy, and SBC polity. . . . [T]he development of a genuine Republican party presence came at roughly the same time as the advent of competing-interest politics in the SBC. In both the SBC and the broader south, opposing the establishment and the bureaucracy of 'good old boys' on principle became morally and politically legitimate [and] respectable."[6]

Farnsley perhaps overstates the matter in giving the SBC conservative faction/conservative (Republican) bloc credit for "opposing 'good ole boys' on principle." The "principle" of Patterson was the "Southern strategy" of Goldwater, Nixon, and Reagan-Bush, using emotional issues to paint an unmistakable picture for Southern whites of the choice they faced in order to pry them from moderate (Democratic) allegiance.

The best explanation of this tactic is found in the writings of Earl Black and Merle Black in describing the methods of Republican strategist Lee Atwater. Atwater used symbolic issues to show conservative Southern Democratic and independent (swing white) voters that they really belonged with the Republicans. Atwater and the Republicans had been forced to undertake this strategy because, without any sizable percentage of the black vote in their column, they needed to win super-majorities of the white vote, the entire white vote—working class, middle class, and upper class—to win elections. With Republicans sure to vote Republican and most Democrats voting Democratic, Republicans were faced with the need to energize (shock?) independents and conservative Democrats (swing whites) to provide the margin of victory against a black-white Democratic coalition. As we have said before, whereas 1950s one-party Democratic conservatism discouraged militant interchange in a *hushed* defense of the status quo, Republican two-party conservatism is militant and *shrill*. Once wedded to this strategy, only militancy and no-holds-barred Atwateresque politics can maximize the white vote to the extent necessary to win elections for the Republicans.

The 1988 presidential campaign is perhaps the best recent example of the Southern strategy on a grand scale. It is remembered for flag burning, the pledge of allegiance, the ACLU, and Willie Horton.[7] Using these symbols, Michael Dukakis was branded by Atwater with the L-word and Bush went on to win the South commandingly and the North convincingly.

Black and Black show the Republicans' skill at unifying working-class white conservatives with middle-class white conservatives for electoral majorities. The alternative is to allow the Democrats to pit the two classes of whites against one another, and attract working-class whites for themselves. The successful Republican merging of different types of conservatism, defined by unifying classes and dividing races, raises a number of questions about modern Southern and American politics—*old* questions.

In some sense, the modern era of Southern politics is not so different from the first era of dramatic change in the New South. In the 1890s, the moderate ex-Confederates, the "marble men" who restored native white rule, were passing off the scene and a new generation was rising. Politics was middle-of-the-road. Opportunities for the African American presented during Reconstruction had been withdrawn, but racism was of a passive, paternalistic type. The upper classes ruled, and sharecroppers had a government run for them.

Then came the new generation.

- In South Carolina the new practitioner came in the form of "Pitch-fork Ben" Tillman. Elected governor in 1890, he led the state in adopting a segregationist constitution. Two years later, Tillman unseated former Confederate general Wade Hampton for U.S. Senate.
- In Arkansas, the demagogic Jeff Davis, spewing racial division, was elected governor in 1901.
- Times were equally grim in Mississippi, where LeRoy Percy faced the most notorious race-baiter of them all, "The Great White Chief," James K. Vardaman. William Alexander Percy's classic memoir, *Lanterns on the Levee*, gives an eloquent and stirring account of this campaign. Percy describes his father's defeat of Vardaman in a special election for U.S. Senate in the Mississippi legislature, only to lose the seat to Vardaman in 1911.

To Percy, Vardaman was "a top-notch medicine man" whose "oratory was bastard emotionalism and raven-tressed rant," stood for all which his father "considered vulgar and dangerous." Of his rhetoric, Percy said that "[Vardaman's] inability to reason was so contagious, it was impossible to determine where his idealism ended and his demagoguery began . . . he had charm and a gift for the reckless phrase."[8]

But the real danger, Percy felt, was that the voters fell for the Vardaman show and the "issues" he popularized. Again, the eyewitness is worth quoting verbatim:

> Father's stand on current legislation . . . held no interest. . . . They were eager to learn if Father was a member of any church, if he hunted on Sunday, if his house was painted, if he had Negro servants, if Mother was a Catholic. . . . [I]t was not a world of honor; it was a new-born, golden age of demagoguery, the age of rabble-rousers and fire-eaters, of Jeff Davis, and Tillman, and Blease, and Heflin, of proletarian representatives of the proletariat . . . an old man wet with tobacco juice and furtive-eyed summed up the result: 'Wal, the bottom rail's on top and it's gwiner stay thar.'[9]

Percy states in narrative sense what W. J. Cash said in a book published in the same year by the same publisher: "The strictly aristocratic type of man tended to vanish from Southern politics after the nineties."[10] A new type of politics was taking shape, one that would be documented and so despised by V. O. Key. It was one-party Southern politics, where true discussion of the issues seldom took place and primaries were won by showmen with mediocre minds. In this world, Percy's "bottom rail" stirred the emotions of a restricted, ignorant electorate. Poor whites were manipulated by paranoid whites of the Black Belt South and by labor organizers and agrarian demagogues who gained a toehold from time to time in the late nineteenth- and early twentieth-century South.

The politics of that era supposedly died with the arrival of a progressive, two-party era, never to rise again. But is that so? Will the new domination of the Republican party, which is consistently winning a majority of the white vote, even in state legislative elections, signal a return to a form of one-party politics? Could it be that the symbolic, immoderate, anti-intellectual, emotional one-party politics of Lee Atwater and Paige Patterson is not so dissimilar from that of the one-party white primaries of Blease or Bilbo?

In this brief comparison of two eras in Southern politics, at least a couple of elements are missing, however. In the latter part of the first one-party era, Southern Baptist Convention conservatism changed from demagogic to the do-nothing, "what injustice?" variety. It became, in effect, *moderate*, silent. "Don't rock the boat." In the modern, one-party Republican South, the SBC has ended its fence sitting and has taken a proactive turn, boldly interjecting its religion into politics. In *this* one-party era in the South, conservatives have an agenda. Now religion and politics *do* mix; indeed, they are fused. According to religion scholar George Marsden, this turn was taken when the moderate consensus simply broke down and the Republicans began to reap the benefits.

> In the face of growing pluralism and moral inclusivism, which became increasingly the trademarks of the Democratic party, one significant wing of Republicanism recovered the ideals of building a consensus around a militant, broadly Christian, anti-secularist and anti-communist heritage. As the end of the twentieth century approaches, this view of the essence of the American consensus conflicts sharply with a more inclusivist moral vision.[11]

The new one-party South, its conservatism, its new form of anti-intellectualism, and its mixing of religion and politics are also illustrated quite accurately in the words of another Mississippian named Percy. William Alexander Percy's nephew, Walker Percy, until his death in 1990, was a physician who became a novelist. The younger Percy, like his uncle, had a great feel for Southern life. In writing *The Last Gentleman* in 1966, Percy could already see the South changing into a fundamentalist Republican Eden. Percy's protagonist in the novel, returning to the region after many years away, finds:

The South he had come home to was different from the South he left. It was happy, victorious, Christian, rich, patriotic, and Republican. . . .

They had a history, they had a place redolent with memories, they had good conversation, they believed in God and defended the Constitution and they were getting rich in the bargain. . . . As he pressed even farther South . . . he passed more and more cars which had Confederate plates on the frontbumper and plastic Christs on the dashboard. Radio programs became more patriotic and more religious. More than once Dizzy Dean interrupted his sportscast to urge the listener to go to the church or synagogue of his choice. "You'll find it a rich and rewarding experience," said Diz. Several times a day he heard a patriotic program called "Lifeline" which praised God, attacked the United States government, and advertised beans and corn.[12]

A number of works, from novelists like the Percys to political scientists like the Blacks, have explored the Southern factor in American life. John Egerton's *The Americanization of Dixie: The Southernization of America*[13] argued that with the end of segregation and the post-World War II boom in economic development, the South was becoming like the rest of the United States. The nation as a whole, in turn, with politics taking on the shrill characteristics just described, began to manifest Southern characteristics. (There are some positive aspects to the book as well. To Egerton's list one can easily add such cultural phenomena as country music and stock car racing, Southern phenomena that are now sweeping the country.)[14]

Similar treatments abound. Michael Lind and others argue that as the Northeastern wing of the Republican party began to atrophy and the Southern wing began to dominate, Federalist-Whig Republicanism became Southern Bourbon-Populist Republicanism. As soon as Southern influence began to take hold in the Nixon and Reagan eras, Republican platforms and campaign themes switched from fiscal responsibility to tax cuts, from strong central government to devolution of powers to the states, and from a progressive policy on the race issue to using race as a wedge. Belief in fair wages and national infrastructure building shifted to an anti-labor, low government service mentality. Belief in party-centered campaigns became personality/money-centered politics. With a rising anti-intellectualism and opposition to public education, thoughtful fiscal debate gave way to anti-intellectual "culture war" rhetoric. Lind writes: "The Southernization of Republican philosophy has done more than transform a once-moderate Republican positions on the economy and race. The politics of 'culture war,' adopted now by mainstream conservatives and neoconservatives as well as the far right, is, like so much else in the GOP, a transplant from the poisoned soil of the Bourbon South."[15]

Lind and those like him seem to make good points, particularly on the types of issues that have taken over the agenda of modern American politics. But his conclusions are a bit reductionistic. For example, his assertion that politics has become candidate centered and that Southerners are to blame seems only half correct. In fact, McGovern-Fraser Commission reforms, a more influential media, the advent of political action committees, and the rise of the primary system have been the true death knell of strong parties and the source of candidate-centered politics.[16] But the willingness of candidates to separate themselves from the pack by attempting the personally outrageous surely seems Talmadge-like. As for campaign strategies and issues, it is indeed hard to picture Lee Atwater in a stiff shirt on the porch at Plymouth Notch, Vermont, calmly planning Coolidge '24, telling him never to attack his opponent and to keep Wall Street happy. Lind's blaming of Rush Limbaugh for Southern-style politics is also a bit misplaced. But Limbaugh and right-wing radio cannot be ignored in any analysis of Republican resurgence, and the Rush Limbaugh phenomenon has surely taken root in the South. It should also be noted that some of the trademarks of Republicanism in the last quarter of the twentieth century may seem Southern but have distinctly Northern roots. The willingness to revolt against native culture, to remain fundamentalist, and the moralizing "do-gooder" aspects of religion's influence on politics are a part of Northern moralistic culture, not of the traditionalistic South.[17]

In light of our summary of the Patterson Southern Baptist, of the one-party Democratic Vardaman, and of the one-party Republican Atwater, it is tempting to follow the line to its ultimate conclusion. Republicans, Southern Baptists, and the politics of each have surely seemed to cross a number of unmarked lines in the last generation, as was the rule in the era of the Southern demagogue. All mention the unmentionable, ask the unspeakable: "Mr. Percy, is your house painted? Is your wife a Catholic?"

In the modern era this parochialism, associated with the rise of the fundamentalist right, has taken on an obsession with "lists," "scores," "contracts," and "confessions." First, there were the Christian voice scorecards in the early 1980s, and the Christian Coalition voter guides in the late 1980s that rated candidates on "Christian issues." Then "the

Contract with America," state versions of the Contract, "The Contract with the American Family," and a revival of interest in the "Baptist Faith and Message." As in Southern Baptist politics of late, there is no gray area in any of these documents.

"Did you sign the Contract?"

"Did you vote against any item in it once elected?"

"Do you believe in inerrancy?"

"Do you hold to the Baptist Faith and Message?"

The issues and the strategy of the scorecards and contracts again are not passive and Brahamin, but populist and Southern: term limits, welfare reform, property-tax cut, local-government spending limits, balanced-budget amendments, "right to carry" handgun legislation, legal reform, truth in sentencing, school choice, anti-pornography, anti-government funding for the arts, and victim's rights—all designed to maximize the white and fundamentalist vote (depending on the venue), just as inerrancy is designed to maximize the vote for conservative faction SBC presidential candidates.

A reporter in South Carolina asked Bob Dole and Phil Gramm their opinions of the Confederate battle flag flying atop the South Carolina statehouse because the reporter knew that in the 1996 South Carolina Republican primary campaign it was an important political issue. The SBC goes after the Masonic Lodge, and after Walt Disney. The complicated issues of gun control and abortion, each allowing for positions in between all and nothing, mean little in this one-party Republican conservative atmosphere.

In religion as in politics, Southernness is concerned with the emotional, the black-white, the yes-no. In this manipulation of class and racial divisions, lower- and middle-class Republicanism has developed, turning Southern and American politics on its head. Similarly, traditional fundamentalist conservatism, in the Southern Baptist psyche from the days of the Convention founding, has taken hold, bludgeoning the moderate faction into submission—a submission felt everywhere but in the White House.

Conclusions

Baptist Republicanism has developed through a complicated history. A South shut off from the rest of the nation by geography and the peculiar institution of slavery generated a special brand of cultural conservatism. Out of that soil, a uniquely democratic, loosely organized denomination with a simple revivalist message grew from sect to cultural dominance. Incorporating defeat and millennialism into its theology and into the culture it began to dominate, and hearing few challenging voices, the church began to thrive in a state of centrist calm, even in the face of social turmoil and divisive attempts at politicization.

But after truly rejoining the nation in the aftermath of the First World War, by the time of the Second the church felt its hold on its native culture begin to slip. As federal authority expanded the electorate, the church incorporated another political defeat into its worldview. But this time, with the end of one-party timidity, the Convention and the culture were presented with a choice of political homes. Each began to yield to the immoderate rhetoric of organized partisan conservatism, rejecting one-party Democratic centrism in favor of two-party Republican militancy. The defeat of one of their own in 1976 (Jimmy Carter) brought a final, resolute closure to the old era, and reaction became the rule.

With an increasingly secular culture closing in, church members first went on the defensive, then on the offensive, drawing the church ever closer to its more sectlike, movement-oriented fundamentalist brethren.

As of this writing, much like in the South or perhaps in the whole nation, the rank-and-file parishioner in the pew is more moderate than the leadership elite. As for that leadership, unlike its separatist and movement brethren, its fundamentalism is emerging in the belief that the church can make one last desperate play for cultural dominance through growth and treaties with like-minded conservatives. The rank and file, though ambivalent to these goals, seem supportive of cooperative efforts denominationally, trusting the new conservative political elites to do the right thing. As for extra-convention political elites, the rank and file continue to send a goodly number of their members to Congress nationally. Though faced with a slow start in the early part of the century, it is difficult to imagine a time when more Southern Baptists were in positions of national leadership than in the present. More Baptists, more Southerners, more Republicans in power have converged, all benefiting the SBC.

It is all the more unique how the Southern Baptist Convention conservative leadership and the Republican congressional leadership stand at a similar political juncture. After years of serving as the restless loyal opposers, each is now struggling with governance. The Republicans organized the House and Senate in 1995, the former after a long interval of forty years. The conservative faction's unchallenged control over Convention affairs was truly consummated only in 1990 with the de facto withdrawal of the moderate faction into the Cooperative Baptist Fellowship and the realization of conservative majorities on each Convention board. The mobilization for politics through the Christian Life Commission began shortly afterward.

In the inauguration of their respective regimes, the conservative elites of the Republican Congress and the conservative SBC leadership moved equally quickly and in similar style. The GOP leadership purged the Congress of numerous standing committees, renamed other committees, fired officers of the House, and changed numerous policies and procedures. In like fashion, the conservative SBC has approved a plan to eliminate a number of agencies and to rename others, has defunded one agency, fired and forcibly retired agency heads, purged seminary faculties, and has created the position of convention CEO.

Similarities also abound in the realm of ideas. In the heartland, polls show that support for Gingrich has been mixed, his personal popularity low but his policies receiving a reception consistent with the respondent's ideology. Support for the Convention leadership is of a policy nature as well, but conservatives seem divided among themselves on some proposals. Unlike the congressional leadership that must face the entire *electorate* every *two* years, the SBC leadership faces *representatives* of member churches *every* year. (Customarily, a new SBC president takes office every two years—a one-year term with traditional reelection for a second.) The appointment of the Speaker of the House is by election of the House. The appointment of the head of the Christian Life Commission is· by the board of that organization appointed by the Convention's president. Much like the Republican Congress, all seem likely to continue in office into the near future.

What then, is the future of Baptist Republicanism? Based on the research discussed in the last seven chapters, its seems that for Baptist Republicanism to survive and remain conservative, it must survive several potential dangers. In this sense, these dangers are somewhat generic. That is, they are the same for the SBC conservative leadership and the conservative bloc (Republican) electoral coalition. The terms are interchangeable.

1. Conservatives are dangerously close to becoming isolated theologically/politically from the rank and file. Part of the reason for the conservative resurgence was due to a feeling of alienation of the mass from

the theology/politics of the leadership. This ideological alienation created a receptive audience for the siren calls of movement conservatives. For example, the SBC's CLC director, who invited the editor of *Playboy* to address the group in 1970, helped create the alienation that subdivided moderate power. In the realm of the national government, Lyndon Johnson's Great Society, and the programs pushed by former Speaker Tom Foley similarly gave rise to the conservative era as a countermeasure. The enemies of one side can grab momentum by the excesses of the other.

2. As with all conservatives, extremists can be dangerous. Conservatives win using symbolic or emotional issues to keep the right and attract enough of the middle to win electoral majorities. This opens the door to reactionary themes that may frighten the centrists (liberal Republicans, pastors of large urban churches, the sizable moderate SBC political rank and file) into the camp of the other side. The rise of Promise Keepers in the SBC and the Buchananesque America First crusade in the GOP are popular, but neither portion must take over the whole. The attempts of the Dole-Kemp ticket to moderate its 1996 convention indicates Republicans are sensitive to this. The SBC is all over the map, apologizing for slavery one year and boycotting Mickey Mouse the next.

3. Conservatives alliances can prove to be damaging. If perceived as too willing to make deals and form alliances with theological/political strangers, conservative leaders could easily find themselves discredited in the eyes of their respective "true believing" powerbase. Had CLC director Land insisted on standing by the Catholic accord, or if Speaker Gingrich were to alienate a branch of the GOP by making a deal with the president on an issue such as campaign finance reform, for example, the Republican coalition would be endangered. Alliances are equally problematic on the starboard side. The right must be kept together; the John Birch Society may not like the Heritage Foundation or Bob Jones may shrink from those who flirted with a Catholic pact.

4. Conservatives' rhetoric can go too far. The Paige Patterson/Lee Atwater "beat 'em up" rhetoric of outsiders wanting to be in could wear thin coming from those who are now in. This is of course a tightrope walk, for conservatives require periodic red meat. The rank and file will nevertheless expect a bit of gravity from their leaders. Judging from the 1996 elections, conservative leaders appear willing and able to present such a face, but time will tell.

5. Conservative egos may come into conflict. The SBC and the GOP will be embarrassed if they are seen as going in opposite directions. The SBC embarrassed itself as well as Presidents George Bush and Ronald Reagan by censuring them in resolutions in the same conventions in which they spoke. Perhaps disagreements over the appointment of an ambassador to the Vatican and over White House astrology cannot be ameliorated, but without coordination of some type, there will be future public relations problems for all concerned. The Christian Life Commission in particular will be under the microscope for years to come as it attempts to sell its agenda to the politicians and its own people.

6. The organization must appear successful. The rank and file must feel that the struggle they have endured and the animosity they have undertaken on behalf of truth, justice, and the SBC leadership has paid off in real change. Should Newt Gingrich or Richard Land merely rearrange the deck chairs, the activists may find other causes to champion. George Bush, without Lee Atwater, was unable to rekindle conservative fire; mediocre leadership in the SBC will be a setback, freezing the SBC at the *Emerging* Fundamentalist Right stage.

The chairman of the RNC or the chief executive officer of the executive committee of the SBC might well be advised to review the last several pages as a policy memorandum rather than abstract political science. The conservative takeover artists of the SBC and the GOP have been adept at calculating the moods of their respective constituencies and adjusting their strategies to them. But they have been less effective at calculating the impact of their rhetoric in the world outside their power bases. It is certain that confidential dialogue would have been preferable to the public outbursts about strategy that took place. (Goldwater planned to "hunt where the ducks are," Paul Pressler intended to "go for the jugular," and Bailey Smith said that God didn't hear Jewish prayers; but certainly each would have happily taken back those words if given the opportunity.)[18]

The conservative movement began in the decade of the 1960s, and it has progressed steadily. But it was both unable to nominate a movement candidate and complete its dominance of the American political system in 1996. The Southern Baptist Convention is in hard right hands even at state levels in many cases. Remaining holdout states are increasingly unable to stem the tide. To plot the future for each is akin to attempting to plot the future of the Republican party at the time of McKinley, or to foresee the future of Protestantism at the height of the Reformation. Though a Democrat sits in the White House, the last year of his first term was dominated by an agenda that was essentially Republican conservatism, and Republicans have elected and reelected a Congress after a forty-year drought. The GOP also dominates state legislatures and governors' mansions. And, after the 1980s and 1990s, an elite network is in place; grass-roots organizing continues, even among the Emerging Fundamentalist Right SBC. Clinton himself, his acknowledged campaign skills notwithstanding, has done less to discourage the conservative bloc and more to motivate them for future battle.

But what of the future? While on the campaign trail in the South, as his presidential campaign stalled, Texas Republican Senator Phil Gramm admitted to his audiences that he trailed in the polls because "I make a poor first impression." The Georgian-turned Texan told them how his wife turned down his first two or three marriage proposals, the response to the first being a simple "Yuk." But, Gramm assured his supporters, his campaign would gain steam, because as the now Mrs. Phil Gramm would testify, though the first impression was poor, after many years of marriage she can truly say that he "wears well."

What is the nature of the conservative resurgence in the Southern Baptist Convention, in the South, and in American politics? Will the new conservative era continue, or is a Democratic-moderate realignment emerging on the horizon? This hesitant observer would lean toward the former. But the deeper question is not unlike the one raised so quaintly by Phil Gramm: regardless of first impression, how well will Baptist Republicanism *wear*? What will be the next step for Baptist Republicanism?

Postmodern Christian Politics?

New strength is often the product of adversity. By that standard, with Bill Clinton in the White House, Baptist Republicanism has become steel belted. There is new ammunition daily for the big guns of the fundamentalist right. The Clinton administration provides daily outrages to stir the conservative masses. A President Dole would never have generated the kind of galvanizing energy. Therefore, the failure to win the White House hasn't left the entire fundamentalist right discouraged. Out of the 1996 defeat has arisen a new, "postmodern" view of Christians in politics. In the postmodern stage, all players shift. The Emerging Fundamentalist Right turns the Movement Fundamentalist Right, and the Movement Fundamentalist Right turns away, finding there is greater fulfillment in rediscovering the Christian gospel than in working doggedly for political power. At least that is one possible path.

As emerging fundamentalist Southern Baptists begin to dabble in education issues, family issues, or even anti-abortion (though the battleground is shifting away from that issue), they begin "backing themselves into" the Movement Right. A leader in rounding up these reluctant activists is Christian psychologist and author James Dobson. He is attractive to Southern Baptists on the edge of Movement activity. Dobson is educated, smooth, even urbane, and has shown an impressive capacity to energize yuppie Republican Southern Baptists, painlessly shifting them from Emerging to Movement status overnight. Dobson communicates his message through his radio programs, his books, and three organizations: the religious Focus on the Family, the political Family Research Council, and the grass-roots state Family Councils. Some Southern Baptists will follow Dobson. Others will take "conventional" channels, setting up Christian Life Commissions in their states and congregations to fight local battles. "Emerging" no more.

But what follows Movement politics? Some are never "cured" of activism once bitten, of course. Others, fed up with internal Republican party struggles and continual warfare against big government and big culture of the progressive bloc, may go underground (as the trend toward home schooling might suggest). Others simply return to a full-time focus on the task assigned over 2,000 years ago: "*Go Ye . . . and preach the gospel.*" (Based on this resurgence, some fundamentalist right leaders even predict a great national spiritual revival not seen in fifty years will take place in the next decade. Back they go to the revivalism that spawned them in the wake of D. L. Moody, and everything old is new again.)

Still others are seeking to reaffirm Christian manhood with rally-style methods, based on the political rally model, to supplement their church activities. These male Promise Keepers, men who fill football stadia and resolve to display Christian manhood, have built the fastest-growing "para-church" organization in Protestant Christianity. Though under fire for its men-only policy, the organization is devoted to making men what they should be by focusing on seven promises derived from scripture and making themselves accountable to each other for adherence to them. Most of the promises reinforce conservative Christian principles and thereby have (like D. L. Moody) a unique, indirect conservative political force.

But whether Baptist Republicanism focuses on conservative politics, home schooling, rallies for manhood, rearing families, soul winning, or a combination of the above, one thing is certain: the SBC is less and less ambivalent about its core identity. It is a large, complex structure with a rock-ribbed conservative agenda certain to have a major impact on the larger American culture. And its capacity to achieve defined goals is growing.

Over the span of two decades, the Southern Baptist conservative faction has increasingly gained organizational sophistication and leadership skills and developed new weapons forged in the heat of battle. To be sure, they have also suffered wounds, some self-inflicted, and the emergence of Baptist Republicanism has at times been slow and irregular. But the general historic pattern has been growth rather than recession.

In a democracy, after all, the final point to be emphasized is numerical. The SBC is an organization that is both theologically and politically conservative (that is to say, its members know who they are). But we must not forget that they are also fifteen million strong. A group that large and that cohesive is fully capable of influencing the national dialogue in significant ways. For the foreseeable future, we can be confident that the moral agenda will remain a staple of Southern and American politics.

The culture war, therefore, is far from over. Arguably it is just beginning, and its outcome will define (or redefine) the nature of the country. Whatever the outcome, the Southern Baptists will be major combatants in the moral struggle for a long time to come.

Appendices

Appendix A: Questions from the South Carolina State Policy Survey, 1990

Question 11: First, some people are interested in state political issues here in South Carolina, while others aren't that interested. How about you? Would you say you are very interested, somewhat interested, or not too interested in political issues in South Carolina?

Question 16: Do you think that abortion should be legal under any circumstances, legal only under certain circumstances, or illegal in all circumstances?

Question 56: Generally speaking, when you think about national politics, and presidential elections, do you usually think of yourself as a Republican, a Democrat, or what?

  IF REPUBLICAN: Would you call yourself a strong Republican or a not very strong Republican?

  IF DEMOCRAT: Would you call yourself a strong Democrat or a not very strong Democrat?

  IF INDEPENDENT OR NO PREFERENCE, OR OTHER: Do you think of yourself as closer to the Republican or to the Democratic party?

Question 58: What is your religion, if any? (Probe: Is it Protestant, Catholic, Jewish, some other religion, or no religion?)

Appendix B: Questions from Research Survey by First Impressions, August 4–5, 1994

Question 1: First, as you know, the Republican primary for governor has three candidates. As of today, are you planning to vote for David Beasley, Tommy Hartnett, or Arthur Ravenel?

Question 2: With what religious denomination are you affiliated?

Question 3: How often do you attend church (every week, almost every week, a few times a year, seldom, or never)?

Question 4: What term best describes you (fundamentalist, evangelical, charismatic, mainline, or something else)?

Appendix C: Questions from the American National Election Study Center for Political Studies, University of Michigan, 1968, 1972, 1976, 1980, 1984, 1988, 1992

Is your religious preference Protestant, Roman Catholic, Jewish, or something else?

IF PROTESTANT: What church or denomination is that?

IF BAPTIST: Is that So. Baptist or something else?

Generally speaking, do you think of yourself as a Republican, a Democrat, an Independent, or what?

Would you call yourself a strong Republican or a not very strong Republican?

Some people don't pay much attention to political campaigns. How about you? Would you say that you have been very much interested, somewhat interested, or not much interested in the political campaign so far this year?

If you were going to vote, whom do you think you would vote for in the election for president? (Probe: We all know the election is some time away and that people are not certain at this point whom they might vote for. Still, whom do you think you would vote for in the election for president?)

Whom did you vote for in the election for president?

There has been some discussion about abortion during recent years. Which one of the opinions on this page best agrees with your view? You can just tell me the number of the opinion you choose.

1. By law, abortion should never be permitted.
2. The law should permit abortion only in case of rape, incest, or when the woman's life is in danger.
3. The law should permit abortion for reasons *other than* rape, incest, or danger to the woman's life, but only after the need for the abortion has been clearly established.

4. By law, a woman should always be able to obtain an abortion as a matter of personal choice.

Do you go to religious services every week, almost every week, once or twice a month, a few times a year, or never?

1992 ONLY: Which one of these words best describes your kind of Christianity: *fundamentalist, evangelical, charismatic or spirit-filled, moderate to liberal?*

Appendix D: *The SBC Controversy, a Chronology, 1961–1997*

1961. Ralph Elliot, a professor at Midwestern Baptist Theological Seminary in Kansas City, Missouri, publishes with the SBC Broadman Press *The Message of Genesis.* The commentary on the first book of the Bible suggests that it cannot be attributed to a particular author and that the book depends on oral traditions.

1962. The Southern Baptist Convention in San Francisco reaffirms infallibility of the Bible, and appoints a committee to redraft the SBC statement of faith adopted in 1925 in the midst of the modernist-fundamentalist controversy during the Scopes-trial era. The convention turns the Elliot issue over to the board of the seminary. The seminary board orders Elliot to withdraw his planned second edition with another publisher, Elliot refuses, is fired for insubordination, and takes an American Baptist Church pastorate in upstate New York.

1963. Southern Baptist Convention in Kansas City adopts the "Baptist Faith and Message," a doctrinal statement declaring that the Bible is "truth without any mixture of error."

1969. Broadman Press publishes *Why I Preach the Bible Is Literally True* by W. A. Criswell, convention president and pastor of the First Baptist Church of Dallas.

Late 1960s. Houston lawyer (later Appeals Court judge) Paul Pressler meets with seminary student (later president of Criswell Biblical Studies Center) Paige Patterson at the Café du Monde in New Orleans. Over café au lait and doughnuts, Pressler and Patterson trade liberal horror stories, and plot to take over the Southern Baptist Convention.

1970. Broadman Press publishes first volume of *The Broadman Bible Commentary*, including a discussion of the Book of Genesis by British scholar G. Henton Davies, which suggests that Abraham might have been mistaken when he thought God wanted him to sacrifice his son Isaac. Before the opening of the annual Southern Baptist Convention meeting in Denver, a conservative conference, entitled "Affirming the Bible," meets. During the convention, presided over by Criswell, a motion by a California delegate for the commentary to be withdrawn and rewritten is passed overwhelmingly. Delegates also criticize the Christian Life Commission seminar held earlier that year in Atlanta, which included a representative of *Playboy* magazine.

1970. First Baptist Church of Dallas votes to establish the Criswell Biblical Studies Center as an alternative to six SBC seminaries.

1971. Conservative leaders establish Mid-America Baptist Seminary in Little Rock. The seminary is soon moved and housed in property near Adrian Rogers's Bellevue Baptist Church in Memphis.

1973. The Baptist Faith and Message Fellowship is formed at First Baptist Church in Atlanta. The Baptist Literature Board and a newsletter, the *Southern Baptist Journal*, edited by Bill Powell, are founded.

1978–1979. Pressler and Patterson speak at rallies in fifteen states on behalf of the conservative agenda.

June 1979. Adrian Rogers, pastor of the Bellevue Baptist Church in Memphis, Tennessee, is elected president of the Southern Baptist Convention in Houston.

June 1980. Bailey Smith, an evangelist from Del City, Oklahoma, is elected president of the Southern Baptist Convention in St. Louis, Missouri. Resolutions are passed opposing abortion and the Equal Rights Amendment.

Fall 1980. At a Republican rally in Dallas, Smith says that God "does not hear the prayer of the Jew."

Late 1980. Cecil Sherman, pastor of the First Baptist Church in Asheville, North Carolina, and seventeen other moderate SBC leaders meet in Gatlinburg, Tennessee, to discuss a fundamentalist takeover. Fundamentalists label this group the "Gatlinburg Gang."

June 1981. Bailey Smith is reelected president of the Southern Baptist Convention in Los Angeles.

June 1982. Jimmy Draper, pastor of the First Baptist Church of Euless, Texas, is elected president of the Southern Baptist Convention in New Orleans.

June 1983. Jimmy Draper is reelected president of the Southern Baptist Convention. Draper is unopposed, which angers Foy Valentine, head of the Christian Life Commission, who vows to organize moderates for 1984.

June 1984. Charles Stanley, pastor of the First Baptist Church of Atlanta is elected president of the Southern Baptist Convention in Kansas City, Missouri.

January 1985. Leaders of the white SBC and the black National Baptist Convention USA note improved relations between their groups.

February 1985. Conservatives fail to eliminate references to ordination of women in Sunday School literature published by the Southern Baptist Sunday School Board.

February 1985. SBC reports that it expects data will show a decline in the number of baptisms that took place during 1984.

April 6, 1985. Fundamentalist Southern Baptists threaten to withdraw financial support from the national SBC unless their candidates are again elected to head the denomination.

April 14, 1985. Presidents of twenty-three state Baptist conventions meet to discuss the dispute between fundamentalists and moderates, expressing concerns over political infighting.

April 21, 1985. Conservatives, led by SBC President Charles Stanley, charge that moderates are covering up a drift toward liberalism in Baptist seminaries and colleges.

April 23, 1985. R. Keith Parks, head of the SBC Foreign Mission Board, announces he will not support the reelection of Dr. Charles Stanley as president of the Convention.

June 10, 1985. Annual Southern Baptist Convention begins in Dallas.

June 11, 1985. Backers of Dr. Charles Stanley claim Billy Graham sends a telegram endorsing their candidate for president of the SBC.

June 13, 1985. Furman University president John E. Johns vows to resist efforts by conservative Baptists to oust liberal professors from the school.

June 13, 1985. Moderates charge fundamentalists with voting irregularities in elections for the leadership of the Southern Baptist Convention. The convention approves creation of a "peace committee" to attempt to resolve tensions; a proposal by the moderate faction to replace the conservative slate of appointees with presidents of state conventions sparks conflict.

June 14, 1985. SBC adjourns in Dallas after electing Dr. Charles Stanley president.

July 20, 1985. Evangelist Billy Graham says his mailgram to Dr. Charles Stanley during the SBC annual meeting was not meant to endorse him for presidency, just to encourage him.

August 3, 1985. Southern Baptist Home Mission Board names the Reverend Janet Fay Fuller as Yale University chaplain.

October 5, 1985. Southern Baptists mark the end of a five-year campaign to boost Sunday School enrollment, with Georgia showing an increase of nearly ten thousand.

November 11, 1985. Dr. Charles Stanley urges membership to pray for upcoming Reagan/Gorbachev summit conference.

January 18, 1986. Stanley says God created AIDS to show his displeasure with homosexuality.

January 23, 1986. Dispute at Wake Forest University and state's Southern Baptists, who founded school.

January 25, 1986. Episcopal bishop of San Francisco criticizes Atlanta Southern Baptist fundamentalist leader Charles Stanley's view that God created AIDS to show his displeasure with the homosexual life-style.

February 2, 1986. Stanley says AIDS is God's "judgment upon sin, not homosexuals."

February 25, 1986. Touring "peace committee" comes to Atlanta with plans to continue efforts to heal the seven-year rift between moderate and conservative factions.

April 5, 1986. Robert Crowder sues Southern Baptist officials, charging they bypassed the church's own rules in overruling the majority at the SBC annual convention on substitution of conservative slate.

April 26, 1986. SBC shows the greatest gain in minority membership among Protestant denominations since 1974.

May 6, 1986. U.S. district judge Robert Hall of Atlanta rules that the First Amendment prevents him from umpiring a dispute over the way Stanley handled SBC's 1985 assembly.

May 8, 1986. Robert Crowder says he will appeal the decision.

May 17, 1986. Gallup Poll finds greater opposition to abortion among Southern Baptists than Catholics.

June 11, 1986. For eighth consecutive year, a fundamentalist is elected SBC president. Dr. Adrian Rogers of Memphis defeats Dr. Winfred Moore of Amarillo, Texas, 54.2 percent to 45.8 percent.

June 12, 1986. Fundamentalists within the SBC are denied an attempt to cut funding for the Baptist Joint Committee for Public Affairs.

July 12, 1986. The vacant presidency of Golden Gate Theological Seminary in Mill Valley, California, is the focus of a fight between fundamentalists and moderates.

August 7, 1986. Fundamentalist trustees of the Home Mission Board force the resignation of its Presidential Search Committee.

August 27, 1986. Jack Harwell keeps his job as editor of the *Christian Index*, the official voice of Georgia Baptists, but the newspaper's board of directors sets up a special "editorial review board" to make sure Harwell's writings conform to recent guidelines.

September 17, 1986. Richard Harmon resigns his position with the Southern Baptist Convention's Home Mission Board.

September 18, 1986. Moderates defeat fundamentalists to take control of the Christian Life Commission, the SBC agency charged with overseeing national political, social, and ethical issues.

September 25, 1986. Southern Baptist conservatives mount an increased attack on the Baptist Joint Committee accusing the agency of focusing on liberal causes.

October 9, 1986. Southern Baptist Home Mission Board votes against women ministers, barring churches from using board money to pay salaries of women pastors.

October 14, 1986. SBC elects the Reverend William Crews president of Golden Gate Seminary. The convention clears G. Temp Sparkman of Midwestern Baptist Theological Seminary of a heresy charge.

November 27, 1986. Mercer University, Macon, Georgia, is ranked among the top ten in *Playboy* magazine's list of the nation's top forty party colleges.

December 6, 1986. SBC Peace Committee comes up with only general proposals on how to end the bitter theological controversy.

December 27, 1986. SBC membership reaches 14.61 million, up 0.9 percent.

January 12, 1987. The *Southern Baptist Advocate* makes a comeback to blast moderates.

January 16, 1987. Moderate seminary dean, N. Larry Baker, is named to head the Christian Life Commission.

February 13, 1987. Southern Baptist moderates announce formation of the Southern Baptist Alliance.

March 14, 1987. Oakhurst Baptist Church of Decatur, Georgia, is the first in the nation to join the Southern Baptist Alliance.

May 16, 1987. Christian Life Commission criticized for its liberal abortion stand.

May 30, 1987. Southern Baptists remain in Baptist Joint Committee on Public Affairs but it is reported that they expect to form another lobby.

June 17, 1987. Dr. Adrian P. Rogers is elected to a second term as president of the SBC in St. Louis, Missouri.

June 27, 1987. The Reverend Bailey Smith, former president of the SBC, publicly reiterates his belief that Jews cannot find salvation without Jesus, renewing a controversy that erupted seven years before.

July 30, 1987. Foreign Missions Board moves against charismatics and divorced persons.

September 24, 1987. Baptist Public Affairs Committee endorses Judge Robert Bork, angering moderates by breaking precedent and endorsing a U.S. Supreme Court nominee. Former SBC executive Porter W. Routh says the endorsement of Bork violates church bylaws.

September 30, 1987. The Reverend Pat Robertson resigns his Southern Baptist ordination in preparation for his presidential campaign.

October 22, 1987. Georgia's Baptist Convention backs Mercer University president R. Kirby Godsey in response to allegations of heresy made by Lee Roberts.

October 23, 1987. The Reverend Nancy Hastings Sehested is called as senior pastor by Prescott Memorial Baptist Church in Memphis. The church is disfellowshipped by the Shelby County Baptist Association.

October 24, 1987. W. Randall Lolley, president of Southeastern Baptist Theological Seminary, and Morris Ashcraft, dean of the faculty, resign in dispute with the fundamentalist faction.

November 12, 1987. Moderate Baptists win elections at conventions in South Carolina, North Carolina, Texas, Louisiana, and Georgia.

February 12, 1988. SBC records its smallest growth in forty-one years.

March 5, 1988. Southern Baptists fire staffer, the Reverend George Sheridan, who said Jews go to heaven.

March 22, 1988. Mercer University president R. Kirby Godsey assails fundamentalists' power.

April 12, 1988. Southern Baptist moderate and conservative trustees disagree on granting tenure to controversial theology professor, Molly Marshall-Green, at Southern Seminary.

May 5, 1988. Southern Baptist leaders consider withdrawing invitation to President Reagan to address its annual convention after reports that Reagan and his wife, Nancy, follow astrology.

May 28, 1988. Decline from (1974–85) in U.S. Sunday School attendance hits all but three groups: Mormons, Baptists, and Assemblies of God.

May 28, 1988. Jack Harwell becomes the editor of a moderate Southern Baptist paper, *SBC Today*.

June 15, 1988. SBC elects conservative president for tenth straight year; the Reverend Jerry Vines of Jacksonville, Florida, defeats the Reverend Richard Jackson by 692 votes out of 32,291 cast.

June 16, 1988. Southern Baptist Alliance agrees to meet in September to weigh its future in the convention.

June 17, 1988. SBC overwhelmingly passes resolution condemning homosexuality as "depraved"; the resolution states that "while God loves the homosexual and offers salvation," homosexuality is "an abomination in the eyes of God."

July 23, 1988. Southern Baptists drop support from Michael Willett, who was scheduled to become a seminary teacher in Venezuela, because of his beliefs.

September 23, 1988. The Christian Life Commission of the SBC decides not to distribute the Surgeon General's report on AIDS because it presents homosexual relations as normal.

September 4, 1988. Southern Baptist Alliance mulls a trust fund as a shelter from fundamentalists.

October 8, 1988. The SBC press service releases a letter considered in violation of IRS tax-exempt rules for being politically biased in favor of Vice-President George Bush.

November 29, 1988. Southern Baptist Alliance hires Stan Hastey as its director and sets up an office in Washington, D.C.

November 30, 1988. Southern Baptist Alliance announces it plans a new seminary.

January 21, 1989. SBC answers that it has no procedure for dismissing trustee Dr. Curtis Caine, who called Dr. Martin Luther King, Jr., a "fraud."

February 18, 1989. Southern Baptist Home Mission Board votes not to support Amy Greene, who plans to start her own inner-city ministry in Atlanta, on the basis that she is a woman.

February 25, 1989. The SBC's executive committee tentatively approves a plan to set up a Washington lobbying office separate from the Baptist Joint Committee.

March 2, 1989. The moderate Southern Baptist Alliance moves toward establishing a theological seminary and becoming a separate denomination from the SBC.

March 11, 1989. Another moderate Baptist group, Baptists Committed to the SBC, is formed as a "resistance movement" against the fundamentalists. The group plans to raise money for moderate causes.

March 15, 1989. Southeastern Seminary in Wake Forest, North Carolina, appoints fundamentalist professor Dr. L. Russ Bush III to be academic vice president and faculty dean.

April 29, 1989. The Southern Baptist Home Mission Board refuses to take part in a national workshop on Christian-Jewish relations because it objects to three Southern Baptist speakers at the workshop.

June 14, 1989. Delegates to the SBC reelect conservative president Jerry Vines.

October 16, 1989. Conservative trustees of Southwestern Baptist Theological Seminary accuse seminary president Russell Dilday of being sympathetic to out-of-favor moderates.

January 27, 1990. Paul D. Simmons of Louisville, Kentucky, is cleared by the Southern Baptist Theological Seminary of charges of teaching students that Jesus Christ was sexually active and may have engaged in homosexual acts.

February 24, 1990. Membership of Southern Baptist churches increases only 0.6 percent in 1989, the second smallest increase since 1936.

June 13, 1990. Conservative Morris Chapman is elected president of the Southern Baptist Convention.

June 15, 1990. About 34,000 of the 38,000 Southern Baptists in New Orleans for their 1990 convention leave before the conference's final day, leaving the convention short of a quorum for conducting business.

June 16, 1990. The fundamentalist camp in the Southern Baptist denomination suggests that dissenters depart from the organization; however, moderate leaders say they will not stage a mass exodus.

July 3, 1990. An official of Jim Edgar's gubernatorial campaign demands that Illinois House Speaker Michael Madigan's press secretary apologize for referring to the Republican candidate's "Southern Baptist conservative mentality" on a public radio broadcast.

July 15, 1990. The virtually all-white SBC launches a campaign to bring four hundred new black congregations to its fold each year.

July 19, 1990. SBC dismisses Al Shackleford and Dan Martin, the two top editors of the convention's news and information service, the Baptist Press (BP).

August 26, 1990. Moderate church leaders choose the Reverend Daniel Vestal of Dunwoody, Georgia, to head a new organization, tentatively called the Cooperative Baptist Fellowship, which is organized to keep their money out of the hands of the conservative leaders of the SBC.

September 22, 1990. Fired Southern Baptist editor Dan Martin is named interim news editor of Associated Baptist Press (APB), an independent news service founded by moderates to report on matters of interest to Baptists.

September 26, 1990. Trustees of Southern Seminary (Louisville, Kentucky) make a literal interpretation of the Bible a condition for future employment, promotion, or tenure at the denomination's oldest seminary.

September 29, 1990. Southern Seminary students gather to discuss the vast differences in beliefs between conservative and moderate factions.

October 21, 1990. The board of trustees at Furman University moves to distance the Baptist-affiliated liberal arts college from doctrinal fighting among Southern Baptists by amending its charter to no longer send nominees for vacant board seats to the South Carolina Baptist Convention for approval.

November 13, 1990. Stetson University, Baptist-affiliated since its founding in 1885, distances itself from the fundamentalist leadership of the SBC, which opposes the university's instruction in evolutionary biology and interpretive theology.

November 17, 1990. The Baptist General Association of Virginia takes half of the state's denominational contributions away from fundamentalist-dominated agencies of the SBC.

November 24, 1990. Southern Baptist state conventions vote overwhelmingly to keep contributing money to the denomination through its Cooperative Program budget, refusing to allow alternative tithing plans.

January 19, 1991. Thomas H. Graves, a former religion professor, is elected president of the Baptist Theological Seminary, a new school being established in Richmond, Virginia, by moderates in the SBC.

February 16, 1991. Membership in the SBC tops the fifteen million mark, fueled in part by the largest increase in baptisms in a decade.

May 9, 1991. Six thousand disaffected SBC members meet in the Omni in Atlanta to form a new Cooperative Baptist Fellowship; some say they view the organization as a liberation movement but many are undecided whether they will declare complete independence from the conservative-controlled SBC.

June 3, 1991. With no major controversial items on the agenda to attract people, attendance at the 1991 SBC in Atlanta drops to twenty thousand from 1990's forty thousand.

June 3, 1991. Former marine lieutenant colonel, Oliver North, calling for prayer in schools and more religious involvement in U.S. politics, receives ovation after ovation from the SBC.

June 4, 1991. Without opposition, fundamentalists retain the presidency of the SBC, taking undisputed control of the nation's largest Protestant denomination. Morris H. Chapman of Wichita Falls, Texas, is reelected easily.

June 5, 1991. One day before he is to address them, the delegates to the SBC rebuke President Bush for his support of the National Endowment for the Arts.

June 6, 1991. Wiping away tears as he recalled praying at Camp David before ordering the start of the Persian Gulf War, President Bush offers a testimony to the annual gathering of the SBC. Bush says his reliance on prayer during the Persian Gulf War relieved him of his Episcopalian worry about "how it looked to others" to pray in public.

November 2, 1991. Paige Patterson, one of the two central strategists in the ascendancy of conservatives to the control of the SBC, is dismissed from the presidency of Dallas's Criswell College by trustees who hold he spent more time on denomination matters than on school matters.

November 11, 1991. Southern Baptist moderates derail fundamentalists and approve Baylor University's attempt to insulate itself from a takeover by the conservative wing of the Baptist General Convention of Texas.

February 23, 1992. Nelson Price, the conservative pastor of the eight-thousand-member Roswell Street Baptist Church in Marietta, Georgia, tells his congregation he will seek the presidency of the SBC at the annual denominational meeting in June.

April 24, 1992. Paige Patterson is nominated president of Southeastern Seminary in Wake Forest, North Carolina, a school that until the mid-1980s was the most moderate of the six Southern Baptist seminaries.

June 5, 1992. Jess Moody, Nelson Price, and H. Edwin Young seek the presidency of the SBC.

June 9, 1992. In a speech to the SBC in Indianapolis that criticizes abortion, homosexual parents, and sex education, Vice-President Dan Quayle portrays the 1992 presidential election campaign as a war between those who hold to traditional values and a cultural elite that mocks families, religion, and patriotism. Quayle says those individuals who criticized him for his comments on the sitcom "Murphy Brown" are elitists and that he "wears their scorn like a badge of honor." After the address, Quayle says that homosexuality is "more a choice" than a matter of biology, but declares that George Bush will not rule out hiring gays for high government posts.

June 10, 1992. The SBC banishes two North Carolina churches for accepting homosexuals and changes its bylaws to mandate the ouster of any church that "acts to affirm, approve or endorse homosexual behavior." The Convention also commissions a year-long study of Freemasonry, as urged by one Baptist who claims the fraternal organization's true purpose is satanic worship.

Southern Baptists also pass resolutions asserting that God is "Father," calling on President Bush to press Kuwait, Saudi Arabia, and Egypt to allow unrestricted Christian worship, cautioning Christians to avoid associating with groups that require secrecy or whose teachings involve mystical knowledge, accusing television networks of promoting immorality and "the moral breakdown in our society," demanding that public schools quit giving out condoms, and supporting a ban on federal funds for experimentation on fetal tissue from spontaneous abortions.

June 14, 1992. Pullen Memorial Baptist Church of Raleigh, North Carolina, is shunned by Southern Baptists for blessing the union of two homosexual men, but mourns its historic expulsion from the Southern Baptist Convention.

July 17, 1992. The 1992 Democratic presidential ticket of Bill Clinton and Al Gore, both of whom are Southern Baptists, is the first such denominational twosome nominated for the nation's top two offices.

Fall 1992. Homosexuality dominates deliberations of the SBC's state associations. Many make it clear that they don't like fellow Baptist Bill Clinton's liberal stance on the issue.

September 15, 1992. After fielding questions about his views on homosexuality, abortion, and women's ordination, and being approved to head the staff of the Georgia Baptist Convention, Gary S. Jones shocks church leaders by turning the job down. Jones declines to serve because he receives only 66 percent of the vote.

October 7, 1992. Analysts examine how the religious factor will play in the 1992 Democratic presidential campaign. One analyst argues that as a part of a new breed of Southern Baptists, both presidential nominee Bill Clinton and his running mate Al Gore are closer to liberal Protestant beliefs than to the SBC.

October 28, 1992. Religious observers suggest that President Bush still commands the affections of a majority of Southern Baptist voters, but that Clinton is getting a boost from his knowledge of "the language of Zion."

November 30, 1992. The Cooperative Baptist Fellowship hires Keith Parks, the SBC's former head of foreign missions, to lead an Atlanta-based independent global missions program.

December 4, 1992. Richard D. Land, a top official of the Southern Baptist Convention Christian Life Commission, asks President-elect Clinton not to name an ambassador to the Vatican.

January 5, 1993. Southern Baptist church leaders plan a campaign to persuade President-elect Clinton to sever diplomatic ties with the Vatican, claiming those ties violate the principle of church-state separation.

January 10, 1993. Beginning his final week in Arkansas, President-elect Bill Clinton bids a tearful farewell to his Southern Baptist church there, crediting it with helping him win the presidency.

January 17, 1993. President-elect Clinton brings pre-inaugural bus tour to Culpeper (Virginia) Baptist Church, asking for God's blessing on the incoming administration, an inaugural tradition.

January 27, 1993. Former president Jimmy Carter declares his support for the fledgling Cooperative Baptist Fellowship.

March 12, 1993. The deacons and pastors of a Georgia church extend an honorary church membership to Paige Patterson after he is denied membership at a church near the Southeastern Seminary campus in North Carolina.

March 17, 1993. Southern Baptists react with a mixture of anger and resignation to the announcement that President Clinton will fill the position of ambassador to the Vatican.

March 17, 1993. After the Home Mission Board studies whether the signet rings and secret handshakes have roots in paganism and the occult, the agency declares that many teachings of the Masonic fraternity are incompatible with Christianity.

March 26, 1993. R. Albert Mohler is elected president of Southern Baptist Theological Seminary in Louisville, Kentucky, in a closed-door trustee meeting near the Atlanta airport.

May 13, 1993. Former president Jimmy Carter officially and publicly declares his support for the Cooperative Baptist Fellowship at the meeting of its third general assembly in Birmingham, Alabama. The assembly draws five thousand registered participants and focuses on social action and missions.

June 1993. Messengers to SBC convention in Houston pass nine resolutions, including a strongly worded resolution calling on President Clinton and Vice-President Gore to "affirm biblical authority in exercising public office" and criticizing their views on homosexuality and abortion. One delegate, referring to the 1992 amendment to the SBC bylaws on homosexaulity, offers a motion to withdraw fellowship from the president and vice-president, another moved that messengers from Clinton's Immanuel Baptist Church in Little Rock not be seated. Delegates from Clinton's church were seated but only after each of the ten appeared before the credentials committee and affirmed his or her opposition to homosexuality. SBC president Ed Young, who stopped the proceedings of the convention to offer a prayer for the president and vice-president, was reelected to a second one-year term.

September 16, 1993. The Reverend Rex Horne, President Clinton's Little Rock pastor; Ed Young, president of the Southern Baptist Convention; and two other Southern Baptist leaders meet with President Clinton and Vice-President Gore to discuss differences over abortion and homosexuality, and to seek common ground. The pastors voiced appreciation for the opportunity to express their views, but did not feel they had changed the president's mind.

October 1, 1993. SBC state conventions release an Evangelism Index, estimating county-by-county numbers and percentages of people who face eternal damnation if they do not recognize Jesus as their savior.

January 1, 1994. Concerned about homosexuals in the military and abortion, the Southern Baptist Convention kicks off a forty-day prayer vigil for President Clinton and Vice-President Gore.

March 9, 1994. Russell H. Dilday, president of Southwestern Baptist Theological Seminary in Fort Worth, Texas, is ousted one day after he was given high marks in a performance review. The firing took place because Dilday refused to take early retirement.

March 10, 1994. Nearly a thousand students at the Southwestern Baptist Theological Seminary gather on the lawn of fired president Russell Dilday's house to show support.

June 14, 1994. Southern Baptist Teenagers plant 103,000 chastity cards at the 137th Annual Southern Baptist Convention. The pledge was part of the SBC teen campaign, "True Love Waits."

June 14, 1994. Though his opponent has the backing of the conservative faction leadership of Orlando, Florida, Jim Henry wins an "upset" victory for the SBC presidency, representing the first loss for the Pressler-Patterson faction since 1978.

June 15, 1994. The Southern Baptist Convention votes 4,730 to 3,342 to reject funds from the Atlanta-based Cooperative Baptist Fellowship.

June 16, 1994. Southern Baptists adopt affirmation of their relationship with Roman Catholics with an internal resolution encouraging "conversation" between the Home Mission Board of the SBC and representatives of the Roman Catholic Church, the first formal endorsement of a dialogue since 1971.

January 1995. Federal prosecutors say that Lewis Nobles, while president of Mississippi Baptist College, skimmed $3 million in donations to the school.

February 1995. Leaders of the SBC ask their 15.4 million members to lobby against the nomination of Henry W. Foster Jr. to be surgeon general.

May 1995. Columbia/HCA Healthcare agrees not to perform elective abortions in its eighteen hospitals and other facilities in the state as part of a sale of Georgia Baptist Hospitals.

June 1995. Charles W. Colson, the former special counsel to President Richard Nixon, addresses the Southern Baptist Pastors' Conference in Atlanta.

June 1995. At its 150th Anniversary Convention, the SBC apologizes to African Americans for racism and slavery. Billy Graham commends its stand.

August 1995. President Clinton speaks on sin to an audience of black Baptists, confessing anger and gluttony to the Progressive National Baptist Convention in Charlotte.

August 1995. By vote of the congregation, Charles Stanley relinquishes his administrative duties at First Baptist Church of Atlanta as he tries to save his marriage.

August 1995. John Killinger sues Baptist-affiliated Samford University for religious discrimination and violation of the conditions of the will that endowed its divinity school. Killinger refused to sign a Baptist statement of faith in 1990.

October 2, 1995. First Baptist Atlanta votes to allow Charles Stanley to remain in the pulpit of the First Baptist Church of Atlanta despite a pending divorce.

October 20, 1995. The Brotherhood organization of the Southern Baptist Convention recruits more than 150 Southern Baptists from Mississippi, Alabama, Louisiana, and Texas as volunteers to complete the Rose of Light Missionary Baptist Church in one of Chicago's poorest African American neighborhoods.

November 10, 1995. Andy Stanley, former preacher at the Dunwoody, Georgia, satellite of the First Baptist Church of Atlanta, says he plans to form a new church in the northern suburbs. Stanley, the son of First Baptist's senior pastor, Charles Stanley, resigns after expressing concern about his father's leadership during his parents' divorce.

November 17, 1995. The Florida Baptist Convention asks its one million members to boycott Walt Disney Company parks and products, saying Disney shows a lack of moral leadership by extending health insurance to the partners of homosexual employees.

November 28, 1996. Herschel Harold Hobbs, a former president of the Southern Baptist Convention and chairman of the committee that wrote the Baptist Faith and Message, dies at the age of eighty-eight.

November 29, 1995. Attorneys for Charles Stanley, the pastor of the First Baptist Church of Atlanta, file papers demanding a jury trial in Stanley's divorce case brought by his wife.

January 16, 1996. President Clinton takes the Martin Luther King Jr. pulpit at Ebenezer Baptist Church in Atlanta to give tribute to the slain civil rights leader and deliver a sermon about the need for racial harmony in the United States.

February 1996. Baylor University, the nation's largest Southern Baptist college, announces its students will be permitted to dance on campus beginning in the spring.

March 17, 1996. Charles Stanley, the pastor of the First Baptist Church of Atlanta, reads a letter to his congregation saying that his wife has withdrawn her divorce petition.

March 28, 1996. SBC leaders denounce supposed efforts by leaders of the Barnetts Creek Baptist Church in Thomasville, Georgia, to disinter the body of a mixed-race baby who was buried the previous week in the church's all-white cemetery. The church abandoned its effort under fierce criticism.

May 26, 1996. The Freedom from Religion Foundation, a 3,500-member organization of atheists, asks Georgia governor Zell Miller to prevent Southern Baptists from "proselytizing" on public property during the 1996 Centennial Olympic Games.

June 11, 1996. Tom Elliff, after being elected president of the Southern Baptist Convention, takes issue with the gay rights policies of the Walt Disney company and argues that the scriptures do not support the ordination of women.

June 12, 1996. The Southern Baptist Convention votes to censure the Walt Disney company for adopting a policy in 1995 of extending health insurance to same-sex partners of employees.

June 12, 1996. The Southern Baptist Convention takes a special collection to benefit the thirty-two predominantly black churches burned across the South.

June 13, 1996. The Southern Baptist Convention adopts a resolution calling for efforts to convert Jews to Christianity and appoints a missionary to undertake such work.

June 1997. Christian Life Commission renamed Ethics and Religious Liberty Commission. Other convention agencies renamed as well.

Appendix E: Resolution on Racial Reconciliation on the 150th Anniversary of the Southern Baptist Convention, 1995

WHEREAS, since its founding in 1845, the Southern Baptist Convention has been an effective instrument of God in missions, evangelism, and social ministry; and

WHEREAS, the Scriptures teach that "Eve is the mother of all living" (Genesis 3:20), and that "God shows no partiality, but in every nation whoever fears him and works righteousness is accepted by him" (Acts 10:34–35), and that God has "made from one blood every nation of men to dwell on the face of the earth" (Acts 17:26); and

WHEREAS, our relationship to African-Americans has been hindered from the beginning by the role that slavery played in the formation of the Southern Baptist Convention; and

WHEREAS, many of our Southern Baptist forbears defended the "right" to own slaves, and either participated in, supported, or acquiesced in the particularly inhumane nature of American slavery; and

WHEREAS, in later years Southern Baptists failed, in many cases, to support, and in some cases opposed, legitimate initiatives to secure the civil rights of African-Americans; and

WHEREAS, racism has led to discrimination, oppression, injustice, and violence, both in the Civil War and throughout the history of our nation; and

WHEREAS, racism has divided the body of Christ and Southern Baptists in particular, and separated us from our African-American brothers and sisters; and

WHEREAS, many of our congregations have intentionally and/or unintentionally excluded African-Americans from worship, membership, and leadership; and

WHEREAS, racism profoundly distorts our understanding of Christian morality, leading some Southern Baptists to believe that racial prejudice and discrimination are compatible with the Gospel; and

WHEREAS, Jesus performed the ministry of reconciliation to restore sinners to a right relationship with the Heavenly Father, and to establish right relations among all human beings, especially within the family of faith.

Therefore, be it RESOLVED, that we, the messengers to the Sesquicentennial meeting of the Southern Baptist Convention, assembled in Atlanta, Georgia, June 20–22, 1995, unwaveringly denounce racism, in all its forms, as deplorable sin; and

Be it further RESOLVED, that we affirm the Bible's teaching that every human life is sacred, and is of equal and immeasurable worth, made in God's image, regardless of race or ethnicity (Genesis 1:27), and that, with respect to salvation through Christ, "There is neither Jew nor Greek, there is neither slave nor free, there is neither male nor female, for (we) are all one in Christ Jesus" (Galatians 3:28); and

Be it further RESOLVED, that we lament and repudiate historic acts of evil such as slavery from which we continue to reap a bitter harvest, and we recognize that the racism which yet plagues our culture today is inextricably tied to the past; and

Be it further RESOLVED, that we apologize to all African-Americans for condoning and/or perpetuating individual and systemic racism in our lifetime; and we genuinely repent of racism of which we have been guilty, whether consciously (Psalm 19:13) or unconsciously (Leviticus 4:27); and

Be it further RESOLVED, that we ask forgiveness from our African-American brothers and sisters, acknowledging that our own healing is at stake; and

Be it further RESOLVED, that we hereby commit ourselves to eradicate racism in all its forms from Southern Baptist life and ministry; and

Be it further RESOLVED, that we commit ourselves to be "doers of the Word" (James 1:22) by pursuing racial reconciliation in all our relationships, especially with our brothers and sisters in Christ (I John 2:6), to the end that our light would so shine before others, "that they may see (our) good works and glorify (our) Father in heaven" (Matthew 5:16); and

Be it finally RESOLVED, that we pledge our commitment to the Great Commission task of making disciples of all peoples (Matthew 28:19), confessing that in the church God is calling together one people from every tribe and nation (Revelation 5:9), and proclaiming that the Gospel of our Lord Jesus Christ is the only certain and sufficient ground upon which redeemed persons will stand together in restored family union as joint-heirs with Christ (Romans 8:17).

Appendix F: Resolution on Disney Company Policy, 1996

WHEREAS, Southern Baptists and their children have for many decades enjoyed and trusted The Disney Company's television programming, feature-length films and theme parks which have reinforced basic American virtues and values; and

WHEREAS, The virtues promoted by Disney have contributed to the development of a generation of Americans who have come toexpect and demand high levels of moral and virtuous leadership from The Disney Company; and

WHEREAS, In recent years, The Disney Company has given the appearance that the promotion of homosexuality is more important than its historic commitment to traditional family values and has taken a direction which is contrary to its previous commitment; and

WHEREAS, In recent years, we have watched the world's largest family entertainment company with growing disappointment as Disney Company's moral leadership has been eroded by a variety of corporate decisions, which have included but are not limited to:

(1) Establishing of an employee policy which accepts and embraces homosexual relationships for the purpose of insurance benefits;

(2) Hosting of homosexual and lesbian theme nights at its parks;

(3) Choosing of a convicted child molester to direct the Disney movie *Powder* through its subsidiary Miramax Productions;

(4) Publishing of a book aimed at teenage homosexuals entitled *Growing Up Gay: From Left Out to Coming Out* through its subsidiary Hyperion, connecting Disney to the promotion of the homosexual agenda;

(5) Producing, through its subsidiary corporations, objectionable material such as the film *Priest* which disparages Christian values and depicts Christian leaders as morally defective;

WHEREAS, These and other corporate decisions and actions represent a significant departure from Disney's family-values image, and a gratuitous insult to Christians and others who have long supported Disney and contributed to its corporate profits; and

WHEREAS, Previous efforts to communicate these concerns to The Disney Company have been fruitless; and

WHEREAS, Boycotts are a legitimate method for communicating moral convictions; Now, therefore,

BE IT RESOLVED, That we as Southern Baptist messengers meeting in annual session on June 11–13, 1996, go on record expressing our deep disappointment for these corporate actions by The Disney Company; and

BE IT FURTHER RESOLVED, That we affirm the employees of The Disney Company who embrace and share our concerns; and

BE IT FURTHER RESOLVED, That we encourage Southern Baptists to give serious and prayerful reconsideration to their purchase and support of Disney products and to boycott Disney Company stores and theme parks if they continue this anti-Christian and antifamily trend; and

BE IT FURTHER RESOLVED, That we encourage the Christian Life Commission to monitor Disney's progress in returning to its previous philosophy of producing enriching family entertainment; and

BE IT FURTHER RESOLVED, That we encourage state Baptist papers and national Southern Baptist publications to assist in informing the Southern Baptist family of these issues; and

FINALLY, BE IT RESOLVED, That the Convention requests the Executive Committee to send a copy of this resolution to Michael Eisner, CEO of The Disney Company, and to encourage the Southern Baptist family to support this resolution with our purchasing power, letters, and influence.

Appendix G: Resolution on Jewish Evangelism, 1996

WHEREAS, Jesus commanded that "repentance and remission of sins should be preached in his name among all nations, beginning at Jerusalem" (Lk. 24:47); and

WHEREAS, Our evangelistic efforts have largely neglected the Jewish people, both at home and abroad; and

WHEREAS, We are indebted to the Jewish people, through whom we have received the Scriptures and our Savior, the Messiah of Israel, and "they are beloved for the sake of the fathers" (Rom. 11:28b); and

WHEREAS, There has been an organized effort on the part of some either to deny that Jewish people need to come to their Messiah, Jesus, to be saved; or to claim, for whatever reason, that Christians have neither right nor obligation to proclaim the gospel to the Jewish people; and

WHEREAS, There is evidence of a growing responsiveness among the Jewish people in some areas of our nation and our world; now, therefore,

BE IT RESOLVED, That we, the messengers of the Southern Baptist Convention, meeting in New Orleans, Louisiana, June 11–13, 1996, reaffirm that we are not ashamed of the gospel of Christ, for it is the power of God unto salvation to every one that believeth; to the Jew first, and also to the Greek (Rom. 1:16); and

BE IT FURTHER RESOLVED, That we recommit ourselves to prayer, especially for the salvation of the Jewish people as well as for the salvation of "every kindred and tongue and people and nation" (Rev. 5:9); and

BE IT FINALLY RESOLVED, That we direct our energies and resources toward the proclamation of the gospel to the Jewish people.

Notes

NOTES TO CHAPTER I

1. Conservative columnist and former Moral Majority official Cal Thomas went so far as to write that "Christianity *is* Politics" (*Fundamentalist Journal*, January 1983, 8).

2. Some of the better international/comparative studies in fundamentalism include Bruce B. Lawrence, *Defenders of God: The Fundamentalist Revolt against the Modern Age* (San Francisco: Harper and Row, 1989); Lawrence Kaplan, *Fundamentalism in Comparative Perspective* (Amherst: University of Massachusetts Press, 1992), and Bronislaw Miztal, ed., *Religion and Politics in Comparative Perspective: A Revival of Religious Fundamentalism in East and West* (Westport, Conn.: Praeger, 1992).

3. A number of sources on party politics and religion are cited elsewhere, but good overall studies include Allen D. Hertzke, *Echoes of Discontent: Jesse Jackson, Pat Robertson, and the Resurgence of Populism* (Washington, D.C.: Congressional Quarterly, 1993); Michael Lienesch, *Redeeming America: Piety and Politics in the New Christian Right* (Chapel Hill: University of North Carolina Press, 1993), and Michael Cromartie, *No Longer Exiles: The Religious New Right in American Politics* (Washington, D.C.: Ethics and Public Policy Center, 1992).

4. Two particularly enlightening studies are Steve Bruce, *The Rise and Fall of the New Christian Right* (New York: Oxford University Press, 1988), and Augustus Cerillo, *Salt and Light: Evangelical Political Thought in Modern America* (Grand Rapids, Mich.: Baker Book House, 1989).

5. These include legal studies such as Rodney A. Smolla, *Jerry Falwell vs. Larry Flint: The First Amendment on Trial* (New York: St. Martin's Press, 1988); more constitutional studies such as Matthew C. Moen and Lowell S. Gustafson, eds., *The Religious Challenge to the State* (Philadelphia: Temple University Press, 1992) and anthologies such as Charles W. Dunn, ed., *American Political Theology: Historical Perspective and Theoretical Analysis* (New York: Praeger, 1984).

6. This field seems to be growing. One of the best is Kathleen Boone, *The Bible Tells Them So: The Discourse of Protestant Fundamentalism* (Albany: SUNY Press, 1989). A densely researched, official statement-oriented approach

is Mark Ellingsen, *The Cutting Edge: How Churches Speak on Social Issues* (Grand Rapids, Mich.: Eerdmans, 1993). Also see David Snowball, *Continuity and Change in the Rhetoric of the Moral Majority* (New York: Praeger, 1991).

7. Though this subfield has not attracted the attention that others have, it has attracted some of the better scholars, with works like Allen D. Hertzke, *Representing God in Washington: The Role of Religious Lobbies in the American Polity* (Knoxville: University of Tennessee Press, 1988); Peter L. Benson and Dorothy L. Williams, *Religion on Capitol Hill: Myths and Realities* (San Francisco: Harper and Row, 1982); and Matthew C. Moen, *The Christian Right and Congress* (Tuscaloosa: University of Alabama Press, 1989).

8. A summary and critique of these early studies can be found at the beginning of chapter 4.

9. I interviewed Michael Brintnall of the American Political Science Association on 11 August 1995. According to Brintnall, the Religion and Politics section of the APSA began in 1987 with 100 members, reaching a high-water mark of 555 in 1991. Current membership is 409. This level of interest among political scientists compares very favorably with the other 31 sections, which average 460 in membership. (Other sections include Comparative Politics, with 1,178 members; Public Administration, with 687 members; History and Politics, with 543 members; Presidency, with 422 members; and Politics and Literature, with 277 members.) A new Christians in Political Science organization, separate from the APSA, has also been founded.

10. Kenneth Wald, *Religion and Politics in the United States* (New York: St. Martin's Press, 1987); Kenneth Wald, Dennis E. Owen, and Samuel S. Hill, Jr., "Churches as Political Communities," *American Political Science Review* 82:531–548.

11. David Leege and Lyman A. Kellstedt, *Rediscovering the Religious Factor in American Politics* (Armonk, N.Y.: M. E. Sharpe, 1993).

12. Andrew M. Greeley, *Religious Change in America* (Cambridge, Mass.: Harvard University Press, 1989).

13. Garry Wills, *Under God: Religion and American Politics* (New York: Touchstone, 1991).

14. Harold Bloom, *The American Religion: The Emergence of a Post-Christian Nation* (New York: Simon and Schuster, 1992).

15. Stephen L. Carter, *The Culture of Disbelief: How American Law and Politics Trivialize Religious Devotion* (New York: Basic Books, 1993).

16. Wills, *Under God*, 18.

17. Lyman A. Kellstedt, John C. Green, James L. Guth, and Corwin E. Smidt, "Religious Voting Blocks in the 1992 Election: The Year of the Evangelical?," paper presented at the Annual Meeting of the American Political Science Association, Washington, D.C., 1–4 September 1993, 18.

18. David C. Leege, "The Decomposition of the Religious Vote," paper pre-

sented at the Annual Meeting of the American Political Science Association, Washington, D.C., 1–4 September 1993.

19. Hertzke, *Echoes of Discontent*.

20. Christopher P. Gilbert et al., "The Religious Roots of Third Party Voting: A Comparison of Perot, Anderson and Wallace Voters," paper presented at the Annual Meeting of the American Political Science Association, New York, September 1994.

21. Lyman A. Kellstedt, John C. Green, James L. Guth, and Corwin E. Smidt. "Tongues of Fire: The Charismatic Movement and American Politics," paper presented at the Annual Meeting of the American Political Science Association, New York, 1–4 September 1994.

22. Southern Baptist Convention Annual, 1993, 109.

23. Ibid., 1986, 81.

24. Will D. Campbell, *The Convention* (Atlanta: Peachtree Publishers, 1988).

25. A pastor at a Charleston, South Carolina, church proclaimed to his congregation that he was proud to be a "wooden-headed conservative." Author's conversation with church member, 20 January 1995.

26. John Lee Eighmy, *Churches in Cultural Captivity: A History of the Social Attitudes of Southern Baptists* (Knoxville: University of Tennessee Press, 1972), ix.

27. Ellen Rosenberg, *The Southern Baptists: A Subculture in Transition* (Knoxville: University of Tennessee Press, 1989), 2–3. As late as 1977, Albert Menendez, in *Religion at the Polls* (Philadelphia: Westminster, 1977), 220, found that though Baptists constitute 14 percent of the population, they form only 11 percent of the Congress. This is in contrast to Episcopalians, who are 2 percent of the population and 12 percent of the Congress; Methodists, who are 5 percent of the population and 16 percent of the Congress; and Presbyterians, who are 2 percent of the population and 12 percent of the Congress. See chapter 7.

28. Rosenberg, *Southern Baptists*, 2–3, 183.

29. Before the fundamentalists took over the Convention, the Christian Life Commission magazine presented a very positive interview with then senator Albert Gore, Jr., of Tennessee (Larry Braidfoot, "Arms Control and Peace: An Interview with Sen. Albert Gore, Jr.," *Light*, October 1985, 1).

30. According to Nancy Ammerman in *Southern Baptists Observed: Changing Perspectives on a Changing Denomination* (Knoxville: University of Tennessee Press, 1993), 4–5, these were the terms invented by the Convention's wire service, the Baptist Press (BP), as compromise terms. This can be very confusing. The title of one moderate book gives the author's preferred nomenclature: Walter B. Shurden, *The Struggle for the Soul of the SBC: The Moderate Response to the Fundamentalist Movement* (Macon, Ga.: Mercer, 1993). Moderate Bill J. Leonard (*God's Last and Only Hope: The Fragmentation of the Southern Bap-*

tist Convention (Grand Rapids, Mich.: Eerdmans, 1990), prefers these terms as well. But the six books by conservative James C. Hefley, beginning with *The Truth in Crisis: The Controversy in the Southern Baptist Convention* (Dallas: Criterion Publications, 1986), use "conservative" and "moderate." Ammerman uses the preferred moderate terms, but suggests that the fundamentalists wanted to move in a "conservative" direction, and often uses the term "progressive" for the moderate group (Ammerman, *Southern Baptists*, 4–5). A survey by the prolific writer Ammerman in *Baptist Battles: Social Change and Religious Conflict in the Southern Baptist Convention* (New Brunswick, N.J.: Rutgers University Press, 1990), 77, indicates that about 10 percent prefer to be called moderate, 10 percent moderate-conservative, 10 percent fundamentalist, 25 percent fundamentalist-conservative, and the rest simply conservative.

31. Jean Miller Schmidt, *Souls or the Social Order: The Two-Party System in American Protestantism* (New York: Carlson, 1991), xiv.

32. James Davison Hunter, *Culture Wars: The Struggle to Define America* (New York: Basic Books, 1991), 306. These terms seem a bit esoteric and would be unrecognizable to members of each bloc, so we have decided to forgo use of them. However, understanding the politics of religion would be incomplete without Hunter.

33. Richard G. Hutcheson, *Mainline Churches and the Evangelicals* (Atlanta: John Knox, 1981), 38. Also, political thinker and Lutheran-turned-Roman-Catholic priest Richard John Neuhaus went so far as to write the article, "Who, Now Will Shape the Meaning of America? The Marriage of Mainline Denominations to the Great Society Caused the Rise of the New Religious Right" (*Christianity Today*, 19 March 1992, 16).

34. Richard Quebedeaux, *The Worldly Evangelicals* (New York: Harper and Row, 1978), passim.

35. To show how far away the SBC and BJU are on the definition of fundamentalist, consider the title of David O. Beale's tract, "The Continuing Battle in the SBC: Are There Fundamentalists in the Southern Baptist Convention?" (Greenville, S.C.: Unusual Publications, 1986). See also Beale's *S.B.C. House on the Sand? Critical Issues for Southern Baptists* (Greenville, S.C.: Unusual Publications, 1985).

36. Nancy Tatom Ammerman's "North American Protestant Fundamentalism," in Martin E. Marty and R. Scott Appleby, eds., *Fundamentalisms Observed* (Chicago: University of Chicago Press, 1991), 29, indicates there was little need for a Southern fundamentalist movement. Martin E. Marty and R. Scott Appleby, eds., *The Glory and the Power: The Fundamentalist Challenge to the Modern World* (Boston: Beacon Press, 1992), 65, list only one Southerner in the fundamentalist top ten. See also George Marsden, *Fundamentalism and American Culture: The Shaping of Twentieth-Century Evangelicalism: 1870–1925* (New York: Oxford University Press, 1982), and William Robert

Glass, "The Development of Northern Patterns of Fundamentalism in the South, 1900–1950," Ph.D. diss., Emory University, 1991.

37. Lawrence, *Defenders*, 14–15, 100–101.

38. Author's interview with Flynn Harrell, February 10, 1994.

39. Shurden, *Struggle for the Soul*, 310.

40. Author's interview with Marion Aldridge, pastor of Greenlawn Baptist Church, Columbia, S.C., July 1993.

41. Shurden, *Struggle for the Soul*, 312, describes the conflicting understandings of the role of the pastor. Martin E. Marty, and R. Scott Appleby, eds., *Glory*, 81, explain the SBC attachment to "bigness" of late.

42. Lawrence, *Defenders*, 15. The media regularly report that SBC attachment to the Bible has diminished little with time, as in "Church Panel Reports Most Baptists Think Adam and Eve Were Real People," *Greenville [S.C.] News*, 13 June 1987, 2.

43. Lawrence, *Defenders*, 7.

44. Ibid., 100–101, 236.

45. Marty and Appleby, *Glory*, 45–68; Lawrence, *Defenders*, 165–169, 182–186.

46. An example of this is the article in a fundamentalist Southern Baptist paper that reacted to the report of a "Peace Commission" ("Peace?? Can There Be Peace While Violations of Our Faith are Called Acceptable?" an unsigned editorial-style article in the Conservative *Southern Baptist Journal* (January–March 1987, 1). George Dollar in *A History of Fundamentalism in America* (Greenville, S.C.: Bob Jones University Press, 1973), appendix, lists in chart form those true fundamentalists (including BJU) under the heading "militant fundamentalists."

47. A version of the women-in-ministry controversy from a moderate point of view is Shirley Radl, *The Invisible Woman: The Target of the Religious New Right* (New York: Delacorte Press, 1983), while "VP's Church Okays Women as Deacons," *Southern Baptist Journal*, February 1983, 12, laments from a conservative point of view the fact that someone in high denominational office would permit women deacons in his church. However, as wire service reporter George W. Cornell's has written, moderate faction Southern Baptists seem to be evening the score ("Ordination Soars among Southern Baptist Women," *The State*, 8 May 1993, 7B).

48. Southern Baptists constantly refer to their "Baptist Life." But often the moderates and the fundamentalists use the same words to mean different things. "Missions" has become a "rallying cry" for the SBC. But "to the fundamentalists, 'missions' means saving souls; to the moderates 'missions' may occasionally involve feeding hungry people and even thinking about changes in social structures that contribute to hunger and sickness" (Rosenberg, *Southern Baptists*, 206).

49. As W. J. Cash wrote in *The Mind of the South* (New York: Alfred A. Knopf, 1941), the typical Southerner does not "think" but "feels." So it is with

Southern Baptist fundamentalists. Similarly, one of the tenets of the failure of Southern politics cited by V. O. Key (*Southern Politics in State and Nation*, New York: Alfred A. Knopf, 1949), was the issueless politics of the South in which a one-party system forced a constrained electorate to focus on "personalities."

50. James Leo Garrett in *Are Southern Baptists "Evangelicals"?* (Macon, Ga.: Mercer University Press, 1983), 111, calls the SBC the country's "strongest evangelical movement." But this was before fundamentalist consolidation. See chapter 2 and Dennis Ray Wiles, "Factors Contributing to the Resurgence of Fundamentalism in the Southern Baptist Convention, 1979–1990," Ph.D. diss., Southwestern Baptist Theological Seminary, 1992.

51. John Shelton Reed, *Surveying the South: Studies in Rural Sociology* (Columbia: University of Missouri Press, 1993), 51–65. On the entire issue of "Southernness," there is no better source than Reed's *The Enduring South: Subcultural Persistence in Mass Society* (Chapel Hill: University of North Carolina Press, 1972), and *Southerners: The Psychology of Sectionalism* (Chapel Hill: University of North Carolina Press, 1983).

52. C. Vann Woodward, *The Burden of Southern History* (New York: Random House, 1960), 3–25.

53. Ibid., 17, and C. Vann Woodward, *Origins of the New South: 1877–1913* (Baton Rouge: Louisiana State University Press, 1957).

54. The best accounts of the travails of the Southern poor white are J. Wayne Flynt, *Dixie's Forgotten People: The South's Poor Whites* (Bloomington: Indiana University Press, 1979), and Gilbert C. Fite, *Cotton Fields No More: Southern Agriculture 1865–1980* (Lexington: University of Kentucky Press, 1984). A good account of the coming economic boom and the slow rise of the region out of poverty is George Brown Tindal's *The Emergence of the New South: 1913–1945* (Baton Rouge: Louisiana State University Press, 1967).

55. Leonard, *God's Last and Only Hope*, 20.

56. V. O. Key, *Southern Politics in State and Nation* (New York: Knopf, 1949), 5. Analyses of the racial politics of this half-century in the South include Harold Stanley's "Race and Realignment," in *The 1984 Election in the South*, ed. Robert P. Steed et al. (New York: Praeger, 1985), and Jack Bass and Walter DeVries, *The Transformation of Southern Politics* (New York: Basic Books, 1976).

57. Leonard, *God's Last and Only Hope*, 20.

58. Earl Black and Merle Black, *Politics and Society in the South* (Cambridge, Mass.: Harvard University Press, 1987), 228–230.

59. Perhaps the best source for understanding the predominance of the English, Scottish, and Irish in the South is David Hackett Fischer's *Albion's Seed: Four British Folkways in America* (New York: Oxford University Press, 1989), 207–418, 605–782.

60. Edward L. Queen, *In the South the Baptists Are the Center of Gravity: Southern Baptists and Social Change, 1930–1980* (New York: Carlson, 1991), 29, 43.

61. Helen Lee Turner, "Fundamentalism in the Southern Baptist Convention: Crystallization of the Millennialist Vision," Ph.D. diss., University of Virginia, 1991. See also Ernest R. Sandeen, *The Roots of Fundamentalism: British and American Millennarianism, 1800–1930* (Chicago: University of Chicago Press, 1970).

62. In addition to Cash's classic treatment of the plight of the Southern working people (*The Mind of the South*, 394–435), there are a number of recent studies of Southern class struggle and the failure of trade unions, including Robert Botsch, *The Politics of the Breathless* (Lexington: University of Kentucky Press, 1993).

63. Charles Reagan Wilson, *Baptized in Blood: The Religion of the Lost Cause* (Athens: University of Georgia Press, 1980), 11.

64. Rosenberg, *Southern Baptists*, 37; Leonard, *God's Last and Only Hope*, 19, 45.

65. Turner, "Fundamentalism," 93.

66. Norman Alexander Yance, *Religion Southern Style* (Danville, Virginia: Association of Baptist Professors of Religion, 1978), 18–23.

67. Turner, "Fundamentalism," 105.

68. Ibid., 120.

69. Ibid.

70. Brooks Hays, *Politics Is My Parish* (Baton Rouge: Louisiana State University Press, 1981), 23.

71. W. Wiley Richards, *Winds of Doctrines: The Origin and Development of Southern Baptist Theology* (Lanham, Md.: University Press of America, 1991), 213.

72. Winthrop Hudson, *Baptists in Transition: Individualism and Christian Responsibility* (Valley Forge, Penn.: Judson Press, 1979), 117.

73. Christian polemicists have gotten in on the act as well: witness evangelical writer Michael B. Smith, "Christians, Democracy: Strange Bedfellows or Blood Relations? Christianity Can Help Cultivate Virtues Essential to Democracy," *World*, 23 November 1991, 7.

74. Because of their democratic spirit, Ellen Rosenberg in *The Southern Baptists: A Subculture in Transition* (Knoxville: University of Tennessee Press, 1989), 2–3, calls Baptists "hyper-Americans." Other sources for Baptist origins include [Congressman] Brooks Hays, and John E. Steely, *The Baptist Way of Life* (Macon, Ga.: Mercer University Press, 1981), 22–27, and Robert A. Baker, *The Southern Baptist Convention and Its People, 1607–1972* (Nashville: Broadman Press, 1974), 15–40. Baptist democracy is described more fully in Leonard, *God's Last and Only Hope*, 81–84.

75. Hudson, *Baptists*, 79–81.

76. Samuel Hill, *Religion and the Solid South* (Nashville: Abingdon, 1972), 24.

77. Jay Reeves, "Lost Souls? Baptists Estimate Half of Alabama Going to Hell," *[Columbia, S.C.] State*, September 18, 1993, 1A.

78. One of the articles in the Christian press addressing this subject is Kim A. Lawton, "Estranged Bedfellows: Are Evangelicals Abandoning the Democratic Party, or Is It Abandoning Them?" *Christianity Today*, 17 August 1992, 40.

79. John Brummett warned his fellow moderate-faction Baptists of this danger in "SBC Seen as Shifting to 'Right-Wing' Republicanism," *Baptists Today*, 6 September 1991, 6. See also Steve Fox, "SBC Tied to the Far Right?" *SBC Today*, October 1988, 7.

80. The important realignment studies include Earl Black and Merle Black, *Politics and Society in the South* (Cambridge, Mass.: Harvard University Press, 1987); Earl Black and Merle Black, *The Vital South: How Presidents Are Elected* (Cambridge, Mass.: Harvard University Press, 1992); James L. Sundquist, *Dynamics of the Party System* (Washington, D.C.: Brookings, 1983), and the still serviceable Kevin P. Phillips, *The Emerging Republican Majority* (New Rochelle, N.Y.: Arlington House, 1969).

81. New Christian Right activism studies, which include discussions of Southern Baptists, include Jerome L. Himmelstein, *To the Right: The Transformation of American Conservatism* (Berkeley: University of California Press, 1990); Robert C. Liebman and Robert Wuthnow, eds., *The New Christian Right: Mobilization and Legitimization* (New York: Aldine, 1983); and the more journalistic Michael D'Antonio, *Fall from Grace: The Failed Crusade of the Christian Right* (New York: Farrar, Straus, Giroux, 1990).

82. These eras are described by Clyde Wilcox in *God's Warriors: The Christian Right in Twentieth-Century America* (Baltimore: Johns Hopkins University Press, 1992), and will be discussed in the next chapter.

NOTES TO CHAPTER 2

1. Phillip E. Hammond, *Religion and Personal Autonomy: The Third Disestablishment in America* (Columbia: University of South Carolina Press, 1992).

2. W. Darrell Overdyke, *The Know Nothing Party in the South* (Baton Rouge: Louisiana State University Press, 1950).

3. Earl Black and Merle Black, *The Vital South: How Presidents Are Elected* (Cambridge, Mass.: Harvard University Press, 1992), 86–90; V. O. Key, *Southern Politics in State and Nation* (New York: Alfred A. Knopf, 1949), 318–329; *A Catholic Runs for President: The Campaign of 1928* (Gloucester, Mass.: P. Smith, 1968).

4. Clyde Wilcox, *God's Warriors: The Christian Right in Twentieth-Century America* (Baltimore: Johns Hopkins University Press, 1992).

5. Ibid.

6. William Wallace Bennett, *The Great Revival in the Southern Armies* (Philadelphia: Claxton, Remsen, and Haffelfinger, 1877); J. William Jones, *Christ in the Camp: Religion in the Confederate Army* (Atlanta: The Martin and Hoyt Co., 1887).

7. Michael Lienesch, *Redeeming America: Piety and Politics in the New Christian Right* (Chapel Hill: University of North Carolina Press, 1993), 4.

8. John Lee Eighmy, *Churches in Cultural Captivity: A History of the Social Attitudes of Southern Baptists* (Knoxville: University of Tennessee Press, 1972), 58.

9. Nancy Tatom Ammerman, *Baptist Battles: Social Change and Religious Conflict in the Southern Baptist Convention* (New Brunswick, N.J.: Rutgers University Press, 1990), 48.

10. Samuel Hill, *Religion and the Solid South* (Nashville: Abingdon, 1972), 24.

11. James Leo Garrett et al., *Are Southern Baptists "Evangelicals"?* (Macon, Ga.: Mercer University Press, 1983), 180.

12. Some have argued that part of the reason for this was the Great Depression that left little time for "bickering"! See W. Wiley Richards, *Winds of Doctrines: The Origin and Development of Southern Baptist Theology* (Lanham, Md.: University Press of America, 1991), 146–147.

13. Samuel S. Hill, "The Story before the Story," in Nancy Tatom Ammerman, ed., *Southern Baptists Observed: Changing Perspectives on a Changing Denomination* (Knoxville: University of Tennessee Press, 1993), 30.

14. James J. Thompson, *Tried as By Fire: Southern Baptists and the Religious Controversies of the 1920s* (Macon, Ga.: Mercer University Press, 1982).

15. Ibid., 76–79, 163.

16. Ibid., 139.

17. Ibid., 139–141; C. Allyn Russell, *Voices of American Fundamentalism: Seven Biographical Studies* (Philadelphia: Westminster Press, 1976); Samuel S. Hill, *Encyclopedia of Religion in the South* (Macon, Ga.: Mercer University Press, 1984), 84, 90, 194.

18. See chapter 1. The newest work on J. Frank Norris is Barry Hankins's *God's Rascal: Frank Norris and the Beginnings of Southern Fundamentalism* (Lexington: University Press of Kentucky, 1996).

19. Garrett et al., *Are Southern Baptists*, 167–168.

20. Thompson, *Tried as by Fire*, 163.

21. Ibid., 164–165.

22. Bible Institute of Los Angeles, *The Fundamentals* (Los Angeles: Bible Institute of Los Angeles, 1917).

23. *Baptist Faith and Message* (Nashville: Sunday School Board, Southern Baptist Convention, 1963).

24. Garrett et al., *Are Southern Baptists*, 180; Jerry Falwell, *Listen America!* (New York: Doubleday), 144.

25. Thompson, *Tried as by Fire*, 101–102.

26. John N. Moore in Marla J. Selvidge, *Fundamentalism Today: What Makes It So Attractive?* (Elgin, Ill.: Brethren Press, 1984), 120.

27. Bruce B. Lawrence, *Defenders of God: The Fundamentalist Revolt against the Modern Age* (San Francisco: Harper and Row, 1989), 185.

28. Garry Wills, *Under God: Religion and American Politics* (New York: Touchstone, 1991), 104, 106, 113.

29. Thompson, *Tried as by Fire*, 127–129.

30. Ibid., 119.

31. Ibid., 136.

32. Ellen Rosenberg in *The Southern Baptists: A Subculture in Transition* (Knoxville: University of Tennessee Press, 1989); Norman Alexander Yance, *Religion Southern Style* (Association of Baptist Professors of Religion, 1978), 31; Eighmy, *Churches*, 49, 53.

33. Rosenberg, *Southern Baptists*, 206.

34. Thompson, *Tried as by Fire*, 32.

35. Ibid., 35.

36. Ibid., 41; Eighmy, *Churches*, 70–71.

37. Thompson, *Tried as by Fire*, 47; Eighmy, *Churches*, 130.

38. Thompson, *Tried as by Fire*, 53.

39. Yance, *Religion Southern Style*, 31.

40. Ibid., 63.

41. Ibid.; Eighmy, *Churches*, 122–125, 132, 136–139.

42. Eighmy, *Churches*, 80–85; George D. Kelsey, *Social Ethics among Southern Baptists, 1917–1969* (Metuchen, N.J.: Scarecrow Press, 1973).

43. Lawrence, *Defenders*, 165–166; H. Leon McBeth, "Fundamentalism in the Southern Baptist Convention in Recent Years," *Review and Expositor*, Winter 1982, 85; John E. Steely, "Current Issues in the Southern Baptist Convention in Historical Perspective," *Faith and Mission* I, Spring 1984, 5.

44. Thompson, *Tried as by Fire*, 183.

45. Ibid., 119.

46. Eighmy, *Churches*, 156.

47. Ammerman, *Baptist Battles*, 50–63; Robert A. Baker, *The Southern Baptist Convention and Its People, 1607–1972* (Nashville: Broadman Press, 1974); William Wright Barnes, *The Southern Baptist Convention, 1845–1953* (Nashville: Broadman Press, 1954).

48. Baker, *SBC*, 384, 413; Winthrop Hudson, *Baptists in Transition: Individualism and Christian Responsibility* (Valley Forge, Penn.: Judson Press, 1979), 113–115; Brooks Hays and John E. Steely, *The Baptist Way of Life* (Macon, Ga.: Mercer University Press, 1981), ix; Rosenberg, *Southern Bap-*

tists, 53; Eighmy, *Churches*, 75–77; Garrett et al., *Southern Baptists*, 163–164.

49. Rosenberg, *Southern Baptists*, 150.

50. C. Stanley Lowell, *Embattled Wall: Americans United: An Idea and a Man* (Washington, D.C.: Americans United, 1966), 1–42.

51. Os Guinness, *The American Hour: A Time of Reckoning and the Once and Future Role of Faith* (New York: Free Press, 1993), 55.

52. Lawrence, *Defenders*, 197. What we have called "Baptist exceptionalism" still exists, I am told. The same deacon who shared with me the new penchant for Convention sloganeering has developed a few suggestions of his own based on the cultural boldness still projected by the SBC and its superchurches. The true slogans of this new confidence, he argues, should be "We Worship a *Big* God," or "*Damn Right* We're Christians."

53. W. A. Criswell, *Standing on the Promises: The Autobiography of W. A. Criswell* (Dallas: Word Publishing, 1990), 184–185.

54. Ibid., 201–204; Baker, *SBC*, 414–415.

55. Eighmy, *Churches*, 192

56. *Economist*, 8 November 1958, 507.

57. *Time*, 17 November 1958, 22.

58. *Newsweek*, 17 November 1958, 30.

59. Ibid.

60. Brook Hays, *Politics Is My Parish: An Autobiography By Brooks Hays* (Baton Rouge: Louisiana State University Press, 1981), 5; see also Brooks Hays, *A Southern Moderate Speaks* (Chapel Hill: University of North Carolina Press, 1959), 130–215.

61. Hays, *Politics*, 64, 67, 66.

62. Ibid., 67.

63. Eighmy, *Churches*, 197; Baker, *SBC*, 415.

64. Eighmy, *Churches*, 190–191; Hays, *Politics*, 96–97; SBC Annual (1954), "Report of Christian Life Commission."

65. Author's interview with Marguerite E. Stafford, February 2, 1995.

66. Ibid.

67. Ibid.

68. Author's interview with Marion Aldridge, pastor of Greenlawn Baptist Church, Columbia, S.C., July 1993.

69. Rosenberg, *Southern Baptists*, 154; Kent B. Blevins, "Southern Baptist Attitudes toward the Vietnam War in the Years 1965–1970," *Foundations*, July–September 1980, 13.

70. Edward L. Queen, *In the South the Baptists Are the Center of Gravity: Southern Baptists and Social Change, 1930–1980* (New York: Carlson, 1991), 1–30.

71. Allen D. Hertzke, *Representing God in Washington: The Role of Reli-*

gious *Lobbies in the American Polity* (Knoxville: University of Tennessee Press, 1988).

72. Author's interview with Dr. James M. Dunn, Washington, D.C., 8 June 1994.

73. SBC *Annual*, 1968.

74. This Land quotation is taken from the transcript of a round-table discussion, "Is the South Still the Bible Belt?" National Review Institute, 25 June 1994, Charleston, S.C., 46. Panelists were Land, Allen Hertzke of the University of Oklahoma, Charles Dunn of Clemson University, and the author.

75. Author's interview with Charles Goolsby, 6 February 1995.

76. Ibid. Other conservative bloc Christians warning of the danger of mixing loyalty to Christ with Caesar include Charles Colson, "Politics, Power, and the Kingdom of God," *Moody*, October 1984, 22; Michael Cromartie, "Fixing the World: From Nonplayers to Radicals to New Right Conservatives: The Saga of Evangelicals and Social Action," *Christianity Today*, 27 April 1992, 23; Daniel Fuchs, "Win Souls Not Elections," *The Chosen People*, June 1981, 5–6.

77. Author's interview with Charles Goolsby, 6 February 1995.

78. Author's interview with Marion Aldridge, pastor of Greenlawn Baptist Church, Columbia, S.C., July 1993.

79. Ibid.

80. The scores of articles in mainstream and evangelical media documenting the dramatic shift to the right of the SBC include Kenneth A. Briggs, "Drift Away from Fundamentalism Splits Ranks of Southern Baptists," *New York Times*, 29 March 1981, A1; James C. Hefley, *The Truth in Crisis: The Controversy in the Southern Baptist Convention*, vols. 1–5 (Hannibal, Mo.: Hannibal Books, 1987–1990); Randy Frame, "Division's Die is Cast," *Christianity Today*, 24 September 1990, 42; James C. Hefley, "Critique of 'House Divided,' Article on the Controversy in the Southern Baptist Convention By R. Gustav Niebuhr Appearing in 'The Wall Street Journal,' April 25, 1990," *Christian News*, 4 June 1990, 14; James C. Hefley, "The Historic Shift in America's Largest Protestant Denomination," *Christianity Today*, 5 August 1983, 38; Mark S. Heim, "Talking on the Truce Line: Southern Baptists in Dialogue." *Christian Century*, 14 April 1993, 402; Roy L. Honeycutt, "Can Southern Baptists Live in Harmony?" *Tie*, May/June 1983, 3; Marjorie Hyer, "Liberal-Conservative Fights Wrench Protestant Churches," *Washington Post*, 29 May 1981, C12; Steve Maynard, "Is the SBC Heading the Way of the Missouri Synod?" *Houston Chronicle*, 22 October 1989, 6; R. Gustav Niebuhr, "Southern Baptists Lose Members and Impetus in an Internal Struggle," *Wall Street Journal*, 25 April 1990, A1; Edward E. Plowman, "Conservative Network Puts Its Stamp on the Southern Baptist Convention," *Christianity Today*, 18 July 1980, 50; "Southern Baptist Division 'Trick of the Devil': Billy Graham," *Religious News Service*, 25 March 1985; Peter Waldman, "Fundamentalists Fight to Capture the Soul of Southern Baptists," *Wall Street Journal*, 7 March 1988, 1A.

81. Jimmy Carter, *Why Not The Best?* (Nashville: Broadman, 1975); "Jimmy Carter Joins Moderate Baptists," *Greenville [S.C.] News*, 22 May 1993, 10A; James C. Hefley, *The Church That Produced a President* (New York: Wyden Books, 1977).

82. Rosenberg, *Southern Baptists*, 177, 188; Plowman, *Christianity Today*, 18 July 1980, 51. For a more complete account, see chapter 5.

83. See chapter 3.

84. Wills, *Under God*, 120; Criswell, *Standing*, 130, 242; Harold Bloom, *The American Religion: The Emergence of a Post-Christian Nation* (New York: Simon and Schuster, 1992), 191–233.

85. Himmelstein, *To the Right: The Transformation of American Conservatism* (Berkeley: University of California Press, 1990), 100; Rosenberg, *Southern Baptists*, 181–190.

86. The moderate faction sounded the alarm about the New Christian Right–SBC connection in James M. Dunn, "Fanatical Fundamentalism and Political Extremism," *USA Today Magazine*, May 1983, 53; Warner Ragsdale, "SBC Mirrors South and Nation in Move to Conservatism," *SBC Today*, August–September 1985, 4; Steve Fox, "SBC Tied to the Far Right?" *SBC Today*, October 1988, 7; Amy Greene, "New Right Groups Exert Influence with Southern Baptists, Others," *SBC Today*, April 1989, 12; Amy Greene, "SBC Tied to Political Right?" *SBC Today*, October 1987, 1. The best discussion of political culture can be found in Daniel Judah Elazar's classic, *American Federalism: A View from the States* (New York: Harper and Row, 1984).

87. Ralph H. Elliott, *The "Genesis Controversy" and Continuity in Southern Baptist Chaos: A Eulogy for a Great Tradition* (Macon, Ga.: Mercer University Press, 1992).

88. Rosenberg, *Southern Baptists*, 139.

89. *Baptist Faith and Message*, 1963.

90. Richards, *Winds of Doctrines*, 163; Ammerman, *Baptist Battles*, 44–71.

91. Leonard, *God's Last and Only Hope*, 131.

92. Conservatives presented their case regularly to rally the faithful. Articles included Paige Patterson, "The Paige Patterson Definition of a Theological Conservative," in the conservative faction's *Southern Baptist Journal*, February 1983, 8, and "Patterson vs. McCall on the Southern Baptist Controversy," in Jerry Falwell's *Fundamentalist Journal*, May 1985, 14. Conservatives also compared their record of baptisms and church membership with the moderate faction in a game of one-upsmanship, "Track Record of Moderates and Conservatives," *Southern Baptist Advocate*, October 1983, 13.

93. Garrett et al., *Are Southern Baptists*, 180.

94. Ammerman, *Baptist Battles*, 12–46.

95. Ibid., 73–87; Rosenberg, *Southern Baptists*, 209; Leonard, *God's Last and Only Hope*, 6.

96. Grady Cothen, *What Happened to the SBC?* (Atlanta: Smyth and Helwys, 1993); Robert U. Ferguson, Jr., *Amidst Babel, Speak the Truth: Reflections on the SBC Struggle* (Macon, Ga.: Smyth and Helwys, 1993); Walter B. Shurden, *The Baptist Identity: Four Fragile Freedoms* (Atlanta: Smyth and Helwys, 1993).

97. Will D. Campbell, *The Convention* (Atlanta: Peachtree, 1988), 383.

98. Brooks Hays and John E. Steely, *The Baptist Way of Life* (Macon, Ga.: Mercer University Press, 1981); Steve Beard, "Religion and Politics: In the '80s, Liberals Said the Two Don't Mix; That Was Then, This Is Now," *World*, 22 May 1993, 10.

99. Leonard, *God's Last and Only Hope*, 53; Rosenberg, *Southern Baptists*, 206.

100. Leonard, *God's Last and Only Hope*, 75.

101. Ibid., 78–80.

102. Ibid., 86.

103. Hinson, *Neo-Fundamentalism*, 164

104. Garrett et al., *Are Southern Baptists*, 166.

105. Leonard, *God's Last and Only Hope*, 146.

106. Ibid., 65.

107. Garrett et al., *Are Southern Baptists*, 121.

108. Ibid., 147.

109. Ibid., 173.

110. Ibid., 125–127.

111. Frances Evans, "Alternative Baptist Group to Meet," *Greenville [S.C.] News-Piedmont*, 25 September 1993, 12A; Stan Hastey, "The Alliance and the Fellowship," *SBC Today*, 3 May 1991, 19.

112. Greg Warner, "Trustees Abuse of Power," *Baptists Today*, 2 February 1995, 1; "Pastors Getting Fired: A Growing Trend among Southern Baptists," *Christianity Today*, 19 March 1982; Russell H. Dilday, "What Kind of Convention?" *SBC Today*, March 1985, 1.

113. R. Albert Mohler, Jr., "Mohler Defends Role of Theological Accountability," *Baptists Today*, 2 February 1995, 4.

114. Larry Witham, "Conservative to Run Venerable Southern Baptist Seminary," *Washington Times*, 17 October 1993, A4; Greg Warner, "Patterson Denied Membership in Wake Forest Church," *Baptists Today*, 18 February 1993, 1.

115. Steve Fox, "Samford University Survives a Close Call," *Baptists Today*, 9 January 1993, 10; Steve Fox, "SBC School Resists Conservatives," *Christian Century*, 1–8 January 1992, 5; Steve Fox, "Why SBC Right Upset with Dunn and Baptist Joint Committee," *SBC Today*, January 1989, 20; Greg Warner, "Close Votes in Texas, South Carolina Bode No Quick End for College Disputes," *Baptists Today*, 28 November 1991, 1; John E. Johns, "Furman Problems Not with Majority of Southern Baptists," *Greenville [S.C.] News-Piedmont*, 9 February 1992, 3C.

116. Greg Warner, "Fundamentalists Make Few Inroads in States," *Baptists Today*, 15 December 1992, 3; Dan Martin, "State Conventions May Face New Blitz by Fundamentalists Who Have Captured SBC," *Baptists Today*, 6 February, 1992, 10; Dan Martin, "Texas Baptist Fundamentalists Launch SBC Style Organization," *Baptists Today*, 23 January 1992, 4.

117. Bill Moyers, "Moyers Calls Baptists to Actively Oppose the Dismissals of Shackleford and Martin," *SBC Today*, September 1990, 12.

118. Jennifer Graham, "Arkansas Lieutenant Governor Putting His Faith into Politics," *[Columbia, S.C.] State*, 22 January 1993, 5E; Paul Greenberg, "Christian Heritage Week Tacky," *Greenville [S.C.] News-Piedmont*, 10 February 1995, 4-A.

119. Christian Life Commission's 1994 annual seminar program.

120. Eugene C. Roehlkepartain, "Fundamentalists Threaten Religious Liberty Watchdog," *Christian Century*, 5 November 1986, 980; "Religious Liberty Council Supports Joint Committee," *SBC Today*, June 1990, 1.

121. James L. Guth, "The Politics of Preachers: Southern Baptist Ministers and Christian Right Activism," in David G. Bromley and Anson Shupe, eds., *New Christian Politics*, 235–250 (Macon, Ga.: Mercer University Press, 1984).

122. Joe Edward Barnhart, *The Southern Baptist Holy War* (Austin: Texas Monthly Press, 1986).

123. Dr. James M. Dunn, interview with the author in Washington, D.C., 8 June 1994.

124. Perhaps the most difficult struggle in recent years for Dunn was his stand against the Moral Majority and others of the religious right who were friendly to the conservative leadership of the Southern Baptist Convention over the school prayer issue. Dunn argued that the measures were anti-Baptist, in that they constituted government entanglement in religion. This incident is best explained in Hertzke, *Representing God in Washington.*

125. The evangelical press reported that conservatives were unhappy that they were not invited (*World* 18:16, September 1993).

126. James M. Dunn, "Shurden Volume Describes Essence of 'Baptistness,'" *Baptists Today,* 26 August 1993, 18.

127. James M. Wall, "Church Leaders Meet with Clinton: A Visit to the White House," *Christian Century*, 7 April 1993, 355; George W. Cornell, "Clinton Meets His Baptist Critics," *Greenville [S.C.] News*, 25 September 1993; Brigid Schulte, "Pastors Seek, but Don't Find Common Ground with Clinton," *[Columbia, S.C.] State*, 17 September 1993, 1B; Greg Warner, "SBC Relations Cool with White House," *Baptists Today*, 26 November 1992, 6.

128. James L. Guth, "Southern Baptists and the New Right," in Charles W. Dunn, ed., *Religion in American Politics*, 177–190 (Washington, D.C.: CQ Press, 1989); Ammerman, *Baptist Battles*, 1993.

129. Barnhart, *Southern Baptist Holy War*, 2.

130. John Brinkley, "Vatican Estranged Truman, Baptists," *Denver Rocky Mountain News*, 13 August 1993, A1.

131. In contrast to the SBC and Bill Clinton, a relationship which began frigid, the relationships of President Harry Truman (1945–53) and President Jimmy Carter (1977–81) to the SBC seemed to start warm but to cool over time. Harry Truman called himself a Baptist from his earliest years but stopped attending the First Baptist Church in Washington when the Southern Baptist Committee on Public Relations, the forerunner of the Baptist Joint Committee on Public Affairs, opposed Truman's appointment of an ambassador to the Vatican in 1951. Truman was particularly annoyed that the director of the committee, Joseph M. Dawson, was active in that congregation. Jimmy Carter always stressed his Baptist roots, that he was born-again, and that he taught Sunday School, and in his first term he enjoyed wide popularity among most Southern Baptists and even the support of Southern Baptist-ordained TV preacher Pat Robertson. The Clinton-SBC relationship, in contrast, has enjoyed none of the early attraction of the Truman and Carter variety.

132. As quoted in Richard John Neuhaus, ed., editorial, *First Things: A Journal of Religion and Public Life* 36 (October 1993): 70.

133. Walter H. Matthews, "Few Called, Few Chosen," *World* 18:16, 14 September 1993, 24, reported that the executive director of the Moderate party's Cooperative Baptist Fellowship, Cecil Sherman, was the lone Southern Baptist present at the August 30 meeting, which took place immediately following the Clinton's vacation. The February and March meetings were free of evangelicals as well, according to Beard, "Religion and Politics," 10–12, and Wall, "Church Leaders," 355–356.

134. Neuhaus, *First Things*, 70.

135. Jack U. Harwell, "Southern Baptists Attack Clinton; Take Middle-Road Stance on Freemasons," *Baptists Today*, 29 June 1993, 1; David Walters, "Southern Baptists Asked to Pray for Clinton and Gore for 40 Days," *Washington Times*, 9 October 1993; Joyce Price, "Catholics, Baptists Find Elders' Apology Lacking," *Washington Times*, 3 September 1993; "Fundamentalists Picket Clinton's Church," *Washington Times*, 14 June 1993; Jill Lawrence, "Clinton Changes Inflame Fundamentalists' Fury," *Seattle Times/Seattle Post-Intelligencer*, 23 May 1993; Kim A. Lawton, "Seeking Common Ground: Evangelicals Hope President-Elect Clinton Will Strive for Consensus on Social Issues, Not Just for Dramatic Change," *Christianity Today*, 14 December 1992, 40.

136. Wills, *Under God*, 60–61. It should also be noted that Albert Gore, Jr., attended the Vanderbilt School of Religion for one year (1972) before entering law school there the following year.

137. According to evangelical observer Mark Noll, Clinton "messed up" I Corinthians 2:9 when he quoted it: "'Our eyes have not seen, nor our ears heard nor our minds imagined . . .' what we can build." The actual verse (by any stretch

of translation) ends "the things which God has prepared for them that love Him." "The Politicians Bible," *Christianity Today*, 26 October 1992.

138. Gustav Niebuhr, "The Language of Zion," *Washington Post*, 28 October 1992, A1; Larry Witham, "Clinton Calls His Job 'A Ministry' in Meeting with Religious Leaders," *Washington Times*, 13 September 1993, A1; Cal Thomas, "Clinton's 'Common Good,'" *Washington Times*, 5 September 1993; "New Ticket Not Squeamish about Using Religious Themes in Campaign," *Knight Ridder*, 27 July 1992; Greg Warner, "Baptists Elected with Little Help from Brethren," *Baptists Today*, 26 November 1992, 1; Albert J. Menendez, "Analysis: Clinton Won Most Religious Votes," *Baptists Today*, 26 November 1992, 1.

139. Best described by Randall Balmer, *Mine Eyes Have Seen the Glory: A Journey into the Evangelical Subculture in America* (New York: Oxford, 1989), and by Ammerman, *Baptist Battles*, 1990.

140. Richard L. Walker, "Baptist Peace Activists Organize to Counter Conservatives," *Southern Baptist Advocate*, Fall 1982, 13.

141. Sam J. Currin, "Dunn's Political Activity," *Southern Baptist Advocate*, June 1988, 7; "Dunn Drags SBC into PAW," *Southern Baptist Advocate*, October 1983, 15; Angela E. Hunt, "Baptist Joint Committee Out of Joint with SBC," *Liberty Report*, April 1987, 20; Linda Lawson, "SBC Messengers Sever Final Ties With BJPCA," *Baptists Today*, 25 June 1992, 3; "Majority Report of SBC Executive Committee on Baptist Joint Committee," *SBC Today*, June 1990, 10; "Minority Report of SBC Executive Committee on Baptist Joint Committee," *SBC Today*, June 1990, 11.

142. "Southern Baptists Break with Tradition; Endorse School Prayer Amendment," *Christian News*, 28 June 1982, 7; Michael Tutterow, "Bork Appointment Stirs SBC," *SBC Today*, October 1987, 1.

143. Matthews, "Few Called," 24.

144. Dunn, "Shurden Volume," 1993, 18; Warner, "SBC Relations," 1992, 1; Menendez, *Baptists Today*, 1992, 1.

145. Moyers, *SBC Today*, 1990, 12.

146. Marse Grant, "Election a Victory for Moderates," *Baptists Today*, 26 November 1992, 6.

147. Mark Wingfield Greg Warner, "Jimmy, Rosalynn Carter Embrace Fellowship," *Baptists Today*, 27 May 1993, 1.

148. Larry Braidfoot, *Light*, October 1985, 1.

149. Will Campbell, "Ministers Can't Be Caesar's Cheerleaders," *USA Today*, 5 April 1983, 12A.

150. Though only a footnote here, Ed McAteer, a member of former convention president Adrian Rogers's Bellevue Baptist Church in Memphis, was one of the leaders of the Christian right from the early eighties. McAteer's Religious Roundtable organization contained most of the preachers associated with the New Christian Right.

151. Don McGregor, "Linking the Political Right and the SBC Right," *SBC Today*, April 1988, 13.

152. Greene, "SBC," 1.

153. *Dallas Morning News*, 26A; "Southern Baptist Convention Split over Two Endorsements," *Greenville [S.C.] News-Piedmont*, 27 March 1988, 26A.

154. Fox, "Why SBC Right Upset," 20.

155. Ibid.

156. Walker L. Knight, "Convention Defied by PAC Action," *SBC Today*, November 1987, 1.

157. "Religious Liberty Award Goes to Senator Helms," *Southern Baptist Advocate*, June 1990, 2.

158. McGregor, "Linking the Political Right," 13.

159. Warner, "SBC Relations," 6.

160. Fox, "SBC School," 6.

161. Tenery, 1; Rob James, ed., *The Takeover in the Southern Baptist Convention: A Brief History* (Decatur, Ga.: SBC Today, 1989); Walter B. Shurden, *The Struggle for the Soul of the SBC: The Moderate Response to the Fundamentalist Movement* (Macon, Ga.: Mercer University Press, 1993); "Liberals Hire Political Consultant," *Southern Baptist Advocate*, March 1986, 1.

162. Welton C. Gaddy, "Precinct Politics Wed to Fundamentalism in 'Takeover' Plan of SBC," *SBC Today*, November 1984, 6.

163. Author's interview with Marguerite E. Stafford, 2 February 1995.

164. Glenn E. Hinson, "Split May Best Bring Peace amid SBC Strife," *SBC Today*, April 1987, 16.

165. Rachel Gill, "Peace Unites ABC, SBC Groups," *SBC Today*, May 1984, 1; "Jackson May Take Church Independent or Cut Support," *Baptist Courier*, 30 March 1989, 6; Walker L. Knight, "Moderate Organizations Fill Vacuums in SBC," *Baptists Today*, 15 December 1992, 7; Nancy Tatom Ammerman, "Why Are We Baptists?" Audiotape of lecture at First Baptist Church, Greenville, South Carolina, 17 November 1991; Nancy Tatom Ammerman, "The Rise of the Progressive Wing of the SBC," audiotape of Lecture at First Baptist Church, Greenville, South Carolina, 4 April 1992.

NOTES TO CHAPTER 3

1. Emile Durkheim, *The Division of Labor* (New York: Free Press, 1933).

2. William Kornhauser, *The Politics of Mass Society*. (Glencoe, Ill.: Free Press, 1959), 177–178, 237–238; Kant Patel, Denny Pilant, and Gary L. Rose, "Christian Conservatism: A Study in Alienation and Life Style Concerns," *Journal of Political Science* 12:17–30 (1985), 18.

3. Richard Hofstadter, *The Age of Reform: From Bryan to F.D.R.* (New York: Knopf, 1956), 97, 96, 63.

4. Ibid., 135, 175.

5. Seymour Martin Lipset, "The Sources of the 'Radical Right,'" in Daniel Bell, ed., *The New American Right* (New York: Criterion, 1955); Richard M. Weaver, *Visions of Order: The Cultural Crisis of Our Time* (Baton Rouge: Louisiana State University Press, 1964).

6. Patel et al., "Christian Conservatism," 19.

7. Sydney Ahlstrom, *A Religious History of the American People* (New Haven: Yale University Press, 1972).

8. "Come out from among them and be ye separate" (II Corinthians 6:17) and "Love not the world neither the things that are in the world . . ." (I John 2:15).

9. It does not necessarily follow that because Southern Baptists have so much cultural influence they cannot have feelings of alienation. This misunderstands the difference between a revolt against *modernism* (liberal theology and its trappings) and *modernity* (economic affluence). In Bruce B. Lawrence, *Defenders of God: The Fundamentalist Revolt against the Modern Age* (San Francisco: Harper and Row, 1989), 17, 169, he argues that fundamentalism is a social movement that protests modernism, not modernity. Southern Baptists are perhaps the most stylistically modern in their work against modernist theology. But they are nevertheless left out, in a sense, in that a more secular culture, even one they greatly influence, is becoming foreign to them. Part of this confusion comes from the commonly held notion that fundamentalists are poor and uneducated and left out of modern life. Ernest Sandeen cleared much of this confusion in *The Roots of American Fundamentalism* as did Miller and Wattenberg (*Public Opinion Quarterly*, 48:308) who wrote: "Contrary to the popular stereotype, conservative Christians are not predominantly less well-educated, elderly, lower class, or Southern. In general, they tend to be relatively well educated, middle-aged, and very similar to the rest of the population in terms of social class."

10. Max Weber, *Economy and Society* (New York: Bedminster, 1968).

11. Ibid., 302–307, 901–940.

12. Lipset, "Sources of the 'Radical Right.'"

13. Joseph R. Gusfield, *Symbolic Crusade: Status Politics and the American Temperance Movement* (Urbana: University of Illinois Press, 1963), 140.

14. Ann Page and Donald A. Clelland, "The Kanawha County Book Controversy: A Study of the Politics of Life Style Concern," *Social Forces* 57:266, September 1978.

15. Roy Wallis, *Salvation and Protest: Studies of Social and Religious Movements* (London: Francis Pinter, 1979).

16. Steve Bruce, *The Rise and Fall of the New Christian Right* (New York: Oxford University Press, 1988).

17. Weber, *Economy and Society*, 302–307, 901–940.

18. Neil J. Smelser, *Theory of Collective Behavior* (New York: Free Press, 1962).

19. Louise J. Lorentzen, "Evangelical Life Style Concerns Expressed in Political Action," *Sociological Analysis* 41:147, 1980:2.

20. Page and Clelland, "Kanawha County," 1978, 267.

21. Ibid., 265–271.

22. Lorentzen, "Evangelical Life Style," 144–154.

23. Page and Clelland, "Kanawha County," 279.

24. Ibid., 266.

25. Lorentzen, "Evangelical Life Style," 147.

26. Nancy Tatom Ammerman, *Bible Believers: Fundamentalists in the Modern World* (New Brunswick, N.J.: Rutgers University Press, 1987), and *Baptist Battles: Social Change and Religious Conflict in the Southern Baptist Convention* (New Brunswick, N.J.: Rutgers University Press, 1990), 486.

27. Page and Clelland, "Kanawha County," 267.

28. Anne N. Costain, *Inviting Women's Rebellion: A Political Process Interpretation of the Women's Movement* (Baltimore: Johns Hopkins University Press, 1992), 16–17; Doug McAdam, *Political Process and the Development of Black Insurgency, 1930–1970* (Chicago: University of Chicago Press, 1992).

29. Bruce, *Rise and Fall*, 16.

30. Jerome L. Himmelstein, *To the Right: The Transformation of American Conservatism* (Berkeley: University of California Press, 1990), 9.

31. Bruce, *Rise and Fall*, 23–24.

32. McAdam, *Political Process*, 25, 29.

33. Mark Silk, "Reagan Stargazing Concerns the Christian Right," *Atlanta Constitution*, 5 May 1988, A7.

34. "Southern Baptists Assail Bush for Stand on NEA," *New York Times*, B11.

35. Ammerman, *Baptist Battles*, 174.

36. Notion of "ripeness" for a political realignment found in Paul Allen Beck, "A Socialization Theory of Realignment," in Richard G. Niemi et al., *The Politics of Future Citizens* (New York: Jossey-Bass, 1974).

37. McAdam, *Political Process*, 1982.

38. Costain, *Inviting Women's Rebellion*.

39. McAdam, *Political Process*, 40; Costain, *Inviting Women's Rebellion*, 12.

40. McAdam, *Political Process*, 40–61.

41. Garry Wills, *Under God: Religion and American Politics* (New York: Touchstone, 1991), 131–132.

42. Michael Lienesch, *Redeeming America: Piety and Politics in the New Christian Right* (Chapel Hill: University of North Carolina Press, 1993), 8–9.

43. *U.S. Census 1930*, General Population Characteristics, table 7; *U.S. Census 1940*, General Population Characteristics, table 7; *U.S. Census 1950*, General Population Characteristics, table 15; *U.S. Census 1960*, General Population Characteristics, table 138; *U.S. Census 1970*, General Population Characteris-

tics, table 138; *U.S. Census 1980*, General Population Characteristics, table 194; *U.S. Census 1990*, General Population Characteristics, table 262; *Statistical Abstract 1941*, 12–13, table 15; *Statistical Abstract 1971*, 12 and 27, tables 11 and 27; *Statistical Abstract 1973*, 13, table 13; *Statistical Abstract 1981*, 9 and 32, tables 8 and 36; *Statistical Abstract 1984*, 11, table 11; *Statistical Abstract 1986*, 12, table 12; *Statistical Abstract 1987*, 22, table 25; *Statistical Abstract 1990*, 20, table 26; *Statistical Abstract 1992*, 22, table 25; *Statistical Abstract 1993*, 28 and 30, tables 31 and 32.

44. Data obtained from the Southern Baptist Convention Historical Commission and the following SBC publications: *Quarterly Review*, July–September 1961, 9; Southern Baptist Handbook (1931), 77–95; SBC Annual (1933), 342–345; SBC Annual (1934), 346–353; SBC Annual (1940), 448–451; SBC Annual (1951), 462–463; Southern Baptist Handbook, 323; Southern Baptist Handbook (1951), 80–97; SBC Annual (1960), 88–91; SBC Annual (1961), 129; SBC Annual (1971), 9, 110; SBC Annual (1981), 9, 86; SBC Annual (1990), 110; Southern Baptist Handbook (1991), 25. The figure we use is for membership. Some argue that the SBC has in recent years padded these membership figures by rebaptizing existing members who had been counted before. We are at the mercy of the Convention for accurate figures in a sense, we but stand by our conclusions as they were reached using data gathered in the same manner and reported in the same way over time.

45. David Leege and Lyman A. Kellstedt, *Rediscovering the Religious Factor in American Politics* (Armonk, N.Y.: M. E. Sharpe, 1993), 4, 277, 300.

46. Ammerman, *Baptist Battles*, 486.

47. James C. Hefley, *The Truth in Crisis: The Controversy in the Southern Baptist Convention* (Hannibal, Mo.: Hannibal Books, 1986), 64–65.

48. McAdam, *Political Process*, 40–61.

49. There is a somewhat interesting parallel in SBC growth in Oklahoma and in GOP growth.

50. See chapter 2.

51. Jean Miller Schmidt, *Souls of the Social Order: The Two-Party System in American Protestantism* (New York: Carlson, 1991).

52. Ibid., xiv.

53. W. A. Criswell, *Standing on the Promises: The Autobiography of W. A. Criswell* (Dallas: Word Publishing, 1990), 217.

54. Robert Wuthnow, *The Restructuring of American Religion* (Princeton, N.J.: Princeton University Press, 1988).

55. Ammerman, *Baptist Battles*, 44–71.

56. James Davison Hunter, *Culture Wars: The Struggle to Define America* (New York: Basic Books, 1991), 67–104.

57. Will Herberg, *Protestant, Catholic, Jew* (Garden City, N.Y.: Doubleday-Anchor, 1960).

58. The very title of one of the early studies of voting behavior, Herberg's *Protestant, Catholic, Jew,* is a powerful summary of the typical partition of the electorate by religion found in both the classic works on voting behavior (Marian D. Irish and James W. Prothro, *The Politics of American Democracy* [Englewood Cliffs, N.J.: Prentice Hall, 1959]; Angus Campbell, Philip E. Converse, Warren E. Miller, and Donald E. Stokes, *The American Voter* [New York: Wiley, 1964]; V. O. Key, *Public Opinion and American Democracy* [New York: Knopf, 1965]; Donald R. Matthews and James W. Prothro, *Negroes and the New South Politics* [New York: Harcourt, Brace, and World, 1966]) and those more recent works that follow in the classic tradition (Robert S. Erikson and Norman Luttberg, *American Public Opinion: Its Origins and Impact* [New York: Wiley, 1973]; Norman Nie, Sidney Verba, and John R. Petrocik, *The Changing American Voter* [Cambridge, Mass.: Harvard University Press, 1976]).

59. James L. Guth, "The Politics of Preachers: Southern Baptist Ministers and Christian Right Activism," in David G. Bromley and Anson Shupe, eds., *New Christian Politics*, 235–250 (Macon, Ga.: Mercer University Press, 1984); Leege and Kellstedt, *Rediscovering the Religious Factor*, 15–18.

60. Charles W. Dunn, "Theology and Politics: Some Modest Propositions about an Immodest Subject," *PS* 19:832–836.

61. Os Guinness, *The American Hour: A Time of Reckoning and the Once and Future Role of Faith* (New York: Free Press, 1993).

62. Stephen L. Carter, *The Culture of Disbelief: How American Law and Politics Trivialize Religious Devotion* (New York: Basic Books, 1993).

63. Lienesch, *Redeeming America*, 20.

64. Ibid., 1–21.

65. Ibid., 4.

66. Phillip E. Hammond, *Religion and Personal Autonomy: The Third Disestablishment in America* (Columbia: University of South Carolina Press, 1992), 1–18.

67. Lienesch, *Redeeming America*, 6, 20.

68. Clyde Wilcox, *God's Warriors: The Christian Right in Twentieth-Century America* (Baltimore: Johns Hopkins University Press, 1992).

69. Peter L. Benson and Dorothy L. Williams, *Religion on Capitol Hill: Myths and Realities* (San Francisco: Harper and Row, 1982).

70. John N. Moore in Marla J. Selvidge, *Fundamentalism Today: What Makes It So Attractive?* (Elgin, Ill.: Brethren Press, 1984), 80.

71. See chapter 2 and Norman Alexander Yance, *Religion Southern Style* (Association of Baptist Professors of Religion, 1978), 31–33.

72. Lienesch, *Redeeming America*, 192.

73. Paul Allen Beck, "A Socialization Theory of Realignment," in Richard G. Niemi et al., *The Politics of Future Citizens* (New York: Jossey-Bass, 1974).

74. V. O. Key, "The Erosion of Sectionalism," *Virginia Quarterly Review* (1955), 161–179; Alexander Heard, *A Two-Party South?* (Chapel Hill: University of North Carolina Press, 1952), 25, questioned Key's sunny assumption that the 1948 campaign would be the "dying gasp" of race as an issue. See also J. Morgan Kousser, *The Shaping of Southern Politics* (New Haven: Yale, University Press, 1974).

75. Earl Black and Merle Black, "The 1988 Presidential Election and the Future of Southern Politics," in Lawrence W. Moreland et. al, *The 1988 Presidential Election in the South* (New York: Praeger, 1991), 255–279.

76. James L. Sundquist, *Dynamics of the Party System* (Washington, D.C.: Brookings Institution, 1983); Earl Black and Merle Black, *Politics and Society in the South* (Cambridge, Mass.: Harvard University Press, 1987).

77. Donald S. Strong, "The Presidential Election in the South, 1952," *Journal of Politics*, August 1955, 382; Kevin P. Phillips, *The Emerging Republican Majority* (New York: Anchor Books, 1970), 232.

78. Earl Black and Merle Black, *The Vital South: How Presidents Are Elected* (Cambridge, Mass.: Harvard University Press, 1992), 29–76; Numan V. Bartley and Hugh D. Graham, *Southern Politics and the Second Reconstruction* (Baltimore: Johns Hopkins University Press, 1975), 185; Black and Black, *Politics and Society*, 178; Phillip E. Converse, "A Major Political Realignment in the South?" in Allan Sindler, ed., *Change in the Contemporary South* (Durham, N.C.: Duke University Press, 1963), 198–202; Sundquist, *Dynamics*, 279.

79. Sundquist, *Dynamics*, 373–375, 367; Phillips, *Emerging Republican Majority*, 187–289.

80. Black and Black, *Vital South*, 30–33.

81. Himmelstein, *To the Right*, 28–62, 75–76; John Shelton Reed, *The Enduring South* (Chapel Hill: University of North Carolina Press, 1972), 44–45; Robert P. Steed and John McGlennon, "A 1988 Postscript: Continuing Coalitional Diversity," in Tod A. Baker et al., eds., *Political Parties in the Southern States* (New York: Praeger, 1990), 204. On the effect of Southern ideology on practical politics, see also Harry Dent, *The Prodigal South Returns to Power* (New York: Wiley, 1978); Jack Bass and Walter DeVries, *The Transformation of Southern Politics* (New York: Basic Books, 1976), and the new edition (Athens: University of Georgia Press, 1995); Dewey Grantham, *The Life and Death of the Old South* (Lexington: University Press of Kentucky, 1988); Harold Stanley, "The 1984 Presidential Election in the South: Race and Religion," in Robert P. Steed, *The 1984 Presidential Election in the South* (New York: Praeger, 1985), 315–326; and Louis Seagull, *Southern Republicanism* (New York: Wiley, 1975), 52–77.

82. Earl Black and Merle Black, "The 1988 Election and the Future of Southern Politics," in Lawrence W. Moreland et al., *The 1988 Presidential Election in the South* (New York: Praeger, 1991), 255–279; Black and Black, *Vital South*, 219–240.

83. Thomas Byrne Edsall and Mary D. Edsall, "Race," *Atlantic Monthly*, May 1991, 58–80.

84. Black and Black, *Politics and Society*, 249–256.

85. Charles L. Prysby, "Realignment among Southern Party Activists," in Tod A. Baker et al., *Political Parties in the Southern States* (New York: Praeger, 1991), 177–190; Lawrence W. Moreland, "The Ideological and Issue Bases of Southern Parties," in ibid., 123–134; Robert P. Steed and John McGlennon, "A 1988 Postscript: Continuing Coalitional Diversity," in ibid., 191–206; Edward G. Carmines and Harold W. Stanley, "Ideological Realignment in the Contemporary South," in Robert P. Steed, et. al, *The Disappearing South? Studies in Regional Change and Continuity* (Tuscaloosa: University of Alabama Press, 1990), 33.

86. Edsal and Edsal, "Race," 73; Black and Black, *Politics and Society*, 218–219.

87. Author's interview with Marion Aldridge, pastor of Greenlawn Baptist Church, Columbia, S.C., July 1993.

88. Page and Clelland, "Kanawha County Book Controversy," 267; Sundquist, *Dynamics*, 369, 383, 389; and Black and Black, "1988 Presidential Election," 265–268.

89. Murray Edelman, *Constructing the Political Spectacle* (Chicago: University of Chicago Press, 1988), 8.

90. Murray Edelman, *The Symbolic Uses of Politics* (Urbana: University of Illinois Press, 1964), 117, 172–173.

91. Ibid., 127.

92. Ibid., 137.

93. Ibid., 190.

94. Ibid., 66.

95. Ibid., 86.

96. Everett Carll Ladd, Jr., with Charles D. Hadley, *Transformations of the American Party System* (New York: Norton, 1978); Sundquist, *Dynamics*, 332–334.

97. Reagan Campaign button, 1980; Sundquist, *Dynamics*, 429.

98. Black and Black, *Politics and Society*, 219–231.

99. Key, 674.

100. Rosenberg, *Southern Baptists*, passim; Bloom, *American Religion*, 224, 229, 231, 233.

101. Stephen L. Carter, *Culture of Disbelief*, 90; black registration, see Black and Black, *Politics and Society*, 138, and Numan V. Bartley, *From Thurmond to Wallace* (Baltimore: Johns Hopkins University Press, 1970).

102. For LBJ as "traitor," see Charles and Barbara Whalen, *The Longest Debate* (New York: New American Library, 1986); Costain, *Inviting Women's Rebellion*, 24.

103. Sundquist, *Dynamics*, 370, 372.

104. Ibid., 424.

105. Albert J. Menendez, *Religion at the Polls* (Philadelphia: Westminster Press, 1977), 207–208.

106. Sundquist, *Dynamics*, 290, 394, 402–409.

107. Himmelstein, *To the Right*, 124–125.

108. Queen, *In the South*, 115–117; Lienesch, *Redeeming America*, 1993, 16; Rosenberg, *Southern Baptists*, 175–179, 188–189.

NOTES TO CHAPTER 4

1. James L. Sundquist, *Dynamics of the Party System* (Washington: Brookings Institution, 1983), 12–13.

2. Leon Epstein, *Political Parties in the American Mold* (Madison: University of Wisconsin Press, 1986), 4–6.

3. Will Herberg, *Protestant, Catholic, Jew* (Garden City, N.Y.: Doubleday-Anchor, 1960).

4. Marian D. Irish and James W. Prothro, *The Politics of American Democracy* (Englewood Cliffs, N.J.: Prentice Hall, 1959); Angus Campbell, Philip E. Converse, Warren E. Miller, and Donald E. Stokes, *The American Voter* (New York: Wiley, 1964); V. O. Key, *Public Opinion and American Democracy* (New York: Knopf, 1965); Donald R. Matthews and James W. Prothro, *Negroes and the New Southern Politics* (New York: Harcourt, Brace, and World, 1966).

5. Robert S. Erikson and Norman Luttberg, *American Public Opinion: Its Origins and Impact* (New York: Wiley, 1973); Norman Nie, Sidney Verba, and John R. Petrocik, *The Changing American Voter* (Cambridge, Mass.: Harvard University Press, 1976); Robert S. Erikson, Thomas D. Lancaster, and David W. Romero, "Group Components of the Presidential Vote, 1952–1984," *Journal of Politics* 51:336–346.

6. Campbell et al., *American Voter*.

7. Ibid.; Erikson and Luttberg, *American Public Opinion*.

8. Erikson and Luttberg, *American Public Opinion*, 1973.

9. Nie et al., *Changing American Voter*.

10. F. Maurice Ethridge and Joe R. Feagin, "Varieties of 'Fundamentalism': A Conceptual and Empirical Analysis of Two Protestant Denominations," *Sociological Quarterly* 20 (1979):37–48.

11. Clyde Wilcox, "Fundamentalists and Politics: An Analysis of the Effects of Differing Operational Definitions," *Journal of Politics* 48 (1986):1041–1051.

12. Stephen D. Johnson and Joseph B. Tamney, "The Christian Right and the 1980 Presidential Election," *Journal for the Scientific Study of Religion* 21 (1982):123–131; Corwin Smidt, "Evangelicals in the 1984 Election: Continuity or Change?" *American Politics Quarterly* 15 (1987):419–444; Corwin Smidt,

"Evangelicals and the New Christian Right: Coherence vs. Diversity in the Issue Stands of Evangelicals," in Corwin E. Smidt, ed., *Contemporary Evangelical Political Involvement*, 75–98 (Lanham, Md.: University Press of America, 1987); Randall Balmer, *Mine Eyes Have Seen the Glory: A Journey into the Evangelical Subculture in America* (New York: Oxford University Press, 1993).

13. Stuart Rothenberg and Frank Newport, *The Evangelical Voter* (Washington, D.C.: Free Congress, 1984).

14. Kenneth Wald, Dennis E. Owen, and Samuel S. Hill, Jr., "Churches as Political Communities," *American Political Science Review* 82 (1988):531–548; Kenneth Wald, Dennis E. Owen, and Samuel S. Hill, Jr., "Political Cohesion in Churches," *Journal of Politics* 52 (1989):197–215; Kenneth Wald, Dennis E. Owen, and Samuel S. Hill, Jr., "Assessing the Religious Factor in Electoral Behavior," in Charles W. Dunn, ed., *Religion in American Politics*, 105–121 (Washington, D.C.: CQ Press, 1989); Corwin Smidt, "Change and Stability among Southern Evangelicals," 147–160, in Charles W. Dunn, ed., *Religion in American Politics* (Washington, D.C.: CQ Press, 1989).

15. Jeffrey L. Brudney and Gary W. Copeland, "Evangelicals as a Political Force: Reagan and the 1980 Religious Vote," *Social Science Quarterly* 65:1072–1079; Johnson and Tamney, "Christian Right."

16. Arthur H. Miller and Martin P. Wattenberg, "Politics from the Pulpit: Religiosity and the 1980 Elections," *Public Opinion Quarterly* 48 (1984):301–317; Tod A. Baker et al., *Religion and Politics in the South* (New York: Praeger, 1983).

17. Ted G. Jelen, "Politicized Group Identificationism: The Case of Fundamentalism," *Western Political Quarterly* 44 (1991):209–219.

18. Robert Booth Fowler, *Unconventional Partners: Religion and Liberal Culture in the United States* (Grand Rapids, Mich.: Eerdmans, 1989).

19. A. James Reichley, *Religion in American Public Life* (Washington, D.C.: Brookings Institution, 1985).

20. Samuel S. Hill, "The Shape and Shapes of Popular Southern Piety," in David Edwin Harrell, ed., *Varieties of Southern Evangelicalism*, 89–114 (Macon, Ga.: Mercer University Press, 1981).

21. Donald R. Stockton, "The Evangelical Phenomenon: A Falwell-Graham Typology," in Corwin E. Smidt, ed., *Contemporary Evangelical Political Involvement*, 45–74 (Lanham, Md.: University Press of America, 1989).

22. Kathleen Murphy Beatty and Oliver Walter, "Religious Preference and Practice: Reevaluating Their Impact on Political Tolerance," *Public Opinion Quarterly* 48 (1984):318–329.

23. Clyde Wilcox, "Evangelicals and Fundamentalists in the Christian Right: Religious Differences in the Ohio Moral Majority," *Journal for the Scientific Study of Religion* 25 (1986):355–363; Clyde Wilcox, "Religious Orientations and Political Attitudes: Variations within the New Christian Right," *American Politics Quarterly* 15 (1987):274–296.

24. James L. Guth, Ted G. Jelen, Lyman A. Kellstedt, Corwin E. Smidt, and Kenneth D. Wald, "The Politics of Religion in America: Issues for Investigation," *American Politics Quarterly* 16 (1988):357–397.

25. Corwin Smidt, "Evangelicals within Contemporary American Politics: Differentiating between Fundamentalist and Non-Fundamentalist Evangelicals," *Western Political Quarterly* 41 (1989):601–620.

26. Ethridge and Feagin, "Varieties"; Nancy Tatom Ammerman, *Bible Believers: Fundamentalists in the Modern World* (New Brunswick, N.J.: Rutgers University Press, 1987).

27. Because of its quantitative nature, much of the failure of voting-behavior literature to adequately analyze the essence of religious differences in politics has been due to poor design of religious questions on recognized surveys like the American National Election Study. Due to the work of religion and politics scholars Lyman Kellstedt, Corwin Smidt, James Guth, John Green, David Leege, and Clyde Wilcox, the ANES questions became much improved beginning in 1990. Because survey design will more accurately reflect reality, these advances will improve research in this field tremendously. See chapter 4 as well as David Leege and Lyman A. Kellstedt, *Rediscovering the Religious Factor in American Politics* (Armonk, N.Y.: M. E. Sharpe, 1993).

28. Southern Baptists are seldom listed as mainline, and we will not consider the SBC this way. Hutcheson writes: "The Southern Baptist Convention, the Lutheran Church, Missouri Synod, and some of the major black Baptist groups, are certainly large denominations with deep roots in American history, but they would be omitted from many 'mainline' lists. Why? Because they are strongly conservative and are not part of the ecumenical movement"; see Richard G. Hutcheson, *Mainline Churches and the Evangelicals* (Atlanta: John Knox Press, 1981), 38.

29. Bob Jones, Jr., refuses to separate religious conservatism and political conservatism. He has written in *Cornbread and Caviar* (Greenville, S.C.: Bob Jones University Press, 1985), 23:

Anyone who takes the Bible seriously, applies its principles, and lives by its standards is going to be regarded as a kook. Everything that is *conservative* is being ridiculed today, and a biblical philosophy is certainly a *conservative* philosophy. I never hesitate to express a conviction, even at the risk of being called a reactionary, a bigot, intolerant, unloving, or just plain mean. (Emphasis mine)

30. See B. Johnson, "On Church and Sect," *American Sociological Review* 28 (1963):539–549, R. Stark and W. S. Bainbridge, "Of Churches, Sects, and Cults: Preliminary Concepts for a Theory of Religious Movements," *Journal for the Scientific Study of Religion* 18 (1979): 117–133; and Robert Wuthnow, *The Restructuring of American Religion* (Princeton, N.J.: Princeton University Press, 1988).

264 | *Notes to Chapter 4*

31. The difference, according to Ammerman (Nancy Tatom Ammerman, ed., *Southern Baptists Observed: Changing Perspectives on a Changing Denomination* [Knoxville: University of Tennessee Press, 1993], 164–165) can be found in H. Richard Niebuhr's *The Social Sources of Denominationalism* (New York: Meridian Books, 1929), who wrote that upper-class Christians were "churchly" while lower-class Christians were "sectarian."

32. This has been stated in general terms in relationship to the decline of the Moral Majority, but little analysis of the religious and political particulars has been undertaken. Green, in reviewing Clyde Wilcox, *God's Warriors: The Christian Right in Twentieth Century America* (Baltimore: Johns Hopkins University Press, 1992) in the *Journal of Politics* 85:3, 816–817, focuses rightly on Wilcox's mention of "religious particularism" as limiting a "mass base for the Christian Right," along with "economic concerns and antipathy to the Christian right leaders themselves." Though economic concerns were probably not at work among the BJU group, both particularism and antipathy toward leaders could be keeping them out of full participation in the New Christian Right as movement. Wilcox said flatly: "[U]ntil conservative Protestants can resolve their religious rivalries, a unified Christian Right is unlikely, in this century or the next" (*God's Warriors*, 232).

33. Bradley Lapiska, morning sermon, Hampton Park Baptist Church, Greenville, S.C., 4 July 1993. It makes sense then that Dr. Bob Jones and Dr. Bob Jones, III, would resist Falwell. The Joneses mailed a 10 June 1980 letter to all BJU ministerial graduates, stating in part: "The devil has been doing everything he can over the last thirty years (that is, for a whole generation) to break down the lines of ecclesiastical separation as set forth in the Scripture, and he has been using first one means then another. We are enjoined not to be ignorant of his devices, and it is well to face Falwell's so-called 'Moral Majority' drive as one of Satan's devices to build the world church of Antichrist. . . . My own personal opinion is that Falwell thinks he can be president of the United States in 1984, and he is building himself a political party" (*Moral Majority Report*, 14 July 1980, 2). See also Bob Jones, III, "What Does America Really Need: Political Maneuvering Cannot Lift God's Judgment on a Nation," *Faith for the Family*, July–August, 1980, 23.

34. Richard Lessner, *Arizona Republic*, 24 October 1981, 1F.

35. George Basler, *[Binghamton, N.Y.] Evening Press*, 20 September 1984, 1A.

36. The doctrine here is "separation." To Jones, Falwell and Graham are not fundamentalists but New Evangelicals, defined by BJU professor David Beale as "the religious mood or attitude that repudiates Fundamentalism's doctrine of separation from false teachers and advocates theological dialogue with Modernism and greater social involvement" (David Beale, *S.B.C. House on the Sand? Critical Issues for Southern Baptists* (Greenville, S.C.: Unusual Publications,

1985), 211. Graham has been known to work with Protestants of all stripes as well as Roman Catholics in his evangelical crusades. Falwell, of course, welcomed all faiths to contribute to his Moral Majority, the only requirement being acceptance of his moral political platform. See the new work by Mark Taylor Dalhouse, *An Island in the Lake of Fire: Bob Jones University, Fundamentalism and the Separatist Movement* (Athens: University of Georgia Press, 1996), for a fuller explanation of BJU separatism.

37. Historically, fundamentalism, which gave birth to Jerry Falwell's Baptist Bible Fellowship and Bob Jones's Fundamental Baptist Fellowship, as well as Pat Robertson's Pentecostalism, have held a millennialist view of the world, expecting the imminent return of Christ to judge the world and rapture his church. Political activity, according to this belief, had the effect of rearranging deck chairs on a sinking ship. The best accounts of the millennialist mentality can be found in George Marsden, *Fundamentalism and American Culture: The Shaping of Twentieth-Century Evangelicalism, 1870–1925* (New York: Oxford University Press, 1982), and Helen Lee Turner, "Fundamentalism in the Southern Baptist Convention: Crystallization of the Millennialist Vision," Ph.D. diss., University of Virginia, 1991; see also chapter 1.

38. Sundquist, *Dynamics*, 288, 290, 291.

39. Jerry Falwell, *Strength for the Journey: An Autobiography* (Nashville: Thomas Nelson, 1987), 320–323. See also Merrill Simon, *Jerry Falwell and the Jews* (Middle Village, N.Y.: Jonathon David Publishers, 1984); Rodney A. Smolla, *Jerry Falwell vs. Larry Flint: The First Amendment on Trial* (New York: St. Martin's Press, 1988); Dinesh D'Souza, *Falwell, before the Millennium: A Critical Biography* (Chicago: Regnery Gateway, 1984); David Snowball, *Continuity and Change in the Rhetoric of the Moral Majority* (New York: Praeger, 1981).

40. Pat Robertson, *America's Dates with Destiny* (Nashville: Thomas Nelson, 1986), 298–304.

41. Jerry Falwell, *Listen America!* (New York: Doubleday, 1980), 245–266.

42. Robertson, *America's Dates*, 302–303. See also other political-religious titles by Pat Robertson: *The Secret Kingdom* (Nashville: Thomas Nelson, 1982); *The New Millennium* (Dallas: Word Publishers, 1990); and *The New World Order* (Boston: G. K. Hall, 1992). Less favorable accounts of the politics of televangelism, and Robertson in particular, include Larry Martz, *Ministry of Greed: The Inside Story of the Televangelists* (New York: Weidenfeld and Nicholson, 1988); Gerard Thomas Straub, *Salvation for Sale: An Insider's View of Pat Robertson's Ministry* (Buffalo, N.Y.: Prometheus Books, 1986). An evangelical view is found in Quentin Schultze, *Televangelism and American Culture: The Business of Popular Religion* (Grand Rapids, Mich.: Baker, 1991).

43. Ralph Reed on *Equal Time*, the Mary Matalin program, CNBC network, 21 October 1994.

44. Richard A. Viguerie, *The New Right: We're Ready to Lead* (Falls Church, Va.: Viguerie Company, 1980). Another account of the early stages of the Moral Majority is included in John L. Kater, Jr., *Christians on the Right: The Moral Majority in Perspective* (New York: Seabury Press, 1982).

45. Os Guinness, *The American Hour: A Time of Reckoning and the Once and Future Role of Faith* (New York: Free Press, 1993), 193–194.

46. Ibid., 196–197. Wald, Owen, and Hill, "Political Cohesion," 215, and Wilcox, *God's Warriors*, 225, report in separate studies that interviews with Christian right supporters revealed a certain lack of respect from the culture at large and a bit of alienation (see chapter 2 for a complete discussion of this phenomenon).

47. Religion writer Dinesh D'Souza wrote that "in the 1950s two preachers, Billy James Hargis and Carl McIntire, urged evangelicals to political activism, but few heeded their appeal. People were comfortable in the fundamentalist enclaves of Sunday church-going and organ music. Who wanted to combat communism, sex education, and pornography when they did not threaten the subculture? Besides, there was a theological reason for political celibacy: fundamentalism suggests that since the world is going to end soon (the doctrine of millenialism) they had better get about the business of saving souls and not exert themselves over ephemeral politics" (*Los Angeles Times* (11 June 1984, II:14). As we saw in chapters 1 and 2, the opposite is true here. Southern Baptists were unlikely to begin political crusading while they dominated the culture.

48. Stephen Carter, *The Culture of Disbelief* (New York: Basic Books, 1993), 3–8.

49. Ammerman writes that in the late 1800s–early 1900s fundamentalist "organizational channels were . . . primarily urban, northeastern, and in the Baptist and Presbyterian denominations. During these formative years, fundamentalism's strength was in New York and Philadelphia, Boston and Chicago, Minneapolis, and Toronto, rather than in Atlanta or Charleston or Birmingham. In the South, liberal theology and social change were not yet factors to be defended against, and Protestantism had not yet been displaced as a dominant community force" (Ammerman, *Bible Believers*, 21).

50. David O. Beale, *In Pursuit of Purity: American Fundamentalism since 1850* (Greenville, S.C.: Unusual Publications, 1986), 268.

51. D'Souza, in *L.A. Times*.

52. Nancy Tatom Ammerman, "The New South and the New Baptists," *Christian Century*, 14 May 1986, 486.

53. A view exemplified by Southern Baptist Progressive Roger Lovette in "Why I Am Not a Fundamentalist," *SBC Today*, October 1985, 14ff.

54. Ellen M. Rosenberg, *The Southern Baptists: A Subculture in Transition* (Knoxville: University of Tennessee Press, 1989), 210.

55. Jerry Falwell, *The Fundamentalist Phenomenon* (New York: Doubleday-Galilee, 1981), 138.

56. *Fundamentalist Journal*, July–August, 1989; "Conservative Surge in the SBC," *Fundamentalist Journal*, February 1983, 24; Carl Diemer, "Southern Baptists: From Where, to Where?" *Fundamentalist Journal*, February 1983, 14.

57. Quentin Schultze, "The Two Faces in Fundamentalist Higher Education," 490–535, in Martin E. Marty, ed., *Fundamentalisms and Society: Reclaiming the Sciences, the Family, and Education* (Chicago: University of Chicago Press, 1993).

58. Bob Jones, Jr., "Can the SBC Be Reclaimed?" *Faith for the Family*, December 1981, 2; Bob Jones, III, "What Is a Fundamentalist?" *Faith for the Family*, October 1985, reprint; J. B. Williams, "The Authority of Scripture vs. the Southern Baptist Convention," *Faith for the Family*, December 1983; James E. Singleton, "The Strange Case of the SBC," *Faith for the Family*, November 1981, 27. Having said what Jones thinks about Falwell and vice versa and stating the differences between Robertson and Falwell, we should also note that Bob Jones, Jr., had this to say about the presidential candidacy of Pat Robertson: "Bush is a trilateralist. The pineapple man—what's his name? Dole?—he's a trilateralist, and Pat Robertson doesn't know which way he's going. Pat Robertson makes a lot of crazy statements. I make them too, but I'm not running for office" (*World* magazine, 21 March 1988, 3.)

59. James C. Hefley, *The Truth in Crisis: The Controversy in the Southern Baptist Convention*, vol. 4: *The State of the Denomination* (Hannibal, Mo.: Hannibal Books, 1989), 6.

60. Beale, *S.B.C.*, 71–72, 132, 139; see also David O. Beale, *The Continuing Battle in the SBC: Are There Fundamentalists in the Southern Baptist Convention?* (Greenville, S.C.: Unusual Publications, 1986).

61. Falwell, *Fundamentalist*.

62. R. L. Hymers, "Why I Left the Southern Baptist Convention," *Baptist Bible Tribune*, 9 May 1986, 4; "Forty-Eight Percent of Southern Baptists Drink," *Baptist Bible Trumpet*, January 1985, 4; Curtis Hutson, "First Baptist Church, Fort Worth, Texas, Seeks Reaffiliation with SBC: Should Independent Baptists Reunite with the SBC?" *Sword of the Lord*, 20 July 1990, 1; John R. Rice, *Southern Baptists Wake Up: Modernism, Neo-Orthodoxy, Unbelief, Compromise, and Worldliness in Southern Baptist Seminaries, Colleges, and Literature* (Murfreesboro, Tenn.: Sword of the Lord, 1963); "Southern Baptist Committee Favors Euthanasia Bill," *Baptist Bible Trumpet*, June 1981, 1; Gerald Thompson, "Why We Must Leave the Southern Baptist Convention," *Sword of the Lord*, 5 March 1976, 1; R. L. Heimers, *Inside the Southern Baptist Convention* (Collingswood, N.J.: Bible for Today, 1990).

63. George W. Dollar, *A History of Fundamentalism in America* (Greenville, S.C.: Bob Jones University Press, 1973).

64. Yance, *Religion Southern Style*, 10.

65. Hill, *Religion and the Solid South*, 49; James C. Hefley, *The Truth in Crisis: The Controversy in the Southern Baptist Convention* (Dallas: Criterion Publications, 1986); idem, *The Truth in Crisis: The Controversy in the Southern Baptist Convention*, vol. 2: *Updating the Controversy* (Hannibal, Mo.: Hannibal Books, 1987); idem, *The Truth in Crisis: The Controversy in the Southern Baptist Convention*, vol. 3: *Conservative Resurgence or Political Takeover?* (Hannibal, Mo.: Hannibal Books, 1988); idem, *The Truth in Crisis: The Controversy in the Southern Baptist Convention*, vol. 4: *The State of the Denomination* (Hannibal, Mo.: Hannibal Books, 1989); idem, *The Truth in Crisis: The Controversy in the Southern Baptist Convention*, vol. 5: *The "Winning Edge"* (Hannibal, Mo.: Hannibal Books, 1990); idem, *The Conservative Resurgence in the Southern Baptist Convention* (Hannibal, Mo.: Hannibal Books, 1991).

66. John Lee Eighmy, *Churches in Cultural Captivity: A History of the Social Attitudes of Southern Baptists* (Knoxville: University of Tennessee Press, 1972), 70–71.

67. Garrett, *Are Southern Baptists*, 119; see also William Robert Glass, "The Development of Northern Patterns of Fundamentalism in the South, 1900–1950," Ph.D. diss., Emory University, 1991.

NOTES TO CHAPTER 5

1. Michael Lienesch, *Redeeming America: Piety and Politics in the New Christian Right* (Chapel Hill: University of North Carolina Press, 1993).

2. Richard Viguerie, *The New Right: We're Ready to Lead* (Falls Church, Va.: Viguerie Company, 1980), 160.

3. Author's interview with South Carolina governor Carroll A. Campbell, 10 May 1993.

4. Karl Hill, "GOP May Mend Wounds or Split Down Center," *Greenville [S.C.] News*, 12 March 1978, 14A; Dale Perry, "Despite GOP Split, Two Groups Get Along Well," *Greenville [S.C.] News*, 19 February 1978, 4B; Dale Perry, "GOP Factions Join to Elect County Chairman," *Greenville [S.C.] News*, 14 March 1978, 1B; and "Two-Year-Old Rift Erupts Again," *Greenville [S.C.] News*, 14 February 1978, 5A.

5. Many of the facts in this section are from my own observations of Greenville County (S.C.) politics.

6. Melton Wright, *Fortress of Faith: The Story of Bob Jones University* (Grand Rapids, Mich.: Eerdmans, 1960), 324–328.

7. Author's interview with Dr. D. B. Verdin, Jr., 2 October 1994.

8. Bob Jones graduates Dell Baker and Terry Haskins were elected to South Carolina House seats in Greenville County with little use of their BJU connections. Baker's campaign literature in District 28 (like his legislative manual biog-

raphy) stressed that he was a graduate of Clemson University, where he received his Master's degree in accounting. Haskins, in the BJU-dominated District 22 (congressional candidate Rigdon's old district), listed himself as a BJU graduate in his literature and in his manual biography. The strongly partisan Haskins became the top Republican in the South Carolina House, rising to the office of minority leader in fewer than two years in Columbia and serving until he was defeated in 1993 by an alliance of "regular" and freshman Republicans who favored a less combative style. They elected a fellow Greenvillian, Howell Clyborne. Dell Baker played a much less partisan role than Haskins, learning the process in Columbia and making enough friends among Democrats to earn himself a subcommittee chairmanship until he was defeated for comptroller general in 1994. Haskins was elected speaker pro-tempore of the South Carolina House after the 1994 Republican takeover of that body. Clyborne was defeated for lieutenant governor that year and serves as Governor Beasley's legislative director.

9. *Bob Jones University* v. *United States of America*, 468 F. Supp. 890, 907 (D.S.C. 1978); *Bob Jones University* v. *United States of America*, 639 F. 2d; "Opinions Announced May 24, 1983," *United States Law Week* 51:45. The case had an impact here in that (1) though BJU paid all the back taxes owed to the IRS from internal sources, it was quite a financial setback, and (2) a number of non-fundamentalist churches filed amicus briefs for BJU. Neither seemed to make BJU less fundamentalist but perhaps it became more politically aware after 1978.

10. Cassette tape copy of David Beasley's speech to Bob Jones University daily chapel service with introduction by Bob Jones, III, 1994. Also Bill McAllister, "Religious Right's Latest Star Is Rising in the South: Former S.C. State Legislator to Win GOP Gubernatorial Nomination in Runoff," *Washington Post*, 22 August 1994, A6.

11. Cindi Ross Scoppe, "Catholic Faith Costing Hartnett Votes, Hartnett Says," *[Columbia, S.C.] State*, 29 March 1994, B4; also, author's informal discussions by telephone with Hartnett campaign manager Walt Whetsell in February and March 1994.

12. Many of the facts in this section are from my conversations with political consultants, campaign managers, and party leaders during the Republican primary campaign of 1994.

13. Many of the facts in this section are from my own observations of South Carolina Republican politics.

14. Michael D'Antonio, *Fall from Grace: The Failed Crusade of the Christian Right* (New York: Farrar, Straus, Giroux, 1990).

15. Ralph Reed, "Casting a Wider Net," *Policy Review* (Summer 1993) 65:31–35; Laurence I. Barrett, "Fighting for God and the Right Wing," *Time*, 13 September 1993, 58–60.

16. "Christian Coalition Voter Guide, 1992," Christian Coalition, Chesapeake, Virginia.

17. Megan Rosenfeld, "Anatomy of a Defeat: How a Middle-of-the-Road Incumbent Got Run Over on Election Day," *Washington Post*, November 1992, D1.

18. Many of the facts in this section are from the author's participant observation of the South Carolina Republican convention, 8 May 1993, and B. Drummond Ayers, Jr., "Christian Right Splits GOP in South," *New York Times*, 7 June 1993, A7; June Shissias and Barry Wynn, "South Carolina Republican Leadership Council," August 1993 newsletter.

19. Cole Blease Graham, Jr., William V. Moore, and Frank T. Petrusak write in "Praise the Lord and Join the Republicans: The Christian Coalition and the Republican Party in South Carolina" (paper presented at the 1994 Annual Meeting of the Western Political Science Association, Albuquerque) that the 1993 South Carolina Republican Convention revealed a distinct split in the party. Delegates who were willing to claim that they were "members or supporters of the Christian Coalition" were much more likely to have chosen the Republican party because of "lifestyle issues," whereas non-Coalition delegates were more likely to respond that they are Republicans because of greater affinity for Republican candidates or because of a feeling that the Democratic party had changed.

One-third of the non-Coalition delegates called themselves fundamentalists, compared to 87 percent of Coalition delegates. Three-quarters of non-Coalition delegates believed that members of churches should get involved in politics, 98 percent of Coalition delegates agreed with the statement. Opposition to marijuana was 73 percent and 89, percent respectively. Opposition to a state lottery was 53 percent and 88 percent, restrictions on abortions was supported 55 percent and 97 percent, and school prayer and Bible reading were supported 79 percent and 94 percent.

20. Author's participant observation, as well as Bill Robinson, "Conservative Coastal Candidates Identified: GOP Chief Denies List Put Forth as a Slate," *[Columbia, S.C.] State*, 2 June 1993, 1B, and Bill Robinson, "Candidates on 'Conservative' List Lose Trustee Bids," *[Columbia, S.C.] State*, 3 June 1993, 1B.

21. Lee Bandy, *[Columbia, S.C.] State*, 13 June 1993, 2D. The author of this book was the lone survivor of those on the McMaster "conservative" list. All other candidates for the Coastal Carolina University board on the list were defeated by wide and narrow margins. The author's opponent dropped out of the contest the day the legislature held the vote.

22. Author's informal conversations with Henry McMaster, South Carolina Republican chairman, June 1993.

23. Graham, Moore, and Petrusak, "Praise the Lord."

24. Lee Bandy, "Hartnett Complains to Christian Coalition," *[Columbia, S.C.] State*, 19 July 1994, B1; Lee Bandy, "Christian Coalition Sparks Inflame GOP Campaigns," *[Columbia, S.C.] State*, 20 July 1994, B5. The third candidate, Arthur Ravenel, was strongest in his tone against the coalition but had on

file a letter dated 12 August 1994 from Philip Charles Bryant, pastor of the French Protestant Church in Charleston, which said in part: "He rarely misses a church service and knowing him as I do, it was no surprise to me to read in a recent newspaper article that he has given more to his church than any other candidate for Governor. Next to his family, his church means more to him than any other thing. After serving for almost a quarter century as a pastor, I wish that every church had a member and leader like Arthur Ravenel."

25. Erik Eckholm, "Clinton Bashing a Growth Industry: 'High Technology Overlay' Propels Diatribes," New York Times service in *[Columbia, S.C.] State*, 26 June 1994.

26. Charlie Rhodes, "America . . . You're Too Young to Die!!" Campaign brochure, South Carolina Republican U.S. Senate primary, 1980.

27. Cindi Ross Scoppe, "Abortion Question Gets Angry Answers," *[Columbia, S.C.] State*, 11 February 1994, 1A.

28. Author's interview with Corning campaign worker John Ward, III, 2 October 1994.

29. Author's interviews with Flynn Harrell, 10 February 1994; 8 January 1997.

30. Matthew 25:34–40 (RSV) reads: "Then the King will say to those at his right hand, 'Come, O blessed of my Father, inherit the kingdom prepared for you from the foundation of the world; for I was hungry and you gave me food, I was thirsty, and you gave me drink, I was a stranger, and you welcomed me, I was naked and you clothed me, I was sick and you visited me; I was in prison, and you came to me.' Then the righteous will answer him, 'Lord, when did we see thee hungry, and fed thee? or thirsty and give thee drink? And when did we see thee a stranger and welcome thee, or naked and clothe thee? And when did we see thee sick or in prison, and visit thee?' And the King will answer them, 'Truly, I say unto you, as you did it to one of the least of these my brethren, you did it to me.'"

31. James L. Guth, "The Politics of Preachers: Southern Baptist Ministers and Christian Right Activism," in David G. Bromley and Anson Shupe, eds., *New Christian Politics*, 235–250 (Macon, Ga.: Mercer University Press, 1984); James L. Guth, "Southern Baptists and the New Right," in Charles W. Dunn, ed., *Religion in American Politics*, 177–190 (Washington, D.C.: CQ Press, 1989); France Evans, "Ministers Switching to GOP: Southern Baptist Clergy Desert Democrats, Survey Shows," *Greenville [S.C.] News*, 28 May 1985, 1B.

32. "Conservatives Encourage Pulling Children from Greenville Schools," *[Columbia, S.C.] State*, 21 September 1993; Jeannie Faris, "National Baptist Rift Filters Down to State," *Greenville [S.C.] News*, 29 September 1991, 1E; Author's interview with former Greenwood County Republican chairman John Ward, III, 2 October 1994.

33. A statewide survey of South Carolina households was conducted by the

Institute of Public Affairs of the University of South Carolina using a random-digit-dialing method during November 1990. A representative sample of 645 state residents, aged eighteen or older, was randomly selected within the household using the "last birthday" method of respondent selection. The data were weighed to correct any potential biases in the samples on the basis of age, race, sex, or number of adults in the household. The sample has a sampling error for the entire population of approximately plus or minus 4 percent. For my purposes, to isolate not only Baptists residing in the South, but those who identify with the Southern Baptist Convention, only whites were selected for this analysis. All missing data were removed as well. The South Carolina survey was selected because of its method of asking for religious preference and of the answers received. After asking the question, "What is your religion, if any?," the only probe attempted consisted of the follow-up question, "Is it Protestant, Catholic, Jewish, some other religion, or no religion?" No specific denominations were given.

34. Survey results based on 640 interviews with a random sample of voters likely to vote in the South Carolina Republican primary. (Because the names were selected from a list of voters who had voted in each of the last two Republican primaries and due to the racial cleavage in the South Carolina electorate, no black South Carolinians were polled.)

The poll was paid for by the Condon for Attorney General campaign and contained an equal number of males and females. The survey was conducted by telephone 4–5 August 1994 by First Impressions Research of Columbia, South Carolina. As an employee of First Impressions, I secured a small grant from the Foundation for American Education of Columbia, South Carolina, which allowed the addition of three religion questions to the Condon survey. The exact wording of the questions, composed by me, is listed in Appendix B. Those conducting the survey were professional pollsters, but I did not train or observe them.

35. Author's interview with David Beasley, 27 August 1994.

36. Author's interview with South Carolina governor Carroll A. Campbell, 10 May 1993.

37. Author's interview with South Carolina governor Carroll A. Campbell, 10 May 1993.

38. Bob Jones, *Cornbread and Caviar* (Greenville, S.C.: Bob Jones University Press, 1985).

39. Author's interview with Governor Carroll A. Campbell, 10 May 1993.

40. Jeff Goldstein, "Christian Coalition Declares War on Clinton Health Plan," *[Columbia, S.C.] State*, 15 February 1994, 7A; Lee Bandy, *[Columbia, S.C.] State*, 11 February 1994, 2D.

41. Of all Falwell's ministries, Liberty University seems to be his favorite.

42. Cody Lowe, "Falwell: Liberty Is Here for Keeps," *Roanoke Times and World News*, 3 September 1992, 1B; Julie L. Nicklin, "Liberty University Avoids

Foreclosure Action in Settlement with Bond Holders," *Chronicle of Higher Education*, 9 December 1992, A28.

43. Nancy Tatom Ammerman, "SBC and the New Christian Right," *SBC Today*, February 1988, 1, 4–5.

44. Author's interview with John Ward, III, former Greenwood County Republican chairman, 2 October 1994.

45. Author's interview with David Beasley, 27 August 1994.

46. The concepts developed in figures 5.1–5.7 are derived in part from frameworks found in classic works such as J. David Greenstone, *Labor in American Politics* (New York: Knopf, 1969), 173–281, and Theodore J. Lowi, *The End of Liberalism: The Second Republic in the United States* (New York: Norton, 1969), 39–99.

47. Oran P. Smith, "Continuity and Change in Dixie's Established Church: Southern Baptists and Politics, 1930–1990," paper presented at the annual meeting of the American Political Science Association, New York Hilton, 1–4 September 1994. See also chapter 1.

48. See chapter 4.

49. See chapter 4; "Christian Life Commission Program, 1994," Christian Life Commission, Southern Baptist Convention, Nashville, Tennessee.

50. Author's interview with Dr. D. B. Verdin, Jr., supporter of Ted Adams for Congress, 2 October 1994.

51. This suggests the theories of resource mobilization discussed in this context in Jerome L. Himmelstein, *To the Right: The Transformation of American Conservatism* (Berkeley: University of California Press, 1990), 120–124, and in chapter 2 of this work. Also, as in any organization, there is always the temptation for leadership of a group to be "co-opted" and made a tool of more moderate forces. In some sense, this is true of the BJU leadership since 1976; see Frances Fox Piven and Richard A. Cloward, *Poor People's Movements: Why They Succeed, How They Fail* (New York: Random House, 1977), 27–37. But then, given BJU's GOP power, the question may be, who is co-opting whom?

52. For a discussion of these reformers, see Jean Miller Schmidt, *Souls of the Social Order: The Two-Party System in American Protestantism* (New York: Carlson, 1991). The difference between conservative and progressive Baptists in the SBC on "soul winning" can be found in Ammerman, *Baptist Battles*, 117–125.

53. Lee Bandy, "Baptists Urge USC to Cancel Course," *[Columbia, S.C.] State*, 2 June 1993, 1A; "Baptists Demand USC Cancel Course," *Charleston Post and Courier*, 3 June 1993; "USC to Review Graduate-Level Religion Course amid Baptists' Protests." *Greenville [S.C.] News*, 4 June 1993; "Christian Schools Grow in SBC," *Moody*, January 1980, 124.

54. Himmelstein, *To the Right*, 45–62.

55. Randall Balmer, *Mine Eyes Have Seen the Glory: A Journey into the Evangelical Subculture in America* (New York: Oxford University Press, 1989), 284.

NOTES TO CHAPTER 6

1. James L. Guth in David Leege and Lyman A. Kellstedt, *Rediscovering the Religious Factor in American Politics* (Armonk, N.Y.: M. E. Sharpe, 1993), 236.

2. Nancy Tatom Ammerman, *Baptist Battles: Social Change and Religious Conflict in the Southern Baptist Convention* (New Brunswick, N.J.: Rutgers University Press, 1990), 486.

3. Stuart Rothenberg and Frank Newport, *The Evangelical Voter* (Washington, D.C.: Free Congress, 1984). James L. Guth, "The Politics of Preachers: Southern Baptist Ministers and Christian Right Activism," in David G. Bromley and Anson Shupe, eds., *New Christian Politics*, 235–250 (Macon, Ga.: Mercer University Press, 1984); James L. Guth, "Southern Baptists and the New Right," in Charles W. Dunn, ed., *Religion in American Politics*, 177–190 (Washington, D.C.: CQ Press, 1989).

4. Nancy Tatom Ammerman, "The New South and the New Baptists," *Christian Century*, 14 May 1986, 486; Nancy Tatom Ammerman, "SBC and the New Christian Right," *SBC Today*, February 1988, 1, 4–5; Clyde Wilcox, "Religious Orientations and Political Attitudes: Variations within the New Christian Right," *American Politics Quarterly* 15 (1987):274–296.

5. For a time, SBC ministers were to the left of their congregations. Most observers estimate that SBC pastors are now to the right of their flocks.

6. I appreciate the assistance of Michael W. Link of the Institute of Public Affairs at the University of South Carolina for 1992 ANES data.

7. African Americans are removed from each sample due to an entirely distinct black religious-political tradition (David C. Leege, "The Decomposition of the Religious Vote," paper presented at the Annual Meeting of the American Political Science Association, Washington, D.C., 1–4 September 1993, 4, 277, 300). However, with the growing number of black Southern Baptist churches that have either left predominately black denominations and joined the SBC or have been "planted" by the SBC, this analysis may have to be adjusted in the not-too-distant future. Additional information on the survey is available from the author.

8. See Appendix D.

9. As the previous chapters have shown, a temporal analysis is essential to understanding the changing politics of the SBC.

10. Based on the analysis of Allen Hertzke, *Representing God in Washington: The Role of Religious Lobbies in the American Polity* (Knoxville: University of Tennessee Press, 1988), 127, and upon the advice of James L. Guth, I have decided to compare church-going samples with non-church-going samples.

11. Angus Campbell, Philip E. Converse, Warren Miller, and Donald E. Stokes, *The American Voter* (Chicago: University of Chicago Press, 1960), 295–332.

12. Michael Cromartie, ed., *No Longer Exiles: The Religious New Right in American Politics* (Washington, D.C.: Ethics and Public Policy Center, 1993), 24.

13. Senator Jesse Helms (R-North Carolina) is equally adamant about his Southern heritage, his Southern Baptist affiliation, and his conservatism. He founded the militantly conservative Congressional Club, is a member of the Sons of Confederate Veterans, and received the Religious Freedom Award from the SBC Public Affairs Committee in 1990 ("Religious Liberty Award Goes to Senator Helms," *Southern Baptist Advocate*, June 1990, 2).

14. Bill J. Leonard, *God's Last and Only Hope: The Fragmentation of the Southern Baptist Convention* (Grand Rapids, Mich.: Eerdmans, 1990).

15. Herchel H. Hobbs, ed., *The Baptist Faith and Message* (Nashville: Sunday School Board, Southern Baptist Convention, 1963), 7.

16. Mark Ellingsen, *The Cutting Edge: How Churches Speak on Social Issues* (Grand Rapids, Mich.: Eerdmans, 1993).

17. BJCPA director and Convention moderate James Dunn suggested that 1968 was a "watershed year for Baptists" (Dunn interview, 8 June 1994).

18. Ellingsen, *Cutting Edge*.

19. Southern Baptist Convention Annual (1971), (1974), (1976–1980), (1982), (1984), (1987), (1989), and (1993).

20. Southern Baptist Convention Annual (1976), 57–58; ibid. (1978), 65; ibid. (1979), 50–51.

21. Ibid. (1984), 66.

22. Ibid. (1989), 53–54.

23. Ibid. (1993), 99–100.

24. Ibid., 99–100.

25. Ibid. (1968–93).

26. Ibid. (1969), 76.

27. Ibid. (1970), 75–76.

28. Ibid. (1976–78), (1980), (1985), (1988), (1993), and (1996).

29. Ibid. (1976), 58.

30. Ibid. (1985), 85.

31. Ibid. (1969–74), (1978), (1981–84), (1986), (1988), (1989), (1993), (1995), and (1996).

32. Ibid. (1982), 64.

33. Ibid. (1972), 75.

34. Ibid. (1978), 63–64.

35. Ibid. (1968), 80–81.

36. Ibid. (1972), 81.

37. Ibid. (1978), 54.

38. Ibid. (1980), 54.

39. Ibid. (1981), 54.

40. Ibid. (1983), 63.

41. Ibid. (1991), 82.

42. Ibid. (1971), 79.

43. However, in passing the resolution to pray for the president, the Mississippi Convention adopted an amendment proposed by Bobby Hood of Laurel and seconded by Lewis Nobles of Clinton, Mississippi to "delete the words 'fellow Southern Baptists' from the resolution" when referring to President Clinton and Vice-President Gore (Annual, Mississippi Baptist Convention (1992), 29–30).

44. *Annual*, South Carolina Baptist Convention (1992), 82.

45. Baptist *Annual*, Florida Baptist Convention (1992), 76.

46. Ellen M. Rosenberg, *The Southern Baptists: A Subculture in Transition* (Knoxville: University of Tennessee Press, 1989), 91–92; Leonard, *God's Last and Only Hope*, 161; chapter 2.

47. Norman Alexander Yance, *Religion Southern Style* (Association of Baptist Professors of Religion, 1978), 39.

48. Robert A. Baker, *The Southern Baptist Convention and Its People, 1607–1972* (Nashville: Broadman Press, 1974); William Wright Barnes, *The Southern Baptist Convention, 1845–1953* (Nashville: Broadman Press, 1954); Edward L. Queen, *In the South the Baptists Are the Center of Gravity: Southern Baptists and Social Change, 1930–1980* (New York: Carlson, 1991).

49. Land is closely associated with Dallas pastor and conservative faction leader W. A. Criswell (Leonard, *God's Last and Only Hope*, 160; Rosenberg, *Southern Baptists*, 91–92, 199).

50. James C. Hefley, *The Truth in Crisis: The Controversy in the Southern Baptist Convention*, vol. 4: *The State of the Denomination* (Hannibal, Mo.: Hannibal Books, 1989), 169–190.

51. Queen, *In the South*, and chapter 3.

52. Yance, *Religion Southern Style*, 53.

53. Frances Fox Piven and Richard A. Cloward, *Poor People's Movements: Why They Succeed, How They Fail* (New York: Vintage, 1977), 30–33, 252–255.

54. James Davison Hunter, *Culture Wars: The Struggle to Define America* (New York: Basic Books, 1991), 306.

55. Hunter, *Culture Wars*, 61–63.

56. Ibid., 306.

57. This is certainly an interesting proposition, but Hunter misses an important distinction here, a point made effectively by Lawrence (Bruce B. Lawrence, *Defenders of God: The Fundamentalist Revolt against the Modern Age* [San

Francisco: Harper and Row, 1989], 2, 39–46), that there is a difference between "modernity" and "modernism." Modernism is a doctrinal shift to the left. Modernity is old wine in new bottles. The question is: Will the SBC be able to face *modernity* without becoming *modernist*?

NOTES TO CHAPTER 7

1. The label "hyper-Americans" is applied to Southern Baptists in Ellen Rosenberg, *The Southern Baptists: A Subculture in Transition* (Knoxville: University of Tennessee Press, 1989).

2. Arthur Farnsley, II, *Southern Baptist Politics: Authority and Power in the Restructuring of an American Denomination* (University Park: Penn State University Press, 1994), 127.

3. James Davison Hunter, *Culture Wars* (New York: Basic Books, 1991), 306.

4. James L. Guth, "Southern Baptists and the New Right," in Charles W. Dunn, ed., *Religion in American Politics*, 177–190 (Washington, D.C.: CQ Press, 1989).

5. Hunter, *Culture Wars*, 306.

6. Joe Edward Barnhart, *The Southern Baptist Holy War* (Austin: Texas Monthly Press, 1986), 251; Michael D'Antonio, *Fall from Grace: The Failed Crusade of the Christian Right* (New York: Farrar, Straus, Giroux, 1989), 202, 214. Perhaps it should be noted here that, in terms of *success*, though Southern Baptists are holding their own in membership, as D'Antonio reported in 1989, 75 percent of United Methodist candidates for the ministry in North Carolina in that year were former Southern Baptists.

7. Herb Hollinger, "Southern Baptists, Assemblies of God Top Congregational Giving Study," *Baptist Press Wire Service*, America Online, 18 June 1995.

8. "Evangelicals and Catholics Together: The Christian Mission in the Third Millennium," *First Things*, May 1994, 15–22.

9. In recent years, "paleo-conservative" has come to mean the Old Right of the *Conservative Mind* author Russell Kirk and politician Pat Buchanan variety that is primarily Anglo and agrarian and purist. "Neo-conservative" has come to mean the type represented by *Commentary* editor Irving Kristol and politician Bill Bennett, which is more urban, less Protestant, and more tolerant.

10. *First Things*, 1994.

11. "Evangelicals and Catholics Together: The Christian Mission in the Third Millennium: A Critique," in *SBCNet* CompuServe Forum, undated.

12. SBCNet.

13. Richard Land, "Evangelicals and Catholics?" in *SBCNet* CompuServe Forum, undated.

14. J. I. Packer, "Why I Signed It," *Christianity Today*, 12 December 1994, America Online.

15. Joe Maxwell, "Evangelicals Clarify Accord with Catholics," *Christianity Today*, 6 March 1995; Martin King, "Catholic-Evangelical Signers Address Areas of Controversy," *Baptist Press Wire Service*, 13 March 1995.

16. Ken Camp, "95 Hispanic Leaders Protest Catholic/Evangelical Document," *Baptist Press Wire Service*, 13 March 1995.

17. "Setback for Evangelical-Catholic Pact," *Christianity Today*, April 1995, America Online; "Land, Lewis Remove Names from Controversial Document," *Light*, July–August 1995, 12.

18. Bill Merrill, "CLC Consultation Yields Stance on Racism," *Baptist Press Wire Service*, 18 June 1995, America Online.

19. Jack E. White, "Forgive Our Sins," *Time*, 3 July 1995, 29; Andrea Stone, "Southern Baptists 'Repent' Past," *USA Today*, 20 June 1995, 3A; Jennifer Graham, "Baptists to Weigh Sins of the Past," *[Columbia, S.C.] State*, 19 June 1995, A1.

20. "Resolution on Racial Reconciliation on the 150th Anniversary of the Southern Baptist Convention," in *SBCNet* CompuServe Forum, June 1995.

21. Wesley Pruden, "When Southern Baptists Freed Their Slaves," *Washington Times*, 23 June 1995, A4.

22. Joe Maxwell, "Black Southern Baptists," *Christianity Today*, America Online, undated.

23. David Winfrey, "Home Mission Board Study: Baptists Losing Ground in the South," *Baptist Press Wire Service*, America Online, undated; Jennifer Graham, "Black Baptists Rate Sincerity, Motive of SBC," *[Columbia, S.C.] State*, 27 June 1995, A1.

24. Carl Rowan, "An Open Letter to the Nation's Southern Baptists," *[Columbia, S.C.] State*, 25 June 1995, D3.

25. Merrill, 18 June 1995.

26. Maxwell, *Christianity Today*.

27. "Resolution on Racial Reconciliation," SBCNet.

28. White, "Forgive Our Sins," 29.

29. Tom Strode, "Blacks Should Oppose Foster, Baptist Pastor Says," *Baptist Press Wire Service*, undated.

30. Sylvester Monroe, "The Gospel of Diversity," *Time*, 24 April 1995, 64.

31. Maxwell, *Christianity Today*.

NOTES TO CHAPTER 8

1. Grady Cothen, *What Happened to the Southern Baptist Convention?* (Macon, Ga.: Smyth and Helwys, 1993), 24; see also chapter 1.

2. Walter B. Shurden, *The Baptist Identity: Four Fragile Freedoms* (Macon, Ga.: Smyth and Helwys, 1993).

3. Cothen, *What Happened?*, 12, 17, 27, 33, 83–89, 148.

4. Ibid., 148.

5. Harold Bloom, *The American Religion* (New York: Simon and Schuster, 1993), 229.

6. Arthur Farnsley II, *Southern Baptist Politics: Authority and Power in the Restructuring of an American Denomination* (University Park, Penn.: Pennsylvania State University Press, 1994), 125, 140–143.

7. Earl Black and Merle Black, *Politics and Society in the South* (Cambridge, Mass.: Harvard University Press, 1987), 292–316; idem, *The Vital South* (Cambridge, Mass.: Harvard University Press, 1992), 176–240, 293–326; Larry Rochelle, "Born-Again Politics: Now the Republicans," *Humanist*, November–December 1980, 18–25, 60.

8. William Alexander Percy, *Lanterns on the Levee* (New York: Knopf, 1941), 140–155. For an extended discussion of Southern demagogic racial rhetoric, see also Earl Black, *Southern Governors and Civil Rights* (Cambridge, Mass.: Harvard University Press, 1976), 342.

9. Percy, *Lanterns*, 148, 153.

10. W. J. Cash, *The Mind of the South* (New York: Knopf, 1941), 254.

11. George Marsden, "Politics and Religion in American History," *Reformed Journal*, October 1988, 15.

12. Walker Percy, *The Last Gentleman* (New York: Farrar, Straus, Giroux, 1966), 177–179. Part of this passage (p. 177) is quoted in the Lind article below. I have chosen to extend the quotation to include material from pp. 178–179 that is more applicable to the thesis here.

13. John Egerton, *The Americanization of Dixie: The Southernization of America* (New York: Harper's Magazine Press, 1974).

14. As we have said, after fifteen years of control, Paige Patterson et al. have changed the Southern Baptist Convention. This rise of the conservative movement has affected the individual churches as well. The current climate at the typical local First Baptist Church is conservative morally, theologically, and politically, but it is also anti-intellectual. This is best reflected in a change in the style of worship that had been used for a century. The style is no longer moderate. Sanctuaries are now Worship Centers, Bach preludes have been replaced by gospel hymns, gospel hymns have been replaced by praise choruses, Vaughn-Williams anthems have been replaced by sing-alongs with taped accompaniment, and expository sermons have been replaced by topical messages designed for television. The annual meeting has taken on a similar cast. Formerly these were gatherings of 10,000 to 20,000 preachers, but attendance has been reaching the 45,000 level during years of hotly contested SBC presidential races.

15. Michael Lind, "The Southern Coup," *New Republic*, 19 June 1995, 26, 29.

16. Martin P. Wattenberg, *The Rise of Candidate-Centered Politics: Presidential Elections in the 1980s* (Cambridge, Mass.: Harvard University Press,

1991); Leon Epstein, *Political Parties in the American Mold* (Madison: University of Wisconsin Press, 1986), 210, 227, 231, 376; L. Sandy Maisel, ed., *The Parties Respond: Changes in the American Party System* (Boulder, Colo.: Westview Press, 1990), 3–17, 137–159, 204–224.

17. Daniel J. Elazar, *American Federalism: A View from the States* (New York: Harper and Row, 1984).

18. Black and Black, *Vital South*, 150; Nancy Tatom Ammerman, *Baptist Battles* (New Brunswick, N.J.: Rutgers University Press, 1990), 174.

Bibliography

AUTHOR INTERVIEWS AND INFORMAL CONVERSATIONS
(INTERVIEWEE, DATE OF INTERVIEW)

Marion Aldridge, Pastor of Greenlawn Baptist Church, Columbia, S.C., July 1993.

David Beasley, Republican nominee for governor/governor of South Carolina, 27 August 1994.

Orin Briggs, Christian lay political leader, 1995.

Carroll A. Campbell, governor of South Carolina, 1987–1995, 10 May 1993.

James M. Dunn, Director, Baptist Joint Committee for Public Affairs, 8 June 1994.

Charles Goolsby, Texas Southern Baptist lay leader, 6 February 1995.

Flynn Harrell, Baptist lay leader, February 10, 1994, July–September 1996.

Eugene G. Hogan II, Baptist deacon and lay leader, 1993–1996.

Henry McMaster, South Carolina Republican chairman, June 1993.

E. Ray Moore, Jr., Robertson for President Operative, August 1996.

Cyndi C. Mosteller, Christian Life Commission, South Carolina Baptist Convention, June–July 1996.

Richard M. Quinn, political consultant, Americans for Robertson, 1993–1996.

Marguerite E. Stafford, Georgia Baptist lay leader, 2 February 1995.

Christopher Morgan Sullivan, Baptist deacon and lay leader, 1993–1996.

Dr. D. B. Verdin, Jr., member of Board of Trustees, Bob Jones University, 2 October 1994.

John Ward III, Chair, Greenwood County Republican Party, 2 October 1994.

Walter Whetsell, Campaign Manager, South Carolina Hartnett for Governor, 31 January 1994, February and March 1994.

ARCHIVES

Baptist History Collection. Furman University, Greenville, South Carolina.

Fundamentalism (Protestantism) File. Bob Jones University, Greenville, South Carolina.

Research Room. South Carolina Baptist Convention, Columbia, South Carolina.

PRIMARY SOURCES

Bob Jones University Bulletin, 1995.

*The Baptist Faith and Message.*1963. Nashville: Sunday School Board, SBC.

"Christian Coalition Voter Guide '92." Christian Coalition, Chesapeake, Virginia, Liberty University Catalog.

Criswell, W. A. 1990. *Standing on the Promises: The Autobiography of W. A. Criswell.* Dallas: Word Publishing.

"Evangelicals and Catholics Together: The Christian Mission in the Third Millennium." 1994. *First Things*, May, 15–22.

Falwell, Jerry. 1980. *Listen America!* New York: Doubleday.

———. 1981. *The Fundamentalist Phenomenon.* New York: Doubleday-Galilee.

———. 1986. *If I Should Die Before I Wake.* Nashville: Thomas Nelson.

———. 1987. *Strength for the Journey: An Autobiography.* Nashville: Thomas Nelson.

Hays, Brooks. 1959. *A Southern Moderate Speaks.* Chapel Hill: University of North Carolina Press.

———. 1981. *Politics Is My Parish: An Autobiography by Brooks Hays.* Baton Rouge: Louisiana State University Press.

Jones, Bob, Jr. 1985. *Cornbread and Caviar.* Greenville, S.C.: Bob Jones University Press.

———. 1981. "Can the SBC Be Reclaimed?" *Faith for the Family.* December, 2.

Jones III, Bob. 1980. "What Does America Really Need: Political Maneuvering Cannot Lift God's Judgment on a Nation." *Faith for the Family*, July–August, 23.

———. 1985. "What Is a Fundamentalist?" *Faith for the Family*, October, reprint.

Reed, Ralph. 1993. "Casting a Wider Net." *Policy Review 65.* Summer 1993: 31–35.

———. 1984. *Equal Time*, the Mary Matalin program, CNBC, 21 October.

Regent University Catalog. 1995.

Rhodes, Charlie. 1980. "America . . . You're Too Young to Die!!" Campaign brochure, South Carolina Republican U.S. Senate primary.

Rice, John R. 1963. *Southern Baptists Wake Up: Modernism, Neo-Orthodoxy, Unbelief, Compromise, and Worldliness in Southern Baptist Seminaries, Colleges, and Literature.* Murfreesboro, Tenn.: The Sword of the Lord.

Robertson, Pat. 1982. *The Secret Kingdom.* Nashville: Thomas Nelson.

———. 1985. *Beyond Reason.* New York: Morrow.

———. 1986. *America's Dates with Destiny.* Nashville: Thomas Nelson.

———. 1989. *The Plan.* Nashville: Thomas Nelson.

———. 1990. *The New Millennium.* Dallas: Word Publishers.

———. 1992. *The New World Order.* Boston: G. K. Hall.

SBC Today. 1985. Fund-raising letter, dated 20 September.

SECONDARY SOURCE BOOKS

Abelman, Robert. 1990. *Religious Television: Controversies and Conclusion.* Norwood, N.J.: Ablex Publishing Corp.

Ahlstrom, Sydney E. 1972. *A Religious History of the American People.* New Haven: Yale University Press.

Ammerman, Nancy Tatom. 1987. *Bible Believers: Fundamentalists in the Modern World.* New Brunswick, N.J.: Rutgers University Press.

———. 1990. *Baptist Battles: Social Change and Religious Conflict in the Southern Baptist Convention.* New Brunswick, N.J.: Rutgers University Press.

———. 1991. "North American Protestant Fundamentalism." In Martin E. Marty and R. Scott Appleby, eds., *Fundamentalisms Observed,* 1–65. Chicago: University of Chicago Press.

———, ed. 1993. *Southern Baptists Observed: Changing Perspectives on a Changing Denomination.* Knoxville: University of Tennessee Press.

Averill, Lloyd. 1989. *Religious Right, Religious Wrong: A Critique of Fundamentalis[m].* New York: Pilgrim Press.

Baker, Robert A. 1974. *The Southern Baptist Convention and Its People, 1607–1972.* Nashville: Broadman Press.

Baker, Tod A., et al. 1983. *Religion and Politics in the South.* New York: Praeger.

———. 1987. "Party Activists and the New Christian Right." In Charles W. Dunn, ed., *Religion in American Politics,* 161–176. Washington, D.C.: CQ Press.

Balmer, Randall. 1993. *Mine Eyes Have Seen the Glory: A Journey into the Evangelical Subculture in America.* New York: Oxford University Press.

Baptist Faith and Message, The. 1963. Nashville: Sunday School Board, Southern Baptist Convention.

Barnes, William Wright. 1954. *The Southern Baptist Convention, 1845–1953.* Nashville: Broadman Press.

Barnhart, Joe Edward. 1986. *The Southern Baptist Holy War.* Austin: Texas Monthly Press.

Barr, James. 1977. *Fundamentalism.* Philadelphia: Westminster Press.

———. 1984. *Beyond Fundamentalism.* Philadelphia: Westminster Press.

Bartley, Numan V. 1970. *From Thurmond to Wallace.* Baltimore: Johns Hopkins University Press.

Bartley, Numan V., and Hugh D. Graham. 1975. *Southern Politics and the Second Reconstruction.* Baltimore: Johns Hopkins University Press.

Bass, Jack, and Walter DeVries. 1976. *The Transformation of Southern Politics.* New York: Basic Books.

Beale, David O. 1985. *S.B.C. House on the Sand? Critical Issues for Southern Baptists.* Greenville, S.C.: Unusual Publications.

———. 1986. *In Pursuit of Purity: American Fundamentalism since 1850.* Greenville, S.C.: Unusual Publications.

———. 1986. *The Continuing Battle in the SBC: Are There Fundamentalists in the Southern Baptist Convention?* Greenville, S.C.: Unusual Publications.

Bell, Daniel, ed. 1955. *The New American Right.* New York: Criterion.

Bennett, William Wallace. 1877. *The Great Revival in the Southern Armies.* Philadelphia: Claxton, Remsen, and Haffelfinger.

Benson, Peter L., and Dorothy L. Williams. 1982. *Religion on Capitol Hill: Myths and Realities.* San Francisco: Harper and Row.

Bible Institute of Los Angeles. 1917. *The Fundamentals.* Los Angeles: Bible Institute of Los Angeles.

Black, Earl. 1976. *Southern Governors and Civil Rights.* Cambridge, Mass.: Harvard University Press.

Black, Earl, and Merle Black. 1987. *Politics and Society in the South.* Cambridge, Mass.: Harvard University Press.

———. 1991. "The 1988 Presidential Election and the Future of Southern Politics." In Lawrence W. Moreland et al., *The 1988 Presidential Election in the South.* New York: Praeger.

———. 1992. *The Vital South: How Presidents Are Elected.* Cambridge, Mass.: Harvard University Press.

Bloom, Harold. 1992. *The American Religion: The Emergence of a Post-Christian Nation.* New York: Simon and Schuster.

Bob Jones University v. United States of America, 468 F. Supp. 890, 907. D.S.C. 1978.

Bob Jones University v. United States of America, 639 F. 2d.

Boone, Kathleen C. 1989. *The Bible Tells Them So: The Discourse of Protestant Fundamentalism.* Albany: State University of New York Press.

Botsch, Robert. 1993. *The Politics of the Breathless.* Lexington: University Press of Kentucky.

Bruce, Steve. 1987. "Status and Cultural Defense: The Case of the New Christian Right." *Sociological Focus* 20:242–246.

———. 1988. *The Rise and Fall of the New Christian Right.* New York: Oxford University Press.

Bryan, Mike. 1991. *Chapter and Verse: A Skeptic Revisits Christianity.* New York: Random House.

Burroughs, P. E. 1934. *The Baptist People.* Nashville: Sunday School Board of the S.B.C.

Campbell, Angus, Philip E. Converse, Warren E. Miller, and Donald E. Stokes. 1964. *The American Voter.* New York: Wiley.

Campbell, Will D. 1988. *The Convention.* Atlanta: Peachtree.

Caplan, Lionel, ed., 1987. *Studies in Religious Fundamentalism.* Albany: State University of New York Press.

Capps, Walter H. 1990. *The New Religious Right*. Columbia, S.C.: University of South Carolina Press.

Carter, Stephen L. 1993. *The Culture of Disbelief: How American Law and Politics Trivialize Religious Devotion*. New York: Basic Books.

Cash, W. J. 1941. *The Mind of the South*. New York: Knopf.

Cerillo, Augustus. 1989. *Salt and Light: Evangelical Political Thought in Modern America*. Grand Rapids, Mich.: Baker Book House.

Clabaugh, Gary K. 1974. *Thunder on the Right: The Protestant Fundamentalists*. Chicago: Nelson-Hall.

Cohen, Norman J., ed., 1990. *The Fundamentalist Phenomenon*. Grand Rapids, Mich.: W. B. Eerdmans.

Commager, Henry Steele. 1950. *The American Mind: An Interpretation of American Thought and Character since the 1880s*. New Haven: Yale University Press.

Conway, Flo. 1982. *Holy Terror: The Fundamentalist War on America's Freedoms in Religion*. Garden City, N.Y.: Doubleday.

Costain, Anne N. 1992. *Inviting Women's Rebellion: A Political Process Interpretation of the Women's Movement*. Baltimore: Johns Hopkins University Press.

Cothen, Grady. 1993. *What Happened to the SBC?* Atlanta: Smyth and Helwys.

Countryman, William. 1981. *Biblical Authority or Biblical Tyrrany?: Scripture and the Christian Pilgrimage*. Philadelphia: Fortress Press.

Criswell, W. A. 1969. *Why I Preach the Bible Is Literally True*. Nashville: Broadman Press.

Cromartie, Michael, ed., 1992. *No Longer Exiles: The Religious New Right in American Politics*. Washington, D.C.: Ethics and Public Policy Center.

Dalhouse, Mark Taylor. 1996. *An Island in the Lake of Fire: Bob Jones University, Fundamentalism and the Separatist Movement*. Athens: University of Georgia Press.

D'Antonio, Michael. 1990. *Fall from Grace: The Failed Crusade of the Christian Right*. New York: Farrar, Straus, Giroux.

D'Souza, Dinesh. 1984. *Falwell, before the Millenium: A Critical Biography*. Chicago: Regnery Gateway.

Dent, Harry. 1978. *The Prodigal South Returns to Power*. New York: Wiley.

Diamond, Sara. 1989. *Spiritual Warfare: The Politics of the Christian Right*. Boston: South End Press.

Dobson, Ed. 1981. *The Fundamentalist Phenomenon: The Resurgence of Conservative Christianity*. New York: Doubleday.

———. 1988. *Seduction of Power*. Old Tappan, N.J.: Revell.

Dollar, George W. 1973. *A History of Fundamentalism in America*. Greenville, S.C.: Bob Jones University Press.

Dunn, Charles W., ed. 1984. *American Political Theology: Historical Perspective and Theoretical Analysis*. New York: Praeger.

———. 1986. "Some Modest Propositions about an Immodest Subject." *PS* 19:832–836.

———. 1989. *Religion in American Politics*. Washington, D.C.: CQ Press.

Durkheim, Emile. 1933. *The Division of Labor*. New York: Free Press.

Edelman, Murray. 1964. *The Symbolic Uses of Politics*. Urbana: University of Illinois Press.

———. 1988. *Constructing the Political Spectacle*. Chicago: University of Chicago Press.

Egerton, John. 1974. *The Americanization of Dixie: The Southernization of America*. New York: Harper's Magazine Press.

Eighmy, John Lee. 1972. *Churches in Cultural Captivity: A History of the Social Attitudes of Southern Baptists*. Knoxville: University of Tennessee Press.

Elazar, Daniel Judah. 1984. *American Federalism: A View from the States*. New York: Harper and Row.

Ellingsen, Mark. 1993. *The Cutting Edge: How Churches Speak on Social Issues*. Grand Rapids, Mich.: Eerdmans.

Elliott, Ralph H. 1992. *The "Genesis Controversy" and Continuity in Southern Baptist Chaos: A Eulogy for a Great Tradition*. Macon, Ga.: Mercer University Press.

Epstein, Leon. 1986. *Political Parties in the American Mold*. Madison: University of Wisconsin Press.

Erikson, Robert S., and Norman Luttbeg. 1973. *American Public Opinion: Its Origins and Impact*. New York: Wiley.

Evans, Rod L., and Irwin M. Berent. 1988. *Fundamentalism: Hazards and Heartbreaks*. LaSalle, Ill.: Open Court.

Evans, Rowland, and Robert Novak. 1981. *The Reagan Revolution: An Inside Look at the Transformation of the United States Government*. New York: E. P. Dutton.

Fackre, Gabriel J. 1982. *The Religious Right and the Christian Faith*. Grand Rapids, Mich.: Eerdmans.

Farnsley, Arthur II. 1994. *Southern Baptist Politics: Authority and Power in the Restructuring of an American Denomination*. University Park: Pennsylvania State University Press.

Finch, Phillip. 1983. *God, Guns, and Guts*. New York: Seaview/Putnam.

Fischer, David Hackett. 1989. *Albion's Seed: Four British Folkways in America*. New York: Oxford University Press.

Fite, Gilbert C. 1984. *Cotton Fields No More: Southern Agriculture 1865–1980*. Lexington: University Press of Kentucky.

Flynt, J. Wayne. 1979. *Dixie's Forgotten People: The South's Poor Whites*. Bloomington: Indiana University Press.

Forsythe, Douglas. 1979. *What Do Southern Baptists Say about Inspiration?* Greenville, S.C.: Bob Jones University Press.

Fowler, Robert Booth. 1982. *A New Engagement: Evangelical Political Thought 1966–1976*. Grand Rapids, Mich.: Eerdmans.

———. 1989. *Unconventional Partners: Religion and Liberal Culture in the United States*. Grand Rapids, Mich.: Eerdmans.

Frankl, Razelle. 1987. *Televangelism: The Marketing of a Popular Religion*. Carbondale, Ill.: Southern Illinois University Press.

Ferguson, Robert U., Jr. 1993. *Amidst Babel, Speak the Truth: Reflections on the SBC Struggle*. Macon, Ga.: Smyth and Helwys.

Garrett, James Leo, et al. 1983. *Are Southern Baptists "Evangelicals"?* Macon, Ga.: Mercer University Press.

Gasper, Louis. 1981. *The Fundamentalist Movement*. Grand Rapids, Mich.: Baker Book House.

Georgianna, Sharon Linzey. 1989. *The Moral Majority and Fundamentalism: Plausibility and Dissonance*. Lewiston, N.Y.: Mellen Press.

Gottfried, Paul. 1993. *The Conservative Movement*. New York: Twayne.

Grantham, Dewey. 1988. *The Life and Death of the Old South*. Lexington: University Press of Kentucky.

Greeley, Andrew M. 1989. *Religious Change in America*. Cambridge, Mass.: Harvard University Press.

Greenstone, J. David. 1969. *Labor in American Politics*. New York: Knopf.

Gritsch, Eric W. 1982. *Born Againism: Perspectives on a Movement*. Philadelphia: Fortress Press.

Guinness, Os. 1993. *The American Hour: A Time of Reckoning and the Once and Future Role of Faith*. New York: Free Press.

Gusfield, J. 1963. *Symbolic Crusade: Status, Politics and the American Temperance Movement*. Urbana: University of Illinois Press.

Guth, James L., and John C. Green. 1991. *The Bible and the Ballot Box: Religion and Politics in the 1988 Election*. Boulder, Colo.: Westview Press.

Hadden, Jeffrey K. 1988. *Televangelism, Power, and Politics*. New York: Henry Holt.

———. 1989. *Secularization and Fundamentalism Reconsidered*. New York: Paragon House.

Hammond, Phillip E. 1992. *Religion and Personal Autonomy: The Third Disestablishment in America*. Columbia: University of South Carolina Press.

Hankins, Barry. 1996. *God's Rascal: Frank Norris and the Beginnings of Southern Fundamentalism*. Lexington: University Press of Kentucky.

Harrell, David Edwin, Jr. 1987. *Pat Robertson: A Personal, Religious, and Political Portrait*. San Francisco: Harper and Row.

———. 1988. "The Evolution of Plain Folk Religion in the South." In Samuel S. Hill, ed., *Varieties of Southern Religious Experience*, 24–51. Baton Rouge: Louisiana State University Press.

Hastings, C. Brownlow. 1981. *Introducing Southern Baptists: Their Faith and Their Life.* New York: Paulist Press.

Hartz, Louis. 1955. *The Liberal Tradition in America: An Interpretation of American Political Thought since the Revolution.* New York: Harcourt, Brace, and World.

Hays, Brooks, and John E. Steely. 1981. *The Baptist Way of Life.* Macon, Ga.: Mercer University Press.

Heard, Alexander. 1952. *A Two-Party South?* Chapel Hill: University of North Carolina Press.

Hebert, Arthur Gabriel. 1957. *Fundamentalism and the Church.* Philadelphia: Westminster Press.

Hefley, James C. 1977. *The Church That Produced a President.* New York: Wyden Books.

———. 1986. *The Truth in Crisis: The Controversy in the Southern Baptist Convention.* Dallas: Criterion Publications.

———. 1987. *The Truth in Crisis: The Controversy in the Southern Baptist Convention,* vol. 2: *Updating the Controversy.* Hannibal, Mo.: Hannibal Books.

———. 1988. *The Truth in Crisis: The Controversy in the Southern Baptist Convention,* vol. 3: *Conservative Resurgence or Political Takeover?* Hannibal, Mo.: Hannibal Books.

———. 1989. *The Truth in Crisis: The Controversy in the Southern Baptist Convention,* vol. 4: *The State of the Denomination.* Hannibal, Mo.: Hannibal Books.

———. 1990. *The Truth in Crisis: The Controversy in the Southern Baptist Convention,* vol. 5: *The "Winning Edge."* Hannibal, Mo.: Hannibal Books.

———. 1991. *The Conservative Resurgence in the Southern Baptist Convention.* Hannibal, Mo.: Hannibal Books.

Heimers, R. L. 1990. *Inside the Southern Baptist Convention.* Collingswood, N.J.: Bible for Today.

Herberg, Will. 1960. *Protestant, Catholic, Jew.* Garden City, N.Y.: Doubleday-Anchor.

Hertzke, Allen D. 1988. *Representing God in Washington: The Role of Religious Lobbies in the American Polity.* Knoxville: University of Tennessee Press.

———. 1993. *Echoes of Discontent: Jesse Jackson, Pat Robertson, and the Resurgence of Populism.* Washington, D.C.: CQ Press.

Hill, Samuel S. 1972. *Religion and the Solid South.* Nashville: Abingdon.

———. 1980. *The South and the North in American Religion.* Athens: University of Georgia Press.

———. 1982. *The New Religious Political Right in America.* Nashville: Abingdon.

———. 1983. *On Jordon's Stormy Banks: Religion in the South.* Macon, Ga.: Mercer University Press.

————. 1983. *Religion in the Southern States: A Historical Study*. Macon, Ga.: Mercer University Press.

————. 1984. *Encyclopedia of Religion in the South*. Macon, Ga.: Mercer University Press.

————. 1988. *Varieties of Southern Religious Experience*. Baton Rouge: Louisiana State University Press.

Himmelstein, Jerome L. 1990. *To the Right: The Transformation of American Conservatism*. Berkeley: University of California Press.

Hinson, E. Glenn. 1981. "Neo-Fundamentalism: An Interpretation and Critique." *Baptist History and Heritage*, April, 33.

Hofstadter, Richard. 1956. *The Age of Reform: From Bryan to F.D.R.* New York: Knopf.

————. 1965. *The Paranoid Style in American Politics and Other Essays*. New York: Knopf.

Hoover, Stewart M. 1988. *Mass Media and Religion: The Social Sources of the Electronic Church*. Newbury Park, Calif.: Sage.

Horsfield, Peter G. 1984. *Religious Television: The American Experience*. New York: Longman.

Hudson, Winthrop. 1979. *Baptists in Transition: Individualism and Christian Responsibility*. Valley Forge, Penn.: Judson Press.

Hunter, James Davison. 1991. *Culture Wars: The Struggle to Define America*. New York: Basic Books.

Hutcheson, Richard G. 1981. *Mainline Churches and the Evangelicals*. Atlanta: John Knox Press.

Ide, Arthur Frederick. 1986. *Evangelical Terrorism: Censorship, Falwell, Robertson, and the Seamy Side of Christian Fundamentalism*. Irving, Tex.: Scholars Books.

Irish, Marian D., and James W. Prothro. 1959. *The Politics of American Democracy*. Englewood Cliffs, N.J.: Prentice Hall.

James, Rob, ed. 1989. *The Takeover in the Southern Baptist Convention: A Brief History*. Decatur, Ga.: SBC Today.

Jelen, Ted G. 1991. "Politicized Group Identificationism: The Case of Fundamentalism." *Western Political Quarterly* 44:209–219.

————. 1991. *The Political Mobilization of Religious Beliefs*. New York: Praeger.

Jones, J. William. 1887. *Christ in the Camp: Religion in the Confederate Army*. Atlanta: Martin and Hoyt.

Johnson, B. 1963. "On Church and Sect." *American Sociological Review* 28.

Johnson, Stephen D., and Joseph B. Tamney. 1982. "The Christian Right and the 1980 Presidential Election." *Journal for the Scientific Study of Religion* 21:123–131.

Jorstad, Erling. 1981. *The Politics of Moralism*. Minneapolis: Augsburg.

————. 1981. *Evangelicals in the White House: The Cultural Maturation of Born Again Christianity, 1960–1981*. New York: Mellen Press.

————. 1987. *The New Christian Right, 1981–1988: Prospects for the Post-Reagan Decade*. Lewiston, N.Y.: Mellen Press.

————. 1990. *Holding Fast and Pressing On: Religion in America in the 1980s*. New York: Greenwood Press.

————. 1993. *Popular Religion in America: The Evangelical Voice*. New York: Greenwood Press.

Kaplan, Lawrence. 1992. *Fundamentalism in Comparative Perspective*. Amherst: University of Massachusetts Press.

Kater, John L., Jr. 1982. *Christians on the Right: The Moral Majority in Perspective*. New York: Seabury Press.

Kelsey, George D. 1973. *Social Ethics among Southern Baptists, 1917–1969*. Metuchen, N.J.: Scarecrow Press.

Key, V. O. 1949. *Southern Politics in State and Nation*. New York: Knopf.

————. 1965. *Public Opinion and American Democracy*. New York: Knopf.

Kornhauser, William. 1959. *The Politics of Mass Society*. Glencoe, Ill.: Free Press.

Kousser, J. Morgan. 1974. *The Shaping of Southern Politics*. New Haven: Yale University Press.

Ladd, Jr., Everett Carll, with Charles D. Hadley. 1978. *Transformations of the American Party System*. New York: Norton.

Lawrence, Bruce B. 1989. *Defenders of God: The Fundamentalist Revolt against the Modern Age*. San Francisco: Harper and Row.

Leege, David, and Lyman A. Kellstedt. 1993. *Rediscovering the Religious Factor in American Politics*. Armonk, N.Y.: M. E. Sharpe.

Leonard, Bill J. 1990. *God's Last and Only Hope: The Fragmentation of the Southern Baptist Convention*. Grand Rapids, Mich.: Eerdmans.

Lienesch, Michael. 1993. *Redeeming America: Piety and Politics in the New Christian Right*. Chapel Hill: University of North Carolina Press.

Lippman, Walter. 1992. *American Inquisitors*. New Brunswick, N.J.: Transaction Publishers.

Lippy, Charles H. 1985. *Bibliography of Religion in the South*. Macon, Ga.: Mercer University Press.

Lipset, Seymour Martin. 1955. "The Sources of the 'Radical Right.'" In Daniel Bell, ed., *The New American Right*, 166–233. New York: Criterion.

Lorentzen, Louise J. 1980. "Evangelical Life Style Concerns Expressed in Political Action." *Sociological Analysis* 41:144–154.

Lowell, C. Stanley. 1966. *Embattled Wall: Americans United: An Idea and a Man*. Washington, D.C.: Americans United.

Lowi, Theodore J. 1969. *The End of Liberalism: The Second Republic in the United States*. New York: Norton.

Maguire, Daniel C. 1982. *The New Subversives: Anti-Americanism of the Religious Right*. New York: Continuum.

Maisel, L. Sandy, ed. 1990. *The Parties Respond: Changes in the American Party System*. Boulder, Colo.: Westview Press.

Marsden, George. 1982. *Fundamentalism and American Culture: The Shaping of Twentieth-Century Evangelicalism, 1870–1925*. New York: Oxford University Press.

———. 1987. *Reforming Fundamentalism: Fuller Seminary and the New Evangelicalism*. Grand Rapids, Mich.: Eerdmans.

———. 1991. *Understanding Fundamentalism and Evangelicalism*. Grand Rapids, Mich.: Eerdmans.

Marty, Martin E. 1976. *A Nation of Behavers*. Chicago: University of Chicago Press.

———. 1987. *Religion and Republic: The American Circumstance*. Boston: Beacon Press.

Marty, Martin E., and R. Scott Appleby, eds. 1991. *Fundamentalisms Observed*. Chicago: University of Chicago Press.

———. 1992. *The Glory and the Power: The Fundamentalist Challenge to the Modern World*. Boston: Beacon Press.

———. 1993. *Fundamentalisms and Society: Reclaiming the Sciences, the Family and Education*. Chicago: University of Chicago Press.

———. 1993. *Fundamentalisms and the State: Remaking Polities, Militance and Economies*. Chicago: University of Chicago Press.

Martz, Larry. 1988. *Ministry of Greed: The Inside Story of the Televangelists*. New York: Weidenfeld and Nicholson.

Matthews, Donald R., and James W. Prothro. 1966. *Negroes and the New Southern Politics*. New York: Harcourt, Brace, and World.

McAdam, Doug. 1982. *Political Process and the Development of Black Insurgency, 1930–1970*. Chicago: University of Chicago Press.

McBeth, H. Leon. 1982. "Fundamentalism in the Southern Baptist Convention in Recent Years." *Review and Expositor*, Winter, 85.

———. 1987. *Four Centuries of Southern Baptist Witness*. Nashville: Broadman Press.

McCuen, Gary E. 1989. *The Religious Right*. Hudson, Wisc.: McCuen Publications.

McPherson, William. 1973. *Ideology and Change: Radicalism and Fundamentalism in America*. Palo Alto, Calif.: National Press Books.

Menendez, Albert. 1977. *Religion at the Polls*. Philadelphia: Westminster Press.

Miztal, Bronislaw, ed. 1992. *Religion and Politics in Comparative Perspective: A Revival of Religious Fundamantalism in East and West*. Westport, Conn.: Praeger.

Moen, Matthew C. 1989. *The Christian Right and Congress*. Tuscaloosa: University of Alabama Press.

———. 1992. *The Transformation of the Christian Right*. Tuscaloosa: University of Alabama Press.

Moen, Matthew C., and Lowell S. Gustafson, eds. 1992. *The Religious Challenge to the State*. Philadelphia: Temple University Press.

Moore, Edmund Arthur. 1968. A *Catholic Runs for President: The Campaign of 1928*. Gloucester, Mass.: P. Smith.

Moore, John N. 1984. In Marla J. Selvidge, *Fundamentalism Today: What Makes It So Attractive?* Elgin, Ill.: Brethren Press, 1984.

Neuhaus, Richard John, and Michael Cromartie, eds. 1987. *Piety and Politics: Evangelicals and Fundamentalists Confront the World*. Lanham, Md.: University Press of America.

Nie, Norman, Sidney Verba, and John R. Petrocik. 1976. *The Changing American Voter*. Cambridge, Mass.: Harvard University Press.

Niebuhr, H. Richard. 1929. *The Social Sources of Denominationalism*. New York: Meridian Books.

———. 1956. *The Kingdom of God in America*. Hamden, Conn.: Shoe String Press.

Overdyke, W. Darrell. 1950. *The Know Nothing Party in the South*. Baton Rouge: Louisiana State University Press.

Percy, Walker. 1966. *The Last Gentleman*. New York: Farrar, Straus, Giroux.

Percy, William Alexander. 1941. *Lanterns on the Levee*. New York: Knopf.

Perry, Ralph Barton. 1944. *Puritanism and Democracy*. New York: Vanguard Press.

Persons, Stow. 1958. *American Minds: A History of Ideas*. New York: Henry Holt.

Peshkin, Alan. 1986. *God's Choice: The Total World of a Fundamentalist Christian School*. Chicago: University of Chicago Press.

Phillips, Kevin P. 1969. *The Emerging Republican Majority* New Rochelle, N.Y.: Arlingon House.

Piven, Frances Fox, and Richard A. Cloward. 1977. *Poor People's Movements: Why They Succeed, How They Fail*. New York: Random House.

Quebedeaux, Richard. 1978. *The Worldly Evangelicals*. New York: Harper and Row.

Queen, Edward L. 1991. *In the South the Baptists Are the Center of Gravity: Southern Baptists and Social Change, 1930–1980*. New York: Carlson.

Radl, Shirley L. 1983. *The Invisible Woman: The Target of the Religious New Right*. New York: Delacorte Press.

Reed, John Shelton. 1972. *The Enduring South: Subcultural Persistence in Mass Society*. Chapel Hill: University of North Carolina Press.

———. 1983. *Southerners: The Psychology of Sectionalism*. Chapel Hill: University of North Carolina Press.

————. 1993. *Surveying the South: Studies in Rural Sociology.* Columbia, Mo.: University of Missouri Press.

Reichley, A. James. 1985. *Religion in American Public Life.* Washington, D.C.: Brookings Institution.

Richards, W. Wiley. 1991. *Winds of Doctrines: The Origin and Development of Southern Baptist Theology.* Lanham, Md.: University Press of America.

Roof, Wade Clark, and William McKinney. 1985. "Denominational America and the New Religious Pluralism." *Annals, AAPSS* 80:24–33.

Rosenburg, Ellen M. 1989. *The Southern Baptists: A Subculture in Transition.* Knoxville: University of Tennessee Press.

Rothenberg, Stuart, and Frank Newport. 1984. *The Evangelical Voter.* Washington, D.C.: Free Congress.

Rowan, Carl. 1995. "An Open Letter to the Nation's Southern Baptists." *[Columbia, S.C.] State,* 25 June 1995, D3.

Russell, C. Allyn. 1976. *Voices of American Fundamentalism: Seven Biographical Studies.* Philadelphia: Westminster Press.

Sandeen, Ernest R. 1970. *The Roots of Fundamentalism: British and American Millennarianism, 1800–1930.* Chicago: University of Chicago Press.

Schmidt, Jean Miller. 1991. *Souls of the Social Order: The Two-Party System in American Protestantism.* New York: Carlson.

Schultze, Quentin. 1991. *Televangelism and American Culture: The Business of Popular Religion.* Grand Rapids, Mich.: Baker.

————. 1993. "The Two Faces in Fundamentalist Higher Education." In Martin E. Marty, ed., *Fundamentalisms and Society: Reclaiming the Sciences, the Family, and Education,* 490–535. Chicago: University of Chicago Press.

————, ed. 1990. *American Evangelicals and the Mass Media.* Grand Rapids, Mich.: Zondervan.

Seagull, Louis. 1975. *Southern Republicanism.* New York: Wiley.

Selvidge, Marla J. 1984. *Fundamentalism Today: What Makes It So Attractive?* Elgin, Ill.: Brethren Press.

Shurden, Walter B. 1993. *The Struggle for the Soul of the SBC: The Moderate Response to the Fundamentalist Movement.* Macon, Ga.: Mercer University Press.

————. 1993. *The Baptist Identity: Four Fragile Freedoms.* Atlanta, Ga.: Smyth and Helwys.

Simon, Merrill. 1984. *Jerry Falwell and the Jews.* Middle Village, N.Y.: Jonathon David Publishers.

Smelser, Neil J. 1962. *Theory of Collective Behavior.* New York: Free Press.

Smolla, Rodney A. 1988. *Jerry Falwell vs. Larry Flint: The First Amendment on Trial.* New York: St. Martin's Press.

Snowball, David. 1991. *Continuity and Change in the Rhetoric of the Moral Majority.* New York: Praeger.

Spong, John Shelby. 1991. *Rescuing the Bible from Fundamentalists: A Bishop Rethinks the Meaning of Scripture*. San Francisco: HarperCollins.

Stevick, Daniel B. 1964. *Beyond Fundamentalism*. Richmond, Va.: John Knox Press.

Stewart, John Mark. 1987. *Holy War: An Inside Account of the Battle for PTL*. Enid, Okla.: Fireside Publishing.

Stockton, Ronald R. 1989. "The Evangelical Phenomenon: A Falwell-Graham Typology." In Corwin E. Smidt, ed., *Contemporary Evangelical Political Involvement*, 45–74. Lanham, Md.: University Press of America.

Straub, Gerard Thomas. 1986. *Salvation for Sale: An Insider's View of Pat Robertson's Ministry*. Buffalo, N.Y.: Prometheus Books.

Streiker, Lowell D. 1984. *The Gospel Time Bomb: Ultrafundamentalism and the Future of America*. Buffalo, N.Y.: Prometheus Books.

Strong, Donald S. 1955. "The Presidential Election in the South, 1952." *Journal of Politics*, August.

Sundquist, James L. 1983. *Dynamics of the Party System*. Washington, D.C.: Brookings Institution.

Thompson, James J. 1982. *Tried as by Fire: Southern Baptists and the Religious Controversies of the 1920s*. Macon, Ga.: Mercer University Press.

Tindall, George Brown. 1967. *The Emergence of the New South, 1913–1945*. Baton Rouge: Louisiana State University Press.

Turner, J. Clyde. 1956. *These Things We Believe*. Nashville: [Southern Baptist] Convention Press.

Viguerie, Richard A. 1980. *The New Right: We're Ready to Lead*. Falls Church, Va.: Viguerie.

Wald, Kenneth. 1987. *Religion and Politics in the United States*. New York: St. Martin's.

Wallis, Roy. 1979. *Salvation and Protest: Studies of Social and Religious Movements*. London: Francis Pinter.

Wattenberg, Martin P. 1991. *The Rise of Candidate-Centered Politics: Presidential Elections in the 1980s*. Cambridge, Mass.: Harvard University Press.

Weaver, Richard M. 1964. *Visions of Order: The Cultural Crisis of Our Time*. Baton Rouge: Louisiana State University Press.

Weber, Max. 1968. *Economy and Society*. New York: Bedminster.

Whalen, Charles, and Barbara Whalen. 1986. *The Longest Debate*. New York: New American Library.

Wills, Garry. 1991. *Under God: Religion and American Politics*. New York: Touchstone.

Wilson, Charles Reagan. 1980. *Baptized in Blood: The Religion of the Lost Cause*. Athens: University of Georgia Press.

———, ed. 1985. *Religion in the South*. Jackson: University Press of Mississippi.

Wilson, K. L., and L. A. Zurcher. 1976. "Status Inconsistency and Participation in Social Movements: An Application of Goodman's Hierarchical Modeling." *Sociological Quarterly* 17:520–533.

Wood, James E. 1982. "The New Religious Right and Its Implications for Southern Baptists." *Foundations*, April–June, 153.

Woodward, C. Vann. 1957. *Origins of the New South, 1877–1913*. Baton Rouge: Louisiana State University Press.

———. 1960. *The Burden of Southern History*. New York: Random House.

Wright, Melton. 1960. *Fortress of Faith: The Story of Bob Jones University*. Grand Rapids, Mich.: Eerdmans.

Wuthnow, Robert. 1988. *The Restructuring of American Religion*. Princeton, N.J.: Princeton University Press.

Yance, Norman Alexander. 1978. *Religion Southern Style*. Association of Baptist Professors of Religion.

Young, Perry Deane. 1982. *God's Bullies: Native Reflections on Preachers and Politics*. New York: Holt, Rinehart and Winston.

SCHOLARLY ARTICLES

Ammerman, Nancy Tatom. 1986. "The New South and the New Baptists." *Christian Century*, 14 May, 486.

———. 1988. "SBC and the New Christian Right." SBC Today, February, 1, 4–5.

Ayers, Jr., B. Drummond. 1993. "Christian Right Splits GOP in South." *New York Times*, 7 June, A7.

Beatty, Kathleen Murphy, and Oliver Walter. 1984. "Religious Preference and Practice: Reevaluating Their Impact on Political Tolerance." *Public Opinion Quarterly* 48:318–329.

Beck, Paul Allen. 1974. "A Socialization Theory of Realignment." In Richard G. Niemi et al., *The Politics of Future Citizens*. New York: Jossey-Bass.

Blevins, Kent B. 1980. "Southern Baptist Attitudes toward the Vietnam War in the Years 1965–1970." *Foundations*, July–September, 13.

Box, S., and J. Ford. 1969. "Some Questionable Assumptions in the Theory of Status Inconsistency." *Sociological Review* 17:187–201.

Brudney, Jeffrey L., and Gary W. Copeland. 1984. "Evangelicals as a Political Force: Reagan and the 1980 Religious Vote." *Social Science Quarterly* 65:1072–1079.

Bullman, Raymond F. 1991. "'Myth of Origin,' Civil Religion and Presidential Politics." *Journal of Church and State*, Summer, 525.

Carmines, Edward G., and Harold W. Stanley. 1990. "Ideological Realignment in the Contemporary South." In Robert P. Steed et al., *The Disappearing South? Studies in Regional Change and Continuity*. Tuscaloosa: University of Alabama Press.

Converse, Phillip E. 1963. "A Major Political Realignment in the South?" In Allan Sindler, ed., *Change in the Contemporary South*. Durham, N.C.: Duke University Press.

Edsall, Thomas Byrne, and Mary D. Edsall. 1991. "Race." *Atlantic Monthly*, May.

Ethridge, F. Maurice, and Joe R. Feagin. 1979. "Varieties of 'Fundamentalism': A Conceptual and Empirical Analysis of Two Protestant Denominations." *Sociological Quarterly* 20:37–48.

Gilbert, Christopher P., et al. 1994. "The Religious Roots of Third-Party Voting: A Comparison of Perot, Anderson, and Wallace Voters." Paper presented at the Annual Meeting of the American Political Science Association, New York, 1–4 September.

Graham, Cole Blease, Jr., William V. More, and Frank T. Petrusak. 1994. "Praise the Lord and Join the Republicans: The Christian Coalition and the Republican Party in South Carolina." Paper presented at the Annual Meeting of the Midwest Political Science Association, Albuquerque.

Green, John C. 1993. Review of *Culture Wars* by James D. Hunter, *The Transformation of the Christian Right* by Matthew C. Moen, and *God's Warriors* by Clyde Wilcox. *Journal of Politics* 55:814–817.

Green, John C., and James L. Guth. 1988. "The Christian Right in the Republican Party: The Case of Pat Robertson's Supporters." *Journal of Politics* 50:150–165.

Guth, James L. 1983. "The New Christian Right." In Robert C. Liebman and Robert Wuthnow, eds., *The New Christian Right: Mobilization and Legitimization*, 31–45. New York: Aldine.

———. 1984. "The Politics of Preachers: Southern Baptist Ministers and Christian Right Activism." In David G. Bromley and Anson Shupe, eds., *New Christian Politics*, 235–250. Macon, Ga.: Mercer University Press.

———. 1989. "Southern Baptists and the New Right." In Charles W. Dunn, ed., *Religion in American Politics*, 177–190. Washington, D.C.: CQ Press.

Guth, James L., Ted G. Jelen, Lyman A. Kellstedt, Corwin E. Smidt, and Kenneth D. Wald. 1988. "The Politics of Religion in America: Issues for Investigation." *American Politics Quarterly* 16:357–397.

Hill, Samuel S. 1981. "The Shape and Shapes of Popular Southern Piety." In David Edwin Harrell, ed., *Varieties of Southern Evangelicalism*, 89–114. Macon, Ga.: Mercer University Press.

———. 1993. "The Story before the Story." In Nancy Tatom Ammerman, ed., *Southern Baptists Observed: Changing Perspectives on a Changing Denomination*, 30. Knoxville: University of Tennessee Press.

Kellstedt, Lyman A., John C. Green, James L. Guth, and Corwin E. Smidt. 1993. "Religious Voting Blocks in the 1992 Election: The Year of the Evangelical?" Paper for the American Political Science Association, Washington, D.C., 1–4 September.

————. 1994. "Tongues of Fire: The Charismatic Movement and American Politics." Paper presented at the Annual Meeting of the American Political Science Association, New York, 1–4 September.

Key, V. O. 1952. "The Future of the Democratic Party." *Virginia Quarterly Review* 28:161–175.

————. 1955. "The Erosion of Sectionalism." *Virginia Quarterly Review* 31:161–179.

Ladestro, Debra. 1993. "Is Fundamentalism Fundamentally Changing Society?" *University of Chicago Magazine*, April.

Langenbach, Lisa. 1989. "Evangelical Elites and Political Action: The Pat Robertson Presidential Candidacy." *Journal of Political and Military Sociology* 17:291–303.

Leege, David C. 1993. "The Decomposition of the Religious Vote." Paper presented at the Annual Meeting of the American Political Science Association, Washington, D.C., 1–4 September.

Liebman, Robert C. 1983. "The Making of the New Christian Right." In Robert C. Liebman and Robert Wuthnow, eds., *The New Christian Right*, 227–238. New York: Aldine.

McConnell, Tandy. 1993. "South Carolina Baptists and Integration: Ideology and Social Change." Paper presented at the Graduate History Symposium, Department of History, University of South Carolina, March.

Miller, Arthur H., and Martin P. Wattenburg. 1984. "Politics from the Pulpit: Religiosity and the 1980 Elections." *Public Opinion Quarterly* 48:301–317.

Miller, Wesley E., Jr. 1985. "The New Christian Right and Fundamentalist Discontent: The Politics of Lifestyle Concern Hypothesis Revisited." *Sociological Focus* 18:325–336.

Moreland, Lawrence W. 1991. "The Ideological and Issue Bases of Southern Parties." In Tod A. Baker et al., *Political Parties in the Southern States*. New York: Praeger.

Page, Ann L., and Donald A. Clelland. 1978. "The Kanawha County Book Controversy: A Study of the Politics of Life Style Concern." *Social Forces* 57:265–281.

Patel, Kant, Denny Pilant, and Gary L. Rose. 1985. "Christian Conservatism: A Study in Alienation and Life Style Concerns." *Journal of Political Science* 12:17–30.

Prysby, Charles L. 1991. "Realignment among Southern Party Activists." In Tod A. Baker et al., *Political Parties in the Southern States*. New York: Praeger.

Simpson, J. H. 1985. "Status Inconsistency and Moral Issues." *Journal for the Scientific Study of Religion* 24:119–236.

Smidt, Corwin. 1987. "Evangelicals in the 1984 Election: Continuity or Change?" *American Politics Quarterly* 15:419–444.

————. 1989. "Evangelicals within Contemporary American Politics: Differentiating between Fundamentalist and Non-Fundamentalist Evangelicals." *Western Political Quarterly* 41:601–620.

———. 1989. "Change and Stability among Southern Evangelicals." In Charles W. Dunn, ed., *Religion in American Politics*, 147–160. Washington, D.C.: CQ Press.

———. 1989. "Evangelicals and the New Christian Right: Coherence vs. Diversity in the Issue Stands of Evangelicals." In Corwin E. Smidt, ed., *Contemporary Evangelical Political Involvement*, 75–98. Lanham, Md.: University Press of America.

Smith, Oran P. 1994. "Continuity and Change in Dixie's Established Church: Southern Baptists and Politics, 1930–1990." Paper presented at the Annual Meeting of the American Political Science Association, New York, 1–4 September.

Stanley, Harold. 1985. "Race and Realignment." In Robert P. Steed et al., eds., *The 1984 Election in the South*. New York: Praeger.

Stark, R., and W. S. Bainbridge. 1979. "Of Churches, Sects, and Cults: Preliminary Concepts for a Theory of Religious Movements." *Journal for the Scientific Study of Religion* 18.

Steed, Robert P., and John McGlennon. 1991. "A 1988 Postscript: Continuing Coalitional Diversity." In Tod A. Baker et al., *Political Parties in the Southern States*. New York: Praeger.

Wald, Kenneth, Dennis E. Owen, and Samuel S. Hill, Jr. 1988. "Churches as Political Communities." *American Political Science Review* 82:531–548.

———. 1989. "Political Cohesion in Churches." *Journal of Politics* 52:197–215.

———. 1989. "Assessing the Religious Factor in Electoral Behavior." In Charles W. Dunn, ed., *Religion in American Politics*, 105–121. Washington, D.C.: CQ Press.

Wilcox, Clyde. 1986. "Evangelicals and Fundamentalists in the Christian Right: Religious Differences in the Ohio Moral Majority." *Journal for the Scientific Study of Religion* 25:355–363.

———. 1986. "Fundamentalists and Politics: An Analysis of the Effects of Differing Operational Definitions." *Journal of Politics* 48:1041–1051.

———. 1987. "Religious Orientations and Political Attitudes: Variations within the New Christian Right." *American Politics Quarterly* 15:274–296.

———. 1992. *God's Warriors: The Christian Right in Twentieth-Century America*. Baltimore: Johns Hopkins University Press.

NEWS ARTICLES

"Author Says Baptists Banned Book about Masons." 1992. *Baptist Courier*, 28 May, 13.

Bandy, Lee. 1993. "Baptists Urge USC to Cancel Course." *[Columbia, S.C.] State*, 2 June, 1A.

————. 1993. "How the GOP Blew It Twice." *[Columbia, S.C.] State*, 13 June, 4D.

————. 1994. "Christian Coalition Espouses Plan to Diversify Following." *[Columbia, S.C.] State*, 11 February, 1A.

————. 1994. "Harnett Complains to Christian Coalition." *[Columbia, S.C.] State*, 19 July, B1;

————. 1994. "Christian Coalition Sparks Inflame GOP Campaigns." *[Columbia, S.C.] State*, 20 July, B5.

"Baptists Demand USC Cancel Course." 1993. *The Charleston Post and Courier*, 3 June.

Barrett, Laurence I. 1993. "Fighting for God and the Right Wing." *Time*, 13 September.

Basler, George. 1984. "Interview with Bob Jones III." *[Binghamton, N.Y.] Evening Press*, 20 September, 1A.

Beard, Steve. 1993. "Religion and Politics: In the '80s, Liberals Said the Two Don't Mix; That Was Then, This Is Now." *World*, 22 May, 10.

Bell, Steve. 1993. "Church Plans Seminar on Religion, Education: Sponsors Say Criticism Obscures Some Programs' Benefits." *Greenville [S.C.] News*, 9 November, 3C.

Braidfoot, Larry. 1985. "Arms Control and Peace: An Interview with Sen. Albert Gore, Jr." *Light*, October, 1.

Briggs, Kenneth A. 1981. "Drift Away from Fundamentalism Splits Ranks of Southern Baptists." *New York Times*, 29 March, A1.

Brinkley, John. 1993. "Vatican Estranged Truman, Baptists." *Denver Rocky Mountain News*, 13 August, A1.

Brummett, John. 1991. "SBC Seen as Shifting to 'Right-Wing' Republicanism." *Baptists Today*, 6 September, 6.

Bush, L. Russ. 1988. "Southern Baptists: What They Believe." *Christianity Today*, 4 November, 22.

Camp, Ken. 1993. "Well-Being of Religious Right Disputed by Activists, Observers." *Baptists Today*, 24 September, 6.

————. 1995. "95 Hispanic Leaders Protest Catholic /Evangelical Document." *Baptist Press Wire Service*, 13 March.

Campbell, Will. 1983. "Ministers Can't Be Caesar's Cheerleaders." *USA Today*, 5 April, 12A.

"Christian Schools Grow in SBC." 1980. *Moody*, January, 124.

"Church Panel Reports Most Baptists Think Adam and Eve Were Real People." 1987. *Greenville [S.C.] News*, 13 June, 2.

"Church-State Issues Surface in Varied Ways." 1991. *SBC Today*, 20 June, 6.

Clapp, Rodney.1988. "America's Southern Baptists: Where Are They Going?" *Christianity Today*, 4 November, 26.

"Conservative Surge in the SBC." 1983. *Fundamentalist Journal*, February, 24.

"Conservatives Encourage Pulling Children from Greenville Schools." 1993. *[Columbia, S.C.] State*, 21 September.

"Controversial Paper's Distribution Was Unauthorized, Patterson Says." 1993. *Baptists Today*, 29 June, 5.

Cornell, George, W. 1993. "Ordination Soars among Southern Baptist Women." *[Columbia, S.C.] State*, 8 May, 7B.

———. 1993. "Clinton Meets His Baptist Critics." *Greenville [S.C.] News*, 25 September.

Colson, Charles. 1994. "Politics, Power, and the Kingdom of God." *Moody*, October, 22.

Criswell, W. A. 1988. "The Curse of Liberalism." *Fundamentalist Journal*, October, 66.

Cromartie, Michael. 1992. "Fixing the World: From Nonplayers to Radicals to New Right Conservatives: The Saga of Evangelicals and Social Action." *Christianity Today*, 27 April, 23.

Currin, Sam J. 1988. "Dunn's Political Activity." *Southern Baptist Advocate*, June, 7.

D'Souza, Dinesh. 1984. "Jerry Falwell." *Los Angeles Times*, 11 June, II:14.

Diemer, Carl. 1983. "Southern Baptists: From Where, to Where?" *Fundamentalist Journal*, February, 14.

Dilday, Robert. 1993. "Spurgeon Leaves FMB Over Trustees' Political Action." *Baptists Today*, 15 April, 14.

Dilday, Russell H. 1985. "What Kind of Convention?" *SBC Today*, March, 1.

"Draper Says 'No': Hierarchical Plan Rejected." 1982. *Southern Baptist Advocate*, Fall, 1.

Dunn, James, M. 1983. "Fanatical Fundamentalism and Political Extremism." *USA Today Magazine*, May, 53.

———. 1986. "The Christian as Political Activist." *Liberty*, July–August, 16.

———. 1993. "Shurden Volume Describes Essence of 'Baptistness.'" *Baptists Today*, 26 August, 18.

"Dunn Drags SBC into PAW." 1983. *Southern Baptist Advocate*, October, 15.

Eckholm, Erik. 1994. "Clinton Bashing a Growth Industry: 'High Technology Overlay' Propels Diatribes." New York Times Service in *[Columbia, S.C.] State*, 26 June.

Evans, Frances. 1985. "Ministers Switching to GOP: Southern Baptist Clergy Desert Democrats, Survey Shows." *Greenville [S.C.] News*, 28 May, 1B.

———. 1987. "Retiring Baptist Leader Cites Differences between North, South." *Greenville [S.C.] News-Piedmont*, 24 January, 10A.

———. 1993. "Alternative Baptist Group to Meet." *Greenville [S.C.] News-Piedmont*, 25 September, 12A.

Faris, Jeannie. 1991. "National Baptist Rift Filters Down to State." *Greenville [S.C.] News* 29 September, 1E.

"Few Called, Few Chosen." 1993. *World*, 14 September.

"Forty-Eight Percent of Southern Baptists Drink." 1985. *Baptist Bible Trumpet*, January, 4.

Fox, Steve. 1988. "SBC Tied to the Far Right?" *SBC Today*, October, 7.

———. 1989. "Why SBC Right Upset with Dunn and Baptist Joint Committee, *SBC Today*, January, 20.

———. 1992. "SBC School Resists Conservatives." *Christian Century*, 1–8 January, 5.

———. 1993. "Samford University Survives a Close Call." *Baptists Today*, 9 January, 10.

Frame, Randy. 1990. "Division's Die Is Cast." *Christianity Today*, 24 September, 42.

Fuchs, Daniel. 1981. "Win Souls Not Elections." *Chosen People*, June, 5–6.

"Fundamentalists Picket Clinton's Church." 1993. *Washington Times*, 14 June.

Gaddy, C. Welton. 1984. "Precinct Politics Wed to Fundamentalism in 'Takeover' Plan of SBC." *SBC Today*, November, 6.

Gill, Rachel. 1984. "Peace Unites ABC, SBC Groups." *SBC Today*, May, 1.

Goldstein, Jeff. 1994. "Christian Coalition Declares War on Clinton Health Plan." *[Columbia, S.C.] State*, 15 February, 7A.

Graham, Jennifer. 1993. "Arkansas Lieutenant Governor Putting His Faith into Politics." *[Columbia, S.C.] State*, 22 January, 5E.

———. 1995. "Baptists to Weigh Sins of the Past." *[Columbia, S.C.] State*, 19 June, A1.

———. 1995. "Black Baptists Rate Sincerity, Motive of SBC." *[Columbia, S.C.] State*, 27 June, A1.

Greenberg, Paul. 1995. "Christian Heritage Week Tacky." *Greenville [S.C.] News-Piedmont*, 10 February, 4A.

Greene, Amy. 1987. "SBC Tied to Political Right?" *SBC Today*, October, 1.

———. 1989. "New Right Groups Exert Influence with Southern Baptists, Others." *SBC Today*, April, 12.

Harwell, Jack U. 1989. "Reports Say Pressler Out as U.S. Ethics Chief." *SBC Today*, November, 1.

———. 1992. "SBC Messengers Approve Conservative Resolutions." *Baptists Today*, 25 June, 3.

———. 1993. "Southern Baptists Attack President Clinton; Take Middle-Road Stance on Freemasons." *Baptists Today* 29 June, 1.

Hastey, Stan. 1991. "The Alliance and the Fellowship." *SBC Today*, 3 May, 19.

Hefley, James C. 1983. "The Historic Shift in America's Largest Protestant Denomination." *Christianity Today*, 5 August, 38.

———. 1990. "Critique of 'House Divided,' Article on the Controversy in the Southern Baptist Convention by R. Gustav Niebuhr Appearing in 'The Wall Street Journal,' April 25, 1990." *Christian News*, 4 June, 14.

Heim, S. Mark. 1993. "Talking on the Truce Line: Southern Baptists in Dialogue." *Christian Century*, 14 April, 402.

Henry, Carl F. H. 1980. "Evangelicals Jump on the Political Bandwagon." *Christianity Today*, 24 October, 1226.

Hill, Karl. 1978. "GOP May Mend Wounds or Split Down Center." *Greenville [S.C.] News*, 12 March, 14A.

Hinson, E. Glenn. 1987. "Split May Best Bring Peace amid SBC Strife." *SBC Today*, April, 16.

Hitt, Russell T. 1982. "The Southern Baptists, an Outsider's View." *Eternity*, March, 17.

Hollinger, Herb. 1995. "Southern Baptists, Assemblies of God Top Congregational Giving Study." *Baptist Press Wire Service*, America Online, 18 June.

Holly, James L. 1990. "Cooperative Program Decline Not Related to Conservative Resurgence." *Southern Baptist Advocate*, June, 3.

————. N.d. "Evangelicals and Catholics Together: The Christian Mission in the Third Millennium: A Critique." In *SBCNet* CompuServe Forum.

Honeycutt, Roy L. 1983. "Can Southern Baptists Live in Harmony?" *Tie*, May–June, 3.

Howard, Judy. 1985. "Outlook for Ethnic Groups in SBC Described as Bright." *Dallas Morning News*, 13 June, 22A.

Hunt, Angela E. 1987. "Baptist Joint Committee Out of Joint with SBC." *Liberty Report*, April, 20.

Hutson, Curtis. 1990. "First Baptist Chruch, Fort Worth, Texas, Seeks Reaffiliation with SBC: Should Independent Baptists Reunite with the SBC?" *Sword of the Lord*, 20 July, 1.

Hyer, Marjorie. 1981. "Liberal-Conservative Fights Wrench Protestant Churches." *Washington Post*, 29 May, C12.

Hymers, R. L. 1986. "Why I Left the Southern Baptist Convention." *Baptist Bible Tribune*, 9 May, 4.

"Intimidation Used by Routh." 1984. *Southern Baptist Advocate*, November, 2.

Jackson, Wesley. 1980. "Southern Baptists 'Cool' Inerrancy." *Times-Picayune*, 14 May, 2.

"Jackson May Take Church Independent or Cut Support." 1989. *Baptist Courier*, 30 March, 6.

"Jimmy Carter Joins Moderate Baptists." 1993. *Greenville [S.C.] News*, 22 May, 10A.

Johns, John E. 1992. "Furman Problems not with Majority of Southern Baptists." *Greenville [S.C.] News-Piedmont*, 9 February, 3C.

Kaufmann, Stephen R. 1984. "Doing Politics: Five Pitfalls for Evangelicals." *Presbyterian Journal*, 19 September, 12–13.

King, Martin. 1995. "Catholic-Evangelical Signers Address Areas of Controversy." *Baptist Press Wire Service*, 13 March.

Kinsella, John. 1992. "A Democratic View of the Bible." *Christian World Report*, November, 3.

Knight, Walker L. 1987. "Convention Defied by PAC Action." *SBC Today*, November, 1.

———. 1992. "Moderate Organizations Fill Vacuums in SBC." *Baptists Today*, 15 December, 7.

Knox, Marv. 1983. "SBC Presidents." *SBC Today*, May, 6.

———. 1992. "Paul Pressler Nominated to Foreign Mission Board." *Baptists Today*, 14 May, 19.

Kondracke, Morton. 1993. "Scope of Clinton's Outreach." *Washington Times*, 4 September.

Land, Richard. N.d. "Evangelicals and Catholics?" In *SBCNet* CompuServe Forum.

"Land, Lewis Remove Names from Controversial Document." 1995. *Light*, July–August, 12.

Lawrence, Jill. 1993. "Clinton Changes Inflame Fundamentalist' Fury." *Seattle Times/Seattle Post-Intelligencer*, 23 May.

Lawson, Linda. 1992. "SBC Messenger Severs Final Ties with BJPCA." *Baptists Today*, 25 June, 3.

Lawton, Kim A. 1992. "Estranged Bedfellows: Are Evangelicals Abandoning the Democratic Party, or Is It Abandoning Them?" *Christianity Today*, 17 August, 40.

———. 1992. "Seeking Common Ground: Evangelicals Hope President-Elect Clinton Will Strive for Consensus on Social Issues, Not Just for Dramatic Change." *Christianity Today*, 14 December, 40.

Leo, John. 1993. "Boxing In Believers." *U.S. News and World Report*, 20 September, 20.

Leonard, Bill J. 1985. "In Search of a Century." *SBC Today*, August–September, 1.

Lessner, Richard. 1981. "Interview with Bob Jones, III." *Arizona Republic*, 24 October, 1F.

"Liberals Hire Political Consultant." 1986. *Southern Baptist Advocate*, March, 1.

Lind, Michael. 1995. "The Southern Coup." *New Republic*, 19 June.

Lovette, Roger. 1985. "Why I Am Not a Fundamentalist." *SBC Today*, October, 14.

"Majority Report of SBC Executive Committee on Baptist Joint Committee." 1990. *SBC Today*, June, 10.

"Many Called, Few Chosen." 1988. *World* magazine, 21 March, 3.

Marsden, George. 1988. "Religion and Politics in American History." *Reformed Journal*, October, 11.

Martin, Dan. 1988. "Pressler, Patterson 'Grieved' By Mailing." *Southern Baptist Advocate*, May, 13.

———. 1992. "Texas Baptist Fundamentalists Launch SBC Style Organization." *Baptists Today*, 23 January, 4.

———. 1992. "State Conventions May Face New Blitz by Fundamentalists Who Have Captured SBC." *Baptists Today*, 6 February, 10.

Maxwell, Joe. 1995. "Evangelicals Clarify Accord with Catholics." *Christianity Today*, 6 March.

Maynard, Steve. 1989. "Is the SBC Heading the Way of the Missouri Synod?" *Houston Chronicle*, 22 October, 6.

McAllister, Bill. 1994. "Religious Right's Latest Star Is Rising in the South: Former S.C. State Legislator to Win GOP Gubernatorial Nomination in Runoff." *Washington Post*, 22 August, A6.

McBeth, H. Leon. 1988. "America's Southern Baptists: Who They Are." *Christianity Today*, 4 November, 17.

McGregor, Don. 1988. "Linking the Political Right and the SBC Right." *SBC Today*, April, 13.

———. 1989. "New Commission Unreasonable." *SBC Today*, March, 28.

McKnight, Edgar V. 1985. "The Crisis in the Southern Baptist Convention." *Furman Magazine*, Spring, 11.

Menendez, Albert J. 1992. "Analysis: Clinton Won Most Religious Votes." *Baptists Today*, 26 November, 1.

Merrill, Bill. 1995. "CLC Consultation Yields Stance on Racism." *Baptist Press Wire Service*, 18 June, America Online.

"Minister Says Southern Baptists Should Consider Changing Name." 1989. *Greenville [S.C.] News*, 20 September, 7B.

"Minority Report of SBC Executive Committee on Baptist Joint Committee." 1990. *SBC Today*, June, 11.

Mohler, Jr., and R. Albert. 1995. "Mohler Defends Role of Theological Accountability." *Baptists Today*, 2 February, 4.

Monroe, Sylvester. 1995. "The Gospel of Diversity." *Time*, 24 April.

Moral Majority Report. 1980. 14 July.

Moyers, Bill. 1990. "Moyers Calls Baptists to Actively Oppose the Dismissals of Shackleford and Martin." *SBC Today*, September, 12.

Neuhaus, Richard John. 1992. "Who, Now Will Shape the Meaning of America? The Marriage of Mainline Denominations to the Great Society Caused the Rise of the New Religious Right." *Christianity Today*, 19 March, 16.

Newsweek. 1958. 17 November, 30.

"New Ticket Not Squeamish about Using Religious Themes in Campaign." 1992. *Knight Ridder*, 27 July; rpt. *New York Times*, 9 November, 1A.

Niebuhr, R. Gustav. 1990. "Southern Baptists Lose Members and Impetus in an Internal Struggle." *Wall Street Journal*, 25 April, A1.

"1958 U.S. Election Report." 1958. *The Economist*, 8 November, 507.

Noll, Mark A. 1992. "The Politicians' Bible." *Christianity Today* 26 October, 16.

"Opinions Announced May 24, 1983." 1993. *United States Law Week* 51:45.

Ostling, Richard N., et al. 1991. "Fundamental Disagreement." *Time*, 13 May, 50.

Packer, J. I. 1994. "Why I Signed It." *Christianity Today*, 12 December, America Online.

"Partisan Politics: Where Does the Gospel Fit?" 1993. Editorial, *Christianity Today*, 9 November, 15.

"Pastors Getting Fired: A Growing Trend among Southern Baptists." 1982. *Christianity Today*, 19 March.

Patterson, Paige. 1983. "The Paige Patterson Definition of a Theological Conservative." *Southern Baptist Journal*, February, 8.

"Patterson vs. McCall on the Southern Baptist Controversy." 1985. *Fundamentalist Journal*, May, 14.

"Peace?? Can There Be Peace While Violations of Our Faith Are Called Acceptable?" 1987. *Southern Baptist Journal*, January–March, 1.

Perry, Dale. 1978. "Despite GOP Split, Two Groups Get Along Well." *Greenville [S.C.] News*, 19 February, 4B.

———. 1978. "GOP Factions Join to Elect County Chairman." *Greenville [S.C.] News*, 14 March, 1B.

Pierard, Richard V. 1984. "The Great Eclipse." *Eternity*, February, 14.

Plowman, Edward E. 1980. "Conservative Network Puts Its Stamp on the Southern Baptist Convention." *Christianity Today*, 18 July, 50.

Prescott, Bruce. 1992. "Two Sermons from Texas Convention Illustrate Gist of Inerrancy Conflict." *Baptists Today*, 9 January, 5.

Price, Joyce. 1993. "Catholics, Baptists Find Elders' Apology Lacking." *Washington Times*, 3 September.

Prince, Eldred E., Jr. 1993. "Commencement Address." Coastal Carolina University, 17 December.

Pruden, Wesley. 1995. "When Southern Baptists Freed Their Slaves." *Washington Times*, 23 June, A4.

Ragsdale, Warner. 1985. "SBC Mirrors South and Nation in Move to Conservatism." *SBC Today*, August–September, 4.

Reeves, Jay. 1983. "Baptists Pick Convention Leader." *Montgomery Advertiser*, 17 November.

———. "Lost Souls? Baptists Estimate Half of Alabama Going to Hell." *[Columbia, S.C.] State*, 18 September, 1A.

"Religion and the Race." 1992. *Christianity Today*, 9 March, 55.

"Religious Liberty Award Goes to Senator Helms." 1990. *Southern Baptist Advocate*, June, 2.

"Religious Liberty Council Supports Joint Committee." 1990. *SBC Today*, June, 1.

Roberts, John E. 1991. "We Chose a Bad Way to Make History." *Baptist Courier*, 28 November, 3.

Robinson, Bill. 1993. "Conservative Coastal Candidates Identified: GOP Chief Denies List Put Forth as a Slate." *[Columbia, S.C.] State*, 2 June, 1B.

———. 1993. "Candidates on 'Conservative' List Lose Trustee Bids." *[Columbia, S.C.] State*, 3 June, 1B.

Robinson, John. 1982. "Study Says New Right to Fail on Legislation." *Raleigh News and Observer*, 8 November, 1A.

Rochelle, Larry. 1980. "Born Again Politics: Now the Republicans." *Humanist*, November–December, 18.

Roehlkepartain, Eugene C. 1986. "Fundamentalists Threaten Religious Liberty Watchdog." *Christian Century*, 5 November, 980.

Rosenfeld, Megan. 1992. "Anatomy of a Defeat: How a Middle-of-the-Road Incumbent Got Run Over on Election Day." *Washington Post*, November, D1.

"SBC and the Panama Canal Treaties." 1978. *Baptist Challenge*, March.

"SBC President Owes $60,000 in Back Taxes." 1993. *[Columbia, S.C.] State*, 4 September.

"SBC Resolutions Deal with Religious Liberties, Art, Other Concerns." 1991. *Indiana Baptist*, 11 June, 9.

Schulte, Brigid. 1993. "Pastors Seek, But Don't Find Common Ground with Clinton." *[Columbia, S.C.] State*, 17 September, 1B.

Scoppe, Cindi Ross. 1994. "Abortion Question Gets Angry Answers." *[Columbia, S.C.] State*, 11 February, 1A.

———. 1994. "Catholic Faith Costing Hartnett Votes, Hartnett Says." *[Columbia, S.C.] State*, 29 March, B4.

Seltz, Johanna. 1978. "Baptists Deny U.S. Request for Hiring Practices Data." *Raleigh News and Observer*, 14 November, 1.

"Setback for Evangelical-Catholic Pact." 1995. *Christianity Today*, April, America Online.

Shurden, Walter B. N.d. "Crises in Baptist Life." Historical Commission, Southern Baptist Convention.

Silk, Mark. 1988. "Reagan Stargazing Concerns the Christian Right." *Atlanta Constitution*, 5 May, A7.

Simmons, Chris. 1986. "Baptists Respect Different Views, Survey Says." *Greenville [S.C.] News*, 10 June, 7B.

Simpson, David. 1983. "SBC Is Turning Right!" *Southern Baptist Journal*, February, 1.

Singleton, James E. 1981. "The Strange Case of the SBC." *Faith for the Family*, November, 27.

"Six Leaders of Conservative Religious Groups Met with White House Chief of Staff." 1992. *National and International Religion Report*, 27 January, 2.

Smith, Ashton. 1993. "Virginia Baptists Form Fellowship." *Indiana Baptist*, 16 February, 9.

Smith, Michael B. 1991. "Christians, Democracy: Strange Bedfellows or Blood Relations? Christianity Can Help Cultivate Virtues Essential to Democracy." *World*, 23 November, 7.

"Southern Baptist Committee Favors Euthanasia Bill." 1981. *Baptist Bible Trumpet*, June, 1.

"Southern Baptist Convention Split over Two Endorsements." 1988. *Greenville [S.C.] News-Piedmont*, 27 March, 26A.

"Southern Baptist Division 'Trick of the Devil': Billy Graham." 1985. *Religious News Service*, 25 March.

"Southern Baptists Break with Tradition; Endorse School Prayer Amendment." 1982. *Christian News*, 28 June, 7.

"Southern Baptists Decry Clinton, Gays." 1993. *[Columbia, S.C.] State*, 16 June, 8A.

"Southern Baptists Disagree." 1980. *Moody*, April, 124.

"Southern Baptists Put Down Gays, Abortion." 1993. *[Columbia, S.C.] State*, 18 June, 14A.

"Southern Baptist Speak out on Alcohol, Sex, Art." 1991. *AFA Journal*, July, 8.

"Southern Baptists Urged to End Division." 1993. *[Columbia, S.C.] State*, 6 June.

"Southern Baptists Widen Gap with Clinton." 1993. *[Columbia, S.C.] State*, 17 June.

Steely, John E. 1984. "Current Issues in the Southern Baptist Convention in Historical Perspective." *Faith and Mission*, Spring, 5.

Stone, Andrea. 1995. "Southern Baptists 'Repent' Past." *USA Today*, 20 June, 3A.

Strode, Tom. N.d. "Blacks Should Oppose Foster, Baptist Pastor Says." *Baptist Press Wire Service*.

"Sweep by 'My Generation': The Children of Modern America Bring An End to the Reagan Revolution." 1992. *World*, 7 November, 6.

Tenery, Robert M. 1987. "Public Affairs Committee Should Be Commended." *Southern Baptist Advocate*, September, 6.

———. 1990. "The Wall Street [Journal] Hoax." *Southern Baptist Advocate*, June, 8.

Thomas, Cal. 1983. "Christianity IS Politics." *Fundamentalist Journal*, January, 8.

———. 1993. "Clinton's 'Common Good.'" *Washington Times*, 5 September.

Thompson, Gerald. 1976. "Why We Must Leave the Southern Baptist Convention." *Sword of the Lord*, 5 March, 1.

Time. 1958. 17 November, 22.

"Track Record of Moderates and Conservatives." 1983. *Southern Baptist Advocate*, October, 13.

Tutterow, Michael. 1987. "Bork Appointment Stirs SBC." *SBC Today*, October, 1.

"Two-Year-Old Rift Erupts Again." 1978. *Greenville [S.C.] News*, 14 February, 5A.

"USC to Review Graduate-Level Religion Course amid Baptists' Protests." 1993. *Greenville [S.C.] News*, 4 June.

"Voting Patterns, the Religious Factor." 1992. *Christian Century*, 18–25 November, 1056.

"VP's Church Okays Women as Deacons." 1983. *Southern Baptist Journal*, February, 12.

Waldman, Peter. 1988. "Fundamentalists Fight to Capture the Soul of Southern Baptists." *Wall Street Journal*, 7 March, 1A.

Walker, Richard L. 1982. "Baptist Peace Activists Organize to Counter Conservatives." *Southern Baptist Advocate*, Fall, 13.

Wall, James M. 1993. "Church Leaders Meet with Clinton: A Visit to the White House." *Christian Century*, 7 April, 355.

Wallis, Roy. 1975. "Relative Deprivation and Social Movements: A Cautionary Note." *British Journal of Sociology* 26:360–363.

Walters, David. 1993. "Southern Baptists Asked to Pray for Clinton and Gore for 40 Days." *Washington Times*, 9 October.

Warner, Greg. 1991. "Close Votes in Texas, South Carolina Bode No Quick End for College Disputes." *Baptists Today*, 28 November, 1.

———. 1992. "Baptists Elected with Little Help from Brethren." *Baptists Today*, 26 November, 1.

———. 1992. "SBC Relations Cool with White House." *Baptists Today*, 26 November, 6.

———. 1992. "Fundamentalists Make Few Inroads in States." *Baptists Today*, 15 December, 3.

———. 1993. "Patterson Denied Membership in Wake Forest Church." *Baptists Today*, 18 February, 1.

———. 1995. "Trustees Abuse of Power." *Baptists Today*, 2 February, 1.

Wentz, Wendell F. 1989. "Missouri Minister Offers Primer on Basic Southern Baptist Polity." *SBC Today*, July, 25.

White, Jack E. 1995. "Forgive Our Sins." *Time*, 3 July, 29.

Whitehead, John. 1982. "The Second American Revolution." *Moody*, July–August, 12.

"Why I Can No Longer Be a Southern Baptist." 1983. *SBC Today*, August–September, 20.

Williams, J. B. 1983. "The Authority of Scripture vs. The Southern Baptist Convention." *Faith for the Family*, December.

Winfrey, David. N.d. "Home Mission Board Study: Baptists Losing Ground in the South." *Baptist Press Wire Service*, America Online.

Wingfield, Mark, and Greg Warner. 1993. "Jimmy, Rosalynn Carter Embrace Fellowship; Fellowship 'Blesses' 25 New Missionaries." *Baptists Today*, 27 May, 1.

Witham, Larry. 1993. "Southern Baptist Panel May Repudiate Clinton." *Washington Times*, 15 June.

———. 1993. "Southern Baptists Chastise Clinton for Liberal Policies." *Washington Times*, 17 June, A6.

———. 1993. "Colson Warns Religions of Secular Myths." *Washington Times*, 3 September, A5.

———. 1993. "Clinton Calls His Job 'A Ministry' in Meeting with Religious Leaders." *Washington Times*, 13 September, A1.

———. 1993. "Conservative to Run Venerable Southern Baptist Seminary." *Washington Times*, 17 October, A4.

Woodward, Kenneth. 1990. "Same Bible, Same Church: Southern Baptist Unity?" *Newsweek*, 23 April.

REFERENCE WORKS

Statistical Abstract of the United States. 1941, 1971, 1973, 1981, 1984, 1986, 1987, 1990, 1992, 1993.

U.S. Census. 1930–90. General Population Characteristics.

DISSERTATIONS

Bledsoe, W. Craig. 1985. "The Fundamentalist Foundations of the Moral Majority." Ph.D. diss., Vanderbilt University.

Bonham, Jerry Lee. 1975. "Fundamentalism and the Radical Right: A Theoretical Exploration and Analysis." Ph.D. diss., University of Illinois.

Earl, Elizabeth Noel. 1992. "A Comparison of Billy Graham and Jerry Falwell: Ministers and Their Presidents." Ph.D. diss., Ohio University.

Freeman, Donald McKinley. 1964. "Religion and Southern Politics: The Political Behavior of Southern White Protestants." Ph.D. diss., University of North Carolina at Chapel Hill.

Glass, William Robert. 1991. "The Development of Northern Patterns of Fundamentalism in the South, 1900–1950." Ph.D. diss., Emory University.

Hendricks, John Stephen. 1977. "Religious and Political Fundamentalism: The Links between Alienation and Ideology." Ph.D. diss., University of Michigan.

Herman, Douglas E. 1980. "Flooding the Kingdom: The Intellectual Development of Fundamentalism, 1930–1941." Ph.D. diss., Ohio University.

Herzog, Albert Anton, Jr. 1983. "Religion and Politics: The Effects of Affiliation with a Religious Denomination on Attitudes and Behavior." Ph.D. diss., Ohio State University.

Hurd, R. Wesley. 1988. "Liberty University: Fortress in the War for a Christian America." Ph.D. diss., University of Oregon.

Southern, James Richard. 1988. "Fundamentalism and Political Activism: A Study of the New Christian Right." Ph.D. Claremont Graduate School.

Turner, Daniel Lynn. 1988. "Fundamentalism, the Arts, and Personal Refinement: A Study of the Ideals of Bob Jones, Sr., and Bob Jones, Jr." Ed.D. diss., University of Illinois.

Turner, Helen Lee. 1991. "Fundamentalism in the Southern Baptist Convention: Crystallization of the Millennialist Vision." Ph.D. diss., University of Virginia.

Wiles, Dennis Ray. 1992. "Factors Contributing to the Resurgence of Fundamentalism in the Southern Baptist Convention, 1979–1990." Ph.D. diss., Southwestern Baptist Theological Seminary.

SBC PUBLICATIONS

Annual. 1992. Alabama Baptist Convention.

Annual. 1992. Arkansas Baptist Convention.

Baptist Annual. 1992. Florida Baptist Convention.

Minutes. 1992. Georgia Baptist Convention.

Annual. 1992. Louisiana Baptist Convention.

Annual. 1992. Mississippi Baptist Convention.

Proceedings. 1992. North Carolina Baptist Convention.

Annual. 1992. South Carolina Baptist Convention.

Texas Baptist Annual. 1992. Baptist General Convention of Texas.

Virginia Baptist Annual. 1992. Baptist General Association of Virginia.

Southern Baptist Convention Annual. 1933, 1934, 1940, 1951, 1954, 1960, 1961, 1968–96.

Southern Baptist Handbook. 1931, 1951, 1991.

SBC Quarterly Review. 1961. July–September.

Annual Seminar Program. 1968, 1969, 1971–94. Christian Life Commission of the Southern Baptist Convention.

AUDIOTAPES

Ammerman, Nancy Tatom. 1991. "Why Are We Baptists?" Lecture at First Baptist Church, Greenville, S.C., 17 November.

———. 1992. "The Rise of the Progressive Wing of the SBC" Lecture at First Baptist Church, Greenville, S.C., 4 April.

———. 1992. "Wandering Together in the Wilderness" Lecture at First Baptist Church, Greenville, S.C., 5 April.

———. 1992. "Organizing to Do God's Work in the 21st Century" Lecture at First Baptist Church, Greenville, S.C., April 5.

Beasley, David. 1994. Speech to Bob Jones University daily chapel with introduction by Bob Jones III.

Lapiska, Bradley. 1993. Morning Sermon, Hampton Park Baptist Church, Greenville, S.C., 4 July.

ONLINE SERVICES

Congressional Quarterly Online. 1995. America Online, 11 April.
SBCNet, CompuServe. 1994–1996.

Index

Accuracy in Academia, 63
Adams, Ted, 119–20, 147
African American alliance with SBC,
  185–90
African American churches, 172
African Americans, 231–32
African Methodist Episcopal Church
  (AME), 195
"Agrarian myth," 69
AIDS, 218, 221
Aldridge, Marion, 12, 46, 91, 241, 247–48
Alford, Clyde, 42
Alienation models, 68–70, 255
Allen, Jimmy, 61, 64
Alliance of Baptists, 54, 60, 220–22
American Baptist Churches (ABC-USA),
  56
American Civil Liberties Union (ACLU),
  34, 200
American Council of Christian Churches
  (ACCC), 39
Americanization of Dixie, 203
American National Election Study
  (ANES), 25, 154, 163, 178, 214, 263
American Political Science Association
  (APSA), 238
Americans for Robertson, 106, 108
Americans United, 39
American Voter, The, 161
America's Dates with Destiny, 107
Amish, 100
Ammerman, Nancy, 31, 72, 102
Anderson, John, 5, 176
Anderson, Marian, 60
Anglo-Catholics, 100
Anti-Communism, 90, 150
Anti-Semitism, 172
Arizona Republic, 103
Armey, Richard, 2, 171

Armey Amendment, 171
Armstrong, Rickey, 189
Arts, government funding of, 205
Ashcraft, Morris, 221
Aspin, Les, 176
Associated Baptist Press (ABP), 55, 223
Atwater, Lee, 116, 125, 200, 202, 204,
  208–9

Baker, Dell, 134, 268
Baker, Howard, 176
Baker, Larry, 220
Balanced budget amendment, 205
Ball, William Bentley, 181
Balmer, Randall, 151
"Bapticity," 20–22, 24, 191
Baptist Bible Fellowship (BBF), 111
"Baptist exceptionalism," 39, 247
Baptist Faith and Message, 34, 36, 52, 93,
  205, 215–16, 230
Baptist General Association of Virginia,
  224
Baptist General Convention of Texas, 225
Baptist Joint Committee on Public Affairs,
  39, 40, 47, 56–57, 61, 63, 175, 219–20,
  252
"Baptist life," 14, 241
Baptists Committed to the SBC, 222
Baptists Today, 52, 60–61, 221
Baptist Theological Seminary at Rich-
  mond, 224
Barnett's Creek Baptist Church, 230
Barton, A. J., 37, 44, 87
Baylor, R. E. B., 40–41
Baylor University, 40, 49, 55, 63, 225, 230
Beale, David O., 111, 264
Beasley, David, 22, 121–24, 128–31, 136,
  140–42, 213
Bennett, William, 56, 176